Employment Policies and Multilevel Governance

KLUWER LAW INTERNATIONAL

BULLETIN OF COMPARATIVE LABOUR RELATIONS – 71

Employment Policies and Multilevel Governance

Editor: Roger Blanpain

Guest Editors: Juan Pablo Landa and Brian Langille

Contributors:

Philippe Auvergnon
Antonio Baylos
Thierry Berthet
Jaime Cabeza
Jo Carby-Hall
Aranzazu Fernández Urrutia
Maximilian Fuchs
Pierre Iriart
Maria Jose Romero
Brian Langille
Julia López López
Philippe Martin
Juan Pablo Landa
Nuria Pumar Beltrán
Giancarlo Ricci
Jean-Michel Servais
Edurne Terradillos Ormaetxea

Wolters Kluwer
Law & Business

AUSTIN BOSTON CHICAGO NEW YORK THE NETHERLANDS

Published by:
Kluwer Law International
PO Box 316
2400 AH Alphen aan den Rijn
The Netherlands
Website: www.kluwerlaw.com

Sold and distributed in North, Central and South America by:
Aspen Publishers, Inc.
7201 McKinney Circle
Frederick, MD 21704
United States of America
Email: customer.care@aspenpubl.com

Sold and distributed in all other countries by:
Turpin Distribution Services Ltd.
Stratton Business Park
Pegasus Drive, Biggleswade
Bedfordshire SG18 8TQ
United Kingdom
Email: kluwerlaw@turpin-distribution.com

Printed on acid-free paper.

ISBN 978-90-411-2866-9

Summary of Contents

Table of Contents

Chapter 6
The Reform of the Public Employment Service in France: Modernization and New Governance Issues **147**
Philippe Auvergnon & Philippe Martin

Acknowledgements

We are in the very fortunate position of being forced to begin by acknowledging the generous and fundamental help of Marta Moreno in the editing of this book. She joined the research team in the Law Faculty of the University of the Basque Country as Associate Researcher four years ago. She has assisted continuously, not only by preparing the chapters for editing, but also by contributing her much appreciated comments.

We also wish to thank María Aragón for her help with the editing. She is a practising lawyer and legal translator. She has dealt with the technical side of the editorial's style guidelines and reviewed the English terminology employed in the translations used by the authors.

We should also give thanks to Sara Lallana, Lecturer of Labour Law in the Law Faculty of the University of the Basque Country, for her efforts in organising last year's meeting in Oñati's International Institute for the Sociology of Law (IISL), to great success. Without this meeting, this book would not have been produced.

We also wish to record our profound thanks to Roger Blanpain and the editorial team at Kluwer, especially our contact Ewa Szkatula, who provided exemplary support in the publication of this volume.

Finally, thanks are due for the financial help to this project from the Subdirectorate for Research Projects of the Ministry for Education and Science of the Kingdom of Spain (Ref SEJ2007-29486-E), as well as for other economic grants from the Basque Government and Kutxa Bank for the meeting in Oñati. In this connection we must mention the management and staff of Oñati's IISL, who provided excellent technical and personal assistance for our meeting.

Juan Pablo Landa and Brian Langille
19 January 2009

Notes on the Authors

Philippe Auvergnon, Professor of Labour Law, Faculty of Law, University of Bordeaux IV, France

Antonio Baylos, Professor of Labour Law, Faculty of Law, University of Castilla-la Mancha, Spain

Thierry Berthet, Senior Researcher Spirit-CNRS, Political Science Institute of Bordeaux University, France

Jaime Cabeza, Professor of Labour Law, Faculty of Law, University of Vigo, Spain

Joseph Carby-Hall, Director of International Legal Research, Centre for Legislative Studies, University of Hull, United Kingdom

Aranzazu Fernández, Lecturer of Labour Law, Faculty of Economics, University of the Basque Country, Spain

Maximilian Fuchs, Professor of Labour & European Law, Faculty of Economics and Management, University of Eichstäet-Ingolstadt, Germany

Pierre Iriart, Senior Lecturer of Labour Law, Faculty of Law, University of Bordeaux IV, France

Juan Pablo Landa, Professor of Labour Law, Faculty of Law, University of the Basque Country, Spain

Brian Langille, Professor of Labour Law, Faculty of Law, University of Toronto, Canada

Julia López López, Professor of Labour Law, Department of Law, University Pompeu Fabra of Barcelona, Spain

Philippe Martin, Senior Researcher Comptrasec-CNRS, University of Bordeaux IV, France

Nuria Pumar, Associate Professor of Labour Law, Faculty of Law, University of Barcelona, Spain

Giancarlo Ricci, Associate Professor of Labour Law, Faculty of Law, University of Catania, Italy

Maria Jose Romero, Associate Professor of Labour Law, Industrial Relations School, University of Castilla-La Mancha, Spain

Jean-Michel Servais, Former Director the ILO, Visiting Professor of Labour Law, University of Girona, Spain & Liège, Belgium

Edurne Terradillos, Associate Professor of Labour Law, Faculty of Law, University of the Basque Country, Spain

Introduction

Juan Pablo Landa & Brian Langille

The essays in this volume have a common, specific, and important focus – the development of effective policies for promoting employment. But the problem which animates our discussion of this issue is a very basic and more general one. It is a question which stalks most policy debates in these times and in our 'globalized' world. That question is: 'who should create and administer such policies?' At one time the answer appeared to be simple – this important policy arena belonged to individual states and their law making bodies. But today that question and its possible answers are seen to be much more complex. We now ask: 'Should employment policy be developed and deployed at the local, national, international, or supranational level?' We also ask: 'If our aim is effective policy making aimed at promoting employment, should this task be undertaken by state or non-state actors?' And these questions lead on to other difficult inquiries such as, 'what types of regulation, beyond formal state law, are conducive to maximizing our desired employment outcomes?' These are the issues which animate this volume. At the core of this enterprise, for many of the authors, is the effect of the so-called 'Europeanization' of employment policies. But, as these essays reveal, there are many other issues as well. These include the varied dynamics of legal and administrative systems in individual states, whether federal in a formal sense of not. Federal states have a long tradition of facing the question of who, in the sense of what level of government, local or central, should have authority over employment issues. But these questions addressed in this volume are now pressing for all states, whether internally federal or not, and whether in Europe or not. Hence our use of the more general term 'multilevel governance'.

We should point out that the rationale for this volume is not, however, a critical review of the suitability of the employment policies developed in certain political systems, nor the legal legitimacy of delegations of authority over them, whether upwards or downwards.[1] The goal of our work is both broader and also rather more modest. We seek to put in context, and then on view, European[2] examples of the struggle with the idea of multilevel governance of employment policies. In other words, we discuss how the idea of multilevel governance has played out within the political and administrative reality of each of the Member States of the European Union (EU) examined in this work and in the context of their efforts to achieve an effective employment policy. With this aim in mind these essays review the legal rules and the administrative procedures regarding employment. They do so taking into account both community and sometimes international law. Some of the essays also assess whether the execution of employment policies by those political systems inspired by, or at least implicated in, multilevel governance is, apart from being efficient, compatible with the traditional goals of the national systems of social protection.

Finally, the scope of this work also includes some analysis of the compatibility of resulting employment and economic policies with the defence of individual rights of a social nature both as guaranteed by the Member States analyzed and by international human rights norms.

The creation of more and better jobs has become one of the indisputable markers of the success of economic policies and the optimization of employment policies is now a challenge that affects all countries to some degree.

It is an issue which is profoundly raised and complicated by economic globalization. As a result, one of the most difficult and central elements in a strategy of economic growth is the development of optimal employment policies. This is demonstrated by the importance attached to it by the EU since the European Employment Strategy (EES) was born in the Council of Essen, later renamed the Lisbon strategy for growth and jobs.

There are, however, and as we shall see, many issues lurking here. Some are substantive. For example, the priority given to the success of economic and employment policies (as set out in the Lisbon strategy integrating employment guidelines with economic policies[3]) faces problems if we consider the defence of individual rights of a social nature. It is also true that there has been a growing introduction of the principles of flexicurity[4] in European employment strategies.

---

1. K. Nicolaidis and R. House (eds), *The Federal Vision* (Oxford University Press,:Oxford, 2001), 4 and 9.
2. Also using one non European example, Canada, as a prism for comparison.
3. Integrated Guidelines for the 2008-2010 period, Brussels European Council, Presidency Conclusions of 14 Mar. 2008, 7652/08.
4. Communication from the Commission to the European Parliament, the Council, the European Economic and Social Committee, and the Committee of the Regions 'Towards Common Principles of Flexicurity: More and Better Jobs through Flexibility and Security' COM (2007) 359 final.

   It is transposed to the Integrated Guidelines for Growth and Jobs (2008-2010) including a Commission Recommendation on the Broad Guidelines for the Economic Policies of the Member States and the Community (under Art. 99 of the EC Treaty) adopted on 11 Dec. 2007, especially in Guideline No. 21.

But, for the moment, this phenomenon seems not to have been accompanied by an inadequate appreciation of the problems posed by the adoption of certain measures. Let us give two examples. One is social benefits made conditional upon the acceptance of employment activation steps (according to the principle of 'make work pay'). A second is social inclusion through employment becoming the yardstick of policies known as 'active social inclusion'. Both examples may illustrate a tendency to forget that the guarantee of minimum resources is an essential condition to keep those with no access to the labour market[5] away from poverty. In any event, this guarantee is essential to the credibility of the European Social Agenda, the European cohesion policy,[6] and, in short, the social dimension of the project of European construction.

Other issues raised are procedural in nature rather than substantive. In states where these policies have been executed at decentralized levels the development, management or evaluation of these policies is at least in part carried out by decentralized entities. Moreover, there may be other social and economic agents participating in the development and execution of these policies. All of this suggests potential for real problems of governability of these policies, whether it is a vertical (from community to local entities) or a horizontal question (with the social partners). More fundamentally, existing complex constitutional rules within federal states mediate any effort to think about multi level governance from first principles, or even in terms of rational allocation of administrative responsibility. Even more basic still there is the profound reality of radically different substantive political and legal orientations to employment policy which reveal different levels of receptivity to redistribution of authority on multiple levels.

The essays in this volume had their origins in a research meeting held in the IISJ at Oñati (Spain) in June of 2007. Some of the contributors to this study, all employment law experts, discuss some of the problematic aspects surrounding the European strategy for employment and its influence upon the decentralization of active employment policies and (albeit to a lesser extent) related elements of social protection. Other authors concentrate on 'built in' problems of existing federal structures allocating competences between central and regional governments. A third group of authors focus upon substantive approaches to employment policies within individual Member States.

---

5. Resolution of the European Parliament on the Social Agenda for the period 2006-2010 (2004/2191(INI)). According to the Communication from the Commission on the 'Proposal for a Joint Report on the social protection and social inclusion 2008' of 30 Jan. 2008 (COM (2008) 42 final), 'there are 78 million of Europeans that risk poverty, of which 19 million are children. They are poor children because they live at the homes of unemployed people who lack sufficient financial aid or because their parents' jobs are not sufficiently paid to avoid or escape from poverty'.
6. The European structural funds (for the period 2007-2013), particularly the ESF, have as main objectives the financial strengthening of the EES, including the re-strengthening of the actions of work insertion for the disadvantaged, the excluded or those in risk of exclusion. See Communication from the Commission of 11 Dec. 2007 'Member States and Regions delivering the Lisbon Strategy for growth and jobs through EU cohesion policy, 2007/2013' (COM(2007)798 final).

One of the first conclusions reached at Oñati was that it was premature to come to anything like a 'theory' of European multilevel governance of employment. Such a theory would have to be capable of revealing common and basic structural truths latent in this diversity of experiences. But in the course of our discussions it became clear that each state has had a unique experience. As these essays make clear, this is true for a host of reasons. But the result is the following truth: there have to be 'multi levels' to any analysis of 'multilevel governance' of employment policies. A single unifying theory is not within our grasp. From a simplistic, but nonetheless useful, point of view this should not come as a surprise because the idea of multilevel governance and related ideas which often accompany it (such as the Open Method of Coordination (OMC)) simply open up, at various levels, more space for local differences to express themselves. These differences may be legal (indeed constitutional), or political, or due to the influence of local traditions, or the tensions brought by the progressive construction of the employment and social European policies marked by the principle of subsidiarity and the OMC since the Essen summit in 1994.[7] This led us to conclude that the best thing to do would be to adopt a more pragmatic and utilitarian line of thought, plural rather than unified.

But having said this we must for the sake of clarity, alert the reader to some functional definitions made necessary for consistency in the various contributions. To begin with, we understand by *employment policies* a rational ensemble of techniques and instruments for developing and achieving employment targets. Secondly, we use the concept of *multilevel governance*,[8] so ample in itself, to refer to a system of coordinated procedures and practices aimed at achieving good employment policies. We see, in common with others, two dimensions of multilevel governance to be coordinated. On the one hand, the vertical partners: from European level to national, regional and local levels. On the other hand, the horizontal level: administrative coordination of networks of civil society stakeholders and private partnerships (business representatives, trade unions, Non-governmental organization (NGOs).

This volume is divided in two parts. Part I assesses the framework or context of developing multilevel governance of national employment policies in Europe. As we have noted, globalization is an inevitable feature of national employment policies. And any reply to globalization has a geopolitical element specific to the EU. The EU acts to a great degree as a supranational power. It is presided over by a Council in a position to face the challenges of globalization in a coordinated manner, with an obvious impact upon the central role assumed by the nation-states during the 20th century. But at the same time it can be argued that the EU's social and economic policy has encouraged a trend towards the decentralization of state policies because the EU has enhanced the participation of the

7. Based on 1993 White Paper on Growth, Competitiveness and Employment. EC Bull. Supp. 6/1993.
8. P. Marginson and K. Sisson, 'Multilevel System of Governance is the Most Appropriate Metaphor of the Emerging EU Polity', in *European Integration and Industrial Relations* (Palgrave McMillan, New York, 2004), 25.

regions and local entities in the development of policy, and the involvement of private and economic agents of different kind in its governance.

In this part of the book many questions are raised, including: Are the regions and local entities capable of acting effectively in the achievement of the goals set by employment and inclusion policies? Are they to be viewed as a real alternative to the functioning of a 'hollowed out' state. Or, are they the recipe needed to bolster states against the blows of globalization?

Part II offers perspective on five national efforts within Europe to regulate employment policies. Part II also includes a chapter on Canada's struggle, within its federal system, to answer the questions 'who does and who should regulate employment policy?', including an analysis of the capacity of this particular model to adapt itself to the new demands posed by globalization. It provides both a sobering reminder of the universality of these issues and also an interesting comparative perspective from which to evaluate the advantages and risks found in employment policies that are more decentralized.

As noted above, Part I of this volume frames, in general terms, the difficulties in having effective management of employment policies given both the internationalization of the economy, and the European dimension of such policies. At the same time, it considers the effects on the levels of social protection traditionally guaranteed by welfare states. In Chapter 1, Servais tackles the different types of response historically given by different countries to the employment policies and the statutory protection for workers and their families. He finishes by pointing out the changes produced at the end of the century. These changes lead him to confirm the relatively minor weight of state policies, and the increasing importance of international political agents in the management of these policies.

Servais restates Europe's urgent needs at present within the complexities of the international regulation of work. Europe is faced with the segmentation of the labour market, the difficulty of integrating the excluded and eradicating poverty, the new design of employment policies (from unemployment insurance to the disappearance of 'work' in the definition of the new policies of social protection) and, even, the new definition of what 'work' means socially in our time. To answer all these problems, the author offers general solutions inspired by the success of the experience of 'social dialogue' and collective bargaining. The goal would be to have a renewed dialogue of multipartite nature, in which civil society can be protagonist and the state assumes a subsidiary role. In his own words, 'the state would thus act more as a source of inspiration than as a guide, a mediator ensuring an adequate climate for... bipartite or multipartite social dialogue'.

In Chapter 2, Landa and Terradillos examine the validity of the OMC as the form of governance that can best guarantee the effectiveness of the EES. The authors stress, however, that the OMC, in practice, and despite its decentralizing impulse, has been implemented in a manner inconsistent with that premise. Execution and evaluation of the OMC targets is allocated to the Member States, since they are responsible for the EES. In particular, only Member States have the task of organizing domestic coordination and cooperation. This task is very complicated as it is not just a question of vertical coordination between the EU and each

Member States's territorial entities, but effective horizontal coordination as well. This includes horizontal integration of social partnerships, both in the formulation and in the application, follow-up, and evaluation of the EES. In addition, the OMC also requires sectoral coordination between employment, social inclusion and social protection with educational and fiscal policies. This may result in a very complex and obscure procedure, without the benefit of either adequate guidance or prior standards. Frequently state administrations intervene which lack capacity or competence in the matter. Sometimes it is impossible to find who exactly is accountable for the execution of a specific measure of an employment policy within the administration of a Member States. This is not simply because the policy may be ill-adapted to the EES, but because in the OMC there is an inadequate and ill-organized distribution of tasks.

The authors also believe that, despite its apparent compatibility with Article 5 of the ECT, some aspects of the OMC violate the very principle of subsidiarity. There are doubts as to the proportionality between the objectives and measures of these community strategies and the effectiveness actually achieved by the OMC's soft law regulations in their application. The authors also stress the 'unbalanced integration of the EES and the social inclusion strategy'. This is due, among other reasons, to the absence of any foundation on the European Community Treaty, with the result that the EU can not apply the OMC for inclusion and social protection policies using the same competences that it has for employment policies. In any event, the powers of political and economic coercion held by the Commission and the Council are rather effective (especially the economic ones) when it comes to the execution of employment policies (for instance, the financial measures of the European Social Fund (ESF)). But these powers are not much present in the social inclusion (and social protection) strategy, which lacks an effective control on the part of the EU.

This last thesis is the starting point for Fernández and Pumar in Chapter 3. They analyze the active measures of the European policy for social inclusion from the point of view of international human rights. They reveal an aspect little known about the EES: its often difficult relationship with international norms currently in force regarding the human rights to dignity and decent work. Only a guarantee of sufficient public resources can ensure those rights effectively. In short, the EES makes those at risk of exclusion even more vulnerable, as it subjects their right to social benefits to availability for a job.

Lastly, López's Chapter 4 is guided by a concern to respond to the questions of whether the OMC can achieve equality for women and, further, whether the introduction of the OMC has not resulted in the weakening of women's presence in the labour market, with less access and less protection than before. In the author's view the gender mainstreaming strategy of the EES implies the delegation of gender politics from EU level to national levels and the EU's renunciation of its leadership on equality policies (in contrast with the latest directives on family friendly policies or on the equality for access to employment). Consequently, she concludes that in reality there is no strategy of multilateral governance on gender equality: the role of collective agreements has been silenced, and with it, that of the social agents. The author challenges the binding nature of the instruments of soft law that characterize the EES, and questions the continuation of the European Court of Justice (ECJ) as the main guarantor of gender equality, undermined, paradoxically it is argued, by the gender mainstreaming strategy itself.

The essays in Part II take as their focus the multilevel regulation of employment policies in individual states.

The analysis contained in these chapters reveal three different sorts, or dimensions, of tension between the reformation impulse promoted by the EES and the traditional legal institutions and political realities of the Member States discussed. These all conduce to a certain resistance, not necessarily conscious, on the part of individual states, when it comes to relinquishing, or sharing, or rationally allocating, regulatory powers within a system of multilevel governance. These three tensions construct the reality and context within which the abstract debate over decentralization or centralization of the management of employment policies takes place. These three tensions may be identified as follows. First, as the chapters on Canada, Spain, and Italy reveal, there is a formidable potential for internal constitutional rules on the distribution of legislative and administrative authority (whether formal rules of federalism or other) to constrain a rational approach to the appropriate level of governance, let alone multilevel governance, of employment policy. This is not simply another layer of 'multilevelness' and might seem an insurmountable barrier to effective re-allocation of authority. Yet what these three essays reveal is a combination of both surprising constraint, and even more surprising potential for innovation, within existing rules. These essays suggest that much more fruitful comparative analysis is available here. Second, as the chapters on the UK and Germany reveal there is the brute fact of the heterogeneity of the fundamental political orientation, as well as the and basic structure, of domestic regulatory policies regarding employment. These differences shatter, or at least cloud, any image of the idea multilevel governance as introducing a homogenizing era in 'on the ground' respect for rights of workers or delivery of entitlements in the labour market. Third, the studies of France reveal a final difficulty which takes us to the heart of the matters raised in the book as a whole – the sheer complexity of multilevel governance within any already developed and entrenched legislative, administrative, and political reality. Here we are introduced, through a well documented and detailed account, to the complexity of the real life tension, struggle, and interaction between the EES and local administrative structures and their reform. Here the level of administrative, legal, political, and cultural intricacy involved in a serious engagement with multilevel governance of employment on the European model is put on full view.

Taken together the seven essays found in Chapters 5 to 11 of this reveal how difficult it is to set in motion the models of multilevel governance.

First, Chapter 5 contains Fuchs' essay on the German federal model. It is worth noting, however, the federal nature of the employment agency. It has favoured the general reform of unemployment insurance in compliance with the principle 'make work pay'. The reform has proceeded to unify in a single instrument the regulation of unemployment benefits and the social assistance for the unemployed. Thus, financial means and employment policy instruments are concentrated in a single state institution. However, this has not prevented the functioning of job centres (on the contrary, it has possibly advanced it), whereby local entities work together with federal employment agencies. These agencies unify all services of orientation and attention to the unemployed. Despite this, there has been a political compromise with the Länder, whereby local authorities shall manage some of the social benefits, mainly non-pecuniary ones.

France has undergone a similar experience. In Chapter 6, Auvergnon and Martin point out that the traditional and obscure share of competences on the instruments for employment policy has not prevented a degree of cooperation and concentration of said instruments at the most suitable and decentralized possible level, the local one. The '*maison d'emploi*' – the French equivalent to the 'job centre' – seeks to concentrate the maximum of competences locally, thanks to, inter alia, the guarantee of coordination from the state's administrative agent (the '*préfet*'). Similarly, the statutory reform recently begun will permit to coordinate the big state institutions for employment (ANPE) and management of unemployment benefits (UNEDIC), with an aim to improve the effectiveness and efficiency of their services. The reform will, at the same time, confirm their nature of state public service (in the former's case) and associative and bipartite character (in the latter's case). In fact, the only truly decentralized and locally managed measure is the '*revenue minimum d'insertion*' (RMI) as income support, together with some aspects of vocational training left in the hands of the regions.

Complementary to the former employment institutional reform in France, Chapter 7 focuses on the reform of vocational training measures in this country. Berthet and Iriart address the important influence of the EES in the governance of vocational training actions, the establishment of goals and the role of financial instruments of the ESF in its development and execution. Multilevel governance applied to vocational training pretends to achieve the best way of governance of the different actors involved: social partners, regional councils and state organizations. According to these authors, governance on this matter must be based on the principle of legitimacy. In this way, the state would deal only with the establishment of minimum standards at national level and would only finance actions of national dimension. Meanwhile, the regional councils would organize, together with the social partners, the actions needed at territorial level for each applicant, depending on his personal profile. In France, however, experience reveals a sort of hybridization of the decision-makers, and confusion between agents and institutional levels when it comes to allocate competences.

On the other hand, Berthet and Iriart underline the definitive nature of the financial instruments for vocational training (New Public Market Codes) put in place by the ESF and the fact that the ESF guidelines direct these resources at local decision levels. However, multilevel governance of vocational funds is not exempted from risk either. The individualization of actions may bring about situations of discrimination, as explained by the authors. The distribution of funds outside the logic of public subsidies, and the subcontracting of training services to non public providers does not guarantee the access to training to all kinds of applicants. In conclusion, efficient solutions may not be the fairest ones.

In both countries, decentralization is not opposed to the markedly state character of the main institutions for the public service of employment. This is quite different in the case of other two European cases examined here. In both the Italian (Chapter 8) and Spanish (Chapter 9) cases, active employment policies and income support measures belong to the sphere of the region. Indeed, in the Spanish case, this decentralization may give rise to a certain unbalance in the quantification of citizens' rights; for example, when it comes to regulating income support by the regions (Baylos, Cabeza and Romero). In Italy, this risk of unbalance in the regulation of citizens' rights is not excluded either, despite the fact that the regulation of the 'essential' level of benefits is competence of the state (Ricci).

Both in Italy and Spain, the decentralization of these competences over to the regions has taken place through their respective constitutional laws. Within this constitutional statutory frame, it has been up to the case law of the constitutional courts to balance the role played by the regions and the state in the management of benefits, in accordance with the constitutional principles of equality, economic unity and solidarity. However, the most interesting thing about these two countries is not this sort of rebalancing function among the regions played by the constitutional case law. The interesting thing is the construction of institutional mechanisms for cooperation and coordination (the inter-administrative sectoral conference in Spain), as well as the renewed impulse given to social dialogue as a means to legitimize the correction by the state of any unbalance in the regulation of regional competences (for example, the social agreement reached in 2007 to reform the financing of vocational training in Spain).

Finally, Chapter 10 explains the British experience on the implementation of the principle of 'make work pay', that is, how to give social protection to the unemployed person so that he keeps actively looking for a job. The British experience is an example of a national strategy aside from the EES and the OMC. In any event, it has also been a particular example of institutional decentralization of the employment services through the creation of the 'job centre plus' at local level. In this sense, Carby-Hall explains at Chapter 10 the essence of Blair's new deal on employment as a result of the 1995 reform of the job seeker's allowance. The Job Seeker's Allowance (JSA) Act of 1995 introduced measures that are still considered a model for an efficient employment policy. The JSA Act encompasses in a single act the economic treatment of unemployment benefits and income support, redesigning the latter as twelve different schemes. Its unified management is based on the 'job centre plus', which controls every aspect of the JSA. There is active commitment (the job seeker's agreement) by the beneficiaries of the JSA combined with sanctions and training tailored to meet skill shortages.

After twelve years of application, the question is as follows: has the reform introduced by the JSA Act served to eradicate long-term unemployment, poverty and social exclusion? According to Carby-Hall, 25% of the beneficiaries of the JSA become unemployed again, which shows the difficulty in finishing with the segmentation of the labour market. In the opinion of the author, this plays down the effectiveness of the JSA. He also casts doubts about the true purpose of the reform: maybe under the cover of encouraging the unemployed back to work there only laid an economic purge of the social security system. Today, in line with the strategy of flexicurity, the UK is debating the effectiveness of the principle of make work pay and is proposing a programme based on a bigger participation by the business community in the insertion of job seekers, in the generation of better jobs and skills and in the anticipation of skill needs.

This variety of national experiences in the implementation of the EES reveals that Europe is far from having achieved a unitary model of reference for the vertical and horizontal coordination of the EES in the Member States. Cooperation and coordination exist where they have already been permitted and established through national laws and customs. It seems unclear whether the EES is advancing this cause in places where it did not already exist.

Our final thought is this. Although the EES has not achieved this uniformity, it may have to do so if it wants to set in motion a new model based on the strategy of flexicurity capable of giving full potentiality to the EES. Here we have in mind the idea that what may be required is nothing less than a basic reformulation of the very notion of work, and of the rights and duties legally configured around it. It is far from clear whether individual European states will or can voluntarily join together to introduce a reform of such importance in their respective legal systems. As a result this may ultimately be both the biggest problem for, but at the same time the largest opportunity for, the credibility of the EES.

In Europe, historically, work has been a symbol of full citizenship. In past times, it was conceived as a duty inherent in the status of citizen. Today, work is, above all, a fundamental source of rights according to the social contract enshrined in the constitutions of most of the European countries during the twentieth century. In virtue of this, every person has the right to work; this is, to freely choose a suitable, professional and decent job.[9] Is this a perspective from which the EES could operate? This is a question best left for another debate, but, probably, an EES without such a modern notion of human work could only be valid only from a certain understanding of economic efficiency, rather than from a social and political perspective. Without a starting point of a modern definition of 'work' legally protected in Europe, in the long term the EES may be incapable of serving effectively as an instrument to drive the modernizing reforms needed for social and employment policies. And as a further result, these policies may remain the exclusive property of the Member States.

9. M. Freedland and N. Countouris, 'Diritti e Doveri nel Rapporto tra Disoccupati e Servizi per L'Impiego in Europa' (2005) *108 Giornale di Diritto del Lavoro e di Relazioni Industriali* 589. G. Mundlak, 'Derecho al Trabajo: Conjugar Derechos Humanos y Política de Empleo' in (2007) 126 No. 3-4 *Revista Internacional de Trabajo*, 222.

Part I

The Framework Context of Europeanization of National Employment and Social Inclusion Policies

Chapter 1

The Impact of Globalization on Employment and Social Inclusion Policies: Experiences and Proposals in Individual European Countries

Jean-Michel Servais

1. INTRODUCTION

The present chapter does not deal with the European Employment Strategy, which is the focus of other contributions to this book. It examines the employment laws of individual European and non-European countries, using material from the International Labour Organization (ILO) as a guide to distinguish between different types of policies. It does, however, observe that the European countries share a specific way of viewing and addressing employment and social protection questions or, more precisely, a set of common institutions and practices, a heritage of history.

Can this heritage be maintained in a globalizing economy? In other words, can the very distinct levels of economic development, the political and social preferences of nations or groups of nations, the national cultures (i.e., the ideas, customs, skills, arts, etc., of a people or group) that are transferred, communicated, or passed along to succeeding generations be still taken into account?[1]

1. This is how culture is defined in the *Webster's New World Dictionary*, 3rd College edn (New York, Prentice Hall, 1984).

Roger Blanpain, Juan Pablo Landa, Brian Langille (eds), *Employment Policies and Multilevel Governance*, pp. 3–31.

This chapter first examines various answers to the so-called social question, with a view to showing whether a better understanding of the differences is of real significance in the elaboration and implementation of a social policy. We revisit briefly the way governments have reacted to the problems of unemployment and the need for financial assistance. This provides a valuable key to understanding the present situation of social uncertainty. We continue by underlining how the political, economic and technological changes have influenced different solutions. This acknowledges both the positive and the negative aspects of the actual globalization. On the one hand, the globalizing process has promoted the principles of freedom (including the freedom to undertake business) and democracy in all parts of the world. On the other, it has put into question the capacity of the state to deal with social problems because it leads to (i) the state's losing its capacity to execute its own policies; and (ii) the inability of traditional social partners to fulfil their functions.

We also review national and international employment laws and the balance they have found between the promotion of decent jobs and the protection of workers, focusing on individual European legislations. This chapter underlines their shortcomings in the present economic environment and further identifies new investigations and experiences aiming to an improved equilibrium between a necessary flexibility and the need for material guarantees for the weakest.

Conclusions will be drawn from this as to the ways and means for the states to reshape their role and for traditional and new actors to contribute to the solution of the social challenges of the day.

2. A VARIETY OF SOCIAL POLICIES

2.1. Historical Perspective

In the past, governments have adopted at least three kinds of policy to maintain or restore social stability among their citizens: enlightened despotism, laissez-faire and the social state.

2.1.1. Enlightened Despotism

The classic example of the first kind of policies just mentioned is the virtuous authoritarianism of Prussia and Austria in the eighteenth century, called 'enlightened despotism'. The government had its own view of the problems encountered and imposed the remedies it deemed appropriate. Modern politicians or high-level civil servants have a similar way to proceed in a number of developing countries, especially in Asia.[2] They sometimes happen to be brilliant technocrats, with PhDs from the best universities. They consider themselves in a privileged position to

2. *See* already J. Schregle, *Negotiating Development. Labour Relations in Southern Asia* (Geneva, ILO, 1982), 184.

understand and solve the difficulties of their people, but without consulting with the people concerned.

The development process of Japan and, later, of South Korea and Taiwan, has been based on this type of social policy. The state and its officials play a very active role in the industrial relations. Their influence appears substantial, but their concern is centred on growth and productivity. To put it very simply, the state deals first with economics before turning its attention to social issues, in the belief that resolving the former takes priority over the latter.[3] However, in the course of the economic development of these countries, greater attention has been devoted to social problems and collective negotiations. It was in this context that the three famous pillars of the Japanese industrial relations system were erected after the Second World War: (i) lifetime employment; (ii) calculation of wages and social benefits based on seniority; and (iii) enterprise-level trade unionism. South Korea and more recently Taiwan appear to be moving towards a fairly similar approach. While Japan and South Korea in particular bear resemblance, in many respects, to the European way to solve social problems (including the practice of collective negotiations at the branch or national inter-branch level), other countries in Asia, like Malaysia, have maintained a more totalitarian approach.

Communist countries adopted a completely different economic policy. Nevertheless, it is also true that their approach to social issues was not very different from that of authoritarian governments in Asia. The leading role was left to the party in power, which saw itself as the enlightened advanced guard of the labour class. Cuba can still be considered as an example of this form of government.

2.1.2. Laissez-Faire

The laissez-faire approach to government could not be more different: the executive lets the 'invisible hand' of the market make the adjustments required, including in the field of labour. No country has completely adopted this form of government, but the United States' approach to labour and employment is probably a good example of little interventionism. In this field as in others, it is rather voluntarist.[4] It values political and economic liberalism. The emphasis is placed on individual freedom and responsibility as well as action by local economic agents and groups, rather than on political power at the state or federal level. Enterprises that dismiss employees pay, for example, increased contributions to the unemployment fund. The law focuses more on civil liberties than on social rights, more on

---

3. ILO, 'Industrial Relations, Democracy and Social Stability' in *World Labour Report 1997-98* (Geneva, ILO, 1997), 224.
4. S. Jacoby, 'American Exceptionalism Revisited: The Importance of Management' in S. Jacoby (ed.), *Masters to Managers: Historical and Comparative Perspectives on American Employers* (New York, Columbia University Press, 1991); S.M. Lipset and N.M. Meltz, 'Canadian and American Attitudes towards Work and Institutions' (1997) 1 (3) *Perspectives on Work. The IRRA's 50th Anniversary Magazine*, 14-19. Earlier, *see* S. McCane Lindsey, 'The Problem of American Cooperation' in J.T. Shotwell (ed.), *The Origins of the International Labor Organisation* (New York, Columbia University Press, 1934), 331-367.

equality of opportunity and treatment than on any levelling of incomes. There is no general recognition of a social question, but rather of a moral, poverty problem to be dealt with firstly by private charities. Hence, the recent school of thought that claims a strengthening of solidarity by making the defense of workers' rights part of human rights.[5]

Historically, the American federal system has made it a complex matter for Congress in Washington to provide workers with the kind of protection granted under the laws of continental Europe or Japan. In the United States, enterprise (or establishment) level collective bargaining has been given preference over labour and social security legislation. In Japan, and in continental Europe, help from the government, civil service and Parliament is expected – although in varying degrees – to improve living and working standards. Moreover, the socialist doctrine of class struggle for state control practically never caught on in the United States. In the past, a trend developed towards greater centralization of authority and greater importance of the federal machinery in labour matters. These efforts to achieve greater uniformity, as well as the similarity between the objectives enshrined in President Roosevelt's New Deal and those of the ILO, finally led the United States to join the ILO in 1934. However, the voluntarist approach of American labour management relations never really changed dramatically. Although federal legislation did evolve significantly in the 1960s, it did so chiefly in the sphere of civil rights (protection of various groups from discrimination, for example).[6]

2.1.3. Social State

The third policy satisfies the citizens' desire to *see* the state establish rules, institutions and practices safeguarding them from social risks, as in a number of European countries. It is based on a recognized duty of solidarity and, more often than not, on the explicit or tacit agreement of the large employers' and workers' federations.

Admittedly, a European 'social dimension' exists already, and it would be wrong to play down its importance. A Community social policy has been built up on treaties as well as on the instruments derived from them: recognition of fundamental principles and rights, including equality of treatment and of opportunities; free movement of workers and persons in general; coordination of employment policies; social security for migrant workers; emergence of minimum social standards regarding enterprise-level labour relations and working conditions; and social dialogue via a number of European collective agreements. This specifically European form of protection, however, remains limited, as a

5. *See*, for example, Committee on Monitoring International Labour Standards, *Monitoring International Labour Standards. Techniques and Sources of Information* (Washington DC, The National Academies Press, 2004), 224 *et seq.*; P. Alston (dir.), *Labour Rights as Human Rights* (Oxford, Oxford University Press, 2005).
6. ILO, above n. 3.

consequence of the principle of subsidiarity enshrined in the Treaty establishing the EC.[7]

In contrast, we can clearly observe at the level of the individual states the social culture shared by many European countries. They believe in the need to go beyond the mere recognition of civil liberties and political rights as enshrined in the 1776 American Declaration of Independence and the 1789 French Declaration of the Rights of Man and Citizen. They are reluctant to accept phenomena of exclusion and excessive inequality. They expect the state to intervene in order to remedy the social consequences of the mechanical operation of the market economy. They wish to find an answer to the social question. They have a strong sense of solidarity in the face of the problems of unemployment and poverty. Most European governments, whether right or left sided, have enacted tax or social security legislation to tackle those problems. Although this has been criticized by some as weakening competitivity, recent history demonstrates that voters continue to prefer this policy, while accepting, as the case may be, limited adjustments.

This common heritage should not mask the clear differences that exist among European countries. In particular, the importance given to job security and social protection varies greatly, as illustrated by the recent debate on the merits of the 'Danish model' which gives preference to the latter. The United Kingdom has traditionally adopted a more voluntarist vision of the world of work. Nevertheless, most European social policies reflect three historical realities.[8]

The first is that of social regulation based on centralized consultation and action in concert, which may be bipartite or tripartite. Whatever the number of parties involved, state institutions are never indifferent to the outcome of talks in which social actors have participated. This practice of collective negotiations (in the broad sense) is generally furthered by a sophisticated system of industrial relations. While it is true that tripartite agreements and other forms of high level social pacts have been, and are, observed in other regions of the world, no other region has resorted as much to dialogue, be it formal or informal, at central level.

The second reality is what is often named 'welfare state' or 'social economy'. Both terms imply an elaborate social security system including, where appropriate, provision for a minimum guaranteed income and other forms of labour protection (minimum wage, for example). They also cover public services provided by the state in the social and economic spheres (industrial, commercial, etc.).

The third reality, related to the other two, is the implementation of Keynesian principles that is of an active state intervention in industrial, economic and social

---

7. On the application of this principle in the field of social policies, *see* R. Blanpain, *European Labour Law*, 10th rev.edn (The Hague, Kluwer, 2006), paras 45-50; P. Rodière, *Droit Social de l'Union Européenne*, 2nd edn (Paris, LGDJ, 2002), paras 30-40.
8. J.M. Servais, 'Quelques Réflexions sur un Modèle Social Européen' (2001) 56 (4) *Relations Industrielles*, 701-719; M. Hansenne, 'The European Social Model and Globalisation of the Economy' in *Labour Relations and Industrial Relations at the Turn of the Century. Liber Amicorum in Honour of Roger Blanpain*, C. Engels & M. Weiss (eds) (The Hague, Kluwer, 1998). 193-200. Cf. R. Boyer, 'Les Quatre Grands Modèles du Capitalisme', (31 Aug. 2005) *Problèmes Économiques*, 34-38.

matters, and, in collaboration with social partners participating in varying degrees, search for consensus in the elaboration and application of policies. For many years, both business and trade unions have been involved, at the governments' invitation, in seeking compromises between the different economic variables: production of wealth, its distribution and job creation.

2.2. Social Policies and Globalization

The revolution in communication and production technologies and in the organization of work, the political changes symbolized by the fall of the Berlin wall, the emergence of newly industrialized countries, the growing interdependence of national economies, have all clearly had telling effects on states, business and trade unions. Some are positive, but there is another side of the coin. Socially speaking, the most important question is probably to ensure a smooth transition to renewed systems: adjustment policies should then involve slowing down the process of alteration to the point where it becomes humanly tolerable.[9]

2.2.1. The Bright Side of the Changes

The softening of national frontiers has spurred the values of freedom and democracy. The victory of the market economy and the use of television, of internet and other cross border means of communication have spilled over the liberal vision of a democratic state and civil liberties, including the principle of equality of opportunities and treatment. The states, even the most remote ones, have faced the impact of western ideas of personal and economic freedoms. The best examples are probably found in the Gulf countries (although the situation differs from one state to another) and in their recent openings with regard to political (women's rights to vote and be elected) and workers' rights (freedom of association or at least of establishment of workers councils). Previously, the democratic revolution in East Germany and in other European communist countries was due, at least partially, and in the opinion of many, to the pictures seen from western television. 1989 was no accident, we were told: that year France celebrated, with a big media display, the bicentenary of its Revolution; its motto *Liberté, Égalité, Fraternité* had a gnawing effect on the still totalitarian structures of central European countries. Generally speaking, globalization implies a weakening of interstate exchange control, freer trade and personal relations.

Freedom to undertake economic activity is seen as an essential factor of long lasting economic success. It fosters private initiative, competition and emulation.

9. K. Polanyi, *The Great Transformation: The Political and Economic Origins of Our Time* (Boston, M.A. Beacon Press, 1957), 33 *et seq.* Along this line, the EU Council of Ministers, together with the European Parliament, has established a fund to help workers adapt to the effects of globalisation (Regulation 1927/2006 on Establishing the European Globalisation Adjustment Fund, OJ L 406, 30 Dec. 2006, 1-6).

It boosts employment. Its links with civil liberties are complex, as exemplified by China. Nevertheless one observes that at a certain stage of their development, previously autocratic states – like South Korea or Taiwan, but also Spain or Portugal before – need to offer more space of liberty for their entrepreneurs. A non-democratic regime tends to impose a monopoly not only in political matters, but frequently on commercial and financial ones as well. Political centralization implies a control by the administration in all respects,[10] favouring friends rather than those with merit, easily accepting nepotism and other forms of corruption. State control affects public life, but quite often extends to private business as well. Red tape becomes a serious obstacle to commercial activities; civil service personnel is selected on the basis of political, rather than technical criteria; and infrastructures suffer from the lack of good management by state agencies. There is a tendency for the public sector to extend or dominate the state. In brief, as underlined several times in some World Bank annual reports, bureaucracy kills emulation and entrepreneurship spirit.

2.2.2. Destabilizing Factors

Political and economic opening is the bright face of the globalization process. There is another side to it. The present economic evolution has negative consequences as well, as it raises a new social question, and brings doubts about the efficiency of present policies.

A first destabilizing factor is the fact that labour and social security legislation often seems ill adapted to today's circumstances, to the extent where it is almost not applied at all. Many consider this as very serious in the case of new members of the European Union (EU).

A related source of destabilization is that employment no longer looks as before: it is less stable, more concentrated in the service sector, increasingly dominated by new technologies, more dependant on communication skills and professional relations frequently built up in smaller enterprises with a much looser structure. Although the new forms of work may boost productivity – though even that is disputed – they may also drive a definitive gap between regular (i.e., more or less permanent) staff and casual workers.

The solutions proposed by governments also vary. Some favour flexibilization of the labour market more than others. Hence, the difficulties for the Member States of the EU to reach a political consensus on labour issues. Countries like Spain or Germany, whatever the colour of their governments, are concerned with maintaining most of the protective rights. The position of more liberal states, including a number of central European countries, is different. Rigidity has a price in economic terms. And yet, and this is a further destabilizing factor,

10. With regard to labour law, *see* M. Sewerýnski and A. Marzal, *Changements Politiques et Droit du Travail. Perspectives Polono-Espagnoles* (Lódz, Wydawnictwo Uniwersytetu Lódzkiego, 1992); COMPTRASEC (Université de Bordeaux I), *Liberté, Égalité, Fraternité. Actualité en Droit Social* (Bordeaux, Editions LC.F.Lycofac, 1990).

experiences show that flexibility is not always the solution, and brings diluting effects as well. More and more voices have been heard, for example at conferences of the World Trade Organization (and elsewhere), even before the present crisis, wondering whether deregulation has gone too far, and whether it is time to restore a little order (including in the capital market). It should also be remembered that the impact of flexibilization depends inter alia on the pre-existing system of law, and on the degree and form of its protective character.

Capital rather than labour mobility has reduced the margin of action for governments that wish to attract foreign direct investment. They have quite often softened companies' fiscal and social obligations, either in free exporting zones or just generally. The globalization of financial and commercial markets has stiffened the competition among private enterprises and countries.[11] There is an ongoing pressure to reduce salaries and social benefits, and threats to move production to cheaper countries, resulting in the weakening of collective bargaining and trade unions.[12]

The internationalization of the market economy, and its regionalization in Europe, has inevitably limited the scope for action of public authorities, in particular with regard to labour affairs.[13] A Keynesian national policy presupposed complete control of economic instruments by the state. It cannot function in the same way if the states lose some of that control. They may even have difficulties to impose the application of their actual law to supranational entities. Labour law is affected in both its content and its implementation. The multinational character of many firms has removed the decision-making power further and further away from the workplace.[14] And yet governments are called on to be active more than ever before, in particular with relation to the problems of employment and social protection.

Governments frequently turn, in Europe, to employers' and trade unions' organizations for help, but the latter are also faced with serious difficulties in the same context. Unions face a well-known predicament, with membership rates falling in many countries. Employers' organizations are also going through a period of upheaval. Diversification and segmentation of interests in the trade unions (the concerns of stable wage earners differ considerably from those of the unemployed and workers in contingent employment) and employers' federations (the interests of small and medium sized businesses may be very much at odds with

11. H.W. Sinn, 'Le Dilemme de la Mondialisation' (2006) 2900 *Problèmes Économiques*, 43-48.
12. I. Rapin, 'Des salariés face à la délocalisation. Notes ethnographiques sur un monde ouvrier en crise' (2007) 6 *Esprit*, 62.
13. *See* for example, A. Martin and G. Ross (eds), *Euros and Europeans: Monetary Integration and the European Model of Society* (Cambridge, Cambridge University Press, 2004).
14. *See* G. Lyon-Caen, 'Sur le Transfert des Emplois dans les Groupes Multinationaux' (1995) 5 *Droit Social*, 489-494. *See also* International Labour Conference, 81st session, *Defending Values, Promoting Changes. Social Justice in a Global Economy: an ILO Agenda. Report of the Director-General* (Geneva, ILO, 1994), 15.

those of multinationals) affect them both to the point that their respective monopoly on representation is open to challenge.

Many companies, especially the bigger ones, seek to preserve their freedom of action when it comes to personnel management. They have nevertheless been known to create relatively informal networks among themselves. Staff policies crop up in the agenda at meetings of CEOs of America's biggest firms or of business councils elsewhere. The leaders of Japan's main enterprises hold sector, inter sector or industrial group coordination meetings, notably in response to the spring labour offensive ritual (the *shunto*). For trade unions, the segmentation of interests has put the tradition of fellowship among workers to the test. Moreover, the group that was most favourably disposed towards union action in the past, the regular wage earners, is shrinking, while a large number of all kinds of organizations claim to represent what are often very specific interest groups (consumers, environmentalists, women, ethnic minorities, local communities, the unemployed, etc.) that overlap with those the unions seek to represent. In short, for employers' associations and workers' federations, the byword is competition rather than unified action.

A parallel phenomenon is the rising strength of new world players, first and foremost the multinationals. Some of them (albeit only a few as yet) no longer have privileged ties with a specific country; their headquarters are located wherever their principal leaders are to be found at any given moment. Regional groups, such as the EU, Mercosur or The North American Free Trade Agreement (NAFTA), constitute other new world players. Non-governmental organizations (NGOs) have for their part used new communication technologies to create transnational networks, which can carry great weight.[15] All of these players have adapted to the opening of borders and trade liberalization more quickly than the more rigidly structured public authorities themselves. Certain groups have an acknowledged ability to make themselves heard in the media.

The diminished role of the state not only reflects the growing importance of international actors. Local and municipal activities are also multiplying. NGO initiatives have changed the local landscape. Increasingly, public authorities entrust NGOs with social tasks that they cannot or no longer wish to carry out, starting a process of privatization that does not involve the business sector but nevertheless relieves the authorities of certain responsibilities. Other public institutions below state level have also been observed to be increasingly active. Most American states have an official observer at the World Trade Organization. The German *Lander*, the Belgian language communities and the British local authorities send representatives to the EU. France's Rhône-Alpes region has established direct relations with Geneva and Turin, with a view to dealing with cross border issues such as seasonal workers. Many large companies endeavour, again more frequently than in the recent past, to develop social activities locally.

15. *See also* J.T. Matthews, 'Power shift' (1997) Jan.-Feb. *Foreign Affairs*, 50-66.

International organizations, like the ILO, are also facing difficulties because their structures and modes of action continue to depend on weakened interstate relations. The efforts of those institutions to bring representatives of the global civil society into the fold express their desire to adapt their objectives to new realities.

2.2.3. Perspectives

None of the social visions mentioned above – and their expression through standards and legal institutions – has managed to mend in any significant way the social questions of the day, that is, (i) the fractures between countries and persons that are able to take advantage of the new economic environment; and (ii) the others, the losers of the upsetting of the status quo that feel more and more marginalized and impoverished. On the contrary, those fractures appear even more pronounced.

The laissez-faire policy has never been able to guarantee a living wage for the most underprivileged, particularly during a slump. In practice, some form or other of a social security system (the 'safety net') often corrected its more heartless consequences. Voices are raised in very liberal states, like in a number of Latin American countries, to correct the absolute freedom of the market in favour of the most destitute; new governments have been elected on 'left' programmes. The modern forms of enlightened despotism have often been mere alibis for personal gain; they do not always – and quite understandably – correspond to the needs and desires of the population; the risks of making a bad policy choice are obvious. And criticism has been heaped on social economies on the grounds that it is too cumbersome to cope with the globalization of the capital, production and labour markets. For social economies to survive unchanged in a world in which trade in capital and goods has been liberalized presupposes an interstate solidarity that does not exist. Both models imply strong public authorities. There is no surprise in observing that they face difficulties to adapt to a process that weakens the role of the state. Social partners also lose strength, as we have seen, in the social states; they are unable, in many cases, to play their expected role, that is, to participate usefully in the adjustment process.

The same may be said of international institutions. They are basically founded on interstate relations, and the decreasing number of centralized states makes their efforts to reshape the economic and social international order less relevant. They are all going through a difficult time, more so those in charge of social matters obviously not at the core of the big players' concerns.

In brief, the traditional channels of labour and social relations are questioned everywhere. More fundamentally, the compromises of political nature that had been established between economic constraints and social protection are being affected in every instance. The pressures brought to bear on the traditional social actors by increased competition and other factors described above have become extremely serious. Wherever we look, people are challenging what used to be taken for granted in a certain society, many policies are being queried; attitudes inherited from the past as well as the structures of social relations themselves are being shaken.

Even in the most industrialized countries, jobs and worker protection are becoming insecure. The diversity of situations and interests undermines the internal cohesion of national societies, moving unrest from the enterprises to the suburbs and, more fundamentally, causing, or risking to cause, the marginalization of important sections of the population. Many political leaders have expressed reservations, stating that man is not a machine – a commodity to use the terminology of the ILO Constitution – and emphasized that the laws of the market, if left to operate unhindered, may well dilute the social cohesion of the human communities. They call for a new international order.

Let us review the present state of employment laws, especially in European countries, before analyzing the search for new solutions.

3. PRESENT EUROPEAN NATIONAL EMPLOYMENT LAWS: A BRIEF OUTLOOK

The promotion of employment lies at the heart of the European countries' programmes. For their governments, the principal route out of poverty is work; poverty cannot be eradicated unless the economy generates opportunities for investment, entrepreneurship, job creation and sustainable livelihoods. Forced inactivity has a devastating impact even in industrialized countries, both on the unemployed and on the undertakings forced to lay workers off. Forced departures leave deep scars in the internal mechanisms of the undertaking and in its workers.

The scars are also psychological. In Western Europe, like in Japan, employment relationships were usually entered into for an unlimited time, that is, for a very long spell if not, as in Japan above all, for the entire working life of the wage earner. A moral bond of loyalty was forged between the employer and the wage earner. Dismissals sever that bond, and destabilize the workers not affected by them. Workers dismissed for economic reasons are sometimes given priority in re-hiring, but this makes little difference. Although those who remain may try to work better so as to protect themselves from dismissal, their perception of work changes: they disengage, or switch their priorities to activities outside work (or take a second job).

The consequences of unemployment go much further than mere cases of staff reduction. It is a serious phenomenon. It pushes people, especially young job seekers, to consume drugs and alcohol, and can have psychosomatic effects. If the unemployment rate grows, the social fabric holding the country together may weaken.

At the Lisbon European Council of March 2000, the EU set itself a strategic goal for the next decade: 'to become the most competitive and dynamic knowledge-based economy in the world, capable of sustainable economic growth with more and better jobs and greater social cohesion'. The strategy was designed to enable the Union to regain the conditions for full employment and to strengthen cohesion by 2010.

How do national labour standards promote fulfilment of this objective? The answer is a complex one because it lies in the grey area between law and economics. All the more reason to be specific and render each discipline its due.

The promotion of full, productive and freely chosen employment should be regarded, as provided in the ILO Employment Policy (Supplementary Provisions) Recommendation of 1984,[16] as the means of giving practical effect to the right to work. In market economies, provisions relating to the right to work tend to be programmatic in nature. They establish obligations of means, not of outcome. The applicable international standards oblige ratifying states to justify their policy in this respect. The ILO Convention on Employment Policy of 1964 (No. 122) contains such an obligation, although it does not expressly mention 'the right to work'. It goes without saying that no legal text will ever do completely away with unemployment: only an economic policy can do this. Such a policy will aim, for example, to restructure undertakings and the national (or local) production machinery as needed. But legal standards can help find a solution if, on the one hand, they set goals, recommend specific policies and programmes, and create appropriate channels for them; and, on the other, provide for very tangible labour market measures and the means of evaluating their effectiveness.

Two kinds of measures may be taken. The first are short term, like public works or subsidies to enterprises facing difficulties that aim to boost recruitment or to avoid dismissals, at least for a brief period. The others lay the groundwork for an active employment policy in the longer term. In this chapter, we shall focus on the latter. The following pages consider common aspects of (i) termination of employment standards; (ii) employment agencies; (iii) social policies and job stimulation; (iv) vocational training and occupational retraining; and (v) the role of social security in an employment policy. They also raise the problem of non-standard forms of employment.

3.1. Employment Security and Dismissal Policies

Dismissal is not the only way to break off the employment relationship, but it is the most used and therefore most of what follows relates to it. The employment relationship may also terminate because it had a fixed term. It has always been considered that a term of employment allows the worker to plan for the future, but there is a risk of abuse: the notice period can be very short, and the use of successive fixed-term contracts can be a means of avoiding the protection against dismissal. European national legislations require adequate guarantees against such procedures.

There are various measures to that end: one is to limit fixed-term contracts to cases where the employment relationship cannot be of indeterminate duration (owing either to the nature of the work, the circumstances under which it is to

16. The ILO Employment Policy (Supplementary Provisions) Recommendation of 1984, (no. 169), para. 1.

be effected or the interests of the worker); another is to deem such contracts, when renewed on one or more occasions, to be contracts of indeterminate duration. Many countries have laws and regulations with provisions of this kind; the rule has in some cases been established by case law as well. However, more than one legislator has encouraged fixed-term contracts, as in France, Germany or Spain, in order to fight unemployment.

Most European national laws require the employer to give a reason for dismissal. They normally distinguish between dismissal grounds based on the capacity or conduct of the worker, and those based on the operational requirements of the employer. Of course, what counts are not the formal grounds but the real reasons for the dismissal. It is up to the courts, when the case is brought before them, to discern where the truth lies.

This is particularly so in the case of reasons that cannot be invoked to justify a dismissal. There are basically two kinds of such reasons.[17] The first involve discrimination of some kind based for example on union activities, race, colour, gender, religion, political opinion, national extraction or social origin, and age. The second are based on the exercise by the worker of rights such as maternity leave, sick leave, or leave for military service or other civic obligations.

Dismissal based on personal grounds reflect the employer's belief that it is impossible to continue the employment relationship. Dismissal based on economic grounds have to do with the undertaking's profits, they affect workers individually and as a group. In the latter case, the decision takes on a special dimension.

Different steps may be taken to prevent collective dismissals or limit their effects. In France and Germany where work committees play a decisive role, the law provides for the establishment of genuine planned redundancy schemes. Both countries have set up insertion enterprises. Measures include a hiring non renewal of temporary contracts, transfers, placement in alternative employment (with retraining and/or mobility assistance as required), temporary layoffs, part time work, early or gradual retirement, voluntary departure (with or without a bonus), reduced overtime, etc.

European national laws usually establish in advance the criteria to select the workers affected, their order of priority and their relative number, giving due weight to the interests of the undertaking or service and the interests of the workers. The criteria used most frequently are seniority, vocational skills, personal capacity and family situation. Others include nationality, age or belonging to a protected category (workers' representatives, the disabled, veterans).[18]

If the employer reduces the size of the workforce, many laws and collective agreements impose priority in re-hiring under certain conditions. One can think of two kinds of measures to attenuate the effects of such dismissals still in use today: compensation, which we will look at later; and assistance in finding other suitable employment.

---

17. For an analysis of national law and practice, *see* in particular ILO, *Termination of Employment Legislation Digest* <www.ilo.org/public/english/dialogue/ifpdial/info/termination>.
18. *See Ibid.*

The procedures for dismissal are, generally speaking, an important aspect of the protection afforded to dismiss workers. They are entitled to a 'reasonable notice period' or compensation in its lieu, unless guilty of serious misconduct – misconduct of such a nature that it would be unreasonable to require the employer to continue the employment during the notice period. The notice period is intended to allow workers to start looking for another job. Many laws provide facilities to that end, in particular free time without loss of pay to be used at times convenient for both parties.

European national laws spell out measures to be taken prior to or during termination of employment. Let us take, for example, the employer's obligation to give the wage earner a prior warning if the dismissal has to do with his conduct. The wage earner has the right to defend himself. Whether immediately or after the notice period, a non-voluntary departure requires a notification indicating the employer's decision to end the contract. Many countries require that this unilateral notice be given in writing, often specifying the date of termination, the reasons therefore, and the applicable legal provisions and remedies (including the right to appeal). The notice periods themselves are sometimes the subject of detailed rules. Lastly, the dismissed wage earner can request from the employer a certificate of employment indicating, as stipulated in the ILO Recommendation on Dismissal of 1982 (No. 166), only 'the dates of his engagement and termination of his employment and the type or types of work on which he was employed'; nevertheless, 'and at the request of the worker, an evaluation of his conduct and performance may be given in this certificate or in a separate certificate'.

Most national laws in Europe contemplate procedures to follow before or against the dismissal: internal appeals that may involve workers' representatives are supplemented with complaints to independent bodies such as a court or arbitral tribunal. If the worker loses his job for economic reasons, many laws and collective agreements, and European law, require prior consultation with the workers' representatives and notice to the public authorities. The laws of some countries go even further and require prior authorization by the labour administration or a joint body, subject to judicial appeal.

The wage earner may find it difficult to prove that the dismissal is unlawful. Therefore, the laws of some countries require the courts to base their findings relating to the reasons for dismissal on the arguments put forth by both parties.

Where a court finds that the dismissal is unjustified, it can annul it and/or order the reinstatement of the worker. That decision, which normally includes the payment of any lost earnings, is obviously difficult to execute in practice. Most countries, therefore, eventually oblige the employer to pay compensation. The solution adopted varies from country to country and from case to case. The compensation may be a lump sum (calculated on the basis of salary and seniority), complete reparation for the damages suffered (in some cases only if the law has been breached) or left to the discretion of the judge.

Custom, collective agreements and individual contracts have gradually introduced the concept of severance pay. This kind of compensation is now part of the laws and regulations of many countries, subject to the principle that there is no serious misconduct on the part of the wage earner and, sometimes, only if there is a reduction in the staff number.

What happens if the employer goes bankrupt? The ILO Protection of Workers' Claims (Employer's Insolvency) Convention of 1992 (No. 173) describes two options: privilege, and guarantee institutions. Privilege is by far the most common method of protecting workers' claims.[19] It is a long-standing legal practice to grant preference to certain creditors over other, non-privileged creditors. The main privileged credits are normally wages and other sums due to workers (paid holidays, paid leaves, severance pay, indemnities, social security and occupational insurance premiums, etc.). The protection may be limited to a maximum amount. In any case, the effectiveness of this privilege requires that the workers' claims be given a high rank amongst the creditors.

The second option is a guarantee institution for payment of workers' claims in cases where the insolvent employer cannot settle them. Funds have been created for that purpose, essentially in Western Europe, and Belgium played a pioneering role in the 1960s. National legislations as well as a European Directive deal with this matter, capping the claims (essentially the same limit as for privileged claims). They also establish the working principles of such funds, which, it has been said,[20] are similar to those of social security schemes: they are mandatory, work on the basis of solidarity, are financed (except in some cases) by payments calculated on the basis of salary, and are managed by institutions that are administrative, financial and legally independent.

In addition, dismissed workers may receive an income from unemployment insurance benefits and unemployment aid. Some countries oblige the employer to notify dismissals to the social security funds.

It is necessary to underline that the dismissal laws of European countries have been at the core of the public debates on the need for more flexibility. They have sometimes been amended.[21] More often, precarious forms of employment relationships have been developed aside from the traditional contract without limit of time.

3.2. Common Aspects to Employment Agencies

In the beginning, public employment services in European countries dealt essentially with vocational guidance and the unemployed. As they grew, their activities became more systematic: they categorized occupations, analyzed positions, looked for and distributed recruitment information. As the state stepped up its role in the

19. *See* ILC, 78th session, *Protection of Workers' Claims in the Event of Insolvency of Their Employer* (Geneva, ILO, 1990), Report V(I); E. Yemin and A. Bronstein (eds), *The Protection of Workers' Claims in the Event of the Employers' Insolvency* (Geneva, ILO, 1991).
20. *See* J.V. Gruat, 'Les Problèmes des Régimes de Protection des Salariés en Cas de Faillite de l'Entreprise (Etude Comparative), Protection contre le Chômage et Politique de l'Emploi' *Documentation de Sécurité Sociale, Série Européenne*, No. 5 (Genève, ISSA, 1981), 171-96.
21. F. Kessler, 'Images de la Flexicurité: le Droit du Licenciement aux Pays-Bas' (2008) 5 *Droit Social* 577.

economic and social fields, it adopted new means of action. After the Second World War in particular, the target of many governments was full employment, and this prompted them to act – or try to act – as employment market regulators. In reality, the results varied according to each country's economic health. In the 1960s, the states further expanded their field of action and integrated these activities into their overall policies and programmes.[22]

More recently, however, the tendency has been for the state to pull back. This has rekindled the discussion of whether placement agencies should be privately or publicly managed. This question has never really been solved. Although those in favour of prohibiting private offices as a matter of principle seemed to hold sway at one time, the situation appears to be reversed today. For the better part of a century, therefore, the public authorities played an active part in the placement of workers in order to put a stop, initially, to well known abuses. Many European countries prohibited private employment agencies, and gave the state a monopoly on this matter.

The debate continued. Doubts were expressed about the effectiveness of certain public employment agencies on the one hand, and the practices of certain private agencies on the other. In 1997, the International Labour Conference finally adopted a new convention (No. 181) and a supplementary recommendation (No. 188) on private employment agencies, allowing these to operate while protecting the workers concerned from possible forms of abuse. The agencies provide temporary workers to firms that do not wish to recruit on a permanent basis. National legislations seek to prevent unscrupulous agencies from reprehensible practices, stipulate the conditions for delivering and withdrawing operating licenses and allow legally recognized agencies to form an association or federation.

Facing significant unemployment rates, European governments feel nevertheless the need to maintain and ensure the maintenance of a free public job service. A public job service calls for improved information on the labour market and occupational guidance and encourages activities promoting geographical and occupational mobility. Workers' and employers' representatives are often associated in the functioning of such services and in policy implementation. Labour administrations act on the mechanisms that regulate the employment market.[23] They do this in different ways: by granting transportation allowances and bonuses for mobility; subsidizing the costs of finding a new job; providing special subsidies for workers said to be a priority; organizing occupational internships, advice for enterprises, priorities with a view to placement, etc. Several of these tasks are part of the basic mission of the modern state. Labour administrations, or more specialized units thereof, are in charge of the vocational rehabilitation and promotion of the recruitment of disabled persons. This stresses the link between the

22. *See* S. Ricca, *Introduction to Public Employment Services* (Geneva, ILO, 1994), 5 *et seq.*; ILO, 'Strategies Developed by the Public Employment Service in Response to Structural Changes in the Labour Market', Acts of the Interregional Technical Meeting (WAPES/ILO, 23-24 Jan. 1997) (Geneva, ILO, 1997).
23. S. Ricca, above n. 3, 41 *et seq.*

training, rehabilitation and placement of disadvantaged workers and the social security system.

In terms of placement in general, many countries require jobseekers to meet certain conditions to register with public agencies, such as an undertaking to accept a job offer of a minimum number of working hours per week.

3.3. Social Policies and Job Stimulation

Traditional objectives of an interventionist employment programme include investment and income policies, promotion of new technologies, regional and agricultural policies, public works, employment of young persons and underprivileged groups, development of small and medium sized enterprises, population policy, international economic cooperation and migration.

Most of the actions proposed are macroeconomic. But it is difficult to oversee the application of those policies. The questions to be solved comprise the relationship between objectives of job creation and other economic and social goals. They refer to policies for general and sectorial development and to measures adopted, for example, in terms of fiscal and monetary policy, trade, prices, wages and social security. They also address the issues of educational and training policies and of labour market policies. Many aspects of employment policy are therefore beyond the immediate purview of labour administrations.

The laws and regulations of many European countries pay special attention to the placement of workers suffering hardship. Among these, the disabled occupy a special place. Often the legislation also deals with the plight of young unemployed people, as unemployment of this type may give rise to other social problems. Legislation may also refer to women, the elderly, the long term unemployed, regular emigrants and workers affected by structural changes. The inhabitants of depressed regions benefit from specific employment programmes, including from the EU.

The means of giving effect to these policies vary: some are legislative, others consensual, and others a combination of the two. Employers, workers, and their associations sometimes (but not always) play a decisive role in the application of programmes. Negotiations are often tripartite and states conclude genuine social pacts with the vocational organizations. However, the efficiency of such policies appears to be limited, at least in the medium or long term, as showed by most European employment statistics.

3.4. Enhancing Occupational Skills

Training seems to be the best guarantee against unemployment. However, other factors, some of them economic, also play a role. But who could deny the usefulness of coupling training with employment? Witness the emphasis put on the issue within the European Employment Strategy and the host of measures devised by governments in recent years, encouraging employers to hire apprentices and trainees by providing financial aid in particular. The decision by several countries to prolong compulsory education is another example. The EU has prompted many European governments to question the quality and effectiveness of their educational systems and introduce what are sometimes thoroughgoing measures of reform affecting the reconversion and ongoing training of adults as well as the education of young people.

Any human resources development policy intended to have tangible results presupposes the implementation of an integrated training and vocational orientation scheme that reflects the choices made in terms of objectives, structures, conditions and sources of financing. Key to the success of such a policy is the definition of specific and concrete objectives for the short and medium term. The aim is not so much to train people for a specific occupation as to teach workers how to adapt to unexpected work situations, tasks and jobs; how to deal, in particular in industrialized countries, with the consequences of technological change and the adjustments and restructuring aimed at enhancing the economy. Occupational training should make wage earners more versatile and enable them to change occupation, even within the company, in the course of their working lives. It is also a means of introducing a degree of long-term flexibility into industry, commerce and offices.[24]

The practice of most European countries reflects the policies promoted by the ILO, as mentioned in particular in Convention No. 142. This instrument requires states to adopt and develop comprehensive and coordinated policies and programmes of vocational guidance and training, and to establish a close link with employment policies. The states undertake to 'extend, adapt and harmonize' their vocational training systems to meet the needs 'throughout the life of both young persons and adults in all sectors of the economy and branches of economic activity and at all levels of skill and responsibility'. Some states have also adopted a policy designed to promote the granting of paid educational leave for training at all levels. This means leave granted to a worker for educational purposes for a specified period during working hours, with adequate financial entitlement.[25] It is conceived in terms of a policy of continuing education and training. Employers' organizations, however, have many times expressed their reservations on such policies.

Most European states have also adopted specific provisions on the vocational rehabilitation and employment of handicapped persons. In line with the ILO Convention No. 159 and Recommendation No. 168, the purpose of vocational rehabilitation is to enable disabled persons to secure, retain and advance in suitable employment and thereby to further their integration or reintegration into society. The trend is now to promote employment opportunities for disabled persons in the

24. *See* P. Auer and B. Gazier, *L'Introuvable Sécurité de l'Emploi* (Paris, Flammarion, 2006); B. Palier, 'Vers un Etat d'Investissement Social' (2006) 2899 *Problèmes Économiques*, 34.
25. According to Art. 11 of the ILO Convention No. 140, a period of paid educational leave shall be assimilated to a period of effective service for the purpose of establishing claims to social benefits and other rights deriving from the employment relation.

open labour market. Many legislations contemplate equality of opportunity with other workers. Special affirmative measures aimed at effective equality of opportunity and treatment are normally not regarded as discriminating against other workers.

The fact that these provisions recommend certain social policies has inevitably prompted questions on the relevance of those policies. More to the point, a number of countries find it difficult to reconcile objectives of equity and effectiveness: they have to choose their priorities and the ensuing investments. The person most in need of training may not be the person whose training will be of greatest benefit to the community: is it not more profitable to allow a skilled worker to enhance his skills? And what about the vocational education of all the workers – sometimes the majority – in declining activities?

3.5. Non-standard Forms of Employment

For many years, contracts without limit of time were the usual form of employment relationship. Later, new methods of organizing work, often born of the desire to give more flexible structures to companies, fostered variations in the forms of employment. The phenomenon grew under the pressure of competition, linked to the internationalization of market economy, and scientific and technical progress. The determination of employers to make their companies more profitable and lower their costs pushed them to explore and use all possible combinations. At the same time, public authorities often encouraged varieties of employment in order to absorb an employment crisis they could not solve by other means.

The circumstances explain, therefore, why many people associate other forms of employment with precarious work, even if that association is not always accurate: a mother can work half time whilst keeping her open-ended contract. Nevertheless, the workers concerned are usually more vulnerable because their job is not secure, their social protection is weak and they find it difficult to organize in trade unions. More specifically, they are often paid less, hardly benefit from any additional social benefits and have only limited access to common social security schemes (pension, unemployment, family allowance, etc.). They tend not to be included in collective bargaining processes and therefore do not enjoy the guarantees that supplement the individual contract. Another aspect is the absence of career prospects and occupational investment. Many women hold jobs of this kind, as do young and elderly workers, immigrants and all those looking for a second or third job when the first one does not pay enough.

In terms of the law, the fact that there is a variety of forms of employment stems chiefly from contractual autonomy, that is, the freedom of anyone to undertake to perform a task for another person and the faculty to give the ensuing relationship the shape the parties wish, subject to the limits of the law. There are many possible combinations. The main variables concern whether the relationship is a subordinate one or not, where the work is done (the case of homework, including telework), the time factor (temporary work, part time work, fixed-term work) and the method of remuneration (in kind, at least partially, for apprentices and for au pair workers).

The terms and conditions of segmented employment – the search for greater flexibility and the often-precarious situation of the workers concerned – explain the difficulties of finding adequate legal provisions for regulation. Many national, European and international labour standards apply to these forms of employment. Some legal provisions, however, exclude them specifically; in other cases, they cannot be implemented for logical (protection against dismissal does not apply to self-employed workers) or practical (duration of work is not easy to control in the case of home-based workers) reasons. Hence, the tendency of the EU to adopt specific standards, especially with regard to fixed term contracts, part time and the type of home-based work called telework.

3.6. Unemployment Benefits and Employment

To be effective, employment programmes must centre around the social security system in force, first and foremost around unemployment benefits.[26] Some consider that the amount of unemployment benefits paid in some countries is a disincentive to find work. No matter how relevant, this affirmation is of little practical value when the jobs are scarce and the job seekers many.

The methods of providing unemployment benefits must contribute to the promotion of employment, and not discourage employers from offering and workers from seeking productive employment contributions to the unemployment insurance scheme.[27] Measures of this kind include assistance for occupational mobility (Spain is an early example), easy access to temporary jobs (the Netherlands), incentives for the unemployed to set up their own businesses or get involved in another economic activity (Italy, Sweden), assistance for return at the worker's own volition (France), and progressive introduction of community services, including healthcare services. In some countries (Greece, Hungary), unemployed workers who receive benefits may be obliged to take a course of vocational training.

Beyond this, social security benefits (sometimes conceived as compensation if the right to work cannot be achieved 'in kind') are, as a rule, tied to an obligation to accept any suitable employment.

26. *See* for example J.A. Sagardoy Bengoechea, 'The Role of Social Security in the Fight against Unemployment', (1994) 10 (1) *The International Journal of Comparative Labour Law and Industrial Relations*, 10 *et seq.*; J. Barthélémy, 'Peut-on Dissocier le Droit du Travail et le Droit de la Sécurité Sociale? Contribution à la Théorie des Vases Communiquants', (2007) 7 *Droit* Social, 787.
27. T. Araki, 'Promotion and Regulation of Job Creation Opportunities', National Report Submitted to the XIV Congress of Labour Law and Social Security (Seoul, 27-30 Sep. 1994) *Reports and Proceedings* (Seoul, Korean Academy of Industrial Relations, 1996), vol I, 414-415.

4. EXPERIENCES, RESEARCH AND PROPOSALS

4.1. 'FLEXICURITY'

Much of the public debate in Europe today focus on the Community's Employment Strategy. Clearly, the various European economies are closely interconnected and have to deal with common problems of unemployment or workers' precarity. Coordination is not only useful, but necessary. It should be underlined however that most of the technical means to promote jobs remains in the hands of national governments.[28] It is still therefore of prime importance to examine how the different states have reacted in front of the social difficulties of the day.

Facing the need to adjust labour laws to new economic developments, the EU promotes 'flexicurity' today. The term has come from the Netherlands and from a legislation that has tried to find a balance between work flexibility and the necessary protection of employees. In particular, the Act of 1 January 1999, based on an informal agreement amongst the social partners, has established a new system for temporary workers: after a certain period of continued work for the work agency (twenty-six weeks in principle), the individuals concerned are considered for all purposes as under the benefit of an employment contract without limit of time.[29] The formula provides some security to the employees concerned, in the sense that they may benefit fully from labour and social security law. It seems well accepted by all parties involved.

The concept, however, has taken a broader significance in the European public debate.[30] It addresses every social policy that aims at reaching the optimal balance between flexibility in the labour market and social protection. It differentiates Nordic countries (especially Denmark) from Southern European countries like Spain, France and Italy. In the first ones, dismissal is relatively easy, but unemployment benefits pretty generous, financed by high taxation; employment policies are active and successful. The second ones have adopted a completely different type of policies; termination of the employment relationship appears to be difficult, but active reintegration policies and unemployment benefits are limited; taxation and social deductions are also less high.[31]

---

28. *See also*, Ch. Erhel, 'Politiques de l'Emploi: entre Compétences Nationales et Coordination Européenne' (2007) 2931 *Problèmes Économiques*, 32.
29. *See* for example, G. Heerma van Voss, 'The "Tulip Model" and the New Legislation on Temporary Work in the Netherlands' (1999) 15 (4) *The International Journal of Comparative Labour Law and Industrial Relations*, 80-84.
30. European Industrial Relations Observatory on-line *EU Countries: Flexicurity and Industrial Relations*, <www.eurofound.europa.eu/eiro/2008/09/index.htm>, 30 Sep. 2008.
31. B. Palier, 'Refonder la Protection Sociale: les Experiences Européennes' (May 2006) *Esprit*, 53-78; D. Anxo et H.Nickclasson, 'The Swedish Model in Turbulent Times: Decline or Renaissance?' (2006) 145 (4) *International Labour Review*, 379.

4.2. Research and Proposals

The limited success of the European and national policies against unemployment and precarity pushed researchers to investigate further on. Some observed that new institutional arrangements increasingly made allowance for vocational training, that the wide variety of individual needs required greater flexibility in the organization of work, and that non-traditional forms of employment called for rethinking the relationship between work and other socially useful activities.[32] They came up with the concept of a 'transitional labour market' as the broad framework within which the new arrangements were being implemented (in terms of organization, income policies, social policies and their fiscal effects).

Another group of researchers, headed by Alain Supiot, sought an alternative to this conceptual approach to the labour market. They pointed out that people could be active in a number of ways in the course of their working lives, for example, wage employment, self-employment, public service employment, training or internship, vocational retraining, sabbatical leave, household work, public office, civic duties (military or social service), etc.

Following this line of thought, some have proposed to construct working life scenarios made up of interlocking modules that alternate working time, training and paid leave – for example, maternity leave, parental leave, leave for military service, etc.[33] Improved skills and greater independence (the latter depends on the former) would allow for more satisfactory coordination of the various activities – work, training and retraining, leave for a specific purpose, voluntary or low paid tasks that have a high social value, such as caring for children or the elderly, assistance to the victims of violence, etc., – and for the planning of such activities over the course of a working life. Conflicts of interest – both in the workers' personal lives and in their employment relationships – would thus be more easily resolved. In particular, this would also lead to a more satisfactory balance between private (family) life and working life.

In practice, however, these proposals come up against major obstacles.[34] The foremost among them relates to the possibility of using such a framework to map out people's life cycle and finance the periods during which they are not engaged in

32. European Academy of the Urban Environment, *New Institutional Arrangements in the Labour Market: Transitional Labour Markets as a New Full Employment Concept* (EAUE, Berlin, 1998); B. Gazier and G. Schmid (eds), *The Dynamics of Full Employment. Social Integration by Transitional Labour Markets* (Cheltenham, Edward Elgar, 2002); P. Auer and B. Gazier, above n. 24.
33. *See* J. Boissonat, *Le Travail dans Vingt Ans* (Paris, Odile Jacob/La Documentation Française, 1995); A. Valli (ed.) *Tempo di Lavoro e Occupazione. Il Caso Italiano* (Rome, La Nuova Italia Scientifica, 1988), 13-38 and 177-197; K.L. Ladear, 'Social Risks, Welfare Rights and the Paradigms of Proceduralisation: The Combining of the Liberal Constitutional State and the Social State', in J. de Munck, J. Lenoble and M. Molitor (eds), *L'Avenir de la Concertation Sociale en Europe* (Louvain, Centre for Philosophy of Law, Catholic University of Louvain, 1995), 145; I. Camos Victoria and E. Rojo Torrecilla, 'À Propos du Rapport Supiot: Réflexions sur les Changements dans le Monde du Travail et en Droit du Travail' (2002), 43 (3), *Les Cahiers de Droit*, 564.
34. R. Castel, 'Droit du Travail, Redéploiement ou Refondation', (1999) 5 *Droit Social*, 438-442.

gainful activity. Indeed, the aim of social protection is to reassure workers and would be workers about their lives, their health, their subsistence and that of their loved ones. It is not intended to eliminate all uncertainties, to provide for every contingency, to organize every single aspect of people's lives. Besides, uncertainty is a spur to enterprise, innovation and creation for the most dynamic people, and hence a factor of progress.

Nevertheless, these ideas offer a fresh perspective on the loss of meaning or centrality of work. They are also helpful in understanding the many forms that work can take. They furnish convincing arguments for a minimum guaranteed income or small loans for training (care of dependants, social work, etc.).[35] Authors reconsider the very concept of work in terms of relationships, market connections and instrumentality in economic security, and as a typically crucial period of human activity.

4.3. *Tempi della Città*

The experiences and ideas mentioned above should help to find new ways of overcoming conflicts such as the controversy surrounding the 35 hour working week in France and to explore the options for better coordinating working time, social life and leisure for the benefit of all. In short, as Italy's *tempi della citta*[36] have showed, employers and wage earners are also consumers, users, clients and taxpayers; they want to purchase the products and services they need at the lowest possible cost and at times that are convenient to them, that is, outside their working hours. They want to have free time to care for their children or elderly parents, either together with their spouse or on the basis of some alternating arrangement with their spouse. Flexible working hours are indeed a very innovative means not only of equalizing opportunities for men and women, but also of stimulating employment. Government policy makers tend to link working time with employment, in order to prevent redundancies and to promote recruitment. In many cases, however, they have failed to take due account of the positive employment effects of keeping shops and offices open longer by having rotating staff – not to mention the implications for economic growth.

4.4. Lessons to Be Drawn

New working time arrangements are only examples of the positive effects deriving from the involvement of the citizens. The mobilization of civil society associations

35. *See* A. Supiot (rapporteur), *Beyond Employment: Changes in Work and the Future of Labour Law in Europe*. Report for the European Commission (Oxford, Oxford University Press, 2001), 56-57.
36. S. Bontiglioli and M. Mareggi (eds) 'Il Tempo della Città fra Natura e Storia. Atlante di Progetti sui Tempi della Città', (1997) 12 Urbanística Quaderni; M.C. Belloni and F. Bambi (eds), *Microfisica della Cittadinanza. Città, Genere, Politiche dei Tempi* (Milan, Franco Agneli, 1997).

and other social groups to give everyone a chance to participate in the organization of the working life raises however a number of questions.

The first concerns the role of the state, which would have to furnish the legal framework required to promote private initiatives in this field. This would connect with the modern tendency for labour law to focus on procedures rather than substance. In this case, it would indeed fall to the law to encourage national, regional or local authorities to recognize truly representative social actors, to help them develop, to provide them with access to useful information, to recognize such groupings as they may establish (or help establish) and to foster relations between the various stakeholders. The law would have to provide for their incorporation into the bodies that plan and implement the systemic organization of social life. It should also broaden the scope for independent negotiations. The state would thus act more as a source of inspiration than as a guide, as a mediator ensuring a favourable climate for dialogue. The EU has initiated means to stimulate such a new vision in its Member States, by fostering for example tripartite social summits for growth and employment, as enshrined in Article 136 bis of the revised treaty on the functioning of the EU.[37]

The second question concerns the type of legal rules that would encourage such interaction and coordination. Preference would of course have to be given to standards that allow the parties themselves to strike their own work and life balance, both individually and collectively – that is, 'programmatic standards' that set objectives and impose only the obligation to strive to attain them, without regulating the process directly. In several countries (including Belgium and France) and at the European level, the social partners have recently been empowered to negotiate collective agreements that liberalize regulatory frameworks or provide for exceptions to the principles laid down in the law, notably with regard to working time arrangements. In some cases, they are given an even greater role: in principle, Italian legislation allows employers and national or local representative trade unions to determine, by collective agreement, the grounds (relating to the organization of production) that justify recourse to casual labour.[38]

This approach could easily be taken one step further. Specifically, instead of restricting the social partners to negotiating the exceptions to a common rule or the safeguards against extreme precariousness, they could be empowered positively and freely to set the terms of work and life balance within a regulatory framework more flexible and comprehensive than the current narrow focus on daily and weekly working time.

The third question concerns the actors who would be called upon to perform regulatory functions. In spite of the well known difficulties they face, workers' organizations remain crucial to social policy making in democratic societies. They are among the most representative bodies in civil society. Which others can claim to have their capacity to mobilize or their number of long standing members?

---

37. As we all know, the amendments to the European Unions Treaties have still to be ratified by some Member States.
38. Article 34 of Legislative Decree No. 276 of 2003 as amended.

The same holds true for employers' organizations. In the recent past, however, other movements have also emerged; they have been instrumental more than once in seeing an initiative through to success.

In all European countries, the states are facing increasing demand upon it. They are called to modernize their institutions in the face of greater competition and to maintain or restore social cohesion seriously weakened by long lasting unemployment or under employment. They are urged to defend jobs and guarantee a minimum income for those who do not have one or have insufficient wages. The issue is whether the traditional collective bargaining can help to solve the acute problems of lack of employment and insecure employment or some other arrangement is needed.

Can bipartite or multipartite social dialogue really create jobs? There is no simple answer. In this respect, the driving force is, undeniably, economic growth. It was an illusion to believe that great social pacts, in European states, could unemployment. Yet negotiations on employment creation, at various levels, can have positive effects. They always lend emphasize to the human dimension of industrial relations, for example the care to avoid abrupt dismissals. In some circumstances, this bargaining also creates a climate conducive to less rigid economic structures and to non-inflationary development, the fruits of which are fairly distributed. It can even prevent job losses, or allow the setting of recruitment targets, especially when it takes a decentralized, enterprise-level form. Above and beyond their direct effects, such negotiations often open up new approaches hitherto considered taboo, like flexibility of working time without compensation or cessation of wage indexation.

The practice has shown not only the multiplicity, but also the growing diversity of social negotiation types. New modes of action in concert have come into existence and are not always sufficiently known. Local level job creation initiatives are under way in a number of French municipalities. In Ireland (especially with the National Economic and Social Forum, but also at the local level), in Italy (with the multipartite collective agreements), additional partners have emerged giving voice to more silent sectors of the population and the economy.

These movements are often the result of a gradual grassroots mobilization effort culminating in the establishment of occupational associations (or of other kind) with a social aim. They are community based rather than centred on the workplace. They often act in close cooperation with institutions that provide support services: local authorities, churches, charities, organizations assisting the unemployed, technical cooperation bodies, and those providing training or assistance to jobseekers. They have also taken on board the concerns of environmental or consumers' associations many times.[39]

No country or supranational institution has yet succeeded in finding wholly satisfactory solutions to the phenomena of impoverishment, marginalization and

---

39. For a more detailed study of those associations and of their action, *see* ILO, 'Industrial relations, democracy and social unity', *World Labour Report 1997-98* (ILO, Geneva, 1997) especially 31-55, 57-67 and 228-229.

exclusion. It appears improbable that the persons concerned would be able to defend themselves alone, because they are scattered, have weak bargaining power and very little ability to take collective action.[40] Almost everywhere however, including in the informal economy of developing countries, groups such as the ones mentioned above have achieved success, defending the interests of the weakest sections of the population. Although the experience cannot be considered as a new trend, it does suggest that it is possible to promote the conclusion of new social pacts that would not replace the traditional collective agreements but would supplement them to benefit those who are covered by them insufficiently or not at all. Even the ILO,[41] in spite of its traditional tripartite structure, has considered that such a step would stimulate and provide a framework for multiple and innovative solutions, often at the local level. It implies the recognition of spokespersons freely chosen by the parties involved, the determination of methods of action that are both flexible yet stable, encouraging social solidarity, as well as specific measures to ensure that the objectives laid down are achieved.

References

Alston, P., (dir), *Labour Rights as Human Rights* (Oxford, Oxford University Press, 2005).

Araki, T., 'Promotion and Regulation of Job Creation Opportunities', National Report submitted to the XIV Congress of Labour Law and Social Security, Seoul, 27-30 September 1994, I *Reports and Proceedings* (Seoul, Korean Academy of Industrial Relations, 1996).

Auer, P. and Gazier, B., *L'Introuvable Sécurité de l'Emploi* (Paris, Flammarion, 2006).

Anxo, D. and Nickclasson, H., 'The Swedish Model in Turbulent Times: Decline or Renaissance?' (2006) 145 (4) *International Labour Review*.

Barthélémy, J., 'Peut-on Dissocier le Droit du Travail et le Droit de la Sécurité Sociale? Contribution à la Théorie des Vases Communiquants' (2007) 7 *Droit Social*.

Belloni, M.C. and Bambi, F., (eds), *Microfisica della Cittadinanza. Città, Genere, Politiche dei Tempi* (Milan, Franco Agneli, 1997).

Blanpain, R., *European Labour Law*, 10th rev.edn (The Hague, Kluwer, 2006).

Boissonat, J., *Le Travail dans Vingt Ans* (Paris, Odile Jacob/La Documentation Française, 1995).

Bontiglioli, S. and Mareggi, M. (eds) 'Il Tempo della Città fra Natura e Storia. Atlante di Progetti sui Tempi della Città' (1997) 12 *Urbanística Quaderni*.

Boyer, R., 'Les Quatre Grands Modèles du Capitalisme' (31 August 2005) *Problèmes Économiques*.

40. *See* the still very indicative article of D. Demazière, 'Des Chômeurs sans Représentation Collective: une Fatalité?' (1996) 11 *Esprit*, 12-32.
41. ILO, above n. 39, 227-229.

Bronstein, A., 'The Protection of Workers' Claim in the Event of the Insolvency of their Employer. From Civil Law to Social Security' (1987) 126 (6) *International Labour Review*.

Camos Victoria, I. and Rojo Torrecilla, E., 'À propos du Rapport Supiot: Réflexions sur les Changements dans le Monde du Travail et en Droit du Travail', (2002) 43 (3) *Les Cahiers de Droit*.

Castel, R., 'Droit du Travail, Redéploiement ou Refondation', (1995) 5 *Droit Social*.

Commission of the European Communities, *Green Paper* COM (2006) 708 final *on Modernising Labour Law to Meet the Challenges of the 21st Century* (Brussels, 22 November 2006).

Committee on Monitoring International Labor Standards, *Monitoring International Labor Standards. Techniques and Sources of Information* (Washington DC, The National Academies Press, 2004).

COMPTRASEC (Université de Bordeaux 1), *Liberté, Égalité, Fraternité. Actualité en Droit Social* (Bordeaux, Editions LCF Lycofac, 1990).

Demazière, D., 'Des Chômeurs sans Représentation Collective: une Fatalité?'(1996) 11 *Esprit*.

Erhel, Ch., 'Politiques de l'emploi: entre compétences nationales et coordination européenne' (2007) 2931 *Problèmes Économiques*.

European Industrial Relations Observatory on-line *EU Countries: Flexicurity and Industrial Relations*, <www.eurofound.europa.eu/eiro/2008/09/index.htm> 30 Sep. 2008.

European Academy of the Urban Environment, *New Institutional Arrangements in the Labour Market: Transitional Labour Markets as a New Full Employment Concept* (Berlin, 1998).

Funk, L., 'European Flexicurity Policies: A Critical Assesment' (2008) 24 (3) *International Journal of Comparative Labour Law and Industrial Relations*.

Gazier, B. and Schmid, G. (eds), *The Dynamics of Full Employment. Social Integration by Transitional Labour Markets* (Cheltenham, Edward Elgar, 2002).

Gruat, J.V., 'Les Problèmes des Régimes de Protection des Salariés en Cas de Faillite de l'Entreprise (Étude Comparative); Protection contre le Chômage et Politique de l'Emploi' (1981) 5 *Documentation de Sécurité Sociale, Série Européenne*.

Hansenne, M., 'The European Social Model and Globalisation of the Economy', *Labour Relations and Industrial Relations at the Turn of the Century. Liber Amicorum in Honour of Roger Blanpain* (The Hague, Kluwer, 1998).

Heerma van Voss, G., 'The "Tulip Model" and the New Legislation on Temporary Work in the Netherlands' (1999) 15 (4) *The International Journal of Comparative Labour Law and Industrial Relations*.

ILC (78th session, 1991) *Protection of Workers' Claims in the Event of Insolvency of their Employer*, Report V (i) (Geneva, ILO, 1990).

– (82nd session, 1995), Protection against Unjustified Dismissal, Report III (Part 4B) (Geneva, ILO, 1995).

ILO, 'Strategies Developed by the Public Employment Service in Response to Structural Changes in the Labour Market', Acts of the Interregional Technical Meeting (WAPES/ILO, 23-24 January 1997) (Geneva, ILO, 1997).

ILO, *Termination of Employment Legislation Digest* <www.ilo.org/public/english/dialogue/ifpdial/info/termination>

– *World Labour Report 1997-98*, Industrial Relations, Democracy and Social Unity (Geneva, 1997).

Jacoby, S., 'American Exceptionalism Revisited: The Importance of Management', in S. Jacoby (ed.), *Masters to Managers: Historical and Comparative Perspectives on American Employers* (New York, Columbia University Press, 1991).

Kaeble, M. and Schmid, G. (eds), *Das Europäische Sozial Modell. Auf dem Weg zum transnationalen Sozialstaat* (Berlin, Sigma, 2004).

Kessler, F., 'Images de la Flexicurité: le Droit du Licenciement aux Pays-Bas' (2008) 5 *Droit Social.*

Ladear, K.L., 'Social Risks, Welfare Rights and the Paradigms of Proceduralisation: The Combining of the Liberal Constitutional State and the Social State', in J. de Munck, J. Lenoble and M. Molitor (eds), *L'Avenir de la Concertation Sociale en Europe* (Louvain, Centre for Philosophy of Law, Catholic University of Louvain, 1995).

Lipset, S.M. and Meltz, N.M., 'Canadian and American Attitudes towards Work and Institutions', (1997) 1 (3) *Perspectives on Work* (The IRRA's 50th Anniversary Magazine).

Lyon-Caen, G., 'Sur le Transfert des Emplois dans les Groupes Multinationaux' (1995) 5 *Droit Social.*

Maggi-Germain N. and Caillaud, P., 'Vers un Droit Personnel à la Formation' (2007) 5 *Droit Social.*

Martin, A. and Ross, G. (eds), *Euros and Europeans: Monetary Integration and the European Model of Society* (Cambridge, Cambridge University Press, 2004).

Matthews, J.T., 'Power Shift' (1997) *Foreign Affairs.*

McCane, L.S., 'The Problem of American Cooperation', JT Shotwell (ed.), *The Origins of the International Labor Organisation* (New York, Columbia University Press, 1934).

Palier, B., 'Refonder la Protection Sociale: les Experiences Européennes' (2006) 5 *Esprit.*

– 'Vers un Etat d'Investissement Social' (2006) 2899 *Problèmes Économiques.*

K. Polanyi, *The Great Transformation: The Political and Economic Origins of our Time*, (Boston, M.A. Beacon Press, 1957).

Rapin, I., 'Des salariés face à la délocalisation. Notes Ethnographiques sur un Monde Ouvrier en crise' (2007) 6 *Esprit.*

Ricca, S., ILO. 'Strategies Developed by the Public Employment Service in Response to Structural Changes in the Labour Market'. Acts of the Interregional Technical Meeting (WAPES/ILO. 23-24 Jan. 1997) (Geneva, ILO, 1997).

Ricca, S., *Introduction to Public Employment Services* (Geneva, ILO, 1994).
Rodière, P., *Droit Social de l'Union Européenne*, 2nd edn (Paris, LGDJ, 2002).
Sagardoy Bengoechea, J. A., 'The Role of Social Security in the Fight against Unemployment' (1994) 10 (1) *The International Journal of Comparative Labour Law and Industrial Relations.*
Schregle, J., *Negotiating Development. Labour Relations in Southern Asia* (Geneva, ILO, 1982).
Servais, J. M., 'Quelques Réflexions sur un Modèle Social Européen', (2001) 56 (4) *Relations Industrielles / Industrial Relations.*
Sewerýnski, M. and Marzal, A., *Changements Politiques et Droit du Travail. Perspectives Polono-Espagnoles*, (Lódz, Wydawnictwo Uniwersytetu Lódzkiego,1992).
Sinn, H. W., 'Le Dilemme de la Mondialisation' (2006) 2900 *Problèmes Économiques.*
Supiot, A., (rapporteur), *Beyond Employment: Changes in Work and the Future of Labour Law in Europe*, Report for the European Commission (Oxford, Oxford University Press, 2001).
Théret, B., *Protection Sociale et Fédéralisme (l'Europe dans le Mirroir de l'Amérique du Nord)* (Montréal, P. U. Montréal et Peter Lang, 2002).
Valli, A., (ed.), *Tempo di Lavoro e Occupazione. Il Caso Italiano* (Rome, La Nuova Italia Scientifica, 1988).
Yemin, E. and Bronstein, A. (eds), *The Protection of Workers' Claims in the Event of the Employers' Insolvency* (Geneva, ILO, 1991).

Chapter 2

Looking at the EES in Search of Effectiveness and Efficiency of National Employment Policies and Social Protection Systems

Juan Pablo Landa & Edurne Terradillos Ormaetxea

1. INTRODUCTION

The reflections made in this chapter are based on the following main question: 'Does the effectiveness of the coordinated European Employment Strategy (EES) necessitate of a new social protection system?' When the European Commission talks about modernizing the systems of social protection it does not seem to suggest a radical change in the traditional systems of Member States. At the moment, modernization is aimed at the mechanisms for fighting exclusion and providing subsidies for the unemployed. The purpose is to reform those mechanisms and make them more proactive, principally by targeting those excluded from the job market and bringing them back in.

The modernization of social protection systems does not stop there. Above and beyond the problem of sustainability of the public pension systems of Member States, there is an attempt to tackle the new requirements of the active population. The current labour market differs a lot from the traditional one of the past century. It is more and more characterized by the segmentation of the workforce and the

Roger Blanpain, Juan Pablo Landa, Brian Langille (eds), *Employment Policies and Multilevel Governance*, pp. 33–64.

transition of employees into other market segments, other unpaid activities (e.g., training, family life, social or political activities), or within the workplace.

The new European strategy for the modernization of labour law – and of employment policies – is based on the mechanism of flexicurity. This mechanism requires a proactive focus by the social protection system. It may also affect the essence of the European social security systems: the public guarantee of protection against risks at work or inherent to the working life. Such risks are guaranteed via the classical mechanism of human solidarity based on collective insurance schemes, predominantly underwritten by public rights.

To examine this we must analyze the current EES as well as its configuration within the framework of the mechanisms based mainly on the theories of flexicurity.

The fight against high unemployment and inactivity rates in most European countries was the reason behind the Employment Title introduced by the Amsterdam Treaty into the European Community Treaty (ECT). Its introduction also meant the surge of an intergovernmental form of governance based on the coordination of policy and the use of non-binding instruments. This was radically different to the use of the traditional Community method based on the recognition of *de minimis* rights common to all workers in the Member States.[1] This new method was officially named Open Method of Coordination (OMC) at the Lisbon European Council, which also launched the EES.

The Amsterdam European Council's Resolution on Growth and Employment provides the basis for an economy founded on the principles of inclusion, solidarity, justice and sustainable environment.[2] Economic efficiency and social inclusion were presented as complements to the social cohesion policy. However, the discussion in the mid nineties was how to increase the Community resources to encourage demand and therefore the employment rate. The Member States refusal to increase the Commission's budget resulted in the 1993 White Paper on Growth, Competitiveness and Employment.[3] It advocated the centralized coordination of the employment policies of the Member States, combined with an active agenda of labour market measures, first put in motion by the Essen Council of 1994 which entailed the move from a passive to an active labour market policy. The priorities set at Essen, before the adoption of the Employment Title at Amsterdam, became the employment guidelines that define the EES since the Luxembourg Council of 1997: nineteen guidelines on four pillars. This was the outline until the approval of the so-called Lisbon Strategy at the Lisbon Council of 2000, where five horizontal objectives were added to the four pillars, in order to reorientate the EES towards the Lisbon Strategy.[4]

More specifically, and in keeping with the spirit of the Essen Council, the Lisbon European Council of 23 and 24 March 2000 included the promotion of

1. C. Barnard, *EC Employment Law* (New York, Oxford University Press, 2006), 105.
2. Resolution 97/C 236/02.
3. EC Bull. Supp. 6/93.
4. C. Barnard, above n. 1, 119.

employment and social inclusion within the first pillar of employability. This pillar is focused on increasing workers' adaptability and employability within the Lisbon strategy for employment. It has formed the basis for the employment policy guidelines of Member States adopted by Council Decision 2001/63/EC. Moreover, the pillar of employability is also Objective 3 of the integrated policy for the structural funds approved in the Regulation 1262/1999 (Article 1) to finance vocational training and promotion of employment.

Thereafter, the Barcelona Council of 2002 reduced the four pillars to three, and synchronized the EES with the Broad Economic Policy Guidelines (BEPG) in a three-year policy cycle. To benefit the effectiveness of the EES, the objectives for the period 2003-2005 became three: (i) full employment, (ii) quality and productivity at work, and (iii) social cohesion and inclusion; besides a greater number of specific targets.

The Commission noted the poor results achieved halfway through the period set for implementing the EES. The European Council of Brussels reviewed its contents on 22 and 23 March 2005 with a view to making it 'more effective'. The outcome of this revision was the merger of the EES guidelines with the BEPG, resulting in the Integrated Guidelines. As a consequence, Member States have been asked to draw up National Reform Programmes (NRP) that respond to country specific needs and socioeconomic features; and reflect an integrated focus between macroeconomic, microeconomic and employment policies.

One conclusion that emerges from the revision of the EES is that the measures that corresponded to social policy have fallen outside its field of action. The problem of exclusion and the fight against poverty belongs to a different strategy, parallel to the EES: the Inclusion and Social Protection Strategy. In future, we will have to differentiate between the measures for active policy of the employment market and the measures that currently make up what is known as the strategy for inclusion. The latter fall within the remit of the objectives set in the social agenda (and the social policy objectives to be developed by 2010), together with the strategy for full employment and measures against poverty and promotion of equal opportunities, in a framework of prosperity and solidarity.[5]

In short, the strategy's measures for inclusion had been excluded from the Integrated Guidelines and were then covered by technical instruments separate from the EES.[6] The tension between the flexibility required by employment measures and the need for social rights in defence of the European social model results now in a technical solution consisting of separating both processes and their techniques in two separate strategies. There remained, however, some connection between both strategies through the principle of 'streaming social cohesion', which projects a general vision of the preservation of social cohesion above all other social, economic, employment and sustainable development policies.

5. Social Policy Agenda 1st phase (COM (2000) 379, 1 Mar. 2004) and 2nd phase (COM (2005) 33 final, 9 Feb. 2005).
6. As approved by the Council of Nice of 7-9 Dec. 2000 and revised in 2002.

The Integrated Guidelines themselves contain an integral strategy for economic and employment policy based on the conviction that a 'harmonious synergy' will be achieved through the development of economic competitiveness and the defence of the European social model. To this end, social protection (especially in the case of unemployment benefits) would have to be modernized under the specific principle of 'making work pay'. This is one of the most visible results of the implementation of the strategy of flexicurity through the EES. This idea was originally introduced by the Commission's Green Paper, called Partnership for a New Organization of Work,[7] and was later allocated to the EES in the 1998 Employment Guidelines under the adaptability pillar. It has now become a fundamental idea – as we examine below – of the current EES.

On the other hand, a complex concept of partnership would also have to be contemplated in the implementation of this employment strategy.[8] This means using the 'OMC' as the chosen instrument for developing the European system of multilevel governance, with the participation of social partners and civil society and the involvement of Member States, regions, local authorities and administrative bodies of public interest services, in coordination through open, flexible and decentralized procedures and institutional mechanisms.

In theory, this approach would advance the role of the regions and local authorities as the main bodies in the implementation of both European strategies. In their favour, the regions already have the policy of the Community structural funds, and in fact the regions have been, until now, the main recipients of the structural funds for social cohesion (Article 158 of the ECT). Currently the reform of the structural funds for 2007-2013 follows its original objective of achieving the socioeconomic convergence of the European regions least developed, thus keeping in line with the original target of the European cohesion policy mentioned above. Moreover, this only confirms the ever-clearer tendency to distribute more than 60% of the public expenditure via the regions and local bodies.

At this moment, the revised EES also counts on the involvement of the regions to turn the EES and other related strategies into more effective policies or actions. For this purpose, the EU approved a Community programme[9] to establish a single record of the EC's financial instruments in the social field. However, this programme does not replace the traditional role of the European Social Fund (ESF) to help Member States strengthen economic and social cohesion by supporting their policies to achieve full employment, promote social inclusion and reduce regional unemployment (Article 2 of ESF Regulation 1081/2006).

Both strategies (the economic and employment strategy on the one hand, and the strategy for social inclusion on the other), are underpinned by the OMC. The employment strategy has relied on the OMC since the Treaty of Amsterdam and, formally, since the Council of Nice of 2000. The OMC has also presided over the

7. COM (97) 127 final.
8. Commission White Paper on European Governance, Brussels, COM (2001) 428 final, 25 Jul. 2001.
9. Known as the Progress Programme (Decision 1672/2006, 24 Oct. 2006).

implementation of the policy against exclusion and poverty (later renamed the social inclusion policy) that is currently part of the reform and modernization of the social protection system.

Together, these European strategies focus on the desire to make the measures of protection an active element of social integration. Their interrelation is not technically predetermined, but based on the smooth running of the Community principle of mainstreaming which supports the preservation of the European social model.

The vague nature of the interrelation between these separate and autonomous Community strategies for employment and inclusion brings us to the heart of this chapter: in the absence of European compulsory mechanisms or clear guidelines, are Member States looking at these complementary measures when it comes to implement the policies? More precisely, who will ensure the implementation of the employment and inclusion strategies: Member States, or regions and local authorities?

There are many formulas of regionalization throughout the Member States. From the federal ones (e.g., Austria, Germany and Belgium) through the *regionalization* whereby certain powers of the state are transferred to the regions or shared with them (e.g., Italy, Spain, UK and France) to administrative decentralization, whether strong (Ireland) or weak (Greece or Portugal).

The OMC respects the idiosyncrasies of the Member States (in line with the subsidiarity principle), but it also seeks to make the EES effective in its results and economic viability, especially when the cost of its social benefits has to be borne and managed by a service of general interest, whether public or private (e.g., employment agencies or social services).

Certainly, Community literature is full of calls for the effectiveness of the EU and its Member States in implementing Community policies within the framework of the respective areas of power at territorial sublevels. The question is this: how can we measure said effectiveness if the regions are the ones empowered to implement and even define those policies (when they have the power to do so, as it sometimes happens) but, in the strict terms of the OMC, it falls on the governments of the Member States to draw up the NRP for implementing and evaluating said policies? Could the regions bring about measurement criteria based on the quality and fairness of these actions, or would they only take into account quantitative measurable results?

We will now look at this general issue in more detail by trying to formulate clearer questions on each of the following points. Firstly, by looking at the specific objectives pursued by the strategies of employment and inclusion. Secondly, by posing questions about the sustainability, success and weaknesses of the OMC in the practical application of both strategies. Thirdly, by describing the problematic effectiveness of the OMC regarding the trend towards modernization of social protection which underlines the strategy of flexicurity. And finally, by rethinking the European strategy for employment and social inclusion from the viewpoint of the different European models of social federalism, drawing a clear line between (i) the discourse on its values and defects; and (ii) the formulae of articulation on a vertical, horizontal and sectoral scale between the different levels of European governance and the respective Member States with regional structures.

2. THE REVISION OF THE EUROPEAN STRATEGIES ON EMPLOYMENT AND INCLUSION: ITS EFFECTS ON NRP

Point 24 of the conclusions of the European Council of Lisbon of March 2000 established that:

> people are Europe's main asset and should be the focal point of the Union's policies. Investing in people and developing an active and dynamic welfare state will be crucial both to Europe's place in the knowledge economy and for ensuring that the emergence of this new economy does not compound the existing social problems of unemployment, social exclusion and poverty.

A central objective of the Commission Communication on growth and employment[10] (which proposed a review of the Lisbon Strategy for 2005-2010), is to 'attract more people into employment and modernize social protection systems'. It concludes that this should be achieved within a framework of objectives aimed at reaching levels of full employment through growth and the promotion of an inclusive social economy, by using active employment policies and appropriate incentives that encourage people (i) to work and remain in the employment market, (ii) to look for work or, (iii) to start a business. To achieve this aim, Member States should in turn 'modernize their systems of social protection' to facilitate mobility between jobs and ensure the sustainability of the social protection schemes.

More precisely, an annex[11] to the Commission Communication mentioned above refers to improving the effectiveness of the Community policy of coordination for encouraging people to continue working and be less dependent on social protection benefits. The measures that Member States are encouraged to take are (i) reinforcement of the conditionality of unemployment benefits; and (ii) development of active labour market policies with selected targets. The few quantified goals set for the Member States by the Employment Guidelines for the period 2005/2008 include offering one of these measures to people under 25 who have received unemployment benefits during six months (twelve months for other unemployed people). Member States are also asked to allow the receipt of pension's benefits whilst remaining an employee.

---

10. Communication to the Spring European Council, 'Working Together for Growth and Jobs: A New Start for the Lisbon Strategy' (Communication from President Barroso in Agreement with Vice-President Verheugen), COM (2005) 24, 2 Feb. 2005, available at <http://eur-lex.europa.eu/LexUriServ/site/en/com/2005/com2005_0024en01.pdf>.
11. SEC (2005) 192.

Moreover, the BEPGs for 2005-2008[12] established the need for reform in the European labour markets, by increasing flexibility, factor mobility and adjustment capacity in labour and product markets, as well as by renewing impetus in tax and benefit reforms and improving incentives to 'make work pay'. This is found in Guideline 5, which is related to Guidelines 18 and 19 of the 2005-2008 EES, which we look at next.

2.1. Strategy for Employment

In our opinion, the EES is visibly inspired by the employment strategy of the OECD of 1994 and relies on two key recommendations. The first is to reform the systems of unemployment benefits and subsidies for the unemployed, and create economic incentives to return to work. The objective is to avoid situations where to accept a job improves someone's income by very little or not at all, considering the quantity and quality of the benefits and the effects of taxation. The second recommendation is to increase and improve the effectiveness of active labour market policies, of job advice and placement programmes and of job training. Moreover, both recommendations are to be seen as closely interrelated.[13]

However, the OECD does not trust everything to the implementation of the principle of making work pay: it is not the only way. In fact, according to the OECD Report on Employment Perspectives for 2005, the subordination of certain benefits to obtaining a job works better when combined with other instruments for improving participation in the labour market, such as setting a suitable minimum salary to prevent employers from abusing the system.[14]

The integrated guidelines for the employment policies of Member States for 2005-2008[15] combine matters of employment with macroeconomic stability and microeconomic reforms by means of an interrelated treatment. These integrated guidelines appear to be slightly more strongly worded than the guidelines of the Lisbon Strategy of 2000, which were much more in line with the OECD Employment Strategy. This change of tack was inspired by the publication of a study made by an independent group of experts known as the Kok Report II in 2004.[16]

Among the new measures for employment, we shall focus specifically on the question of incentives for returning to work. Currently, the unemployed person must show an active disposition to return to work not only as a condition for obtaining unemployment benefits or subsidies, but (in a wider context) for having

12. Council Recommendation 2005/601/EC of 12 Jul. 2005 on the Broad Economic Policy Guidelines of the Member States and the Community 2005-2008, OJ L 205 of 6 Aug. 2005.
13. OCDE, *Perspectivas de Empleo* (Madrid, MTAS, 2006), 75-76.
14. OCDE, *Perspectivas de Empleo* (Madrid, MTAS, 2005), 271.
15. Council Decision of 12 Jul. 2005 (OJEU 6/8/2005).
16. W. Kok, *Facing the Challenge. The Lisbon Strategy for Growth and Employment* (Luxemburg, Office for the Official Publications of the European Communities, 2004) available at <http://ec.europa.eu/growthandjobs/pdf/2004-1866-EN-complet.pdf>.

personalized advice plans and social services specialized in inclusion as well. This can be seen in Guideline 19, which refers to:

> early identification of needs; job search assistance, guidance and training as part of personalised action plans; provision of necessary social services to support the inclusion of those furthest away from the labour market and contribute to the eradication of poverty.

However, the vagueness of the measures proposed, and the fact that these guidelines are still based on general objectives and principles with very few quantified targets, leave the exact definition of concrete measures and the most suitable pace of priorities for these general objectives in the hands of each Member States. In short, the application of the employment strategy continues to leave ample leeway for each Member State to draw up their own NRP and progress reports for the Commission. Many would probably argue that this is the only way to ensure the principle of subsidiarity.

Guideline 19 also contemplates the 'continual review of the incentives and disincentives resulting from the tax and benefit systems, including the management and conditionality of benefits and a significant reduction of high marginal effective tax rates, notably for those with low incomes, while ensuring adequate levels of social protection'.

The guideline raises the question of something that we will look at later in more detail: the possible influence on this phase of the EES of the approval by the European Council in December of 2007 of its conclusions on the common principles of flexicurity for the development of more and better employment, intended to be instrumental in the implementation of the next cycle of the Lisbon Strategy by 2008.[17]

Indeed, tax schemes and the regulation of social service benefits (unlike the social inclusion activities), usually fall, to a great extent, under the central responsibility of the states rather than the regions and local councils. As a result, there would be, in our opinion, an obvious disconnection between the regional, federal or quasifederal administrative bodies responsible for social and employment policies and the Member States charged with other cross-border policies. Equally, it would favour a recentralization of state powers in social policies by taking away competences from the regions, for example, active labour market insertion measures seduced by state aid policy.[18] Although it may seem contradictory, this recentralization could nonetheless be justified by more effectiveness in implementing the EES.

17. European Council, *Towards Common Principles of Flexicurity-Council Conclusions* (16201/07), 6 Dec. 2007.
18. *See* M. Moreno Marcos, 'Medidas de Fomento al Empleo y Reglamento 2204/2002/CE de la Comisión de 12 de Diciembre de 2002, sobre la Aplicación de los Artículos 87 y 88 del Tratado de CE a las Ayudas Estatales para el Empleo (A Propósito de la Sentencia del Tribunal de Justicia de las Comunidades Europeas de 14 de abril de 2005)' (2006) 62 *Revista del Ministerio de Trabajo y Asuntos Sociales*, 261-276.

2.2. Strategy for Social Inclusion

As for the Strategy for Social Inclusion (Nice 2000), its four general objectives were, and continue to be: (i) to promote the insertion of the excluded into employment; (ii) to give them access to social service resources; (iii) to provide access to goods and services; and (iv) to achieve the same level of recognition of rights for everyone (with the final objective of eradicating poverty by 2010).

This strategy has traditionally been complemented by a policy of cohesion, but the reorientation of the objectives of the structural funds proposed by the Council to meet the priorities of the new EES[19] has reduced the objectives to three: (i) to make the regions and cities more attractive to investors; (ii) to encourage innovation, entrepreneurship and the growth of a knowledge based society; and (iii) to attract more people into jobs or entrepreneurial activity by improving their adaptability to change. In our opinion, this revision of the strategy of inclusion, which was much more in line with the objectives of the EES, dilutes its special connotations, as it had become truncated and subordinated to the success of the real EES priorities, with the subsequent danger of undermining the interests of inclusion.

Further, the Social Agenda has declared that it is complementary to the EES. When it mentions the modernization of social protection, it underlines the fact that it will act on the basis of solidarity but will also strengthen the role of the systems of social protection as a productive factor.[20] The Renewed Social Agenda issued by the Commission on 2 July 2008[21] calls for an improved efficacy of the social expenditure in line with the objectives set by the Lisbon Strategy, which include a successful completion of the EES by 2010. This Agenda, including its actions and instruments, will be reviewed together with the Lisbon strategy in preparation for the post 2010 period.

Consequently, there has been a real risk that (i) the objectives of social justice and cohesion may become dependent on the realization of the objectives of the strategy for growth and employment; and that (ii) this main objective of the EES, inspired unconditionally and unthinkingly on the principle of activation, may end up undermining the basis of the national systems of social protection and their quite distinct inspiration: that of intergenerational solidarity and human solidarity between active and passive members of society.

Without appearing to recant, but conscious perhaps of the political danger of a negative interpretation of this strategy by European citizens, the Council of Ministers, meeting on 22 February 2007, declared that active inclusion does not create a conflict of interest with the obligation to provide an adequate level of social services and minimum resources for all (balancing the guarantee of protection with the principle of making work pay), ensuring permanent and adequate levels of

---

19. Commission Communication, 'Cohesion Policy in Support of Growth and Jobs: Community Strategic Guidelines 2007-2013', COM (2005) 0299, 5 Jul. 2005.
20. Commission Communication on the Social Agenda, COM (2005) 33 final, 9 Feb. 2005.
21. Renewed Social Agenda: Opportunities, Access and Solidarity in 21st century Europe COM (2008) 412.

minimum resources for the disadvantaged.[22] However, the conclusions from the European Council of March 2008[23] confirmed the validity of the integrated guidelines approved in 2005 for the 2008-2010 period, with a warning, however, to establish specific and quantifiable objectives in order to ameliorate their efficacy and improve the transparency of the methodology for monitoring the NRP.

Nevertheless, our initial observation still stands. The strategy for inclusion, like the strategy for employment, holds Member States responsible for the difficult task of clarifying the close links between protection and inclusion policies and economic and employment policies; and for trying to improve their interaction and 'harmonious synergy'. Member States have to reflect this in the NRP for growth and employment, alongside the strategies of protection and social inclusion.

These strategies of protection and social inclusion should be focused towards 'active inclusion' to be consistent with the priorities of the employment strategy, that is, measures of protection for the population at risk of exclusion which favour labour supply by making benefits more strictly conditional on active availability for work and by improving incentives through tax and benefit reforms. In addition, Member States are encouraged to set up tax allowances and tax credits for low paid jobs to encourage participation of the disadvantaged in the labour market, and reinforce active labour market policies in a balanced policy mix for active inclusion.

Commission Communication 'Working together, working better: A new framework for the open coordination of social protection and inclusion policies in the European Union',[24] emphasized that the OMC of inclusion should go hand in hand with the revised Lisbon strategy (the integrated guidelines for this strategy will incorporate those aspects of social protection that reinforce its objectives), whilst facing the challenge of differences in application. As for the latter, the progress programme[25] will provide assistance in this separate but parallel and partly integrated activity, but Member States have to guarantee a healthy relationship between these diverse strategies.

22. Following the philosophy established by the Commission in its Communication 'Opportunities, Access and Solidarity: Towards a New Social Vision for 21st century Europe', of 20 Nov. 2007 (COM (2007) 726), in which the Renewed Agenda Social has also been based.
23. Conclusions 14/3/2008, Suppl.7652/08.
24. COM (2005) 706 final, 22 Dec. 2005.
25. The decision 1672/2006 of the President and the Council of 24 Oct. 2006, sets out a unique Community programme for employment and social solidarity, called 'Progress' (for the period 2007/2013), designed to give financial support to the implementation of the European Union's objectives in the fields of employment and social solidarity affairs, as set out in the Commission Communication on the Social Agenda, and thereby contribute to the achievement of the goals of the EES as well (Art. 1). This programme will serve to finance 'monitoring and evaluating the implementation of the European Employment Guidelines and Recommendations and their impact, notably through the Joint Employment Report and analysing the interaction between the EES and general economic and social policy' (Art. 4b), and separately, it will be used to finance 'monitoring and evaluating the implementation of the OMC in the field of social protection and inclusion and its impact at national and European Community level' (Art. 5b).

According to this Communication, the objectives of the OMC on the strategy for social inclusion centre on ensuring social inclusion by promoting labour market participation, good coordination of inclusion policies (so that they become not only effective but efficient too), and integration of these into the relevant public policies (such as economic, training, ESF and so on). It is a multidimensional focus, so that employment and social economic policies may both benefit, and social protection may function effectively as a productive factor.[26]

Moreover, the Commission also commits itself to integrating the inclusion social services into the Services of General Interest (SGI) recently excluded from the scope of the directive on the free provision of services (known – at some stage – as the Bolkestein Directive). As a result, the specific regulation of the SGI now being drafted will, in the Commission's opinion, exempt these services from the application of the regulations relating to the internal market, in particular from the regulations on free provision of services. Thus, we can say that the definition of the SGI will include services offered directly to a person, consisting of personalized aid for their inclusion in society and guarantee of full enjoyment of their fundamental rights (for example activities of social and work insertion, housing benefits, cultural integration and so on).[27]

However, for those furthest removed from the labour market, those who really are in a situation of social exclusion, the programmes for a minimum income may be the only real way to escape extreme poverty.[28] The Commission seems to want to correct the conditionality of benefits in the development of the strategy for active social inclusion, which ties in with what was planned in the Social Agenda (2005-2010). The truth is that the latest employment guidelines for Member States[29] for the period 2008-2010 align themselves with the European Council's political decision to strengthen the social dimension of the Lisbon Strategy through the reinforcement of the territorial, economic and social cohesion. The aim is to consolidate social inclusion and the fight against poverty, as well as the interaction of the EES with the OMC in the area of protection and social inclusion. On the other hand, according to these new guidelines for 2008-2010, Member States have to guarantee the good governance of employment and social policies, through the creation of a wide partnership with local and regional entities and the civil society.

Besides, the EES is given more quantifiable objectives in favour of a higher efficacy and accountability. For instance, employability measures for every unemployed person, four months prior to finishing his studies – in the case of young people – or after twelve months of unemployment in other cases; with a

26. Joint Decision of the Social Protection Committee and the Economic Policy Committee of 27 Feb. 2006, 6801/06.
27. Commission Communication on the Community Programme of Lisbon Social Services of General Interest in the European Union of 26 Apr. 2006, COM (2006) 177 final.
28. Communication Concerning a Consultation on Action at EU Level to Promote the Active Inclusion of the People Furthest from the Labour Market, COM (2006) 44 final, 8 Feb. 2006.
29. Council Decision 2008/618/CE of 15/7/2008.

25% rate of participation in job promotion measures among the long term registered unemployed. All to be achieved before 2010 (Guideline No. 18).

But it is also true that the most promising measures for a strategy of active inclusion seem to have been those that are close to the average worker, combined with a level of income sufficient to lead a decent life and with better access to the sort of social services that permit social integration. Guideline No. 19 of the EES for 2008-2010 looks to ensure inclusive labour markets, enhance work attractiveness and make work pay for job seekers, whilst ensuring affordable access to basic services and providing adequate levels of minimum resources to all.[30]

Abuses in the implementation of the minimum income or low wage benefits schemes – and its poor efficacy to prevent and fight against poverty – have given rise to the fears that lie behind many of the growing criticisms in the Member States over the decentralization of the means of application.

One alternative which the Commission is yet to consider is the recognition of a citizen's right to a basic unconditional income benefit (a sort of moral right derived from human dignity and recognized by each national law).[31] The obligation for Member States and the EU[32] to ensure a basic income for their citizens (either through more unemployment benefits or through a basic income universally guaranteed) will become even more urgent given the likely slide into recession of the economies of the majority of Member States.[33] From the perspective of the Lisbon Strategy the danger of implementing – albeit gradually – this class of measures lies in the fact that the individuality of these types of income could cause a lack of motivation for work, and most of all, a lack in the demand for less qualified or paid jobs in the labour market.

The recent Spanish experience is an example of how in the medium term this objective of social policy can make gradual inroads. But it is still far from being an efficient strategy because of its heavy cost – one high fiscal rate – and besides, it would be necessary to redefine the whole social protection system. This is too big a task for the medium and short term of the Lisbon Strategy.[34]

---

30. This also seems to be the conclusion which follows from the holistic approach taken by the Commission when including the three main axis of active inclusion: minimum income, active measures for the labour market and social services. *See* Commission Communication 'Modernising social protection for greater social justice and economic cohesion: taking forward the active inclusion of people furthest from the labour market' COM (2007) 0620 final.
31. Y. Vanderorght and Ph. Van Parijs, *L'Allocation Universelle* (Ed. La Dcouverte, Paris 2005); D. Raventós, *El Derecho a la Existencia* (Ed. Ariel Practicum, Barcelona, 2007).
32. Let us not forget that the EU's Charter of fundamental rights recognises in its Art. 34(3) the fundamental right to social and housing assistance to ensure a decent existence to all European citizens.
33. A truly inclusive and fair policy should recognize the minimum right to subsistence autonomy and freedom, intrinsic in a society that aims to be fair and egalitarian. J.A. Noguera, 'Ciudadanos Trabajadores? La Renta Básica frente a las politicas de activacisn laboral' in G. Pisarello and A. del Cabo (eds), *La Renta Básica como Nuevo Derecho Ciudadano* (Madrid, Trota, 2006), 221.
34. The Act on Dependent People (Law 39/2006) provides for *inter alia*, a social income for the caregivers of dependent relatives. Another benefit that has been created is the so-called basic emancipation income aimed at young people between 22 and 30 to help them rent their own

In any case, nowadays the 'principle of activation' or that of 'making work pay' has to be compatible with the new European strategy of flexicurity. This is the emerging set of principles[35] in the context of the economic, social and employment policy, and to a great extent the integrated guidelines of the EES are already being designed around it. If the strategy of flexicurity wants to be credible and socially acceptable to the citizens of Europe, it must be able to ensure a basic level of income during periods of unemployment, training or unpaid social activities in transitions between jobs. The best way of providing security for those looking for a decent job is to guarantee minimum benefits or income in kind (such as public housing, health and education).

This strategy would be morally more dignified than that of workfare. Employment is not always a guarantee against poverty.[36] Putting unemployed people to work at the risk of turning them into *poor* workers, or offering temporary workers to companies in exchange for public incentives, may result in workers without a real, dignified salary: second-class workers without hope for a decent future.[37]

Furthermore, this vision of providing minimum resources to all European citizens, through measures implemented by each Member State (income support, benefit, subsidies, basic rents or tax deductions) would be more in line with the doctrine of the European Court of Justice (ECJ) on equality, which has ended up recognizing the right of Community residents to the same treatment as nationals when it comes to the entitlement to social benefits, irrespective of whether the benefit is a social security payment or not.[38] Nor would this social objective be incompatible with the policy being pursued by the Commission, as it claims that:

> the policies of social protection should contribute effectively to the mobilisation of those people capable of working, but without forgetting at any moment the wider objective; that of guaranteeing a decent quality of life for those who find themselves outside the labour market and whose situation does not look as if it will change.[39]

---

accommodation. In any event, and even though the Act on Gender Equality (Law 3/2007) extends paid leave for parents, all of these measures remain insufficient, since as soon as the Act was implemented there was a call for a new regulation to declare the state's obligation to ensure public pensions for those who give up their jobs to look after their families. In fact, there is a Bill for a basic income for universal and unconditional citizenship (basic income benefit), although this initiative has yet to succeed in the Spanish Parliament.

35. Commission Communication 'Towards Common Principles of Flexicurity: More and Better Jobs through Flexibility and Security' of 20 Oct. 2007 COM (2007) 359.
36. As the Commission itself has recognized in its Communication on the social protection and social inclusion report 2008 of 30 Jan. 2008 (COM 2008 42 final). Eight percent of workers in the EU are at risk of poverty, so promoting quality in work is also important, as well as offering adequate income support, access to inclusive labour markets and quality social services. *See* <http://ec.europa.eu/employment_social/emplweb/news/news_en.cfm?id301>.
37. B. Friot, 'La Jurisprudence de la Cour de Justice des Communantés européennes eu matiére des peurious de retraite et les réformer du financement de émploiet de la protection rociale', in P. Hassenteufel and S. Hennion-Moreau, *Concurrence et Protection Sociale en Europe* (Rennes, Presses Universitaires de Rennes, 2003), 161.
38. A.P. Van der Mei, *Free Movement of Persons within the European Community* (Oxford-Portland, Hart Publishing, 2003), 177.
39. Commission Communication, COM (2006) 44 final, 8 Dec. 2006.

The construction of the internal market cannot be carried out at the cost of fundamental social rights. That would be morally reprehensible and a political hazard for the future of the EU. The regulation at Community level of a minimum wage for active workers and a basic income benefit for all European citizens – and (legal) residents – is, in the medium and long term respectively, the best answer for more and better jobs in a framework of growth and sustainable development which perfectly complements the European social cohesion policy objectives according to the principle of solidarity.

3. THE OMC'S VALIDITY TO REACH THE OBJECTIVES OF THE EES EFFECTIVELY AND EFFICIENTLY

By 'effectiveness' of an action, or of the measure adopted to undertake an action, we understand its aptitude or suitability for reaching its desired objective.[40] By 'efficiency' we understand the estimated economic cost of achieving the objectives of an action, in the assumption that the more efficient an action or policy is, the less financial and economic cost will be required to reach its goals (optimization of resources).

A useful definition of the OMC is that put forward by Zeitlin (originally based on a comment by the Belgian Minister Frank Vandenbroucke in 2002):[41] 'an experimentalist approach to EU governance based on interactive benchmarking of national progress towards common European objectives and organized mutual learning'.[42] However, 'there is no single OMC methodology'.[43] Minister Vandenbroucke also said that it is not 'some kind of fixed recipe that can be applied to whichever issue, but is instead a kind of cookbook that contains various recipes, lighter and heavier ones'.[44]

In the specific context of the Lisbon strategy,[45] the OMC is predominantly institutionalized (based on Title VIII of the ECT) and backed up by soft law sanctions. The EES seeks to favour European integration through 'mutual learning' and the promotion of 'multilevel governance', translating the EU objectives into

40. A. Jeammaud, 'Le Concept d'Effectivité du Droit' in P. Auvergnon (ed.), *L'Effectivité du Droit du Travail: À Quelles Conditions*? (Bordeaux, COMPTRASEC, 2006), 49.

41. According to the Commission, the OMC is 'a means of spreading best practice and achieving greater convergence towards the main EU goals', COM (2002) 629, para. 14.

42. G. De Búrca, *EU Law and the Welfare State* (New York, Oxford University Press, 2005), 215. The OMC has also been defined as 'a post-modern polity, as a form of polymorphic governance distributed network-wise over several interdependent and interconnected levels without any predefined hierarchies', *see* S. Giuboni, *Social Rights and Market Freedom in the European Constitution*' (Cambridge, Cambrigde University Press, 2006), 247.

43. C. Barnard, above n. 1, 141.

44. J. Zeitlin, P. Pochet and L. Magnusson, *The Open Method of Coordination in Action: The European Employment and Social Inclusion Strategies* (PIE/Peter Lang, Brussels, 2005), intro.

45. Point 38 of the conclusions of the Lisbon European Council of March 2000 defined the OMC as a 'fully decentralised approach [to] be applied in line with the principle of subsidiarity in which

national/regional policies and promoting further cooperation and exchange of good practices.[46] Furthermore, the OMC is a specific European expression of multilevel governance for employment and social inclusion[47] which seeks to involve in the decision making several public and private agents and which is also beginning to show its worth as a structure for the management of economic reforms in Europe. This is nothing more than the reflection of the very ideas of multilevel governance of the EU through a singular structure where along with sovereign nations, sub-national and supranational actors intervene.

The OMC also promotes European convergence via a particular process, which essentially consists of a combination of soft law measures, such as sharing common objectives, improving political coordination at various levels and carrying out evaluation processes that are suitable for the designed objectives.

As the OMC consists of a group of soft law measures, it is not possible to use the typical hard law instruments of control, because there is little scope for legislative solutions. The Community sanction par excellence in the correct implementation of the OMC by the Member States in matters of employment and social inclusion is essentially political, and eventually financial, and meeting the objectives pursued by the structural funds (especially the ESF but also the Cohesion Fund and other funds) would also serve as an instrument for integrating the functionally separate strategies of employment and social inclusion.[48]

The OMC falls clearly into the category of systems of *regulation by goals*, distancing itself radically from the system of *regulatory harmonisation* typical of the classic Community legislative method. This leads necessarily to insecurity about the way in which the Member States and the regions, and other territorial bodies, should implement these policy guidelines. It entrusts much to the statistical comparison of the goals reached, but little to the evaluation of the suitability of the measures used and (even less) of the appropriate level at which these measures should be used or of its faithfulness to the requirements of decent work and social justice that should follow from its application.

In reality, it is very difficult to distinguish between the measures that the Member States would have adopted anyway and those that they adopted under pressure from the EES.[49] Also, it is not easy to judge whether the rise in

---

the Union, the Member States, the regional and local levels, as well as the social partners and civil society, will be actively involved, using variable forms of partnership'. See S. De la Rosa 'Stratégie européune pour l'emploi: les nouvelles orientations' (2005) 12 Droit Social, 128.

46. J.A. Noguera, above n. 33, at 142.
47. The literature on the OMC agrees that it should be classed among the theories on multilevel governance, *see* C. De La Porte and P. Pochet, 'The European Employment Strategy, Existing Research and Remaining Questions' (2004) 14 *Journal of European Social Policy*, 71.
48. For example, this is reflected in the guidelines for the cohesion policy (2007-2013), as presented in the Commission Communication, where the prevalent focus within the guideline 'more and better jobs' is to attract more people to join and stay in the labour market and to modernise the systems of social protection to this end (COM (2005) 0299, 5 Jul. 2005).
49. J. Goetschy, 'The European Employment Strategy, Multilevel Governance, and Policy Coordination: Past, Present and Future' in J. Zeitlin and D. Trubeck (eds), *The European Employment Strategy. Governing Work and Welfare in a New Economy: European and American*

employment is due to the structural reforms in the market (linked to the EES) – that is, microeconomic reforms – or to the macroeconomic growth of the economy. In spite of everything, what seems clear is that there is a tendency to emulate the employment policies that are most efficient from an exclusively financial viewpoint.[50] In December of 2006[51] the Commission noted that 'there is a clearer recognition that, in modernizing social protection and inclusion, it is not possible to separate the suitability of the protection from its financial sustainability'. Guidance based on primarily economic indicators leads us into a perpetual search for efficiency, which appears to gain prominence over any desire for redistribution.[52]

All of which is damaging for the credibility of the OMC, because it not only attempts to be a guarantee of effectiveness (quantifiable results) but also because it should generate greater efficiency of the national and community resources at the disposal of Member States to achieve these results (quality of results).[53] This efficiency of results is urgent, if, as intended by the European Social Agenda, our social European model is to be preserved through the reform of the labour markets so that they provide work as a real option for each and every European citizen; and if, at the same time, our social protection systems are to be modernized so that they can fight better against poverty.[54] However, economic growth does not necessarily contribute to fighting effectively against poverty if, along with the demand for qualified and well paid jobs, it also results in a large number of low qualified and badly paid jobs, jobs that are, moreover, rejected by the majority of European citizens because they cannot see a comfortable future via that kind of employment.

It is not clear whether the OMC for the policies of social inclusion and employment is making labour markets more efficient – even less whether it is bringing modernization of social protection for the improvement of social justice and access to decent jobs for most citizens. Moreover, it is not easy to measure the real effects that the OMC is having on the various different participants and on national policies.[55] Besides, the construction of a partnership between the state, regional and local public authorities, both among themselves and horizontally with the social and economic partners competent in these matters in each territory or administrative level, is still far from functioning operatively, since normally regions and

---

Experiments (Oxford, Oxford University Press, 2003), 68-69; *see also* S. Sciarra, 'La Constitucionalización de la Europa Social: Derechos Fundamentales y Procedimientos de Soft Law' (2004) 2 *Revista de Relaciones Laborales*, 1215.

50. Goetschy, *Ibid* at 75.
51. COM (2006) 816 final, 12 Dec. 2006.
52. R. Dehousse, 'The Open Method of Coordination: a New Policy Paradigm?', presented at the First Pan European Conference on EU Politics, The Politics of European Integration: Academic Acquis and Future Challenge, Bordeaux, 26-28 Sep. 2002, at 7.
53. Among other reasons, the genesis of the OMC responded to a call for efficiency, to ensure decisions of greater quality and to improve the way they were applied, *see* Goetschy, above n. 49.
54. Declarations by the Commissioner Vladimir Spidla IP/05/152, 9 Feb. 2005.
55. Goetschy, above n. 49, at 65-66.

cities tend to be subcontractors or whatever is decided on at national level. A better design for the tasks and responsibilities that correspond to each agent and each level of action of the public powers is still needed.

The complexity and number of coordination procedures, at so many levels, not only complicate the existing system, but also seem to give it serious problems of governability.[56] Also, the introduction of levels of experts and of interrelationships between public servants within and outside the relations between the Commission and the Member States helps to depoliticize the handling of the subject, but kills any real public debate to the detriment of the democratic legitimacy of the OMC as a decision-making procedure. At the same time, this transverse functioning between agents and institutions promoted by the OMC affects the schemes of relationships and responsibilities, more or less vertical or cooperating, and causes tension between the existing meeting spaces within each Member State (e.g., the legitimacy of the partners in the social dialogue), impeding the implementation of the OMC in the internal practicality of each Member State.[57]

As long as the OMC does not become an impediment to any future resort to the usual techniques of Community law it will be useful, in particular as a formula of multilevel governance of the European strategies of employment and social inclusion. The opposite would mean that the Union was washing its hands of the task of getting to grips with the internal division of responsibilities between the EU and the Member States. At the moment, the definition of each of the multiple competences that make up the complex process of employment is a task which falls to the Member States. The EES does not even require the decentralization of those competences to the regional and local powers, nor stipulate the type of commitment that the social and economic stakeholders should have in the process.

This has resulted in the OMC being called a type of 'exercise of symbolic politics where national governments repackage existing policies to demonstrate their apparent compliance with EU objectives'.[58] If this were to be the final outcome of the implementation of the EES by the Member States via the OMC (modernizing the national systems of social protection to reduce their workload and therefore becoming more proactive and efficient, with all that this entails in savings in the social budget), it would certainly be a great success in terms of net figures in job creation (the question of effectiveness). However, this success would not be complete if it were not accompanied by an improvement in quality for the people helped by the social protection system. In other words, the success of the active policy for employment should be analyzed alongside the results of the policy

56. Goetschy, above n. 49, at 75.
57. The Committee of Regions pointed this out when it said that 'apparently, the cross-section approach of the EES obfuscates the correlation between the labour market related activities at European level and the responsibilities affected by these activities at the national, regional and local level. For that reason it is extremely difficult to draft a systematic survey clearly assigning tasks in the field of employment policy – as understood at European level to the different levels of government within the EU Members States'. *See* Committee of the Regions, 'Regional and Local Powers in Europe' (Belgium, Office for Official Publications of the EC, 2001), 104.
58. *See* Zeitlin *et al.*, above n. 44.

of inclusion, and the real improvement in the social welfare of European society as a whole. The active employment policy must not turn out to consolidate itself by removing funds and benefits from the social protection systems, to the detriment of its solidarity and the very objectives of the welfare system.

4. THE EUROPEAN URGE FOR DECENTRALIZATION: THE KEY FOR EFFECTIVENESS IN THE FLEXICURITY IDEAL

The notion of regional and local democracy, as a complement to national democracy, was put forward by the Council of Europe before the EU did so. Nowadays, the basic instrument of the promotion of democracy at territorial level is still the European Charter of Local Self Government, an international agreement ratified by the immense majority of the members of the Council of Europe. A similar charter should be approved for regional autonomy, although none has been drafted yet.

The notion of 'multilevel governance' as used at European level is not a proper theory but rather an approach. Terminologically it is nothing more than a semantic footnote to the Anglo Saxon idea of 'governance', which differs from the institutional idea of 'government' (a coherently organized structure of institutions for conducting the affair of governing). It has been translated as *gobernanza* in Spanish and defined as 'the art or manner of governing, of relation between the different levels of government, which promotes a healthy balance between the state, civil society and the market'. In practice, what characterizes multilevel governance is the diversity and asymmetry between the levels of government (in many cases the actual experimental character of these relationships), as well as the tendency to invert the impulse for greater autonomy from top down to bottom up.

The first Kok Report[59] encouraged the implementation of an OMC between the levels of national and regional government in the case of countries with decentralized political structures. This would involve bringing in an open, transparent negotiation between the national and regional governments in the hope of agreeing on regional targets and mechanisms of information and control.

What is attractive in this new method is the fact that it contributes to the construction of a formula of supranational coordination,[60] although there do exist doubts about the alleged add on effects of further uniting Europe beyond the intergovernmental relations of the interested parties. If it had more depth, the OMC could be exported as a formula for coordination to federalist style countries within, of course, the framework of the relationships between the central state and

59. W. Kok, 'Jobs Jobs, Jobs. Creating More Employment in Europe', Report of the Employment Taskforce, Nov. 2003 available at <http://ec.europa.eu/employment_social/employment_strategy/pdf/etf_en.pdf>.
60. *See* S. Sciarra, above n. 49, at 1217.

the regions, or even between the regions themselves. This is, however, a hypothetical situation, as there is not sufficient proof of the real scope, in this area, of the new cycle of governance which began with the Lisbon Strategy.[61] On the contrary, the call for new governance seems to be due to the need to present the OMC within a legitimate discourse.[62]

If, in the opinion of the immense majority of citizens of western countries, the state is the guarantor of national solidarity and coherence, and a national system of social security guaranteed by the state by law is its core raison d'être; how will the improvement of the effectiveness and efficiency of that social security and social protection, fundamental principle of the welfare state, favour the development of regional and local democracy? Until this question is satisfactorily answered, the principle that the state is the best and only guarantor of national security and solidarity will prevent the development of other actions that are uneven and decentralized despite being, theoretically at least, more effective.

However, the main question to be answered is not whether local government is more democratic or effective, but to demonstrate that it is also more efficient 'in the allocation of administrative and financial resources',[63] as good governance would require.

4.1. The Horizon of Flexicurity

Finally, the possible negative effects of the application of the OMC do not end with the implementation of the EES and the other social policies that hinge on the OMC. The need to concentrate means and resources at Community level and in the Member States towards highly defined priority goals has another great challenge in the near horizon. The buzzword for sustainable growth in the European social model is 'flexicurity', a concept that hinges essentially on the ability of the individual to manage – in a context favoured by public authorities – the transitions between employment and unemployment, or between jobs in different categories, thanks to public authorities allowing the sustainable incorporation of the individual to a flexibilized job market.

It is hard to understand how it is possible to reach this goal without an institutional system of support and suitable protection on the part of the public authorities. If it is a question of reducing the levels of labour regulation (especially external flexibility at the cost of undermining labour rights) in exchange for the reinforcement of social protection measures (such as using the whole range of benefit resources, active instruments and measures for job advice and placement,

61. *See* the Resolution of the European Economic and Social Committee of 16 Feb. 2007 on the implementation of the renewed Lisbon Strategy (EESC 298/2007).
62. C.M. Radaelli, 'The OMC: a New Governance Architecture for the European Union?', Swedish Institute for European Policy Studies, Rapport No. 1, 2003 at 7.
63. As found in the Council Decision on the guidelines for the employment policies of the MS (Guideline No. 17) into the integrated guidelines for growth and jobs 2008-2010.

lifelong learning, housing benefits, public health, increases in the minimum guaranteed income), does this not mean that the employment and the inclusion strategies should be rerouted towards this one single central objective of flexicurity?

The flexicurity model is far from having been defined in a way universally accepted. In our opinion, if it wants to be socially acceptable in the EU it should not be so much focused towards the implementation of the principle of activation. Rather, it should point towards the creation of a favourable context for adaptation to the changing circumstances of the labour market, within a process of transitions that the individual would not undertake on his own, but backed by the public powers and services.

5. THE IMPLEMENTATION OF THE EUROPEAN STRATEGIES BASED ON THE OMC CERTAINLY IMPLIES THE DEVELOPMENT OF AN OPEN TYPE OF SOCIAL FEDERALISM

The idea of social federalism is an open concept, still in creation. It could be defined alongside the more extensive notion of fiscal federalism as a model for public intervention in the economy:[64] it is not a simple decentralization of certain tax competences from the central state to the regions, but an entire reorganization of the vertical tax system (i.e., of the fiscal instruments and responsibilities for the same) between the three decision making levels: central, regional and local. Through a clear scheme of division of competences between the central state and the local and regional sublevels within that state, a fiscal federalism model meets the criteria of equity, efficiency, autonomy and coordination on fiscal responsibility of each territorial sublevel and the central level, plus unity of economic policy. This notion therefore requires a differentiating focus between subnational levels, although corrected by the compensatory transferences spread among the territorial authorities by the federal or central government.

If this idea were transferred to the field of social protection, a system of social federalism would mean a (i) reordering of the protection resources and techniques (with the criteria of maximum efficiency) (ii) between the three levels of governance (central, regional and local), (iii) according to criteria of autonomy and self sufficiency in the management of the benefit resources, and (iv) based on principles of equity and solidarity. It would carry responsibilities defined at each level of the regional and local powers with the state and via coordination with the EU. In short, hypothetically, social federalism could be defined as a move by fiscal federalism to the social field.

64. J.P. Landa Zapirain, 'La Política Social en España y el Federalismo Social' (2003) 24 *Revista de Derecho Social*, 70-71.

The traditions of the national systems of social security in the Member States have produced varying results in the spread of competences for technical and financial measures of social protection within the different levels of state government. In Europe, Germany, Austria and Belgium are usually classed as federal states. In spite of their different evolution (from unitary state to federal – Belgium –, or from federal to unitary decentralized state under a model of horizontal cooperation between the autonomous regions and the federal authority (Austria)), in all three cases the regions have autonomous competences in training, employment and social services (although in Germany, social assistance is fully financed by the federal government), and the federal level covers all other matters expressly recognized by federal law. Another group of countries like Spain, Italy, France and the United Kingdom are not strictly federal states, although final decisions on all these matters lies with the regions in the first two, while only partially so in France (vocational training and social services) and in the United Kingdom (training). In these four cases, it is the central state which has proceeded to hand over the functions and competences of the central state to the regions, by transferring the power and means for their implementation. In the background, the central state continues to regulate any matter not developed by the regions within the distribution framework established by the state legal system. A third group of countries consists of the *municipalist* or *provincialist* states (two or three of them), that have adapted their strongly decentralized structure of local powers to the regional model promoted by the EU policy of the structural funds (the majority of the Scandinavian countries).[65]

The Commission Communication of 1998 'A European Strategy for Encouraging Local Development and Employment Initiatives' identified nineteen job areas where the local initiatives were judged appropriate and having a future. Since the start of the EES (Process of Luxembourg of 1997), the implication of the regional and local authorities has become an integral part of the Community strategy for employment. Their involvement is declared to be ideal for making territorial employment pacts, for building public-private partnerships and developing an efficient labour market.

In any case, the regionalizing impulse is consistent with the development of the common market, since, with the exception of Germany and Austria, the other Member States of the EU began reforming their internal structures in a decentralizing way (politically or administratively, depending on the country) in the mid 20th century. The new countries of the EU have quickly adapted their institutional structures to the regionalization which is a general tendency in Europe: Portugal (1976), Greece (1986), Ireland (1994), Czechoslovakia (1997), Hungary (1999) or Poland (1999).[66]

65. There is frequently a sharing of competences in employment matters where most issues of labour law, taxation and social security belong to the national level, while the regional and local level is at least coresponsible for implementation tasks in fields like teaching and (vocational) training, placement and guidance of job seekers, as well as back to work programmes for the unemployed and the payment of social benefits. *See* above n. 48, at 108.

66. M. Caciagli, *Regiones en Europa* (Valencia, Tirant lo Blanch, 2006), 78 *et seq.*

However, it is not clear whether this process of regionalizing the institutional structures of the Member States, backed by the EU, has resulted in local and regional structures as the main pillar of the employment and social inclusion strategy. The privileged interlocutor of the EES is still the central state, and the political action of the regions appears to be subordinate to that central state both in carrying out the NRP and in the use of Community funds or in communicating with the Council or the Commission.

Perhaps part of the responsibility for the persistence of this state of affairs lies with the OMC's problems to function properly, as observed earlier. A positive step would be to look into the possibility of making a clear proposal for the generalized institutionalization of federalist mechanisms for implementing employment and inclusion strategies in Europe. And, in this way, to fix the levels of competence (or sovereignty) and responsibility that have to be undertaken by the different institutional levels involved in the OMC: supranational, central state, regions and local authorities.

5.1. A Model of Social Federalism for an Effective OMC Strategy Means Good Multilevel Coordination and Efficient Interadministrative Cooperation

In matters of employment, the OECD report on the perspectives of work for 2005 admitted that:

> the adaptation of the employment programmes to regional needs may stimulate local initiatives and improve the effectiveness of the employment policy, but following the Canadian experience started up in 1996, that focus should be adopted within a common framework agreed between the central and the regional authorities.[67]

The so-called model of the *Estado de las Autonomías* in Spain has enabled the Spanish Constitutional Court to establish case law definitions of the principles of smooth functioning of the administration (aimed at the so-called autonomous communities) when developing the services of public interest (in particular the social services), in a framework of decentralized competences.[68] Essentially, the basic principles are those of coordination and cooperation.

The principle of coordination has been defined as:

> the setting of means and systems of relationship, which allow for reciprocal information . . . and the joint action of the state and autonomous communities in the exercise of their respective competences, in such a way as to achieve the

67. OECD, *Perspectivas del Empleo 2005* (Madrid, MTAS, 2005), 183.
68. J.P. Landa Zapirain, 'La Organización de la Sanidad Pública ante la Jurisprudencia Constitucional: una Reflexión sobre este Modelo de Reparto Competencial entre Estado y Comunidades Autónomas' (1999) 6 *Revista de Derecho Social*, 131-132.

> integration of the partial acts (of the autonomous communities) with the overall benefits system . . . avoiding reiterations and contradictions, and reducing dysfunctions . . . (Decision of the Constitutional Court, STC 32/1983).[69]

Again, according to the ruling of the Spanish Constitutional Court, the principle of cooperation would not involve:

> management power, consequence of the position of superiority in which the coordinator finds himself; on the contrary, cooperation has a voluntary base' (STC 118/1996). Cooperation therefore requires prior collaboration at political level, through 'technical instruments for collaboration and cooperation that allow a technical task to be carried out jointly when reasons of efficiency call for it', as established in previous decisions (STC 76/1991 and STC 67/1996).[70]

The development of the OMC as a model of multilevel governance applied to such matters as employment, inclusion and social protection policies, requires Member States to effectively resolve the problems of starting up efficient mechanisms of coordination and cooperation, whether on a vertical, horizontal or sectorial axis, as the OMC may need.

5.2. Multilevel Governance on a Vertical Plane: Europe-Member States-Regions-Local Authorities

The procedure promoted by the OMC pursues the objective of vertical, horizontal and sectoral integration of the public bodies and private agents involved, as well as reinforcement of the capacity of the Member States' institutions, both in terms of effectiveness and efficiency.[71] According to Serrera and Sacchi, the vertical integration of the central state with the regional and local bodies requires 'virtuous' coordination and commitment by the state sublevels. The technique used is that of economic incentives within a framework of institutional relations predetermined at central state level.[72]

---

69. The most usual instrument of coordination which is centralised or directed by the central state is that of the sectoral conference. However, the coordination intended has not been able to prevent dysfunctions in the central state regulations of the active instrumentation of unemployment benefits (e.g., the programme run by the Ministry of Employment known as active income for insertion of the unemployed) and the policy on benefits led by the regions (the programme for a minimum income for the insertion of those excluded from the labour market). *See* M. Rodríguez Piñero, 'La Normalización de la Renta Activa de Inserción' (2007) 3 *Revista de Relaciones Laborales*, 10-11.
70. In Spain, examples of this cooperation between administrations are the collective conventions of collaboration, the arbitration bodies that resolve conflicts of authority, the reciprocal systems of information and communication, or the interterritorial councils.
71. M. Ferrera and S. Sacchi, 'Il Metodo Aperto di Coordinamento e la Capacita Istituzionali: l'Esperienza Italiana', (2005) 105 *Giornale di Diritto del Lavoro e di Relazioni Industriali*, 52.
72. *Ibid.*

In its White Paper on European Governance,[73] the European Commission proposed greater participation at state sublevels, both in the phase of preparing the European regulations, and in their subsequent implementation. One of the instruments proposed for this new governance was permanent dialogue between the European Commission and associations previously constituted at sub-state level (e.g., the experience of 'Eurocities'). Another instrument used by the European Commission has been the tripartite agreements between itself, the territorial authority and the Member States, such as that signed by the Commission, Italy and the region of Lombardy, on 15 October 2004, for the improvement of the implementation of European environmental, transport and energy policies. We do not know whether any of these instruments of collaboration has been used in matters of employment and social inclusion, nor whether this new dynamic has effectively replaced the intervention of lobbies from the regions or large cities at the headquarters of the European institutions in Brussels.

Furthermore, anyone can see that a proper incorporation of this new level of intervention into the European decision making processes would mean added cost and loss of efficiency in the political and administrative management of such matters. It would be different if the initial loss of efficiency were to be compensated by subsequent improvement in the results achieved. Here, correct measurement criteria are essential to the defence of the EES's processes of regionalization.

The NRP of Spain for 2005-2008 indicated that the annual assessment will be forwarded to 'the national parliament, the autonomous communities, the Spanish federation of municipalities and provinces and the social interlocutors'. This cannot be called true coordination, but it is rather a simple technique of information for the purpose of possible future consultation by the government, or for later publication of opinions.

According to the European Economic and Social Committee Report on the application of the Lisbon Strategy of March 2006 (1468/2005) cited above, an authentic decentralization of the Lisbon objectives to the territorial authorities should not leave Member States open to experiment freely. It recommends that the tasks and responsibilities be apportioned more clearly between the various levels and participants.[74]

This would involve clear guidelines from the Member States on the different sublevels of governance of the EES, with adequate recognition of a degree of decisional autonomy but without renouncing to joint action to prevent any localized act which might break away from the general state and European action. Such guidelines would bring in clear methods, precise individualized measures and realistic and measurable deadlines for implementation.[75]

---

73. COM (2001) 428, 27 Jul. 2001.
74. An opinion which is echoed by the Spanish ESC; *see* the summary report of the ESC of 23 and 24 Mar. 2006 on the application of the Lisbon strategy: 'it would be convenient to share out the tasks and responsibilities clearly between the different levels and actors to fix the responsibilities of the different European, national, regional and local public powers'.
75. '*La decentralisation ne signifie pas l'abandon par l'Etat de sa fonction de fixation d'objectifs essentials des politiques* (decentralisation does not mean that the State should abandon its

In the case of Spain for example, the NRP annual progress report for the country, approved by the Council of Ministers on 13 October 2006, lays emphasis on the techniques of coordination between the autonomous communities and the central state. The initiative of the regions is based on the regional programmes for reform of those areas in which they have competences, such as 'increasing opportunities for employment, driving business potential forward, especially at the level of small and medium sized enterprises, investing in innovation, etc.' All of which is communicated in turn to the Spanish Parliament.[76]

5.3. Deep Cross Level Governance on a Horizontal Plane: Cooperation and Civil Partnership

The OMC also works on a horizontal level. The presentation of the OMC made by the European Council of Lisbon, defines it as a:

> totally decentralised approach in line with the principle of subsidiarity, in which the Union, the Member States and the regional and local levels, as well as the social stakeholders and civil society, will participate actively via various different forms of collaboration.

Maybe this conglomeration of public and private participants, rather than meeting a particular need of functionality and efficiency in social and employment policies, fulfils only a vague idea of participative democracy, dressed up as the formulation of a legal principle which is nothing more than a new attempt to restore the 'participation myth'.[77]

This principle of subsidiarity that results from a period of grave institutional crisis in the EU (but also from the territorial and qualitative expansion of its activities in social matters following the Agreement on Social Policy annexed to the Treaty of the EU), shows up in our field of study on another axis, the horizontal one. By virtue of the principle of subsidiarity the social stakeholders have priority to make proposals in the area of social policy. Article 138 ECT says that the Commission commits itself to promoting consultation with the social partners at Community level and enabling dialogue between them.

The OMC puts forward a process of policy making that is horizontally integrated via social partnership. This requires a good representation of the civil population and major presence of their social interests in the decision making

---

function of setting the main objectives for policies)' *see* D. Giorgi and V. Saintoyant, 'Gouvernance des Politiques d'Action Sociale Décentralisées et MOC'(2007) 7/8 *Droit Social*, 891.

76. In line with the opinion of the Committee of Regions: '[d]evolution of competences in the field of vocational training should be accompanied by the transfer of autonomous decision making powers in the field of regional and local economic development to achieve synergic effects' *see* above n. 48, at 298.

77. *See* J.A. Noguera, above n. 33, at 141.

process at all stages of the EES, and not only in subsequent monitoring and evaluation.

In the opinion of many, the lack of democratic legitimization of the OMC would be overcome by the participation of the civil society in the formulation of the EES, in its effective application, in the choice of the instruments of implementation, in its follow up, in the evaluation of its results and, if need be, in its reorientation. Some actions are producing a relatively positive result. For example, the European Economic and Social Committee (EESC) has created an interactive network made up of the national ESCs and open to other social organizations, to promote the application of the Lisbon strategy. In its opinion, the European organizations of civil society have the means and capacity to assume their obligations and cooperate with the public and private sector. According to the EESC, these institutions of participation are suitable for the sought after objective of partnership and they also 'generate in civil society a feeling of owning the actions undertaken, favour the assumption of responsibilities, constitute useful laboratories of social innovation and encourage the spirit of commitment between diverse groups and interests in society'.[78]

Another example of this participation is social dialogue, whose influence over government action, if we look at the Spanish experience at least, is greater than the official intervention of the national ESC. Indeed, in Spain, the participation of the social partners is channelled by the technique of social dialogue which often gives rise to national agreements like that of 9 May 2006, for the improvement of growth and employment. These national agreements are sometimes complemented by similar agreements made at regional level.

From the renewed perspective of flexicurity, the EES should also demand a more effective involvement of the social interlocutors in the modernization of the social protection systems of Member States. Scandinavian models of flexible labour markets are associated with high social security for the unemployed in systems characterized by high trade union membership. Modernization of labour law should reinforce trade union membership and trade union engagement in unemployment insurance systems.[79]

5.4. Idiosyncratic Differences Would Get in the Way of Transnational and Intranational Cooperation Promoted and Directed by EU

The OMC also pursues sectoral integration, that is, promotes more effective forms of coordination between policies of employment, social inclusion and social protection with educational or fiscal policies. We are looking here at an ambition of

78. *See* the EESC Resolution 298/2007, 16 Feb. 2007.
79. B. Bercusson, 'Employment and Social Protection: A New Relationship?', Working Paper for the International Seminar on Comparative Labour Law, Industrial Relations and Social Security, Bordeaux, 2-13 Jul. 2007, 6.

the OMC that fundamentally concerns the hard core of national competences. At European level, that interaction is resolved by the OMC. Is this an invitation to transfer the procedure to the internal policies of each Member State? Would this not be a direct violation of the principle of subsidiarity?

The introduction of instruments to get the unemployed back to work (for example using the jobseekers allowance), combined with measures to flexibilize the labour market (such as part time contracts, etc.) would not work equally well in countries with a system of flexicurity based on flexible regulation of the work market and a strong, prolonged regulation of unemployment benefits (Denmark, Switzerland); and countries with tight regulations and smaller unemployment benefits (such as those in the south of Europe – France, Italy, Spain). In the latter, a strong dose of determination and social consensus is needed to promote reforms that meet the needs for growth in their labour markets.[80]

A lack of direct powers of coercion could be damaging and prevent the effectiveness of the European social model on this point. The apparent good will of Community objectives in matters of inclusion becomes irrelevant in practice when it comes to Member States applying this strategy. This may be the most relevant consequence of an unbalanced integration in favour of activation measures for work and the economy over and above other more caring and fair considerations.

6. CONCLUSIONS

A European model of welfare and social security should not only seek effectiveness and efficiency, but should also be fair in line with the principle of solidarity that governs it. A current criticism levelled at the Anglo-Saxon models of social security systems is that, although they are efficient, they are not fair. The process of modernization of social security schemes that is under way in Europe contains a seed of seeking efficiency principally, even if this means reducing the levels of equity that to a greater or lesser degree maintain the immense majority of the continental social security systems.

The concept of solidarity is not unknown in European law. It can be seen in a number of EU texts, for example, Article 86(2) ECT on SGIs, Article 16 ECT on SGEIs or, generally, in the European Union Charter of Fundamental Rights of 2000. In the Geraets-Smits v Peerbooms (C-157/99) and Watts (C-372/04) cases, the ECJ attempted to recognize 'a nascent transnational solidarity that flows from the exercise of economic freedoms'.[81] The recognition of this European principle of solidarity at a constitutional level (the ECT) is the best antidote against

80. W. Eichhorst and R. Konle-Seidt, 'The Interaction of Labour Market Regulation and Labour Market Policies in Welfare State Reform' (2007) 28 (1) *Review of Comparative Labour Law & Policy Journal*, 40-41.

81. M. Ross, 'Promoting Solidarity: from Public Services to a European Model of Competition', (2007) 44 *Common Market Law Review*, 1064-1065.

the EES threatening the maintenance of national systems of social security, based, *inter alia*, on that very intergenerational and human solidarity.

The modernization of social protection currently discussed in Europe should limit its objectives to, wherever possible, the adaptation of its protection mechanisms for the personal situation of active employment to the individual circumstances of the various transitions in the working life of each person. In addition, the modernization of the system should help to stimulate each person to join the labour market.[82]

We are conscious that 'it is not possible to reform employment protection without considering its effects on the whole of the social protection system'.[83] But we believe that modernizing the national systems of social security to favour employment policy objectives does not necessarily have to cause a wholesale change in the basis of the social security and protection system. What is needed is to talk about whether it is a good idea to externalize totally or partially the financing and management of unemployment benefits.

From a financial point of view, it should be possible to convert unemployment benefits into a new technique for active employment policies transferred to regional or local sublevels by keeping their finance by the state. At first, it might be necessary to combine state financing with partial financing by enterprises, which would continue to contribute to an independent fund for unemployment benefits. If active workers were to contribute to this fund – which would not be a bad idea to justify the involvement of trade unions in its management – then their contribution should be made on the premise of capitalization rather than distribution. This would guarantee a future complement to income (e.g., to pay for training to improve employability or become self employed) should the work terminate, whether for voluntary or involuntary reasons.

Moreover, coherent management of the unemployment benefits through effectiveness and efficiency of the active employment policies would need a change in such management to improve its effectiveness, and ideally, its efficiency too. This should be the objective in sight if the present administrative resources in the public services are finally transferred to the appropriate local sublevels without thereby increasing the administrative bureaucracy required for their management. This improvement would include the transfer of the corresponding resources (technical as well as financial) to the regional and local sublevels. It would be down to the cooperation between the state and regional administrations to decide on the best location for managing these services within the geographical framework – the French experience of the *bassin d'emploi* (travel to work areas) is a good example of the idea of most efficient location. This would be the level at which it would be most necessary to articulate horizontal cooperation with the social and employer partners.

---

82. 'Each individual is the first person in charge of his own welfare' in F. Míguelez Lobo, 'Flexiseguridad, Bienestar y Cohesión Social' (2007) No Extraordinario *RMTAS*, 158.
83. Cf. J. Gautié, 'Les Économistes contre la Protection de l'Emploi: de la Déregulation à la Flexicurité' (2005) No. 1 at 10.

In our opinion, any other mechanism for the protection of the social security systems that might be put into practice would seriously endanger the survival of the principles of equity and solidarity that have upheld the success and longevity of these systems. Any reform might turn into a crisis of the traditional fundamentals and of the feeling of solidarity among those who support it. This would lower the acceptance not only of the European social model but of the basis of the modern state itself (its justification before its sovereign people), in particular because the state ensures the security and welfare of its citizens.

However, no modernization of the social protection systems will be effective if, at the same time, the financial independence of the individual citizen is not guaranteed in the systems of social security and the 'new' social benefits. In Denmark, the model of state that is used as the main reference for flexicurity, 25% of the population aged 16 to 64 is not employed; they are living on public support outside the labour market. The public emphasis on active labour market policies means, principally, 'some kind of artificial employment in the form of subsidized or sheltered employment, or some kind of skill upgrading through job training or education'.[84] Faced with this persistent reality, guaranteeing the financial autonomy of the passive class (citizens who do not work) and of the unemployed (citizens who have lost their jobs) is, in the long term, the most effective way of ensuring that no one comes up against the perpetual risk of falling into poverty and marginality.

Hypothetically, the guarantee to the right of a universal basic income benefit is not only fair but proves to be the most effective mechanism in the fight against poverty. At the same time, the progressive achievement of this objective through the fiscal and social policy of the Member States would be (i) the best guarantee that the European social model of protection and social inclusion is not an obstacle to trying to ensure the access of all citizens to decent work, as well as (ii) a guarantee of good social welfare for its citizens in any of the situations of transition throughout their working life: from study to work, from study to unemployment, during training to improve employability and during times of conciliation between work and family life.

In addition, the generalization of an instrument like the citizen's basic income benefit would be a good example of 'social federalism' in action. Its finance would require vertical fiscal co-responsibility between the different levels of state institutions (central, regional and local) and of any future European funds. This would swing things in favour of the level of governance responsible for the management of that universally basic income, essentially an individual right to a new system of public assistance benefits (whether at central level as in Germany, or at regional level as in Spain).

Moreover, that co-responsibility would have to extend horizontally too, and would affect all citizens and their social and civil organizations, albeit to a lesser

84. P. Abrahamson, 'Employment and Social Protection in Denmark: the Active Turn in Danish Welfare Policy', Working Paper for the International Seminar on Comparative Labour Law, Industrial Relations and Social Security, Bordeaux, 2-13 Jul. 2007 at 19-20.

degree. Certainly the most effective technique would be to use a new solidarity tax on enterprise profits and on saving financial schemes of an individual character. As for the citizens, all recipients of the basic income of an active age would however be subject to contribution to the public pensions system.[85] This obligation would provide an incentive to take a paid job to be able to access the pensions system.

Right at this moment, the European model of 'multilevel governance' (OMC) is not yet, in our opinion, aimed at guaranteeing equity and solidarity between European citizens, but is rather at the service of the development of an economic policy of sustained growth, which has to be supported politically. However, economic development has to be environmentally and socially sustainable too. If we want to defend the European social model we will have to consume differently and also grow in a different way, not through continuous increases in production. Thus, to use the present OMC not to define the level of public responsibilities of the different levels of government in the state, regional, local and European institutions, but to do, instead, precisely the opposite (to dilute those public responsibilities, both vertical – as there is no effective model of social federalism – and horizontal – by making a rhetorical – empty call to the effective co-responsibility of the social organizations and business in the management of the NRP) may be effective for a short term political strategy but is inefficient in the long term. In lieu of resulting in public savings, it brings, sooner or later, greater public expense and, what could be even worse, an incalculable political cost.

References

Abrahamson, P., 'Employment and Social Protection in Denmark: the Active Turn in Danish Welfare Policy', Working Paper for the International Seminar on Comparative Labour Law, Industrial Relations and Social Security, Bordeaux, 2-13 Jul. 2007.

Auvergnon, P., (dir) *L'effectivité du Droit du Travail: A Quelles Conditions*? (Bordeaux, COMPTRASEC, 2006).

Barnard, C., *EC Employment Law* (New York, Oxford University Press, 2006).

Bercusson, B., 'Employment and Social Protection: A New Relationship?', Working Paper for the International Seminar on Comparative Labour Law, Industrial Relations and Social Security, Bordeaux, 2-13 Jul. 2007.

Caciagli, M., *Regiones en Europa* (Valencia, Tirant lo Blanch, 2006).

Committee of the Regions, *Regional and Local Powers in Europe* (Belgium Office for Official Publications of the EC, 2001).

Dehousse, R., 'The Open Method of Coordination: A New Policy Paradigm?' Paper at First Pan European Conference on EU Politics on the Politics of

85. It would be a question of a well defined contribution into an individualised account of the public pensions scheme, following the new orientation of the reform of the social security system – in particular of the retirement pensions – tried out in Sweden. *See* O. Settergren, 'Balance de la Reforma de la Seguridad Social Sueca' (2007) No extraordinario. *Revista del Ministerio de Trabajo y de Asuntos Sociales*, 165-166.

European Integration: Academic Acquis and Future Challenge, Bordeaux, 26-28 Sep. 2002.

De la Porte, C. and P. Pochet, 'The European Employment Strategy: Existing Research and Remaining Questions' (2004) 14 *Journal of European Social Policy*.

De la Rosa, S., 'Stratégie Européenne pour l'Emploi: Les Nouvelles Orientations' (2005) 12 *Droit Social*.

Eichhorst, W. and R. Konle-Seidt, 'The Interaction of Labour Market Regulation and Labour Market Policies in Welfare State Reform' (2007) 28 (1) *Review of Comparative Labour Law & Policy Journal*.

Ferrera, M. and S. Sacchi, 'Il Metodo Aperto di Coordinamento e la Capacita Istituzionali: l'Esperienza Italiana', (2005) 105 *Giornale di Diritto del Lavoro e di Relazioni Industriali*.

Friot, B., 'La Jurisprudence de la Cour de Justice des Communantés européennes eu matieére des peurious de retraite et les réformer du financement de émploiet de la protection rociale', in P. Hassenteufel and S. Hennion-Moreau, *Concurrence et Protection Sociale en Europe* (Rennes, Presses Universitaires de Rennes, 2003), 161.

Gautié, J., 'Les Économistes contre la Protection de l'Emploi: de la Déregulation à la Flexicurité' (2005) No 1.

Giorgi D. and V. Saintoyant, 'Gouvernance des Politiques d'Action Sociale Décentralisées et MOC'(2007) 7/8 *Droit Social*.

Giuboni, S., *Social Rights and Market Freedom in the European Constitution* (Cambridge, Cambrigde University Press, 2006).

De Búrca G., (ed.), *EU Law and the Welfare State* (New York, Oxford University Press, 2005).

Goetschy, J., 'The European Employment Strategy, Multi-level Governance, and Policy Coordination: Past, Present and Future' in J. Zeitlin and D. Trubeck (eds), *The European Employment Strategy. Governing work and Welfare in a New Economy: European and American Experiments* (Oxford, Oxford University Press, 2003).

Hassenteufel, P. and S. Hennion-Maureau, *Concurrence et Protection Sociale en Europe* (Rennes, Presses Universitaires de Rennes, 2003).

Jeammaud, A.,'Le Concept d'Effectivité du Droit' in P Auvergnon, *L'Effectivité du Droit du Travail: À Quelles Conditions*? (Bordeaux, COMPTRASEC, 2006).

Landa Zapirain, J.P. 'La Organización de la Sanidad Pública ante la Jurisprudencia Constitucional: una Reflexión sobre este Modelo de Reparto Competencial entre Estado y Comunidades Autónomas' (1999) 6 *Revista de Derecho Social*.

– 'La Política Social en España y el Federalismo Social' (2003) 24 *Revista de Derecho Social*.

Míguelez Lobo, F., 'Flexiseguridad, Bienestar y Cohesión Social' (2007) No extra-ordinario *Revista del Ministerio de Trabajo y Asuntos Sociales*.

Moreno Marcos, M., 'Medidas de Fomento al Empleo y Reglamento 2204/2002/ CE de la Comisión de 12 de Diciembre de 2002, sobre la Aplicación de los Artículos 87 y 88 del Tratado de CE a las Ayudas Estatales para el Empleo (A Propósito de la Sentencia del Tribunal de Justicia de las Comunidades Europeas de 14 de abril de 2005)' (2006) 62 *Revista del Ministerio de Trabajo y Asuntos Sociales.*

OCDE, *Perspectivas del Empleo 2005* (Madrid, MTAS, 2005).

OCDE, *Perspectivas del Empleo 2006* (Madrid, MTAS, 2006).

Pisarello, G. and A. del Cabo, (eds) *La Renta Básica como Nuevo Derecho Ciudadano* (Madrid, Trotta, 2006).

Radaelli, C.M., 'The OMC: a New Governance Architecture for the European Union?' (2003) Rapport 1 Swedish Institute for European Policy Studies at <www.sieps.su.se/_pdf/Publikationer/CR20031.pdf>.

Raventós, D., *El Derecho a la Existencia* (Ed. Ariel Practicum, Barcelona, 2007).

Rodriguez Piñero, M., 'La Normalización de la Renta Activa de Inserción' (2007) 3 *Revista de Relaciones Laborales.*

Ross, M., 'Promoting Solidarity: from Public Services to a European Model of Competition' (2007) 44 *Common Market Law Review.*

Settergren, O., 'Balance de la Reforma de la Seguridad Social Sueca' (2007) No extraordinario *Revista del Ministerio de Trabajo y de la Seguridad Social.*

Sciarra, S., 'La Constitucionalización de la Europa Social: Derechos Fundamentales y Procedimientos de Soft Law' (2004) 2 *Revista de Relaciones Laborales.*

Van der Mei, A.P., *Free Movement of Persons within the European Community,* (Oxford-Portland, Hart Publishing, 2003).

Vanderorght, Y. and Ph. Van Parijs, *L'Allocation Universelle* (Paris, La Dcouverte, 2005).

Zeitlin, J., P. Pochet, and L. Magnusson, *The Open Method of Coordination in Action: The European Employment and Social Inclusion Strategies* (Brussels, PIE/Peter Lang, 2005).

Chapter 3

EES and European Social Inclusion Policy: Employment as a Means of Social Inclusion in an International Human Rights Perspective

Aranzazu Fernández Urrutia &
Nuria Pumar Beltrán

1. INTRODUCTION

Given the debate, which has arisen in European Labour Law[1] on how fundamental rights can affect the European social policies in the Open Method of Coordination (OMC), we need to review the OMC on social inclusion in the light of international human rights. To do this we must first cover the main characteristics of the OMC on social inclusion as a political process, together with the latest developments regarding the contents therein by highlighting the relevance of employment policies and employment as a means towards social inclusion. In the second part of this chapter, we will show how poverty and social exclusion, according to international norms issued by the United Nations, are examples of violations of

1. This debate became more significant following the ratification of the Charter of Fundamental Rights in 2000 and its future inclusion in the European Constitution. *See* for all S. Sciarra, 'Fundamental Labour Rights after the Lisbon Agenda' (2005) 36 *Working Papers Centro Studi di Diritto del Lavoro Europeo 'Massimo d'Antona'*.

Roger Blanpain, Juan Pablo Landa, Brian Langille (eds), *Employment Policies and Multilevel Governance*, pp. 65–103.

fundamental human rights and we will examine the human right to decent employment as a means to fight these phenomena. International standards serve to analyze European Union (EU) policies, which focus mainly on the fight against poverty from the viewpoint of economic growth and employment. We finally conclude that the contents of these policies need to be reviewed in the light of international commitments undersigned by Member States of the EU poniéndolo en relación con el papel que juegan los derechos sociales fundamentales en el actual marco jurídico y político de la Unión Europea.We finally conclude that the contents of these policies needs to be reviewed in the light of the international commitments undersigned by Member States of the EU.

2. ACTION TAKEN BY UNION INSTITUTIONS REGARDING SOCIAL EXCLUSION

2.1. Background and Development

Although the EU's first programmes to fight poverty were introduced in the 1980s, it was not until the early 1990s, under the presidency of Jacques Delors, when they were finally accepted by the European authorities after they emerged as an issue of 'common concern'.[2] An important breakthrough in consolidating the fight against social exclusion in the EU occurred when it was first included in social-policy objectives in EU Treaties following the signing of the Amsterdam Treaty.[3] Article 137 of this Treaty states that the EU 'shall support and complement the action by Member States' in the fight against social exclusion. The Council could promote cooperation, exchange data among Member States and even dictate Council Directives to be used as a way to help people excluded from the labour market find employment.

At the European Council meeting held in Lisbon in March 2000 the future EU strategy was drawn up with a view to turning it into a superpower in the new world economy based on knowledge. In pursuing this ambitious project, the political strategies in the field of socioeconomics had to focus mainly on the area of economic reforms, employment and social cohesion. Precisely in order to promote social inclusion, the Council of Europe announced at this summit the EU's commitment 'to make a decisive impact on the eradication of poverty'.

By acknowledging this, social policy became part of the three vertices of the triangle upon which the Lisbon Strategy was based and developed through the OMC, that is, economic policies (through the Broad Economic Guidelines

2. M. Ferrera, M. Matsaganis and S. Sacchi, 'Open Coordination against Poverty: the New EU Social Inclusion Process' (2002) 1 (2:3) *Journal of European Social Policy*, 228.
3. M. Ferrera, M. Matsaganis and S. Sacchi, 'Open Coordination against Poverty: The New EU Social Inclusion Process' (2002) 1 (2:3) *Journal of European Social Policy*, 230. J. O'Connor, 'Policy Coordination, Social Indicators and the Social-Policy Agenda in the European Union' (2005) 15 *Journal of European Social Policy*, 348.

(BEPGs)), employment policies (through the so called European Employment Strategy (EES)) and social protection (which essentially includes social inclusion and pensions with the recent inclusion of healthcare and long-term care). In this renewed political commitment, the Social Protection Committee plays an important role as a consultation institution created in 2000 whose main purpose is to promote cooperation between the EU and Member States.[4]

It is worth highlighting the fact that the fight against social exclusion has been included in the Lisbon Strategy, which means broadening the EU's viewpoint on social-policy issues that, until recently, had focused almost exclusively on employment policies. Social cohesion was only seen from a viewpoint of the employability of long-term unemployed and for those in situations of exclusion. This change implies that 'while unemployment remains a central concern, policy should no longer confine itself to labour markets but should tackle poverty and social exclusion'.[5]

Through this new cooperation framework, the EU aims to coordinate social-policy actions of Member States on a European level, whereby they converge towards medium and long term commonly-agreed objectives set by the Commission and the Council. This would be an attempt to encourage all levels of the population to gain access to the goods and rights considered to be basic, such as education, housing, employment, healthcare or minimum incomes. Sustained economic growth would promote employment and social cohesion. This would also contribute to achieving economic expectations. There is therefore a strong dependency among these three facets.

The political commitment to promote social inclusion begun in Lisbon was consolidated at the Nice summit in December 2000,[6] which approved the Social Agenda for 2000-2005 and also the first set of commonly-agreed appropriate objectives in the fight against social exclusion and the eradication of poverty previously adopted by the Council (Employment and Social Policy) on 17 October 2000 –, and that Member States had to include in their policies on social inclusion. These objectives were: to facilitate participation in employment; to facilitate access by all to the resources, rights, goods and services; to prevent the risks of exclusion; to help the most vulnerable; and to mobilize all relevant bodies. Given the complex nature of social exclusion and the need to involve authorities, civil society and those affected, each of these objectives came with a set of detailed guidelines, forming a strategy described as pluridimensional. One of the proposed actions was to organize the systems of social protection so as to ensure to everyone the resources necessary to live with dignity; and the creation of policies to allow access to decent housing, healthcare, education, justice, culture, sport and

4. Council Decision 2004/689/EC of 4 Oct. 2004, Establishing a Social Protection Committee and Repealing Decision, OJ L 314, 8-10.
5. S. Middelton, M. Barnes and J. Millar, 'Introduction: The Dynamic Analysis of Poverty and Social Inclusion', in *The Dynamic of Social Exclusion in Europe*, E. Apostori and J. Millar (eds) (London, Edward Elgar Publishing, 2003).
6. *See* Presidency Conclusions of Nice European Council Meeting, 7, 8 and 9 Dec. 2000, <www.consilium.europa.eu/ueDocs/cms_Data/docs/pressData/en/ec/00400-r1.%20ann.en0.htm>.

recreational activities. Another proposal, to prevent exclusion, was to promote access to information technologies, and to implement policies to avoid excessive indebtedness, exclusion from school or loss of housing. It also proposed to implement corporate social responsibility. Nonetheless, priority was given to employment as 'the best safeguard against social exclusion' so that, with the EES in mind, Member States were called to:

(a) promote access to stable and quality employment for all women and men who are capable of working, in particular:
   - by putting in place, for those in the most vulnerable groups in society, pathways towards employment and by mobilizing training policies to that end;
   - by developing policies to promote the reconciliation of work and family life, including the issue of child and dependent care;
   - by using the opportunities for integration and employment provided by the social economy; and

(b) prevent the exclusion of people from the world of work by improving employability, through human resource management, organization of work and life long learning.[7]

These initial common objectives were revised by the Council in December 2002, including in the same three new aspects proposed by the Social Protection Committee and to be contemplated by Member States in their National Action Plans (NAPs): (i) targets for significantly reducing the number of people at risk of poverty and social exclusion by 2010; (ii) the role of gender; and (iii) the high risk of poverty and social exclusion faced by some men and women as a result of immigration.[8]

The first NAPs on Social Inclusion were presented in June 2001 and contained forecasts for two years. A year later, the OMC on Adequate and Sustainable Pensions was set up until the Commission and Council decided to join both processes in 2005 in a Joint Report on Social Protection and Social Inclusion.[9] It encouraged a higher exchange of information on health care and long-term care.

Also in 2005, the Commission included its first guidelines on economy and employment through so-called 'integrated guidelines' in order to achieve greater simplicity and coherence.[10] The three coordination processes (social inclusion,

---

7. Full text of the first commonly agreed objectives in the fight against social exclusion and the eradication of poverty available at <http://ec.europa.eu/employment_social/spsi/docs/social_inclusion/approb_en.pdf>, 12 Dec. 2008.
8. Available at <http://ec.europa.eu/employment_social/spsi/docs/social_inclusion/counciltext_en.pdf>, 12 Dec. 2008.
9. Joint Report on Social Protection and Social Inclusion, COM(2005) 14 final, 27 Jan. 2005.
10. *See* Presidency Conclusions of Spring European Council, Brussels, 22 and 23 Mar. 2005; European Commission, Integrated Guidelines for Growth and Jobs (2005-2008), COM(2005) 141 final, 12 Apr. 2005; and Council of the European Union Recommendation on the Broad Guidelines for the Economic Policies of the Member States and the Community (2005-2008) available at <ec.europa.eu/growthandjobs/pdf/integrated_guidelines_en.pdf>.

adequate and sustainable pensions and high quality and sustainable healthcare and long-term care) were merged into one single Social OMC, and the Commission proposed a structure for reporting and evaluation across the three fields and a timetable synchronized with the BEPGs and Employment Guidelines since 2006.[11]

In 2006, new common objectives were established and updated by the European Council (which confirmed their validity during its 2008 spring session). At that session, the European Council declared that 'the policies for social protection and social inclusion have to be closely coordinated with the Partnership for jobs and growth, both at national and European level in order to ensure that economic, employment and social policies interact in a positive way', and insisted that the 'social protection is regarded as a productive factor'.[12] Thus, the overarching objectives of the OMC for social inclusion and social protection are to promote:

> (a) social cohesion, equality between men and women and equal opportunities for all through adequate, accessible, financially sustainable, adaptable and efficient social protection systems and social inclusion policies; (b) effective and mutual interaction between the Lisbon objectives of greater economic growth, more and better jobs and greater social cohesion, and with the EU's Sustainable Development Strategy; (c) good governance, transparency and the involvement of stakeholders in the design, implementation and monitoring of policy'.

However, in contrast with those approved in 2000, more detailed and pluridimensional, the new objectives aimed at achieving 'a decisive impact on the eradication of poverty and social exclusion' were more generic and geared towards:

> (d) access for all to the resources, rights and services needed for participation in society, preventing and addressing exclusion, and fighting all forms of discrimination leading to exclusion; (e) the active social inclusion of all, both by promoting participation in the labour market and by fighting poverty and exclusion; (f) social inclusion policies well coordinated and involving all levels of government and relevant actors, including people experiencing poverty, being efficient and effective and mainstreamed into all relevant public policies, including economic, budgetary, education and training policies and structural fund (notably ESF) programmes.[13]

To monitor progress towards the commonly-agreed objectives of the Social OMC, the Social Protection Committee agreed a set of common indicators in 2006,

11. *See*, Communication from the Commission, Strengthening the Social Dimension of the Lisbon Strategy: Streamlining Open Coordination in the Field of Social Protection, COM(2003) 261 final, 27 May 2003; and Communication from the Commission, Working Together, Working Better: A New Framework for the open Coordination of Social Protection and Inclusion Policies in the European Union, COM(2005) 706 final, 22 Dec. 2005.
12. Brussels European Council, 23-24 Mar. 2006, Presidency Conclusions, paras 70 and 71.
13. The text of all the new common objectives on social protection and social inclusion is available at <http://ec.europa.eu/employment_social/spsi/docs/social_inclusion/2006/objectives_en.pdf>, 12 Dec. 2008.

to which another specific group of indicators to monitor the healthcare and long-term care objectives in 2008 has been added. These indicators are used for the overall National Reports on Strategies for Social Protection and Social Inclusion and the specific National Reports on the three different strands as well as for the joint report presented by the European Commission and the Council.[14]

Finally, the OMC was completed with Community action programmes to fight social exclusion,[15] though the main EU action mechanisms supporting social cohesion are its structural funds and, particularly, the European Social Fund whose main priority is to promote employability.[16]

All in all, the level of maturity and development of these processes has been rather unequal. Thus, Treaty regulations show greater institutional importance to employment policies, as they dedicate an entire chapter to employment – unlike the general views on social policy matters.[17]

The lack of balance between the development of a European economic and social model lies deep in the origins of the EU, since the main reason for its existence was to create a common market of goods, services, capital and employment. So it should come as no surprise to *see* that the most advanced process of policy convergence has been economic through BEPGs, to the extent that a breach of the objectives set in the Stability and Growth Pact by any Member State can lead to sanctions (Article 104.11 ECT).

It is also a fact that the OMC on social inclusion issues began later and this process has always lagged behind the initiatives on employment and economic policies. As the Commission acknowledged in its report titled 'Building an inclusive Europe' (2000), the EU has taken on a commitment of 'promoting transnational co operation and appropriate benchmarking mechanisms, building on knowledge, experience and efforts in Member States. The purpose is to encourage open and flexible forms of cooperation between Member States, not to set up a heavy coordination process'.

Coordination of the various national policies is less exacting, so that inspections and controls carried out by Brussels on actions by Member States are more flexible in social inclusion issues.

---

14. Indicators can be accessed at <http://ec.europa.eu/employment_social/spsi/common_indicators_en.htm>, 12 Dec. 2008.
15. *See* Decision No. 50/2002/EC of the European Parliament and of the Council of 7 Dec. 2001. Establishing a Programme of Community Action to Encourage Cooperation between Member States to Combat Social Exclusion, OJ L 010, 1-7; and Decision No. 1672/2006/EC of the European Parliament and of the Council of 24 Oct. 2006 Establishing a Community Programme for Employment and Social Solidarity – PROGRESS, OJ L 315, 1-8.
16. *See* Council Regulation (EC) No. 1083/2006 of 11 Jul. 2006 Laying Down General Provisions on the European Regional Development Fund, the European Social Fund and the Cohesion Fund and Repealing Regulation (EC) No. 1260/1999, OJ L 210, 25-78; and Council Decision of 6 Oct. 2006 on Community Strategic Guidelines on Cohesion 2007-2013 (2006/702/EC), OJ L 291, 11-33.
17. J. Zeitlin, 'The Open Method of Coordination and the Future of the European Employment Strategy', Hearing of the European Parliament, Employment and Social Affairs Committee, 8 Jul. 2002.

However, key rules in the OMCs are repeated in this process, so European authorities periodically set guideline objectives and common indicators which Member States must follow in their respective national policies. In turn, these policies must assess and review the way they are carried out through the national plans presented by each Member State. Thus, the Commission sets common key strategies in its Joint Reports and highlights the good practices among the initiatives presented.

Below, we refer briefly to the parameters used by European authorities to determine situations of poverty or social exclusion. Later, we describe the peculiarities of the OMC process. And, finally, we will *see* the EU's predominant approach to or philosophy in the fight against poverty and social exclusion: the active inclusion through employment.

2.2. Defining the Problem of Social Exclusion and the Main Political Aspects

One of the main difficulties for the social policies aimed at the most disadvantaged is building a term and concept framework basis for the occurrences that we identify as poverty and social exclusion. Poverty and social exclusion are not equivalent, even though they can overlap.[18] They both share a common feature, the violation of personal dignity and human rights, as highlighted by international human right organizations.

To begin with poverty, the EU indicator of poverty is the so called 'at-risk-of-poverty rate', which is part of the portfolio of indicators adopted by the Laeken European Council (2001). It shows the percentage of persons with an equivalized disposable income below the at-risk-of-poverty threshold, which is set at 60% of the national median equivalized disposable income after social transfers. Se considera que estos resources are so low that they risk exclusion from full participation in the society in which they live. It is estimated that these resources are so low that they risk exclusion from full participation in the society in which they live.

According to EU statistics for 2006, 79 million people or 16% of the EU population are at risk of poverty, ranging from 10% in the Czech Republic and the Netherlands to 21% in Greece and 23% in Latvia. 41% of the unemployed live under the poverty threshold (so that unemployment is one of the main factors of poverty and exclusion); but 8% of people at work are at risk of poverty. This in-work poverty is linked to low pay, low skills, precarious employment and often-involuntary part time working. This figure is worth recalling when relating EU social inclusion and employment policies.[19]

18. Extensively, on the use of the term 'social exclusion' mainly in Europe and the different perceptions regarding the concept of poverty, *see* P. Spicker, 'Exclusion and Rights', in *Law and Poverty – The Legal System and Poverty Reduction*, L. Williams, A. Kjønstad and P. Robson (eds) (London: Zed Books, CROP International Studies in Poverty Research, 2003), 124-136.

19. In summary, it is estimated that 'out of the 78 million people living at risk of poverty in the EU, one fourth are children, one fifth are elderly, one fifth are working poor, 12% are unemployed

Regarding social exclusion, there is general agreement that despite being identified with poverty, social exclusion is more complex. Many factors may be involved in its roots (for example long-term unemployment, unstable employment, health problems, lack of emotional stability or qualifications, the level of development in the area or region, etc.) and the groups involved are very heterogeneous (long-term unemployed, single mothers, immigrants, ethnic minorities, the disabled . . .).

As the EU authorities have highlighted on numerous occasions, to completely grasp the phenomenon of social exclusion we need to consider the lack of resources but, due to its multidimensional characteristics,[20] other equally important aspects such as access to employment, education, housing and health, the level of meeting basic needs and the power to participate fully in society.[21] Furthermore social exclusion is a dynamic problem so, along with social change, new risks of poverty or exclusion arise, as occurs for instance with immigration.

The Commission defines social exclusion as:

> a process whereby certain individuals are pushed to the edge of society and prevented from participating fully by virtue of their poverty, or lack of basic competencies and lifelong learning opportunities, or as a result of discrimination. This distances them from job, income and education opportunities as well as social and community networks and activities. They have little access to power and decision making bodies and thus often feeling powerless and unable to take control over the decisions that affect their day-to-day lives.[22]

The Social Protection Committee and the Commission have made an effort to develop both social indicators reached by consensus and a pan European base of statistics with the purpose of measuring situations of poverty and social exclusion more accurately. Only common indicators used in the NAPs will allow the Commission to identify the best practices and assess the progress made. The importance of selecting the right common indicators to test the multiple facets

---

and one fourth are inactive people of working age'. *See* Commission Staff Working Document. Monitoring Progress Towards the Objectives of the European Strategy for Social Protection and Social Inclusion, SEC(2008), Brussels, 6 Oct. 2008, 11, 17, 23, 24 and 38. Also, O. Lelkes and E. Zólyomi, 'Poverty Across Europe: The Latest Evidence Using the EU-SILC Survey', European Centre for Social Welfare Policy and Research, 2008. It states that 'two thirds of the total poor population in the European Union live in six countries: Germany, France, the United Kingdom, Italy, Poland and Spain', and that 'jobless households show the highest rates of poverty in the majority of the EU Member States', 2, 7 and 13. Also, L. Bardone and A.-C. Guio, 'In-Work Poverty – New Commonly Agreed Indicators at the EU Level', Eurostat, Luxembourg, Statistiques en Bref, Population et Conditions Sociales, No. 5/2005. This study defines the in-work poor 'as those individuals who are classified as employed (according to their most frequent activity status) and whose household equivalised disposable income is below 60% of national median equivalised income', an estimated 14 million people of the EU 25 (1, 6, and 11).

20. Communication from the Commission, Building an Inclusive Europe, COM(2000) 79 final, 1 Mar. 2000.
21. Joint Report on Social Inclusion, Council document (15223/01) of 12 Dec. 2001.
22. Joint Report on Social Inclusion, COM(2003) 773 final, 12 Dec. 2003.

of social exclusion led to later shaping the indicators that were agreed in the Laeken summit in 2001[23] and these refer to four areas: income poverty, long-term unemployment, health and lifelong learning.

As regards the most vulnerable groups, social inclusion programmes must prioritize those who suffer social exclusion or a greater risk of poverty. Different reports on social protection have highlighted long-term unemployed, children and youths who drop out of school early (early school leavers), handicapped workers, immigrants and people who belong to ethnic minorities (particularly gypsies) as well as prisoners or ex prisoners as particularly vulnerable.[24] They also recommend analyzing the various effects of social exclusion depending on gender, bearing in mind the fact that there are three situations which increase the risk of poverty for women: single mothers, pensioners who have never contributed or did so insufficiently and women who are victims of domestic violence.[25] There is thus a need to extend policies on equality and non-discrimination to a large number of the aforementioned groups.

2.3. The Strengths and Weaknesses of the OMC in Social Inclusion Issues

The strengths and main deficiencies of the OMC's and the EU's method of governance have already been covered in great depth in EU publications. We therefore mention it very briefly, so as to focus on the OMC on social inclusion.

Perhaps the main argument used in favour of the OMC as a political action tool is that it allows the EU to act in matters upon which it has no powers or which require rules of unanimity or qualified majority to pass as laws. Furthermore, those in favour of the OMC compare the flexibility of political coordination techniques to the inflexibility of European legislation since with the former it is possible to manage various areas of EU interest while respecting the diversity of national situations. Otherwise, this method promotes a key quality in European governance design[26] such as greater participation by the agents involved. In this sense, the method of multi-level governance, inherent to the OMC, may involve other

23. After including social protection and social inclusion in one OMC, indicators which the NAPs must contain are classified in the following way: overarching indicators which reflect the social, economic and demographic context to carry out the social protection and inclusion policies and the three strands – social inclusion, pensions and health – primary indicators have been agreed on and defined 'as a condensed set of lead indicators which cover all essential dimensions of the defined objectives and/or highlight the social situation of key sub-populations' and secondary indicators that 'would support these lead indicators by having a greater insight into the nature of the problem'. European Commission, Portfolio of Overarching Indicators and Streamlined Social Inclusion, Pensions, and Health Portfolios', 7 Jun. 2006 D(2006). Regarding criteria for adopting the social indicators *see* T. Atkinson et al., *Social Indicators. The EU and Social Inclusion* (Oxford University Press, 2002).
24. Commission of the European Communities, Joint Report on Social Protection and Social Inclusion. Supporting Document, SEC(2007) 329, 6 Mar. 2007.
25. Joint Report on Social Inclusion, Council document (15223/01) of 12 Dec. 2001.
26. European Governance. A White Paper, COM(2001) 428 final.

separate agents from national governments such as subnational institutions, social agents and NGO's designing and executing their actions. Also, greater flexibility would promote decentralized policies which would better adapt to the different levels of national, regional or local political responsibility.[27]

Despite all these advantages, many qualify this way of governance as insufficient since putting these objectives into practice depends greatly on the degree of commitment taken on by the various national governments. This is the OMC's Achilles' heel since if no commitment exists there is a risk that the OMC will have no impact 'outside the political and administrative elite'.[28] To this can be added the difficulty to measure the impact of this process on national policies.[29] It is then an insufficient means to achieve social-policy objectives and must necessarily be completed by approving directives which will create minimum legally binding social contents.[30]

However, a more sceptical view will highlight a conscious abandonment by EU authorities regarding legislation on social matters on a European level, at the expense of leaving the land ripe for promoting neoliberal dictates in policies from Brussels. The change of the EU's action model which devolves judicial legislative activity to Member States avoids establishing minimum legally binding contents for all as well as deactivating the role carried out by the European Court of Justice (ECJ).[31]

However, through common objectives, the Social OMC permits to reorientate and bring together the contents of various social policies starting from the wide diversity of social protection models, ways of organizing and political decentralization, etc. As highlighted so often, the really important feature of the OMC is the outcomes which can be seen in the various social indicators regardless of the means used to achieve them.

Also, Commission reports and objectives set by the Council encourage the exchange of knowledge and experiences between the Member States, and this allows the various territorial institutions and other organizations, such as social agents or NGO's, to participate in Member States decisions. Applying this open method would not only allow European guidelines to be territorialized so that NAPs can be linked to different territorial levels down to local ones but also, in

27. C. De La Porte and P. Pochet, 'Social Benchmarking, Policy Making and New Governances in the EU' (2001) 11.4 *Journal of European Social Policy*, 300.
28. J. O'Connor, *see* n. 3.
29. E. Terradillos, 'The Validity and Limits of the Open Method of Coordination in Community Social Policy', paper given at the Conference 'The Implementation of Community Employment and Social Inclusion Policies in the Model of Social Federalism' (21-22 Jun., Oñati, 2007).
30. J. Goetschy, 'The European Employment Strategy, Multi-level Governance, and Policy Coordination: Past, Present and Future', in *Governing Work and Welfare in a New Economy*, J. Zeitlin and D. M. Trubek (eds) (Oxford, Oxford University Press, 2003). B. Cantillon, 'European Subsidiarity versus American Social Federalism: Is Europe in Need of a Common Social Policy?', Paper for the Second Annual ESPAnet Conference (9-11 Sep., Oxford, 2004).
31. J. López, 'Beyond the National Case: The Role of Transnational Labor Law in Shaping Domestic Regulation' (2008) 28 *Comparative Labor Law & Policy Journal*, 547.

a bottom up process, non governmental institutions could contribute with their political practices and experience to NAPs.

This complexity, as we shall *see*, is shown most clearly in matters of social inclusion precisely due to its comprehensive nature, since it is present in all areas of social policy. Another factor concerning this complexity is the large number of agents involved on different levels. And the same heterogeneity is present between those groups considered to be in a situation of or risk from social exclusion (disabilities, immigrants from outside the EU, single mothers and ethnic minorities), where gender and age plays a decisive role moreover.

Developing objectives and establishing benchmarking and indicators has clearly contributed to improving the understanding of situations of social exclusion. This approach also contributes, through mainstreaming, by including the objectives of social inclusion in the Member States' political actions. It also helps Member States detect deficiencies in their political actions, such as, for example, the existence of a lack of coordination with other institutions or the absence of statistical data on certain indicators.[32]

However, doubts are growing as to the practical effectiveness of the OMCs, that is, as to their influence on national policies when they concern social inclusion. And this occurs because, despite efforts to develop common objectives, they continue to suffer from an obvious lack of specification because they are not quantified and their compliance is not subject to deadlines.

In the first Joint Report on Social Inclusion,[33] the Commission and the Council already detected a series of deficiencies in the NAPs, such lack of specific objectives (since they were not quantifiable), scant attention paid to gender or not including regional and local policies.[34]

To this may be added the complexity of applying the method of mainstreaming in such wide-ranging policies. No less important, to the necessary open style of social inclusion policies is added the failure to agree on common terminology and meaning in the EU to define social protection issues, social care, social services, etc. In fact, the use of political language distances itself from the traditional legal terms used in international rules and regulations. Agreement on these documents should be reached by consensus to find an open but necessarily common meaning for all national legal systems.

But the success of implementing this type of policies and their influence on national policies depend, above all, on the level of commitment taken on by the EU and Member States. And, as we have seen, the fight against poverty and exclusion was left out of the Lisbon Strategy and of the integrated guidelines for economy and employment.[35]

---

32. Social Protection Committee, Fight Against Poverty and Social Exclusion: Common Objectives for the Second Round of National Action Plans, Brussels 25 Nov. 2002.
33. Joint Report on Social Inclusion, Council document (15223/01) of 12 Dec. 2001.
34. Of the same opinion, Committee of Regions, Decision Taken by the Committee of Regions on Re-Launching the Lisbon Strategy (2005/C 164/13), OJ C 164, 91-94.
35. J.P. Landa Zapirain, 'Looking at the EES in the Search for Efficacy (and for Efficiency) in the National Systems of Social Protection: the Balance of Social Federalism Models', paper given

In fact, several indicators show the secundary role of the fight against social exclusion as compared to economic and employment policies in the Lisbon Strategy has grown over time coinciding with a more integrating approach of these processes.[36]

However, in the context of the recently approved Social Agenda for 2008-2010, the European Commission aims to correct the policy approach in the future and proposes to strengthen the Social OMC by improving its visibility and working methods, strengthening its interaction with other policies (e.g., competition, internal market, economic policy, health, immigration, trade, agriculture, etc.),[37] reinforcing its analytical tools and evidence base, and enhancing ownership in Member States through peer review, mutual learning and involvement of all relevant actors (regional and local authorities, and civil society) throughout the full policy (this is, including its implementation phase). The reinforcement will be achieved by adopting progressively, in agreement with the Member States, some of the successful methods applied under the Lisbon strategy. In particular, by the introduction of quantitative targets for the reduction of poverty in general as well as for specific forms of poverty, such as child poverty, in-work poverty, long-term poverty and poverty of older people, which is also an indicator of pension adequacy. And also by the introduction of quantified targets supported by the commonly-agreed indicators related to a minimum level of income provided through pensions, whether publicly or privately provided; related to access and quality of healthcare and social care; and health status related targets, since 'health status is decisive for active participation in the labour market, longer working lives and for reducing poverty'. At the same time, it is possible for Member States to define national targets, making it possible for groups of countries with similar situations to work together, and taking into account the diversity, particular national context and different points of departure of each Member State.[38]

at the Conference, 'The Implementation of Community Employment and Social Inclusion Policies in the Model of Social Federalism' (21-22 Jun. 2007, Oñati).

36. On this process *see* mainly in European Commission, Strengthening the Social Dimension of the Lisbon Strategy: Streamlining Open Coordination in the Field of Social Protection, COM (2003) 261 final; and European Commission Working Together for Growth and Jobs: A New Start for the Lisbon Strategy, COM (2005) 24 final.

37. The Social Protection Committe and Employment Committe 'welcome' this 'holistic approach embraced by the Renewed Social Agenda as it contributes to open ways to mainstream employment and social goals in all EU policies, and sets instruments to act in synergy with the Lisbon Strategy.' *See* Joint SPC-EMCO opinion on the Renewed Social Agenda, adopted by the two Committees on 14 and 27 Nov. 2008, respectively, <http://register.consilium.europa.eu/pdf/en/08/st16/st16495.en08.pdf>, 23 Dec. 2008.

38. *See* Communication from the Commission to the European Parliament, the Council, the European Economic and Social Committee and the Committee of the Regions, Renewed Social Agenda: Opportunities, Access and Solidarity in twenty-first century Europe, COM (2008) 421 final, 2 Jul. 2008. And also Communication from the Commission to the European Parliament, the Council, the European Economic and Social Committee and the Committee of the Regions, A Renewed Commitment to Social Europe: Reinforcing the Open Method of Coordination for Social Protection and Social Inclusion, COM (2008) 418 final, 2 Jul. 2008.

2.4. PREDOMINANT POLICY APPROACH: EMPLOYMENT AS THE MAIN FACTOR OF SOCIAL INCLUSION

In their quest to liberalize the European market, European institutions *see* the role of public policies, whether employment or social protection, subordinated to the needs of the economy and market.[39]

It is precisely on the fulfilment of economic convergence objectives that success in the fight against unemployment and social exclusion will depend, so such social policies cannot obstruct them.

The idea is that social protection, in the Commission's words, will contribute 'to guaranteeing that systems will reinforce, instead of obstructing, economic development and create employment'.[40]

It is necessary, as the White Book on European governance points out, for greater coordination among the different policies to make them more coherent and efficient with a view to complying with the Lisbon strategy.

As stated by the Commission, the material link between economic guidelines and employment and those of social protection are clearly visible in two aspects: first, in the convenience of national strategies on matters of pensions that are financially feasible and subject to the Stability and Growth Pact to cover an ageing population and also social protection; secondly, besides complying with the traditional function of compensating for social risks and providing a minimum level of subsistence, they must promote employment and an open labour market which includes the most disfavoured.[41]

It could be said there are two trends in the OMC which are, in principle, contradictory: first, they cut expenses in social protection matters reducing the pensions and emphasizing the criteria of contributions. and then, they reinforce the mechanisms of solidarity and therefore social cohesion. One key factor of social cohesion is clearly the universal provision of healthcare and long-term care which enable people from less privileged groups to have equal conditions. It is also necessary to reinforce factors of social protection by essentially improving coverage of guaranteed minimum incomes, minimum contribution pensions and other kinds of benefits.

However, this approach to solidarity must lie in the context of budgetary balance and control of social spending. The prospects of the European population ageing and the foreseeable problems of the Social Security's financial feasibility

39. A. Atkinson, 'La Pauvreté et la Exclusion Sociale en Europe', *Pauvreté et Exclusion* (La Documentation Française, 1998); M. Rhodes, 'Globalization, Welfare States and Employment: is There a European 'Third Way'? in N. Bermeo (ed.), *Unemployment in the New Europe* (Cambridge University Press, 2001).
40. Social Protection in Europe, Report, 1997. Social protection is even seen as a 'productive factor'. Communication from the Commission to the Council, the European Parliament, the Economic and Social Committee and the Committee of the Regions, Social Policy Agenda, COM (2000) 379 final.
41. European Commission, Strengthening the Social Dimension of the Lisbon Strategy: Streamlining Open Coordination in the Field of Social Protection, COM (2003) 261 final.

are decisive factors which affect a switch towards inclusive policies of employment and social cohesion. And, in this context, one way to save costs in social benefits lies in integrating groups who have greater employment problems into the labour market. Therefore measures can be highlighted which encourage women to join the labour market and lengthen the working life of people at the age of retirement.

Here active employment policies are mixed with the passive ones of social protection so the latter must contribute most to 'making work pay'[42] and make it easier for people who are temporarily unemployed or inactive to join the labour market, in line with policies of 'flexicurity'.

To foment 'making work pay' one starts from the premise that high levels of social protection and taxation discourage a person from finding work. EU authorities recommend a review of fiscal policies and benefits 'so they lower the risk of inactivity, unemployment and poverty traps', following in the wake of studies on employment published by the Organization for Economic Cooperation and Development (OECD) in 1994. According to the Commission, we must find a balance between designing benefits and taxes which discourage the unemployed from finding work while guaranteeing sufficient income. These actions must be complemented with policies which offer support and training as well as services which contribute to the work-life balance.[43]

The proposal of 'making work pay' has received different warnings. For instance, in 2003, the Social Protection Committee stated that such 'guideline could be formulated differently regarding the focus on the incentives of benefit systems'. It should have a broader focus 'emphasizing also the need for entitlement to benefit to be accompanied by improved access to activation measures to support employability and the search for a job'.[44] And, bearing in mind the need for a good

42. The background to this strategy is the Essen European Council of 9-10 Dec. 1994, which stated that 'the effectiveness of employment policy must be increased by avoiding practices which are detrimental to readiness to work, and by moving from a passive to an active labour market policy'. It recommended to act in favour of a 'more flexible organization of work', in line with the proposals of the White Paper on Growth, Competitiveness, and Employment COM (93) 700 final/A and B, 5 Dec. 1993, and of the White Paper on European Social Policy COM (94) 333 final, 27 Jul. 1994. Later, 'making work pay' was the fourth key objective set out by the European Commission in its Communication on a Concerted Strategy for Modernising Social Protection COM (1999) 347 final. This goal is also issued by the employment and the broad economic policy guidelinesand continues in the integrated guidelines for economy and employment, which call for Member States to act to 'ensure inclusive labour markets, enhance work attractiveness, and make work pay for job-seekers, including disadvantaged people, and the inactive'. *See* Council Decision of 12 Jul. 2005 on Guidelines for the Employment Policies of the Member States 2005/600/EC, OJ L 205, 21-27, guideline No. 19; and Council Decision of 15 Jul. 2008 on guidelines for the employment policies of the Member States, OJ L 198, 47-54, aslo employment guideline No. 19.
43. *See* European Commission, Modernising Social Protection for More and Better Jobs: a Comprehensive Approach Contributing to Making Work Pay, COM (2003) 842 final, 21-22.
44. Opinion of the Social Protection Committee on the Proposal for the 2003 Employment Guidelines and the 2003 Broad Economic Policy Guidelines, <http://ec.europa.eu/employment_social/spsi/docs/social_protection_commitee/opinion_bepg_en.pdf>, 12 Dec. 2008.

articulation between the OMC for social inclusion and pensions processes and the EES, the Committee noted the need for 'strong mutually reinforcing interaction between employment and social protection policies' to ensure, *inter alia*:

> 'that social inclusion is promoted by facilitating participation in employment for those wanting and able to work and by ensuring possibilities to progress in terms of pay and qualifications; that social protection systems offer the right *incentives* and *conditions* for employment participation; that work is brought within the formal employment system where it can properly support social protection systems by generating tax and contribution income and where the objective of a high quality of work can be promoted'; and 'that employment practices do not shift the costs of poor labour management and working conditions to social protection systems in the form of invalidity and early retirement pensions, unemployment benefits, sickness pay for workers suffering excessively high levels of stress or poor working conditions'.[45]

In turn, the OECD warned in its 2006 employment programme of the obvious social effect that such aggressive employment policies would have since cuts in unemployment benefits would compel workers to accept low skilled, low-paid jobs, so employees could fall into the trap of temporary, low-paid employment, and not be given the chance to find a better job.[46]

On the other hand, in parallel to the strategy of 'making work pay' we have the proposal to modernize the regulation of the labour market and the systems of social protection through 'flexicurity'.[47] Combining job flexibility with security leads to a wider interpretation of labour law which adapts to a company's needs (for example through regulating atypical employment, reducing the cost of dismissals or promoting professional mobility, etc.). In contrast – and this would be a factor of security – the public authorities must offer workers support mechanisms so that

---

45. Opinion of the Social Protection Committee on the Commission's Synthesis Report to the Spring European Council, Choosing to Grow: Knowledge, Innovation and Jobs in a Cohesive Society and on the Communication The Future of the European Employment Strategy, available at <http://ec.europa.eu/employment_social/spsi/docs/social_protection_commitee/opinion_synthesis_en.pdf>, 12 Dec. 2008.
46. OECD Employment Outlook, Ch. 5 'Social Implications of Policies Aimed at Raising Employment', 2006. Previously, on the negative effects of the 'neoliberal approach' to the labour market and social protection systems in relation to social excusion, using data from the first half of the nineties, *see* D. Meurs and J. Prelis, 'Western Europe thematic employment report', in *The Human Dignity And Social Exclusion Initiative* (Strasbourg, Council of Europe,1997).
47. *See* Report of the Employment Task Force chaired by Win Kok, Jobs, Jobs, Jobs, Creating More Employment in Europe, Nov. 2003, 27-32 on Promote Flexibility Combined with Security on the Labour Market, 33-46 and on Attracting More People to the Labour Market: Making Work a Real Option for All, available at <http://ec.europa.eu/employment_social/employment_strategy/pdf/etf_en.pdf>. In 2004 the European Council accepted the recommendations of said Report and called Member States to implement them within the framework of the Broad Economic Policy Guidelines and the European Employment Strategy. *See* revised version of the Presidency Conclusions of the Brussels European Council (25 and 26 Mar. 2004), paras 34-40, at <http://ue.eu.int/ueDocs/cms_Data/docs/pressData/en/ec/79696.pdf>, 12 Dec. 2004.

they can find new jobs in times of inactivity between jobs throughout their working life through policies of education, training to improve professional skills and providing necessary income, support and guidance measures in the search for employment, etc.[48] This is not the place to analyze this new approach to labour law in depth. But it could be said that promoting these labour policies will raise – not lower – barriers for inclusion, especially for the most underprivileged groups who, despite finding employment, will not be able to gain access to basic rights such as, for example, the right to decent housing.

The specific guideline on 'making work pay' was not part of the first set of commonly agreed appropriate objectives in the fight against social exclusion and the eradication of poverty approved in 2000. Its philosophy, however, was used for and adapted to the Social OMC through the Social Agenda (2005-2010), which also activated the debate on the role of the national minimum income schemes.[49] In line with this, since 2006 the Social OMC has among its specific objectives in the fight against exclusion 'the *active social inclusion* of all, both by promoting participation in the labour market and by fighting poverty and exclusion'.

Under this tag, the European Commission has developed a strategy complementary to the flexicurity approach, whose final goal is to help Member States to move the people furthest from the labour market towards quality work. In summary, after public consultation under Article 138 EUT,[50] the European Commission considers that to achieve that aim it is necessary that Member States ensure those in exclusion situations the effective access to social services related to social and economic policies of active inclusion; including services of social assistance, health, employment, training, housing and care (children and long duration). Equally, it considers necessary to promote the employability of those apt to work and link their public benefits to their active inclusion; whilst acknowledging an 'adequate income' for those in exclusion situations but not capable of active work. In short it is about finding the middle ground between the two goals of alleviating poverty and increasing labour supply incentives, taking account of the budgetary costs that any tax and benefit reform may involve.

Thus, the European Commission first defined active social inclusion as a holistic treaty based on three main pillars: (i) a link to the labour market through job opportunities or vocational training; (ii) income support at level that is sufficient for people to live in dignity; and (iii) better access to services that may help some individuals and their families in entering mainstream society, supporting their reintegration into employment.[51]

---

48. Concerning this concept *see* Commission of the European Communities, Green Paper, Modernising Labour Law to Meet the Challenges of the 21st Century, COM (2006) 708 final, Brussels, 22 Nov. 2006.
49. Commission of the European Communities, Communication on the Social Agenda, COM (2005) 33 final, 9 Feb. 2005, 9-10.
50. Consultation documents available at <http://ec.europa.eu/employment_social/spsi/active_inclusion_en.htm>, 12 Dec. 2008.
51. Communication from the Commission to the Council, the European Parliament, the European Economic and Social Committee and the Committee of the Regions, Concerning a Consultation

After the first open consultation, the European Commission has suggested to perfect the OMC through the adoption of principles common to all aspects of active inclusion, with the participation of the Social Protection Committee, aimed at Member States and irrespective of the principle of subsidiarity to allow their evaluation. Said principles are based on three main points: income support sufficient to avoid social exclusion, link to the labour market and link to better access to quality services. Similarly, it has proposed to strengthen the role of the European Social Fund in the development of active inclusion measures and in the establishment of a Network of Local Observatories, in partnership with EU networks of local authorities, service providers and NGOs, to monitor and promote best practices, especially in relation to access to quality services.[52]

In this line, the Renewed social agenda for 2008-2010 keeps the strategy of active inclusion as the main tool in the fight against social inclusion. But it stresses the integration into the labour market, productivity of work, and permanent training; especially for those furthest from the labour market – whilst it recognizes that poverty among those who work is in the increase. It also foresees the adoption of a 'recommendation on active inclusion covering questions of income support, links with the labour market and better access to quality services'.[53]

Finally, the European Commission approved Recommendation of 3 October 2008 on the active inclusion of people excluded from the labour market[54] under Article 211 of the Treaty establishing the European Community. Its aim is that Member States organize and implement integrated active inclusion policies in accordance with the common principles and guidelines established for each of the three lines of the strategy of active inclusion, while respecting the principle of subsidiarity, the necessary policy coordination among local, regional, national and EU authorities, and the active participation of all other relevant actors,

---

on Action at EU Level to Promote the Active Inclusion of the People Furthest from the Labour Market, COM (2006) 44 final, 8 Feb. 2006.

52. Communication from the Commission to the Council, the European Parliament, the European Economic and Social Committee and the Committee of the Regions, Modernising Social Protection for Greater Social Justice and Economic Cohesion: Taking Forward the Active Inclusion of People Furthest from the Labour Market, COM (2007) 620 final, 17 Oct. 2007.
53. Together with the strategy of active inclusion, the Commission selects these lines of action for 2010: (i) the development of social services of quality, accessible and viable, in a single market and under competition rules; (ii) the extension of a programme of food subsidies as a response to the increase in food prices; (iii) the development of information technology and access to the same, in particular for the disabled; and (iv) the promotion of universal access to financial services. *See* Communication from the Commission to the European Parliament, the Council, the European Economic and Social Committee and the Committee of the Regions, Renewed Social Agenda: Opportunities, access and solidarity in 21st century Europe, COM (2008) 421 final, 2 Jul. 2008.
54. OJ L 307, 18 Nov. 2008, 11-14. This Recommendation is complemented by Communication from the Commission to the Council, the European Parliament, the European Economic and Social Committee and the Committee of the Regions on a Commission Recommendation on the Active Inclusion of People Excluded from the Labour Market, COM (2008) 639 final, 3 Oct. 2008.

including these affected by poverty, in the development, implementation and evaluation of strategies.

With regards to adequate income support, this recent Recommendation comes from Council Recommendation 92/441/EEC of 24 June 1992[55] – which called upon Member States to recognize 'the basic right of a person to sufficient resources and social assistance to live in a manner compatible with human dignity' – and stresses those elements more in line with the new active inclusion strategy – its *common principles* listed in paragraph B and its *practical guidelines* in paragraphs C (1), C (2), and C (3) – so that income support may become an active factor in social and labour market inclusion, without its eventual discouraging effect.

With this aim, the European Commission calls upon Member States:

(i) To review their social protection systems. The right to sufficient resources should be combined with active availability for work or for vocational training with a view to obtaining work in the case of persons whose conditions permit such active availability; or be subject, where appropriate, to economic and social integration measures in the case of other persons; and be combined with policies deemed necessary, at national level, for the economic and social integration of those concerned.

(ii) To take into account living standards and price levels by type and size of household to determine the resources necessary to lead a life of dignity, using the appropriate national indicators. But it also says that 'within an active inclusion framework, an incentive to seek employment for persons whose condition renders them fit for work should be safeguarded and the amounts adjusted or supplemented to meet specific needs'.

With respect to the strand on inclusive labour markets, it encourages to promote, as *common principles*, *inter alia*, the response to the needs of people excluded in order to facilitate their progressive reintegration into society and into the labour market and to enhance their employability; and also to promote quality jobs (including pay and benefits and other aspects) with a view to preventing in-work poverty; and tackle labour market segmentation by promoting job retention and advancement. Those common principles should be implemented through the main *practical guidelines* contemplated in the same Recommendation. For instance, expand and improve investment in human capital, including effective lifelong strategies, and adapt education and training systems to digital skills; active and preventive labour market measures, including support involving early identification of needs in job search; continually review the incentives and disincentives resulting from tax and benefit systems, in particular for those with low incomes, while ensuring adequate levels of social protection; provide support for the social economy and sheltered employment; promote microloans and financial incentives for employers to recruit; and the development of new jobs in services, particularly at local level.

55. OJ L 245, 26 Aug. 1992, 46-48.

In contrast with the European Parliament, the Recommendation of the European Commission does not call for income levels above the level of poverty risk. Nor does it want to rethink 'activation policies' that are based on 'too restrictive eligibility and conditionality rules for benefit recipients and force people into low quality jobs that do not provide a decent living standard', or to reduce fiscal pressure on the middle classes to avoid non declared revenues.[56] It does not call either for the adoption of agreements between social agents which could regulate the role of enterprises (mainly private ones) in the policies of active inclusion.

Finally, on the issue of access to quality services, it is interesting to note its holistic approach, and the need to ensure its territorial availability, physical accessibility, affordability, and due account for diversity of users. As for resources, it will be necessary to take into account 'the economic and budgetary constraints, the priorities set by national authorities and the state of public finances', without mention of the destiny of resources against poverty and exclusion.

3. A RATHER MORE WHOLE APPROACH: THE HUMAN RIGHTS STRATEGY

At the end of the 1980s, the United Nations system began to look in detail into the issue of poverty including its social exclusion aspect, as a situation hindering the actual exercise of human rights as a whole and of basic freedom which violates the dignity of people. General consent in this matter is seamless in regards to what is called 'extreme poverty' as well as 'social exclusion'.[57]

Since then, this issue has been a reason for concern among several institutions of the United Nations (bodies of the United Nations system) and specific reports performed by Special Reporters on realization of economic, social and cultural rights,[58] by Independent Experts on human rights and poverty appointed by the

56. *See* European Parliament Resolution of 9 Oct. 2008, on Promoting Social Inclusion and Combating Poverty, Including Child Poverty, paras 5-19 and 38-54, <www.europarl.europa.eu/sides/getDoc.do?pubRef=//EP//TEXT+TA+P6-TA-2008-0467+0+DOC+XML+V0//EN>.
57. The starting point of this approach can be found on the appearance of Father Joseph Wresinski before the Human Rights Commission. *See* L. Despouy, Preeliminary Report on Human Rights and Extreme Poverty (document E/CN.4/Sub.2/1993/16), para. 33. *See also* Resolution 1989/10 of the Human Rights Commission.
58. *See*, D. Türk reports contained in United Nations documents E/CN.4/Sub.2/1989/19; E/CN.4/Sub.2/1990/19; Charters III and IV; E/CN.4/Sub.2/1991/17; and in particular, document E/CN.4/Sub.2/1992/16. Also L. Despouy reports contained in documents E/CN.4/Sub.2/1993/16; E/CN.4/Sub.2/1994/19; E/CN.4/Sub/1995/15; and his final report in document E/CN.4/Sub.2/1996/13, paras 98-219. Regarding this report, the General Assembly Resolution of 12 Dec. 1996 (document A/RES/51/97), called 'upon states, the specialized agencies, United Nations bodies and other international organizations, including intergovernmental organizations, to give the necessary attention to this problem and to the necessary follow-up to the recommendations of the Special Rapporteur as contained in his final report' (para. 4).

Commission on Human Rights Human and the Rights Council,[59] as well as by independent experts from other specific fields.[60] It was also widely researched by the Working Group on the implementation of existing human rights norms and standards in the context of the fight against extreme poverty,[61] and was at the centre of the multilateral debate for further Social Forum meetings.[62] It is also the object of the reports by the Secretary General[63] and by the United Nations High Commissioner for Human Rights.[64]

The severity and relevance of this issue was documented in several Resolutions adopted, such as the already obsolete Sub-commission on the Promotion and Protection of Human Rights[65] and the Commission on Human Rights,[66] among others, by its successor the Human Rights Council,[67] and by the General Assembly.[68]

---

59. *See* Reports submitted by A.-M. Lizin, Independent Expert, contained in documents E/CN.4/1999/48, E/CN.4/2000/52, E/CN.4/2001/54, E/CN.4/2002/55, E/CN.4/2003/52, E/CN.4/2003/52/Add.1, E/CN.4/2004/43, and E/CN.4/2004/43/Add.1. Also reports submitted by A. Sengupta contained in documents E/CN.4/2005/49, E/CN.4/2006/43, E/CN.4/2006/43/Add.1, A/HRC/5/3 (2007), and A/HRC/7/15 (2008). And more recently by M. Sepúlveda, Interim Report contained in document A/63/274 (2008).
60. These reports focus on specific issues such as the impact of foreign debt, the fundamental right to food, the human right to the highest attainable standard of physical and mental health, and the minority rights. For a summary of their contributions *see* United Nations High Commissioner for Human Rights, Background Report, document A/HRC/SF/2008/2, 6 Aug. 2008 (para. 20-29), submitted to the World Social Forum 2008.
61. *See* working papers contained in documents E/CN.4/Sub (2003), E/CN.4/Sub.2/2004/25/Add.1, E/CN.4/Sub.2/2004/25, and E/CN.4/Sub.2/2004/44.
62. *See* Human Rights Council Resolution on Social Forum of 28 Sep. 2007 (document A/HRC/RES/6/13). The contributions to the World Social Forum sessions up to date since its beginning in 2002 and up to the last session in Sep. 2008 are available at <www2.ohchr.org/english/issues/poverty/sforum.htm>.
63. Recently, Implementation of the 1st United Nations Decade for the Eradication of Poverty (1997-2006): Report of the Secretary General (document A/62/267, 17 Aug. 2007).
64. *See* Report of the United Nations High Commissioner for Human Rights on the draft Guiding Principles on Extreme Poverty and Human Rights : the Rights of the Poor (document A/HRC/7/32, 11 Feb. 2008), and Implementation of Human Rights Council Resolution 6/13 of 28 Sep. 2007 entitled 'The Social Forum' : Background Report/submitted by the United Nations High Commissioner for Human Rights pursuant to para. 8 of Human Rights Council Resolution 6/13 entitled 'The Social Forum' (document A/HRC/SF/2008/2, 6 Aug. 2008).
65. *See* Sub-Commission on the Promotion and Protection of Human Rights Resolutions on Human Rights and Extreme Poverty 1992/27, 1993/35, 1994/41, 1995/28, 2001/8, 2005/9, and 2006/9.
66. *See* Comission on Human Rights Resolutions contained in documents E/CN.4/RES/1988/23, E/CN.4/RES/1989/10, E/CN.4/RES/1990/15, E/CN.4/RES/1991/14, E/CN.4/RES/1992/11, E/CN.4/RES/1993/13, E/CN.4/RES/1994/12, E/CN.4/RES/1994/12, E/CN.4/RES/1995/16, E/CN.4/RES/1996/10, E/CN.4/RES/1997/11, E/CN.4/RES/1998/25, E/CN.4/RES/1999/26, E/CN.4/RES/2000/12, E/CN.4/RES/2001/31, E/CN.4/RES/2002/30, E/CN.4/RES/2002/39, E/CN.4/RES/2003/24, E/CN.4/RES/2004/23, E/CN.4/RES/2005/16.
67. *See* Human Rights Council Resolutions on Human rights and Extreme Poverty of 9 Jan. 2007 (document A/HRC/RES/2/2), of 25 Mar. 2008 (document A/HRC/7/L.32), and of 18 Jun. 2008 (document A/HRC/RES/8/11), and Resolution 7/27 of 28 Mar. 2008.
68. *See*, among others, General Assembly Resolutions contained in documents A/RES/46/121, A/RES/47/134, A/RES/47/196, A/RES/48/183, A/RES/48/184, A/RES/49/110, A/RES/50/107,

In short, the development of this approach has lead to the General Assembly to state in its Resolutions on Human Rights and Extreme Poverty that 'extreme poverty is a violation of human dignity and might, in some situations, constitute a threat to the right to life'.[69] '[S]urmounting extreme poverty constitutes an essential means to the full enjoyment of political, civil, economic, social and cultural rights', so there is an 'interrelationship among these goals'.[70] And vice versa, 'extreme poverty and exclusion from society constitute a violation of human dignity' – and therefore 'urgent national and international action is therefore required to eliminate them': '[T]he existence of widespread absolute poverty inhibits the full and effective enjoyment of human rights and renders democracy and popular participation fragile.' The above-mentioned statements are based on the express recognition that the 'extreme poverty persists in all countries of the world, regardless of their economic, social and cultural situation'.[71]

3.1. Poverty and Social Exclusion as a Violation of International Human Rights

At the moment, a general consensus has not yet been reached regarding the definition of poverty and social exclusion linked to the violation of human rights within the United Nations, (which could serve as the common basis for international and national action).[72] Nevertheless, and although not binding, the experts in this field and the relevant institutions (bodies) have outlined the meaning of both terms.

As it is not possible to gather here the whole evolution of the definition of these three levels – poverty, extreme poverty and social exclusions – we will describe the most recent proposals and those which have gained the most relevance.[73]

As a sample, the latest report from the independent expert Mr. Sengupta, published in 2008 provides new criteria based on the integration of the poverty

---

A/RES/52/193, A/RES/52/194, A/RES/53/146, A/RES/53/198, A/RES/54/232, A/RES/55/210, A/RES/56/207, A/RES/57/266, A/RES/58/222, A/RES/59/246, A/RES/60/209, A/RES/61/213, A/RES/61/214, A/RES/62/205, and A/RES/63/274.

69. Among others, General Assembly Resolutions of 18 Dec. 1992 (document A/RES/47/134), and of 23 Dec. 1994 (document A/RES/49/179).
70. *Ibid*, and also General Assembly Resolutions of 12 Dec. 1996 (document A/RES/51/97), of 4 Dec. 2000 (document A/RES/55/106), and of 18 Dec. 2002 (document A/RES/57/211).
71. *Ibid*, and also, among others, General Assembly Resolutions of 18 Dec. 2002 (document A/RES/57/211), of 20 Dec. 2004 (document A/RES/59/186), and of 19 Dec. 2006, which highlights, among other tools, 'the critical role of both formal and informal education in the achievement of poverty eradication (. . .), especially for girls and women' (document A/RES/61/157).
72. In this regard, *see* the United Nations High Commissioner for Human Rights, *Background Report* (document A/HRC/SF/2008/2, of 6 Aug. 2008), para. 10.
73. The first contributions to the concept can be found on L. Despouy's reports contained in documents E/CN.4/Sub.2/1993/16 (paras 8, 32-38) and E/CN.4/Sub.2/1996/13 (paras 175-179, 180, 183, 217-218, and Annex III).

phenomenon into several interdependent dimensions, and which can be mutually overlapped.[74] The first one is 'income poverty', which means, 'being below an agreed level of minimum disposable income or expenditure required for leading a sustainable life'. He warns that a relative interpretation of income poverty would take into account the sociocultural background of a country.[75] The second dimension is the lack of human development or 'human development poverty', which means that the person is 'without access to, or availability of, certain basic goods and services to make it possible for them to lead a meaningful life', measurable by similar indicators such as the ones applied by the United Nations Development Program (UNDP).[76]

And the third dimension is 'social exclusion', defined as:

> the opposite of social integration, where the poor, the unemployed, ethnic minorities and vulnerable groups have remained 'outsiders' in the social hierarchy. It is this relational aspect of social exclusion which brings in a distinct added value in identifying problems associated with poverty. The relevant issues, then, concern the nature and causes of the disruption of social bonds, inability of the group to participate in society, the discrimination they faced, or the denial of their rights within the existing legal system.[77]

And following Father Joseph Wresinski, further adds 'it is this exclusion that traps poor families... any effort to reduce poverty cannot be successful unless it addresses the effects of exclusion'. It is also worth highlighting that Sengupta gathers on his report the definition provided by Tony Atkinson, which identifies among the key elements of social exclusion, the external factor, which is the fact that 'people are excluded by acts of some agents'.[78]

Finally, Sengupta considers that 'extreme poverty can therefore be identified with people suffering from income poverty and people suffering from human development poverty as well as people in social exclusion'; which means that 'extreme poverty should be regarded as the combination of income poverty, human development poverty and social exclusion'.[79] Based on this definition and from a pragmatic point of view, he proposes 'establishing eradication of extreme poverty as a human right, particularly by confining it to a smaller fraction of the population', which in his view, 'enhances the possibility of reaching a social

74. Last Report of the Independent Expert A. Sengupta on the question of human rights and extreme poverty, document A/HRC/7/15, 28 Feb. 2008 (paras 23-34), which was reflected by the Human Rights Council Resolution 8/11 on Human Rights and Extreme Poverty, of 12 Jun. 2008 (document A/HRC/RES/8/11).
75. A. Sengupta *Final Report*, *Ibid.*, document A/HRC/7/15, of 28 Feb. 2008 (paras 23-25).
76. *Ibid.*, paras 26 and 27. The indicators used by the UNDP are considered as suitable for the purpose of the measure used in his study.
77. *Ibid.*, paras 28 and 29.
78. *Ibid.*, paras 44 and 47.
79. *Ibid.*, paras 31 and 40. The Human Rights Council Resolution contained in document A/HRC/8/L16 of 12 Jun. 2008 'acknowledges' this report and 'in particular the proposed definition of extreme poverty as the combination of income poverty, human development poverty and social exclusion' (p. 1), without adopting it.

consensus and will ensure its social acceptance, enabling a higher prioritization in domestic affairs and the international community of policies to achieve that right'.[80]

Nevertheless, in 2001 the Committee on Economic, Social and Cultural Rights (CESCR) decided to promote a poverty notion linked to the deprivation of human rights but not limited to extreme poverty in its Statement on Substantive issues arising in the implementation of the International Covenant on Economic, Social and Cultural Rights (ICESCR): poverty and the International Covenant on Economic, Social and Cultural Rights,[81] to which we refer in the following section.

The CESCR takes the wide and multidimensional understanding of poverty which was reached by consensus in the World Summit on Social Development in 2005,[82] as 'the lack of the basic capability to live with dignity', including among its features 'hunger, a lack of education, discrimination, vulnerability and *social exclusion*' [emphasis added]. It adds that:

> in the light of the International Bill of Rights, poverty may be defined as a human condition characterized by sustained or chronic deprivation of the resources, capabilities, choices, security and power necessary for the enjoyment of an adequate standard of living and other civil, cultural, economic, political and social rights . . . , this multi-dimensional understanding of poverty, . . . reflects the indivisible and interdependent nature of all human rights.[83]

It is also worth considering the document prepared in 2006 by the Office of the United Nations High Commissioner for Human Rights (OHCHR), Principles and Guidelines for a Human Rights Approach to Poverty Reduction Strategies which contemplates a broader notion of poverty as a situation where human rights are violated, which allows to act beyond the poorest of the poor.[84] It states that:

> from a human rights perspective, poverty can be described as the denial of a person's rights to a range of basic capabilities – such as the capability to be

80. *Ibid.*, paras 34-37, 40-42, and 85-89. Along the same strategic line, the Draf Guiding Principles on Extreme Poverty and Human Rights: the Rights of the Poor, approved by Resolution 2006/9 of Sub-Commission for the Promotion and Protection of Human Rights adopted on 24 Aug. 2006 and annexed to it (both in final report of the fifty-eighth session, document A/HRC/SUB. 1/58/36, 27-38).
81. *See* document E/C 12/2001/10.
82. Copenhagen Declaration and the Programme of Action (1995), Ch. II on Eradication of Poverty, para. 19.
83. CESCR, *Statement on Substantive Issues* . . . , n. 68, paras 7 and 8.
84. Developed at the request of the CESCR, and contained in Document HR/pub/06/12. However, it must be taken into account as the document warns, that 'the primary focus of these *Guidelines* is on poverty in poorer countries. In part, this is in recognition of the obvious fact that poverty is a much more serious problem in these countries. But it is also partly because poverty in rich countries has special features that need to be addressed separately' (para. 5). The Summary of the OHCHR Draft Guidelines on a Human Rights Approach to Poverty Reduction Strategies (2004), and the publication entitled Human Rights and Poverty Reduction: A Conceptual Framework (2004) preceded the above mentioned documents and are available at <www2. ohchr.org/english/issues/poverty/guidelines.htm>.

> adequately nourished, to live in good health, and to take part in decision-making processes and in the social and cultural life of the community. In the language of rights, one may say that a person living in poverty is one for whom a number of human rights remain unfulfilled – such as the rights to food, health, political participation and so on.

However it also points out that 'only those capability failures that are deemed to be basic should count as poverty, and these should be rated in some order of priority', acknowledging that 'as different societies may have different orders of priority, the list of basic capabilities may differ from one society to another'.[85]

3.2. The International Human Rights Normative Framework

The human rights recognized in international treaties are the basis and aims of the UN system strategy to eliminate poverty and social exclusion globally.[86] In order to facilitate the inclusion of human rights in the national policies of Member States, interpretative documents regarding its required content and scope have been developed, both within the scope of the CESCR,[87] as well as the OHCHR,[88] and of the Sub-Commission for the Promotion and Protection of Human Rights,[89] referred to below.[90] The Human Rights Council continues to develop this work 'with a view to a possible adoption of guiding principles on the rights of persons living in extreme poverty'.[91]

In fact, based on the common foundation of the defence of the human dignity, with the precedent of the founding texts in the International Labour Organization (ILO),[92] this conception can be traced back to the early international treaties on

85. OHCHR, Principles and Guidelines . . . , paras 7 and 30-32.
86. An early research of this approach can be found in W. Van Genugten and C. Perez-Bustillo, 'Human Rights as Source of Inspiration and Instrument for the Eradication of Extreme Poverty: the Need for an Integrated Economic, Political and Legal Approach', in W. Van Genugten and C. Perez-Bustillo (eds), *The Poverty of Rights: Human Rights and the Eradication of Poverty* (CROP International Studies in Poverty Research, Zed Books, 2001).
87. *See* CESCR document E/C.12/2001/10, of 10 May 2001, and its general comments adopted since 1989, available at <www2.ohchr.org/english/bodies/cescr/comments.htm>.
88. *See* the last document HR/pub/06/12.
89. *See* Draft Guiding Principles Approved by the Sub-Commission for the Promotion and Protection of Human Rights annexed to its Resolution 2006/9 (Document A/HRC/Sub.1/58/36, of 24 Aug. 2006, 28-40).
90. The document created in 1986 by experts in international law preceded the above mentioned, The Limburg Principles on the Implementation of the International Covenant on Economic, Social and Cultural Rights, on 'The Nature and Scope of the Obligations of State Parties'. Based on the above mentioned, in 1997 The Maastricht Guidelines on Violations of Economic, Social and Cultural Rights, on 'Nature and Scope of Violations of Economic, Social and Cultural Rights and Appropriate Responses and Remedies' were adopted. Both are included in UN document E/C.12/2000/13, of 2 Oct. 2000.
91. Resolution 7/27, of 28 Mar. 2008, para. 4 (b).
92. ILO Constitution (1919) and Declaration concerning the aims and purposes of the International Labour Organisation (Declaration of Philadelphia, 1944).

human rights which were passed following the Second World War. Recognition of 'dignity and value of all humans' lies in the preamble of the founding agreement, the Charter of the United Nations (1945),[93] whereby Member States are obliged to promote universal and effective respect for human rights and freedoms which are built on this recognition. They are also found in the Universal Declaration of Human Rights[94] and other international agreements and protocols which make up the International Bill of Human Rights.

Notwithstanding the independent and irreversible nature of all human rights, and of the consideration that the use of a multidimensional strategy that incorporates the defence of all human rights is therefore crucial to fighting poverty in all its many dimensions,[95] from the outset the specific reports issued by the experts gave particular attention to the economic, social and cultural rights dimensions of anti-poverty strategies, in as much as the same consideration as the standard of civil and political rights.[96]

This approach was undertaken by the CESCR in its Statement on Substantive issues arising in the implementation of the International Covenant on Economic, Social and Cultural Rights: poverty and the International Covenant on Economic, Social and Cultural Rights of 2001, which states that 'the rights to work, an adequate standard of living, housing, food, health and education, which lie at the heart of the Covenant, have a direct and immediate bearing upon the eradication of poverty'.[97]

Focusing on the rights pertaining directly to the economic and social protection realms and without aiming to be comprehensive, we would like to mention the Universal Declaration of Human Rights which recognizes, among other rights, that the family 'is entitled to protection by society and the state', as 'the natural and fundamental group unit of society' (Article 16.3); that 'everyone has the right to own property alone as well as in association with others' (Article 17.1); the need for a minimum level of 'indispensable' rights for human dignity which is independent from other rights recognized for 'all people' such as the right to 'social security' (also in Article 22); that 'everyone has the right to work, free choice of work... and protection for unemployment' (Article 23.1); the 'right' of 'all who work... to fair and satisfactory pay, which ensures for the worker and also his family, a living in accordance with human dignity and will be complemented,

93. Signed on 26 Jun. 1945 in San Francisco.
94. Adopted and proclaimed by General Assembly Resolution 217 A (III) of 10 Dec. 1948, in Paris.
95. United Nations Secretary General Report on Eradicating Poverty and Other Issues Concerning Development: Observation of the First Decade of the United Nations for the Eradication of Poverty (1997-2006), document A/61/308 of 5 Sep. 2006 (para. 7).
96. In this sense, specifically highlighting the right of families to be protected, among others, *see* D. Türk *Progress Report*, document E/CN/.4Sub.2/1990/19 of 6 Jul. 1990 (paras 189-217), and his *Final Report*, document E/CN.4/Sub.2/1992/16 of 3 Jul. 1992 (paras 8-132). Also, *see* A.-M. Lizin *Report* (document E/CN.4/2000/52 of 25 Feb. 2000), which among other things concluded that '[l]egislation establishing a guaranteed minimum income is one of the most effective weapons for fighting extreme poverty' (para. 80).
97. Document E/C.12/2001/10 of 10 May 2001 (paras 1, 3 and 10).

when necessary, by any other means of social protection' (Article 23.3); and 'an adequate standard of living which ensures health and welfare for both him and his family, above all food, clothing, housing, health care and necessary social services' (Article 25.1, first clause).

Also, the International Covenant on Economic, Social and Cultural Rights (ICESCR)[98] recognizes 'the right of all people to social security, even social insurance'; (Article 9)[99] 'the right of all to an adequate standard of living for him and his family, even adequate food, clothing and housing, and to a continuous improvement of living conditions', being obliged to adopt 'appropriate measures to ensure the efficacy of this right' (Article 11.1);[100] 'the fundamental right of all people to be protected against hunger . . . ' (Article 11.2);[101] and the right to education (Articles 13 and 14).[102] 'The right to work' was also recognized as a human right with its effects being widely curtailed (Article 6),[103] and 'the right of everyone to the enjoyment of just and favourable conditions of work' (Article 7). In addition, the Member States of ICESCR assumed the obligation to ensure that the rights stated therein 'will be exercised without discrimination of any kind as to race, colour, sex, language, religion, political or other opinion, national or social origin, property, birth or other status' (Article 2.2).[104]

Later the link between fulfilling the various human rights including economic, social and cultural ones, and the development of human welfare was backed in several commitment programmes such as the Proclamation of Teheran (1968);[105] the Declaration on Social Progress and Development (1969);[106] the Declaration on

98. Adopted and opened for signature, ratification and accession by General Assembly Resolution 2200A (XXI) of 16 Dec. 1966.
99. CESCR General Comment 19 (2007), on the right to social security (Art. 9 ICESCR).
100. *See* CESCR General Comment 4 (1991), on the right to adequate housing (Art.11.1 ICESCR), and General Comment 7 (1997), on the right to adequate housing: forced evictions (Art. 11.1 ICESCR).
101. *See* the later Universal Declaration on the Eradication of Hunger and Malnutrition, adopted on 16 Nov. 1974 by the World Food Conference. It today occupies the first of the eight Objectives foreseen in the United Nations Millennium Declaration 2000.
102. *See* CESCR, General Comment (1999), On the Right to Education (Art. 13 ICESCR), para.1.
103. *See* CESCR, General Comment 18 (2005), on the right to work (Art. 6 ICESCR).
104. In addition to its predecessors, they also support the fight against poverty and exclusion as in Art. 6.1 of International Covenant on Civil and Political Rights (1966); Art. 5 of the International Convention on the Elimination of All Forms of Racial Discrimination (1965); Arts11, 12, 13 and 14 of the Convention on the Elimination of All Forms of Discrimination against Women (1979); Arts 24 and 27 of the Convention on the Rights of the Child (1989); Arts 24 to 30 and 43 of the International Convention on the Protection of the Rights of All Migrant Workers and Members of their Families (1990); and Art. 28 of the Convention on the Rights of Persons with Disabilities (2002).
105. Proclaimed by the International Conference on Human Rights at Teheran on 13 May 1968 (para. 13).
106. Proclaimed by General Assembly Resolution 2542 (XXIV) of 11 Dec. 1969. *See* Arts 6 and 7 (Part I, principles), Arts 10 and 11.a (Part II, objectives), Arts 14 at 19, and 19.b (Part III, means and methods).

the Right to Development (1986);[107] and the Vienna Declaration and Programme of Action (1993) which specifically proclaimed that extreme poverty and social exclusion are a violation of human dignity and inhibit one's enjoyment of human rights.[108] Regarding specific rights, the World Summit for Social Development (Copenhagen, 1995) is worthy of mention since it focuses on the fight against poverty, unemployment and social isolation which resulted in the approval by consensus of the Copenhagen Declaration and the Programme of Action on 12 March of the same year,[109] and was later accepted by the UN General Assembly.[110] Finally, the Millennium Declaration (2000), whose eighth objective includes as one of its goals 'drawing up and applying strategies which provide the young with decent productive work', taking into account that the young are an increasingly larger part of the population, a goal the ILO is working on.[111]

Both instruments recognize, amongst others the right to 'effective access to [....] social assistance' (Part I, paragraph 13, and Part. II, Article 13). Despite lack of binding value, the explanatory report to this charter adds that the 'effective access to social assistance' includes 'the guarantee of minimum resources' and that the states subscribing to the right to protection against poverty and social exclusion 'are encouraged to restrict financial benefits to those who cannot help themselves by their own means' (paragraphs 115 and 116). These provisions 'shall not prejudice the provisions of domestic law or of any bilateral or multilateral treaties, conventions or agreements which are already in force, or may come into force, under which more favourable treatment would be accorded to the persons protected' (Part V, Article H).[112] In addition to the above, the Revised Social Charter reinforces the obligations of the Member States in favour of the most disadvantaged when it includes, for the first time, the acknowledgement that 'everyone has the right to protection against poverty and social exclusion' (Part I, paragraph I, paragraph 30, and Part 30, and Part II, Article 30), as well as two other new rights which strengthen the effectiveness of the former: 'every elderly person has the right to social protection' (Part. I, paragraph 23, and Part. II, Article 23) and 'everyone has the right to housing' (Part I, paragraph 31, and Part II, Article 31).

107. Adopted by General Assembly Resolution 41/128 of 4 Dec. 1986.
108. Adopted by the World Conference on Human Rights in Vienna on 25 Jun. 1993. *See* paras 14 and 25. Along these lines, among others, Resolutions of the Human rights Commission no. 2002/3029 and no. 2005/16.30, and United Nations General Assembly Resolution no. 59/186.31.
109. A/CONF.166/9.
110. Resolution passed at the 98th plenary meeting, 22 Dec. 1995 (document A/RES/50/161).
111. Likewise, the aim of the reduction of poverty in the context of globalisation is also present in the General Assembly Resolution 60/1 on 2005 World Summit Outcome (document A/RES/60/1 of 24 Oct. 2005). And is part of the Declaration of the Summit on Financial Markets and the World Economy (15 Nov. 2008), paras 2, 12, 14 and 15, available at <www.whitehouse.gov/news/releases/2008/11/20081115-1.html>.
112. This Explanatory Report is available at <http://conventions.coe.int/Treaty/EN/Reports/HTML/163.htm> 12 Dec. 2008.

3.3. The Added Value of Human Rights Strategy and Its Influence on the Member States

The aforementioned international agreements and declarations form the basis of the United Nation's strategy to eradicate poverty and exclusion based on the effective fulfilment of human rights. The CESCR was the first to fully formulate this strategy based on the broad definition of poverty already stated in its Statement on Substantive issues arising in the implementation of the International Covenant on Economic, Social and Cultural Rights: poverty and the International Covenant on Economic, Social and Cultural Rights ratified in 2001, 'aimed at encouraging the integration of human rights into poverty eradication policies by outlining how human rights generally, and the Covenant in particular, can empower the poor and enhance anti-poverty strategies' (paragraph 3). Nevertheless, this task is not exclusive of CESCR, as it has also been developed by other bodies of the United Nations, which also have emphasized the benefits of this strategy. We summarize its main components as follows.

Firstly, it not only describes the end result but also how it must be carried out: it must respect all human rights as equal. Secondly, it requires the active involvement of those affected by poverty, their participation in the transmission of the knowledge of the situation suffered by them, in designing policies against poverty and how these are carried out ('empowerment'). This specific request, initially defended by Father Wresinski was further echoed by the experts appointed ad hoc,[113] and recognized by the bodies of the United Nations as one of the key elements in the fight against poverty.

Actually, this strategy requires an upgrading of the decision-making capabilities, turning them into actions and participating in the institutions which affect their lives, by negotiating and influencing them, controlling them and requiring them to account for their actions ('authorization'). This authorization is achieved by 'introducing the concept of real rights . . . in the area of policy making'; that is, the 'reasons for reducing poverty no longer simply lie in the fact that people living in poverty have needs, but also that they have rights and this creates legal obligations for third parties'.[114]

Third, this approach highlights the opinion that a rise in one's income does not necessarily imply a reduction in situations of poverty and exclusion, which are present in all countries of the world to a greater or lesser degree;[115] but the

113. *See* D. Türk, *Realization of Economic, Social and Cultural Rights. Progress* Report, document E/CN.4/Sub.2/1990/19 (paras 150-158, 175, and 186); *see* also L. Despouy, *Preliminary Report*, document E/CN.4/Sub.2/1993/16 (paras 18-21). More recently, regarding the poor and nevertheless 'vital' involvement of the people who live in poverty, not only formally but inclusive of marginalised groups even among the poor (with a express mention of women), M. Sepúlveda, *Report on the Question of Human Rights and Extreme Poverty*, document A/63/274 of 13 Aug. 2008 (paras 42-45).

114. OHCHR, *Principles and Guidelines for Human Rights . . .*, paras 18 and 19.

115. Hence, as regards data from 2005 the US came second in the ranking of countries according to its GDP per capita and seventeenth in the Index of Human Poverty. *See* Report on Human

fulfilment of human rights also requires firm political will.[116] What is more, it offers solid support to this political will: compliance with the legal obligations that states have signed by virtue of their membership to international human rights organizations and ratification of international agreements on human rights.[117]

Based on this, the CESCR recommends that international regulations on human rights be included in national plans to eradicate poverty in all states, regardless of the stage of their economic development, and recalls that, in addition to states, 'non governmental agents' also have great responsibilities in the fight against poverty; among these, 'international organizations, national human rights institutions, civil society organizations and private companies'.[118]

Among other aspects regarding the level of obligations taken on in virtue of the ratification of ICESCR, in accordance with the General Recommendations adopted by the CESCR, states that are party to this agreement are reminded that they have 'a minimum obligation to ensure at least the *basic levels* of each of its rights are met' – a breach of which violates the ICESCR –[119] and once this objective is reached, they must still strive to improve... towards the complete fulfilment of all rights consecrated in the ICESCR[120] by the use of 'every available resource' (Article 2.1 ICESCR), 'both the resources existing within a state and those available from the international community through international cooperation and assistance',[121] and in such manner that 'due priority shall be given to the realization of rights recognized in the Covenant, mindful of the need to ensure to everyone the satisfaction of subsistence requirements as well as the provision of essential services'.[122]

The state's obligation to effectively guarantee these rights includes its responsibility to 'ensure that private enterprises or individuals' under its jurisdiction, including multinational companies, 'do not deprive anybody of his economic, social and cultural rights', so states 'are responsible for violations of these rights... due to the omission of due diligence to correct the behaviour of non governmental

---

Development 2007-2008, United Nations Development Programme, 2007, pages 243, 244, 247, 359, 368, and 369. Also in 2006, the mortality rate for children under five in the USA was higher than countries such as Cuba or Spain. *See* The State of World's Children 2008, UNICEF, Dec. 2007,1, 2, 8, 113 to 117, 149, and 150-153.

116. In this sense, for all, Report by the Secretary General of the United Nations on 'Eradicating poverty and other issues concerning development: observation of the first decade of the United Nations for the Eradication of Poverty (1997-2006), document A/61/308 of 5 Sep. 2006, 4-10.
117. CESCR, *Statement on Substantive issues*..., paras 9-18.
118. CESCR, *Statement on Substantive issues*..., paras 19 and 20.
119. This obligation does not wane even when the resources available are insufficient, nor in times of economic recession where 'the vulnerable members of society can and indeed must be protected by the adoption of relatively low cost targeted programmes'(CESCR, *General Comment* no. 3, paras 10-12). In particular, there are core obligations to ensure the satisfaction of minimum essential levels of the rights to food, education and health (last these non-derogable), in CESCR General Comments no. 11, 13 and 14, respectively.
120. CESCR, *Statement on Substantive Issues*..., above n. 117, paras 15 and 18.
121. The Limburg Principles..., para. 26, and CESCR General Director-General: Comment no. 3, para. 13.
122. The Limburg Principles..., para. 28.

agents'. Particularly, regarding the right to work recognized by Article 6 ICESCR, states which fail to guarantee that private employers comply with the basic rules may be in breach of this Agreement.[123]

The obligation of states to guarantee these rights includes 'taking part in international organizations where they act together', so they must strive 'to ensure there are no violations as a consequence of the programmes and policies of the organizations to which they belong'.[124]

Finally, all victims shall also have 'access to effective legal recourse or other channels of appropriate remedies, both nationally and internationally', and also to 'adequate remedy, which may be in the form of reinstatement, compensation and satisfaction or a guarantee that it will not be repeated'.[125]

3.4. Brief Reference to the Human Right to Decent Employment as a Means against Poverty and Social Exclusion

The initial definition of the right to decent work took place within The ILO in 1999,[126] where it continues to be further developed as a poverty fighting tool,[127] once generally assumed by the other bodies of the UN.[128] This conviction is reinforced with the general affirmation of the declining progression of employment and social protection in the context of globalization,[129] as well as by the fact that the strong economic growth experienced during the 1997-2006 decade did not prevent the rise in global unemployment figures and that most people living in poverty are not actually unemployed, but working on 'low productivity jobs where they are unable to earn enough money'. Therefore, the international community has been encouraged to create a global economic environment to promote employment, particularly in developing countries, with the aim to promote national initiatives against poverty which must include the aspects of productive work and decent work.[130] However, as previously mentioned, the statistics show that the phenomenon of poor workers is also present within the EU.

123. The Maastricht Guidelines . . . , para. 6.
124. The Maastricht Guidelines . . . , para. 19.
125. The Maastricht Guidelines . . . , paras 22 and 23.
126. Regarding its initial formulation, *see* Report of the Decent Work, International Labour Conference, 87th Session Geneva, Jun. 1999.
127. *See* ILO, Office of the DG, Decent Work and Poverty Reduction in the Global Economy, 2000. And, Decent Work and Strategies to Fight Poverty: Reference Handbook for Civil Servants and Mandators of the ILO, Geneva, ILO, 2005.
128. *See*, among others, document A/62/267 of 17 Aug.2007 (para. 33), and General Assembly Resolution 60/1 on World Summit 2005, document A/RES/60/1 of 24 Oct. 2005 (para. 47). Also, on the activity of the various bodies of the UN system in cooperation with the ILO, *see* Report on The Role of the United Nations System in Promoting Full and Productive Employment and Decent Work For All, document E/2007/49 of 26 Apr. 2007.
129. Report on the World Social Situation. 2007, Employment Imperative, document A/62/168 of 30 Jul. 2007.
130. Report of the Secretary General, document A/62/267 of 17 Aug. 2007 (paras 33-37 and 74-76).

With regards to the definition of this right, the CESCR considers that work as specified in Article 6 of the ICESCR must be *decent work*, which is defined in summary as the work 'that respects the fundamental rights of the human person as well as the rights of workers in terms of conditions of work safety and remuneration. It also provides an income allowing workers to support themselves and their families as highlighted in Article 7 of the Covenant', and 'also include respect for the physical and mental integrity of the worker in the exercise of his/her employment'.[131]

From the perspective of an effective human right against poverty, the definition provided by the OHCHR is similar to the one mentioned above. It also includes the creation of social, economic and material conditions in which all people have the chance to prosper, fairly and equally with their own efforts which is compatible with their dignity, and that it includes the right of each person to enjoy fair and favourable labour conditions, in particular fair salaries, equal pay for jobs with equal value, equal opportunities, enough income to ensure decent living conditions for the worker and his family, safe and healthy work conditions, reasonable work and rest times and the right to join a union and to collective bargaining. It may be added that all employment opportunities and activities creating income must be 'culturally adequate and compatible with human dignity'. Lastly, the right to decent employment also implies creating adequate social security mechanisms to cover situations such as economic crises and policies, where people 'cannot get stable employment'. It is also an instrumental right which serves other human rights, such as the right to food and housing.[132]

Regarding unemployment, it is worth noticing that the CESCR has included as part of the regulatory content of the right to social security that 'the states parties must endeavour to provide benefits to cover the loss or lack of earnings due to the inability to obtain or maintain suitable employment. In the case of loss of employment, benefits should be paid for an adequate period of time and at the expiry of the period, the social security system should ensure adequate protection of the unemployed worker, for example through social assistance. The social security system should also cover other workers, including part time workers, casual workers, seasonal workers and the self employed'. And this 'in addition to promoting full, productive and freely chosen employment.'[133] The general consent over the existence of direct links between failure to ensure human rights and fundamental freedoms and situations of poverty and exclusion reaches also the lack of realization of the right to decent employment.[134] The access to formal employment is

131. *See* General Comment n. 18 (2005), on the right to work, para. 7.
132. OHCHR, Principles and Guidelines for Human Rights Approach to Poverty Reduction Strategies, Geneva, 2006 (HR PUB/06/12), *see* paras 110-116.
133. CESCR, General Comment no. 19 (2007), on the Right to Social Security (art. 9 ICESCR), *see* paras 9, 10, 16, 33 and 34.
134. United Nations Secretary General, Report on Eradication of Poverty and Other Development Issues: Implementation of the first United Nations Decade for the Eradication of Poverty (1997-2006), Observance of the International Day for the Eradication of Poverty, document A/61/308 of 5 Sep. 2006, 4-7.

often impossible for the poor or those excluded due to social discrimination, or a lack of housing or education. This leads them to search for employment in the underground economy which is characterized by unskilled work, insecurity, dangerous conditions and low pay which fails to guarantee an adequate standard of living. So, bearing in mind that most of these people have no assets other than their work, the United Nations strategy calls for them to be employed in decent jobs to access food, health and housing.[135]

In this regard, the CESCR includes as normative content of the human right to work of Article 6 ICESCR, the obligation of the participating states to adopt:

> the requisite measures, legislative or otherwise, to reduce to the fullest extent possible the number of workers outside the formal economy, workers who as a result of that situation have no protection. These measures would compel employers to respect labour legislation and protect their employees, thus enabling the latter to enjoy all the rights of workers, in particular those provided for in Articles 6, 7 and 8 of the Covenant. These measures must reflect the fact that people living in an informal economy do so for the most part because of the need to survive, rather than as a matter of choice. Moreover, domestic and agricultural work must be properly regulated by national legislation so that domestic and agricultural workers enjoy the same level of protection as other workers.[136]

Regarding its impact on the ICESCR participating states, it is worth highlighting that among other aspects, the CESCR states as its main obligation 'to ensure the progressive realization of its exercise', and 'must therefore adopt, as quickly as possible, measures aiming at achieving full employment'. It is also an integral part of the minimum content of this right which must grant the obligation of the participating states 'to adopt and implement a national employment strategy and plan of action based on and addressing the concerns of all workers on the basis of a participatory and transparent process that includes employers' and workers' organizations'. And in particular, that 'such an employment strategy and plan of action should target disadvantaged and marginalized individuals and include indicators and benchmarks by which progress in relation to the right to work can be measured and periodically reviewed'.[137] In addition, it warns the participating states that 'specific measures to increase the flexibility of labour markets must not render work less stable or reduce the social protection of the worker'.[138]

Finally, decent work also involves a human right which must be included in the states' economic and social policies, since doing so will mean complying with international law, particularly the following regulations: the Universal Declaration of Human Rights (Article 23); ICESCR (Articles 6, 7, and 9); International Covenant on Civil and Political Rights (Article 8); Convention on the Elimination of All

135. *Ibid.* 6 and 8.
136. General Comment 18 (2005), On the Right to Work, para. 10.
137. *Ibid.*, paras 19 and 31 (c).
138. *Ibid.*, para. 25.

Forms of Discrimination against Women (Articles 6 and 11); Convention on the Rights of the Child (Articles 32, 34, 35 and 36); ILO Minimum Age Convention (1973); ILO Worst Forms of Child Labour Convention (1999); ILO Forced Labour Convention (1930); and Abolition of Forced Labour Convention (1957). The Copenhagen Declaration and the Programme of Action (1995)[139] and the ILO Declaration on Fundamental Principles and Rights at Work (1998) also promote the fulfilment of these.

4. FINAL CONCLUSIONS: THE NEED TO INTEGRATE THE HUMAN RIGHTS STRATEGY AGAINST POVERTY AND EXCLUSION IN OMC PROCESSES

As shown in this chapter, acknowledging the fight against social exclusion in the Union Treaty and the Lisbon Strategy has led to the EU widening its view of social objectives and the policies of open coordination have also contributed positive characteristics to this process.

As regards the above, the OMC on social inclusion has developed a methodology for Member States whereby they can detect situations of social exclusion by setting common indicators and statistics that can contribute to Member States agreeing on new areas of exclusion. Drawing up NAPs can also help introduce improvements in the efficacy of these policies through the Commission's multilateral process of supervision or by exchanging information on good practices or by 'mutual learning'.

As several studies have highlighted, it is difficult to gauge the role that European coordination policies have played in the positive results of economic growth and employment in recent years. We have noticed that since these were set up, the level required for compliance with the objectives set by the OMC on social inclusion has been lower than the two other processes.

What is more, since the OMC on social inclusion began it has always played a less significant role than BEPG policies and employment. This situation has become more patent following the renewal process of the Lisbon strategy which first included the OMC on social protection and social inclusion and then went on to cover economy and employment. In this new stage, the aim is to relaunch the objective of economic growth and employment and this has also placed the EES in the spotlight regarding social inclusion policies.

However, as the OECD pointed out in 2006, growth in the employment rate does not always mean less poverty but rather this will depend on a fairer redistribution of income.

Labour and employment policies which follow the maxims of 'making work pay' and 'flexicurity' aim to encourage the inclusion of people in situations of social exclusion in the labour market, but over these maxims hang a greater number

139. Chapter III on 'Expansion of productive Employment and Reduction of Employment', para. 47.

of traps surrounding temporary and low-paid jobs. It is necessary to counteract this situation with active policies which foment aspects of training, education and guidance for these workers and to help the unemployed with sufficient benefits. If, on the contrary, priority is given to more flexible policies in the field of labour which recommend cutting unemployment benefits to encourage the unemployed to look for work, there is a risk that some workers will suddenly find themselves in a 'poverty trap' and will remain caught up in the 'temporary employment trap' in a situation of social exclusion. Many of these workers – who do not even belong to particularly vulnerable groups – will have to do jobs in conditions of poverty without being entitled access to the most basic rights, including the right to decent employment. We should not forget that resorting to sub-employment is the same as excluding workers from many important areas of social, economic and cultural human rights.

The thesis we uphold in this work is that European policies on social inclusion have placed employment and economic growth at the epicentre, without integrating the notion of poverty and social exclusion as a violation of human dignity and of lack of compliance of human rights – among others, the human right to decent employment.

In fact, its is worth remembering that in the current framework, the EU 'is founded on the principles of liberty, democracy, respect for human rights and fundamental freedoms, and the rule of law, principles which are common to the Member States' (Article 6, paragraph 1 EUT); that the observance of such rights is the mandatory prior requirement for any European state applying to join the EU (Article 49 EUT); and that the Council is empowered to act against any Member State in case of the 'existence of a serious and persistent breach by a Member State of the principles mentioned in Article 6 paragraph 1)' (Article 7 EUT).

However, regarding its own remit, the level of commitment for the EU seems to be weaker, as the Union only states as general principles of Community law those fundamental rights 'guaranteed by the European Convention for the Protection of Human Rights and Fundamental Freedoms . . . and as they result from the constitutional traditions common to the Member States' (Article 6.2 EUT). The express mention to the above mentioned fundamental rights implies that other fundamental rights which are recognized by other international treaties are left outside, even if Member States have ratified them. Therefore, as social objectives are concerned, the ECT only encourages the Community and the Member States to '*having in mind* fundamental social rights such as those set out in the European Social Charter signed at Turin on 18 October 1961 and in the 1989 Community Charter of the Fundamental Social Rights of Workers' (Article 136). On the other hand, the commitment of observance of 'the Human Rights and Fundamental Freedoms as they result from the constitutional traditions common to the Member States' entails the first hurdle which is to determine what should be conceived as common constitutional traditions, given the diversity of contents and formulations included in the constitutional texts of the Member States.

The general consensus is that the European Union human rights protection system is still in an 'embryonic'[140] state as the EU fails to take on positive obligations regarding such matters, whilst the Court of Justice does not deal with fulfilment control. As De Schutter[141] states, the fundamental European code rights have been traditionally created with a clearly defensive approach, that is, they have only been considered as limits outside the exercise framework of the European authorities. An example of this are the multiple cases[142] presented before the European Union Court of Justice which has examined whether or not a fundamental right protection justified Member State had made the economic liberties envisaged in the Treaties vulnerable.

Nevertheless, despite all the above, Member States are not prevented from adopting the broadest strategy possible regarding human rights against poverty and exclusion, and from integrating this into their NAPs along with the guidelines issued by the EU institutions, in compliance with the obligations undertaken through the ratification of human rights international treaties (above). As we have specifically referred to in relation to the ICESCR, and although it also applies to other treaties, 'states are obliged in accordance with the Vienna Convention on the Law of Treaties of 1969 (Article 31) to interpret the convention in good faith, taking into account the object and purpose, the ordinary meaning, the preparatory work and the relevant practice'.[143] This obligation not only pertains to national policies in relation to social inclusion, but also to all areas,[144] so, it must be incorporated into the national policy related to economic growth and unemployment, social protection, and education and training.

Several factors contribute to the adoption of the strategy of human rights by, and may also make harder eventual opposition by the EU institutions or by other Member States. First of all, the multidimensional notions regarding poverty and social exclusion issued by the Social OMC are not opposed to the ones developed in the realm of the United Nations,[145] even though the latter can be technically

140. G. de Bùrca, 'Beyond the Charter: How Enlargement Has Enlarged the Human Rights' (Jan. 2004) *Fordham International Law Journal*, 679-682.

141. O. de Shutter, 'The Implementation of the EU Charter of Fundamental Rights through the Open Method of Coordination', The Jean Monnet Program, NYU School of Law, NY 10012.

142. These are three cases, due to their repercussion in the Labour Law Scholarship, amongst many other possible cases: the Albany Case (Case C-67/96, Albany, 1999, I-5751); Webb Case (Case 279/80, Webb, 1981, ECR 3305) and more recently due to the controversy over the Viking Case (C-438/05).

143. *See*, The Maastricht Guidelines on Violations of Economic, Social and Cultural Rights, document E/C.12/2000/13, para. 4. Also, E. Asbjørn, 'Human Rights and the Elimination of Poverty', in *Law, Power and Poverty* (K. Asbjørn and J. H. Veit (eds) (International Social Science Council, CROP, Bergen, Norway, 1997), 126.

144. In addition, a human rights approach imposes a duty to ensure that the rights of people living in poverty and their concerns are prioritized when any policy or other initiative is formulated and implemented. International human rights law, therefore, does not negate, but it narrows, the discretion of states and other entities to formulate policy'. M. Sepúlveda, Interin Report on the Question of Human Rights and Extreme Poverty, document A/63/274 of 13 Aug. 2008, para. 11.

145. On this question, *see* A. Sengupta, *Report on the Question of Human Rights and Extreme Poverty*, document A/HRC/7/15 of 28 Feb. 2008, para. 48.

considered as being more perfected as they incorporate the idea of the violation of human rights as a defining factor for poverty and exclusion, once its association to those who suffer these situation is generally acknowledged. Secondly, EU institutions are subject to the principles proclaimed in Article 6.[146] Thirdly, both the Social OMC and the strategy of human rights of the United Nations system identify the state itself as the main responsible for the fight against poverty and exclusion within its jurisdiction. In fourth place, the human rights strategy against poverty supplements and reinforces the Union law designed to combat discrimination based on grounds of 'nationality' (Article 12 EUT), 'sex, racial or ethnic origin, religion or belief, disability, age or sexual orientation' (Article 13 EUT). Indeed, this strategy has demonstrated that discrimination is an existing factor in poverty and exclusion situations. According to the independent expert Magdalena Sepúlveda, 'people living in poverty are typically victims of discrimination' and 'patterns of discrimination keep people in poverty which in turn serves to perpetuate discriminatory attitudes and practices against them. In other words, discrimination causes poverty but poverty also causes discrimination'.[147] And finally, this approach does not contradict the European Commission Recommendation of 3 October 2008, on the active inclusion of people excluded from the labour market, grounded on the 'respect for human dignity as a foundig principle of the European Union'. It recommends to Member States to ensure that active inclusion policies 'support the implementation of fundamental rights'. And it is also backed by the European Parliament, who in their recent Resolution of 9 October 2008 on promoting social inclusion and combating poverty, including child poverty, recommends that the Commission should adopt a more holistic approach to proactive social inclusion policies, which must be 'to implement fundamental rights in order to enable people to live with dignity and participate in society and the labour market'.[148]

To the above arguments in support of this strategy, it must be added the prevailing nature of the international commitments assumed by the Member States regarding human rights, as opposed to the Union guidelines issued through the OMC, given its soft law nature. As regards to social inclusion policies, we wonder about the likelihood of enforcing any of the Human Rights International Treaties faced with national practices which following the EU policies may violate the international human right to decent work. Some Member States may incur in the violation of fundamental social rights in the application of these social exclusion policies based around the principle 'make work pay'. Just imagine that a particular Government drastically cuts back unemployment protection, regulates employment contracts without the required social coverage, or discontinues the regulation on the minimum wage. We believe that the response of the national

146. C. Fabre, 'Social Rights in European Constitutions', in G. de Búrca and B. de Witte (eds), *Social Rights in Europe* (Oxford University Press, 2005), 16 and 28.
147. M. Sepúlveda, Interin Report *(...)* *see* paras 20, 29 to 31, and 33.
148. *See* n. 40.

judges in the event of a violation of these rights will be important, by applying the international commitments assumed by the Member States.

Resides, the incorporation of the strategy of human rights would oblige to allocate available resources to the fight against poverty and exclusion, to encourage other actions aimed at covering basic needs and services. It would have particularly positive effects in the eradication of poverty among the under aged, who cannot access work yet. It also implies the obligation to foster the creation of productive work and the employability of workers; and to ensure that said work is carried out in conditions that eliminate the risk of poverty. Finally, it encompasses the need to execute impact assessments of all Community policies, especially those that directly or indirectly affect the labour market, including competition policy.

However, it cannot be ignored that significant differences continue to exist among the Member States in regards to their international commitments to fundamental human rights. In view of this situation, the European Commission has encouraged Member States – particularly most recently joining the EU – to ratify certain ILO Treaties, continuing its commitment to campaign in favour of decent work.[149] The differences are also apparent in the scope of the instruments adopted by the European Council. For example, at the moment, only a small group of Member Status have ratified the Revised European Social Charter without posing any reservations, neither to the 'right to protection against poverty and social exclusion' nor to the recognition that 'everyone has the right to housing' (above).[150]

Despite this, the trend towards a higher harmonization of fundamental social rights within the EU will increase, in any event, if the Treaty of Lisbon finally comes into force, at least in relation to the fundamental social rights recognized in the Charter of Fundamental Rights, covered mainly in its Chapter IV, dedicated to 'solidarity rights'.[151] One of the rights benefiting from this initiative is 'the right to social and housing benefits so as to ensure a decent life for all those who lack sufficient resources, in accordance with the rules laid down by EU and national laws and practices' (Article 34.3).[152] And equally or more importantly, the fight

149. *See* Commission Staff Working Document. Report on the EU Contribution to the Promotion of Decent Work in the World, COM (2008) 421 final, 31-35, available at <http://ec.europa.eu/social/main.jsp?catId=323&langId=en> 12 Dec. 2008.

150. These countries are Finland, France, Italy, Portugal, and Slovenia. The ratification status is available at http://conventions.coe.int/Treaty/Commun/QueVoulezVous.asp?NT=163&CM=8&DF=11/3/2008&CL=ENG> 12 Dec. 2008.

151. Article 6 of the new EUT after the Lisbon Treaty states that 'the Union recognises the rights, freedoms and principles set out in the Charter of Fundamental Rights of the European Union of 7 Dec. 2000, as adapted at Strasbourg on 12 Dec. 2007, which shall have the same legal value as the Treaties'.

152. Regarding para. 3 of Art. 34, the Explanations relating to the Charter of Fundamental Rights clarifies that it draws on Art. 13 of the European Social Charter (On the Right to Social and Medical Assistance) and Arts 30 and 31 of the revised Social Charter (On the Right to Protection Against Poverty and Social Exclusion, and On the Right to Housing, respectively), and point 10 of the Community Charter of the Fundamental Social Rights of Workers (on social protection).

against exclusion would cease to be an objective of the social policy,[153] to become an objective penetrating through the whole Union action under the principle of mainstreaming in accordance to the new Article 9 TFUE.

References

ASBJØRN E., 'Human Rights and the Elimination of Poverty', in Asbjørn K. and Veit J. H. (eds), *Law, Power and Poverty* (Bergen, International Social Science Council, 1997) available in <www.crop.org/publications/files/cpubl/LAP97book.pdf#page=121>, 12 Dec. 2008.

Atkinson, A., 'La Pauvreté et la Exclusion Sociale en Europe', *Pauvreté et Exclusion* (La Documentation Française, 1998).

Atkinson, T. et al., *Social Indicators. The EU and Social Inclusion* (Oxford University Press, 2002).

Cantillon, B., 'European Subsidiarity Versus American Social Federalism: Is Europe in Need of a Common Social Policy?' (2004), Paper for the second Annual ESPAnet Conference, <www.spsw.ox.ac.uk/fileadmin/static/Espanet>.

De Búrca, G., 'Beyond the Charter: How Enlargement Has Enlarged the Human Rights' (2004) *Fordham International Law Journal.*

De Schutter, O., 'The Implementation of the EU Charter Of Fundamental Rights Through the Open Method of Coordination' (2004) 07/04, *Jean Monnet Working Paper* <ideas.repec.org/p/erp/jeanmo/p0160.html>, 12 Dec. 2008.

FABRE, C., 'Social Rights in European Constitutions' in De Búrca, G. and De Witte B. (eds), *Social Rights in Europe* (Oxford, Oxford University Press, 2005).

Ferrera, M., Matsaganis and M.; Sacchi, S., 'Open Coordination Against Poverty: The New EU Social Inclusion Process' (2002) 1. 2:3, *Journal of European Social Policy.*

Goetschy, J, 'The European Employment Strategy, Multi-Level Governance, and Policy Coordination: Past, Present and Future', in J., Zeitlin and D. M. Trubek (eds) *Governing Work and Welfare In A New Economy* (Oxford, Oxford University Press, 2003).

Landa Zapirain, J.P., 'Looking At the EES In the Search For Efficacy (And For Efficiency) In The National Systems of Social Protection: The Balance of Social Federalism Models', Paper given at the conference 'The Implementation of Community Employment and Social Inclusion Policies In the Model of Social Federalism' (Oñati, Jun. 21 and 22 2007).

López López, J., 'Beyond the National Case: The Role of Transnational Labor Law in Shaping Domestic Regulation' (2006) 28 *Comparative Labor Law & Policy Journal.*

---

153. *See* Art. 137 ECT, whose content will be included in Art. 153 of the Treaty on the Functioning of the European Union, once the Lisbon Treaty comes into force.

Meurs, D.; Prelis, J., 'Western Europe Thematic Employment Report', *The Human Dignity and Social Exclusion Initiative* (Strasbourg, Council of Europe, 1997).

Middelton, S., Barnes, M. and Millar, J. 'Introduction: The Dynamic Analysis Of Poverty and Social Inclusion', in Millar, J., Apospori, E., *The Dynamic Of Social Exclusion In Europe* (London, Edward Elgar Publishing, 2003).

O'Connor, J., 'Policy Coordination, Social Indicators and the Social-Policy Agenda in the European Union' (2005) 15 *Journal of European Social Policy.*

Rhodes, M., 'Globalization, Welfare States and Employment: Is There A European "Third Way?" ', in N. Bermeo (ed.), *Unemployment In the New Europe* (Cambridge, Cambridge University Press, 2001).

Sciarra, S., 'Fundamental Labour Rights After the Lisbon Agenda' (2005) 65, *Working Papers Centro studi di Diritto del Lavoro Europeo 'Massimo d'Antona'.*

Spicker, P., 'Exclusion and Rights', in Williams, L., and Robson, P. (eds), *Law and Poverty – The Legal System and Poverty Reduction*, (London: Zed Books, CROP International Studies in Poverty Research, 2003), <www.crop.org/publications/files/cisprserie/CROPZED2003WILLIAMSETAL.pdf>, 12 December 2008.

Terradillos, E., 'The Validity and Limits of the Open Method of Coordination in Community Social Policy', paper given at the Conference on 'The Implementation of Community Employment and Social Inclusion Policies in the Model of Social Federalism' (Oñati, June 21 and 22 2007).

Van Genugten, W. and Perez-Bustillo, C, 'Human Rights As Source of Inspiration and Instrument For the Eradication Of Extreme Poverty: The Need for an Integrated Economic, Political and Legal Approach', in W. van Genugten and C. Perez-Bustillo (eds), *THE Poverty of Rights: Human Rights and the Eradication of Poverty*, (London, CROP International Studies in Poverty Research, Zed Books, 2001).

Zeitlin, J., 'The Open Method of Coordination and the Future of the European Employment Strategy' (2002), Hearing of the European Parliament, Employment and Social Affairs.

Chapter 4

The OMC as Decentralization of Regulations and Case Law: A Gender Mainstreaming Perspective

Julia López López

1. THE IMPLEMENTATION OF THE LISBON STRATEGY: DOES IT WORK FOR WOMEN?

One of the main questions that any analysis of the Lisbon Strategy should be addressing is the role played by women in its implementation.[1] This question is framed in the context of the transformation imposed by globalization, where societies are 'cosmopolitan communities of citizens that have complex layers of national and international governance and legal regulation'.[2]

The point of departure for the Lisbon Strategy and the European Employment Strategy (EES) is the assumption that if the current demographic trends continue, it will be impossible to maintain the European Union's (EU's) welfare

1. For a general descriptive *see* F. Beveridge and S. Velluti (eds), *Gender and Open Method of Coordination : Perspectives on Law , Governance and Equality in the EU* (Ashgate, 2008).
2. *See* C. Joerges, 'Introduction and Overview' in C. Joerges and E.U. Petersmann (eds), *Constitutionalism, Multilevel Trade, Governance and Social Regulation* (Oxford and Portland OR, Hart Publishing, 2006), xxii.

Roger Blanpain, Juan Pablo Landa, Brian Langille (eds), *Employment Policies and Multilevel Governance*, pp. 105–122.

state systems beyond 2050. A new strategy is therefore necessary to increase the employment rate and the number of contributors to the welfare state systems. One of the goals is to increase women's participation in the labour force. This implies both the elimination of all forms of discrimination against women and an implementation of family friendly policies. The Lisbon Strategy acknowledged the need for better family friendly polices, but the strategy combined with the Open Method of Coordination (OMC), introduced an important change in how EU policies would be implemented. In this context we need to explore the relationship between the Lisbon Strategy and the OMC in the generating process of decentralization of regulations and case law, and the resulting impact on women's rights as seen from the perspective of gender mainstreaming.

The goal of the Lisbon Strategy is to reach a 60% employment rate for women by 2010.[3] In 2005 the gap between women's and men's employment in the EU was 15%. It is important to note that there are important differences across countries, with a gap below 10% in Finland, Sweden, Denmark, the Baltic countries, Bulgaria and Slovenia; but exceeding 20% in Cyprus, Spain, Italy, Greece and Malta. Although the gap between women's and men's unemployment rates narrowed from 2.8% in 2000 to 2% in 2005, women were still more likely to be unemployed that men; the unemployment rate was 9.9% among women in 2005 compared to 7.9% among men. More women than men work part time: in 2006 that percentage was 32.8 of women in the EU against 7.7% of men. There are differences among Member States: the percentage of female part timers exceeded 30% in France, Denmark and Luxembourg, 40% in Sweden, Austria, Belgium, the United Kingdom and Germany, and even reached 75% in the Netherlands. Among the new Members States, however, that percentage is very low in Bulgaria, Hungary, Slovakia and Latvia. The EU Commission recognized that the participation of women in the labour force is affected by their predominant role in the care of children and other dependent persons. The difficulty for women in reconciling their professional and private lives is evidenced by the strong impact of parenthood on employment rates. In 2005 the employment rate for women aged 20-49 was 61.1% when they had children under 12, compared to 76% when they did not. For men with children under 12, the employment rate was actually higher (91.5%) than that of men without children (85.5%).

Historically the EU has recognized that female workers are at a disadvantage as caregivers and that it is therefore necessary to implement policies to reduce discrimination against women in order to encourage them to participate in the labour market. The process of implementation of EU policies on equality and anti-discrimination by gender started in the 1970s.

3. *See* Report from the Commission to the Council, 'The European Parliament, the European Economic and Social Committee and the Committee of the Regions on Equality Between Women and Men 2007', Brussels 7 Feb. 2007, COM (2007) 49 final.

1.1. The Starting Point of Reference: Directives versus Guidelines on Equality and Anti-Discrimination Policy

During the 1970s the enactment of an important package of directives played a crucial role in the construction of an EU level of hard and binding regulations. The directives have created a large body of case law from the Court of Justice which has effectively transformed labour equality law in the Member States. The influence of these directives and their application by the Court of Justice have resulted in important national laws concerning equality and gender discrimination, and a creative national case law to reduce discrimination in working conditions, for example with regard to salary, holidays, part-time work, welfare state entitlements and so on.[4]

The directives on equality totally prohibited all discrimination by gender including harassment. From the first directive in 1975 to the last in 2006, the progress in the field of equality has been enormous. The role of the EU has been very important in the transformation of the national systems on equality and anti-discrimination.

On a special note, two more directives deal with maternity protection and parental leave. Both have far-reaching implications not only for family polices but also for equality between women and men.[5] Council Directive (EEC) 92/85

---

4. Council Directive (EEC) 75/117 on the Approximation of the Laws of the Member States Relating to the Application of the Principle of Equal Pay for Men and Women [1975] OJ L 45; Council Directive (EEC) 76/207 on the Implementation of the Principle of Equal Treatment for Men and Women as Regards Access to Employment, Vocational Training and Promotion, and Working Conditions [1976] OJ L 39 as amended by Directive 2002/73 of the European Parliament and of the Council [2002] OJ L 269; Council Directive (EEC) 79/7 on the Progressive Implementation of Equal Treatment for men and Women in Matters of Social Security, [1979] OJ L 6; Council Directive (EEC) 86/378 on the Implementation of the Principle of Equal Treatment for Men and Women in Occupational Social Security Schemes [1986] OJ L 225 as amended by Council Directive (EC) 96/97 [1996] OJ L 46; Council Directive (EC) 97/80 on the Burden of Proof in Cases of Discrimination Based on Sex [1998] OJ L 014 C/6; Council Directive (EC) 98/52/on the Extension of Directive (EC) 97/80 on the Burden of Proof in Cases of Discrimination Based on Sex to the United Kingdom of Great Britain and Northern Ireland [1998] OJ L 205/66; and Council Directive (EC) 2006/54 on the Implementation of the Principle of Equal Opportunities and Equal Treatment of Men and Women in Matters of Employment and Occupation (recast) [2006] OJEU L 204/23.
5. Council Directive (EEC) 86/613 on the Application of the Principle of Equal Treatment Between Men and Women engaged in Activity, Including Agriculture, in a Self-Employed Capacity, and on the Protection of Self-Employed Women During Pregnancy and Motherhood [1986] OJ L 359; Council Directive (EEC) 92/85 on the Introduction of Measures to Encourage Improvements in the Safety and Health at Work of Pregnant Workers and Workers Who Have Recently Given Birth or are Breastfeeding (tenth individual directive within the meaning of Art 16(1) of Directive 89/391/EEC), [1992] OJ L 348; Council Directive (EC) 96/34 of 3 June 1996 on the Framework Agreement on Parental Leave Concluded by UNICE, CEEP and the ETUC [1996] OJ L 145 4); Council Directive (EC) 97/75 Amending and Extending to the United Kingdom of Great Britain and Northern Ireland Council Directive (EC) 96/34 on the Framework Agreement on Parental Leave Concluded by UNICE, CEEP and the ETUC [1998] OJ L 010/24; Council Directive (EC) 97/80 on the Burden of Proof in Cases of Discrimination Based on Sex [1998]

encourages improvements in the safety and health at work of pregnant workers and workers who have recently given birth or are breastfeeding. Article 8 of this directive recognizes a maternity leave of fourteen uninterrupted weeks in which – as is to be established in the legislation of Member States – women workers will not lose their employment rights and will maintain their right to receive their salary or an allowance, so long as they meet the requirements stipulated by the relevant national laws. Women workers are not required to have paid social security taxes for more than one year to be entitled to this paid maternity leave. The point to underline is that this directive understands maternity leave as a health issue separate from equality and no discrimination.

The second legal reference at the EU level, as mentioned above, is Directive 96/34 on parental leave. It recognizes an individual right to parental leave for workers, men and women both, who have a work contract or labour relationship as defined by the law, collective bargaining contract or practice within each Member State. This right is applicable in the case of birth or adoption, for the parent to take care of the child for a minimum of three months and up to a given age – no more than eight years old – to be determined by Member States and/or the social negotiating partners.

The non-transferability of their right stands as another important element, in an effort to define parental leave from the standpoint of equal treatment. Thus, it is established that, in order to promote equal opportunity and equal treatment for men and women, the right to parental leave should be, in principle, non transferable. The fixing of both modalities of parental leave and their conditions are to be defined by law and collective bargaining within the Member States in accordance with the *de minimis* dispositions set forth in the directive.

Member States can decide if parental leave is to be awarded as a full working day, a half-day, day parts, or in the form of time credits. They also may elect to subordinate the right to parental leave to the length of service or seniority not greater than one year; adjust the conditions for eligibility and the modalities of parental leave to the circumstances of adoption; establish the notice period to claim parental leave, with explicit mention of the beginning and ending dates; define the circumstances under which the employer may postpone it (for example, where the work is of a seasonal nature, where no replacement can be found during the notice period, where a significant proportion of the workforce applies for parental leave at the same time, or when the employee's job is of strategic importance). The employee is guaranteed the right to return to the same job, or, if that is not reasonably practicable, a similar job that has the same or better status, terms and conditions. The rights in existence or in the process of being acquired by the worker at the time of taking parental leave are to be maintained without change. At the end of parental leave those rights – including changes derived from national legislation, collective bargaining agreements or practice – are to be applied. Member States

OJ L 014//6; Council Directive (EC) 98/52 on the Extension of Directive 97/80/EC on the Burden of Proof in Cases of Discrimination Based on Sex to the United Kingdom of Great Britain and Northern Ireland [1998] OJ L 205/66.

and/or social negotiating partners are to define the rules applicable during the period of parental leave.

As mentioned above, all these EU regulations on equality have been transforming national law in this field. Moreover, it is not possible to understand the dynamic relations of these directives in the construction of a European social model without reference to the implementation and interpretation by the Court of Justice. Some authors maintain that the Court of Justice has played a crucial role in the 'constitutionalization' of the EU model.[6] Enacting the directives was only the first step; the case law of the Court of Justice has been the motor of change in their implementation.[7] The case law of the Court of Justice has consolidated directives as an instrument to enact rights involving the national courts. The spillover process that some authors[8] have called 'conversation between the courts' is a source of progress in issues of equality and no discrimination by gender.

Despite all this progress, it is necessary to emphasize that the anti-discrimination and equality model should be evaluated from the gender mainstreaming principle which requires more provisions for family care. I argue that the conceptualization of maternity as a health risk and the framework that the EU offers for parental leave is not enough to transform the current scenario for women, and that the OMC design on family friendly policies will not help much. The OMC transfers the implementation of these polices to Member States and this in turn implies a future movement of case law from the EU level to the national level, reducing the benefits that the multilevel legal spillover has had thus far.

1.2. Multilevel Governance and the OMC: Subsidiarity and Proportionality in Social Policies

Focusing on reforming governance in the EU, the White Paper on European Governance[9] is a main reference for the implementation of criteria and principles of governance in Europe and an important key to understanding the effects of changes in policies and regulations on labour law.

The White Paper addresses the question of how the EU uses its powers on the basis of the principles of openness, participation, accountability, effectiveness and

6. *See* J.A. Caporaso, *The European Union. Dilemmas of the Regional Integration; Dilemmas in World Politics* (Notre Dame, University of Notre Dame, 2000), 72-73.
7. *See* in this sense the introduction of the Council Directive (EC) 2006/54 of the European Parliament and Council of 5 Jul. 2006 on the Implementation of the Principle of Equal Opportunities and Equal Treatment of Men and Women in Matters of Employment and Occupation (recast).
8. *See* S. Sciarra, 'Integration Through Courts: Article 177 as a Pre-Federal Device' in S. Sciarra (ed.) *Labour Law in the Courts: National Judges and the European Court of Justice* (Oxford and Portland, OR, Hart Publishing, 2001). There is a very interesting scholarly debate about the role of judges in the society, *see* R. Hirschl, *Towards Juristocracy: the Origins and Consequences of the New Constitutionalism* (Harvard, Harvard University Press, 2004).
9. *See* COM (2001) 428 final. of 25 Jul. 2001.

coherence.[10] The declaration of multilevel governance in the White Paper and the five principles described reinforce two structural principles of EU labour policies: subsidiarity and proportionality. Together these are the key for understanding the current state of labour law and more specifically the EU policy on equality and no discrimination by gender.[11] According to the principle of subsidiarity, the objectives of the proposed action cannot be sufficiently achieved by the Member States and are therefore better achieved by the Community. In accordance with the principle of proportionality, EU regulations should not go beyond what is necessary for the purpose. The proportionality principle offers an extended level of flexibility for the EU in the distribution of competences between the EU and Member States. In the case of the EU's equality policies, both principles reinforce the Member State – the national level – as the main player in the process of initiating and developing policies on labour rights, as we will see in detail.

The multilevel approach implies taking into account several territorial jurisdictions (the EU, as a whole, national and local), actors (for example, institutions and unions), and the judiciary, to identify the role that each one has to play regarding governance. The transformation of governance described as a process starting with the Lisbon Strategy is the scenario in which to start the analysis of the EU's call for a process of modernization of labour law.

The Lisbon Strategy and the Green Paper on modernization of labour law form part of the process that the EU calls 'modernization' of labour law and welfare systems. They represent milestones in the construction of a new way of regulating labour relations[12] characterized by the combination of classic forms of regulation, by hard and binding instruments that imply a role for the judiciary, with non-binding instruments such as Papers or Guidelines. The latter presuppose the decentralization of hard and binding labour law regulations, from the EU level to the national level. Here, the increasing role of the subsidiarity principle and the self-imposed limits on the EU according with the principle of proportionality, are crucial. Transferring hard law from the EU to the Member States has the result

10. The White Paper defined five principles of: (i) openness: the institutions should work in a more open manner, it is necessary to strengthen communication with the Member States and use a language accessible and understandable for the general public; (ii) participation: improved participation from the conception of the policies to their implementation; (iii) accountability: each of the EU institutions and Member States have to take responsibility for developing and implementing EU policy at whatever level; (iv) effectiveness: policies must be effective and timely and the EU depends on implementing EU polices in a proportionate manner and at the most appropriate level; and (v) coherence: policies and action must be coherent and easily understood.
11. The White Paper maintains that 'the Commission alone cannot improve European governance, nor can this Paper provide a magic cure for everything. Changes required concerted action by all the European institutions, present and future Member States, regional and local authorities, and civil society. Elected officeholders at the various levels, in particular at the national level, have a crucial role in this context'.
12. About the new way of regulating labour law *see* S. Fredman, 'The Ideology of the New Labour Law' in C. Barnard, S. Deakin and G.S. Morris (eds), *The Future of Labour Law. Liber Amicorum* (Oxford and Portland, OR, Hart Publishing, 2004).

of diminishing the role of the European Court of Justice as a builder of European workers' rights.

The critical change here is that the EU has moved from a labour law model that integrated a number of important Council Regulations and Directives to a model that reduces the amount of hard and binding regulations in favour of techniques of coordination among Member States. The most relevant consequence is the use of guidelines (which are not directives), to eliminate hard law (and, as a consequence, the role of the Court of Justice) at the EU level.

The process of transformation from the first model to the second model starts in Lisbon in 2000. With the Lisbon Strategy the EU launched the goal 'to convert the EU economy into the most competitive economy in the world and full employment by 2010'. The Lisbon Strategy has three pillars. The economic pillar prepares the transition to a more dynamic and competitive economy based on a knowledge economy in the information society. The social pillar calls for the 'modernization' of the social model with the implication that the Member States will invest in education and training and active policy for employment. The third pillar is environmental, in accordance with the Goteborg European Council. All these goals are to be achieved through the OMC.

The techniques to organize national and supranational level regulations in a multilevel approach to governance are becoming increasingly more complex. The OMC shares with other mechanisms the definition of coordination techniques, which have as a point of departure the respect for the different national systems and the renunciation to harmonization,[13] understood as a tendency to unify systems.

A coordination mechanism has been developed in Luxembourg for employment; in Cardiff for the functioning of markets, goods, services and capital; and in Cologne for a process of macroeconomic dialogue. The principal difference that the OMC presents is that these techniques propose, in many cases, the decentralization of regulations – that is of, hard and binding law – which implies the elimination of the role of the Court of Justice in these fields.[14]

The OMC is a very sophisticated coordination technique that works as a complete programme for Member States, fixing very clear goals together with route maps to assess their accomplishment. The Lisbon Strategy is summarized in (a) Employment Guidelines, proposed by the Commission and setting out

13. The renunciation to harmonization is very clear in the EU among other issues on social rights, *see* P.C. Schmitter, *How to Democratize the European Union and Why Bother?* (Oxford, Rowman & Littlefield Publishers, 2000), 45; by contrast, currency harmonization presents a clear sign of the EU's determination to achieve an economic goal; *see* R. Fishman, 'Introduction' in R. Fishman and A. Messina (eds), *The Year of the Euro. The Cultural, Social and Political Import of Europe's Common Currency* (Notre Dame, University of Notre Dame Press, 2006).
14. The OMC proposes a new way to coordinate policies totally different from other mechanisms of coordination at the EU level, which involve hard and binding EU law, such as the Council Regulation 1408/71 on social security and mobility for workers. It has been the origin of a very relevant core of workers' rights through the interpretation by the Court of Justice, for example, in anti-discrimination policy by nationality.

common priorities for employment policies; (b) National Reform Programmes produced by every Member State to define the design and implementation of the guidelines; (c) Joint Employment Reports adapted by the Council; and (d) Recommendations by the Council upon a proposal from the Commission and the EU annual progress report.

The EU understands the OMC as a coordination mechanism based on five principles: subsidiarity, convergence, concerted action, mutual learning and exchange of good practices. The OMC affects areas such as employment, social protection, social inclusion, education, youth and training.

Supporters and opponents of the OMC defend passionately its advantages and disadvantages with respect to the participation of the social actors. The increase of participation inside a model of deliberative democracy is one of the most robust arguments used by its supporters, but other scholars and social actors have stressed the weakness of the OMC as an extreme manifestation of the principles of subsidiarity and proportionality.[15] At the same time the EU is still able, despite important transfers of legal hard instruments from the EU to the national level, to condition the national legal framework through the control of national budgets.[16]

2. UNDERSTANDING EQUALITY IN A HOLISTIC FRAMEWORK: THE GENDER MAINSTREAMING STRATEGY

The gender mainstreaming strategy established as a global strategy by the United Nations in Beijing in 1995, places gender equality issues at the centre of the policy decisions. It involves more than just an increase in women's participation, demanding the penetration of women in spaces where they are not yet present.

The EU gender mainstreaming, as stated in Articles 2 and 3(2) of the Treaty, establishes that in all of its actions the EU will have as objectives the elimination of inequalities between men and women and the active promotion of equality. The EU regards the gender mainstreaming strategy as a cohesive instrument to achieve the goals of the EES and maintains that combating discrimination and promoting gender mainstreaming are essential for making progress towards achieving full employment.[17]

Gender mainstreaming implies a holistic conception of equality integrating not only the policies related to equality and anti-discrimination but also parental leave and family friendly policies.

---

15. For a complete study of the OMC and the different scholars' approach *see* B. Caruso and M. Barbera, 'In Search of a New Language: Italian Labour Law Scholarship in the Face of the European Integration' (2007) *The Jean Monnet Working Papers Series*, NYU School of Law. *See also* D. Ashiagbor, *The European Employment Strategy: Labour Market Regulation and New Governance* (Oxford, Oxford University Press, 2005).
16. *See* G. Ross and A. Martin, 'European Social Democracy and Monetary Integration' in R. Fishman and A. Messina (eds), above n. 13, 218-219.
17. *See* Community Strategic Guidelines COM (2005) 299.

2.1. The Problem of Reading Equality Policies as an Employment Issue

As noted already, the OMC combines, under the principles of subsidiarity and proportionality, a wide spectrum of hard and binding regulations with other soft instruments such as books and papers which are not binding in a legal sense. Some of the effects that this coordination system presents are very clear if we analyze equality and anti-discrimination by gender from a holistic perspective under the gender mainstreaming strategy, and also integrate other policies related to equal opportunities.

The point of reference is how the EU and the OMC have distributed, under the principle of subsidiarity and proportionality, the power of regulations between the EU and the Member States. Table 4.1[18] illustrates two trends of the ESS in attracting more people into employment and modernizing social protection systems. The first one shows how the OMC places the promotion of equal opportunities and the necessity of increasing female participation in the labour force. The second one shows how family friendly policies are devolved to the Member States because the instruments are not directives or binding law.

As seen in the Table 4.1, the policy of equality and anti-discrimination by gender, (a EU goal in promoting equality of opportunities), will be implemented by hard and binding legislation such as directives. This strategic decision made by the EU implies that the Court of Justice and the national courts will participate in the application of these regulations. The spillover between EU and national regulations and from the Court of Justice to the national courts will continue. By contrast, family friendly polices in regard to childcare and care for the elderly and disabled will be implemented by expenditure legislation, social dialogue and the ESS. The latter implies a delegation of the responsibility to adopt these policies from the EU to the Member States. The EU agenda does not contemplate more binding regulations on this issue, and the decentralization of these policies implies a halt in the activism of the Court of Justice in the future.[19]

In the context of the OMC the plan is to transfer to the Member States the responsibility to enact family friendly polices referring to promotion of equality between women and men. The transfer of policies implies that in the future there will be no more directives on this issue and consequently the active relation between EU regulations and the Court of Justice will come to an end. This scenario makes it difficult to implement the principles of gender mainstreaming and empowerment as axes of the equality policy. The principles of gender mainstreaming and empowerment for women in the evolution of social and gender policies in

18. The Lisbon Action Plan incorporating the EU Lisbon Programme and Recommendations for actions to Member States for inclusion in their national Lisbon programmes, companion documents to the Communication to the Spring European Council 2005, *Working Together for Growth and Jobs*, SEC (2005) 192.
19. It is interesting to *see* in G. Flakner, O. Treib, M. Hartlapp and S. Leiber, *Complying with Europe. EU Harmonization and Soft Law in the Member States* (Cambridge, Cambridge University Press, 2005) the defense that the number of directives has not declined, and how these authors understand that the OMC could mean a reduced role for the Court of Justice.

Table 4.1.

Policy measure at community level	*Instrument*	*Roadmap*	*Progress indicator*	*Impact on jobs and growth*
Promote equal opportunities	Ensure full implementation of acquis Legislation	Adoption of pending recast proposal on implementation of equal opportunity and equal treatment of men and women in matters of employment and occupation	Gender gaps including pay gap	Increase participation rates Social cohesion
Increase female participation in the labour market	Expenditure legislation Social dialogue European Employment Strategy	Childcare facilities and care facilities for elderly and disable Extension of parental leave to fathers	Female participation employment rate Provision childcare facilities (90% for children between 3 and school age; 33% for 0 to 3 years old) Care facilities for elderly and disabled	Increase labour market participation and employment Social cohesion

the EU have emerged as a capital reference in the construction of equality and anti-discrimination by gender in the 21st century, and face an erosion of rights because of the demand for flexibility imposed by the markets.

2.2. The Risk of an Individualistic Approach to Labour Law

There is no doubt that women are the most vulnerable workers in the marketplace, and that the risk of social exclusion is higher for women than for men. Because of women's special vulnerability, it is important to establish the effect that the Green Paper[20] could have on women's rights.

20. Green Paper on Modernising Labour Law to Meet the Challenges of the 21st century, COM (2006) 708 final.

The first point to emphasize is the individualistic reading of workers' rights by the Green Paper's strategy for labour law. The paper focuses on the guidelines of labour law at the individual level and omits any reference to collective rights. This is, in our opinion, the biggest failure of the Green Paper. By ignoring collective rights the Green Paper conflicts with the Charter of Fundamental Rights. Furthermore, the non-existence of collective rights in the Green Paper contradicts the role that the unions have in the configuration of policies at the national level and conflicts with the strong tradition of the ILO (International Labour Organization) Convention on Freedom of Association among Member States.[21] It does not make sense to design OMC policies in which social dialogue has a crucial role whilst ignoring, at the same time, the unions as major actors in the Green Paper. This is one of the main difficulties for the successful implementation of family friendly policies.

The approach that the Green Paper offers for the future of labour law is based on the idea of flexicurity. Flexicurity is defined in the EU as a strategy to enhance both flexibility and security in the labour market. Flexibility means increase of mobility from school to work, from one job to another, from unemployment or inactivity to work, and from work to retirement. For employers, this EU version of flexibility is not limited to more freedom for companies to recruit or dismiss. It also means flexible work organization, new productive needs and skills, and new means to combine family and work. Security in this context refers to employability; it no longer implies a job for life but, rather, training to help workers to have more possibilities in the labour market combined with a welfare state for the transition periods.[22]

One important aspect to underline in the Green Paper's model is the openness to different instruments to regulate the relationship between labour and capital, not limited to the employment contract. The promotion of other ways to regulate the labour relationship signifies a diminution of the classic model of rights attached to the employment contract and more segmentation of the workers' rights. The Green Paper requires Member States to offer more flexibility – understood as the elimination of guarantees and redundancy pay for workers – with the goal to increase employment. There is a very clear tendency in all Member States[23] to amend the current regulation of employment termination, and to facilitate the way for layoffs accompanied by the elimination of redundancy pay.

Another element of flexicurity in the Green Paper is the treatment of employability and unemployment benefits. Temporary contracts and easier layoffs create an enforced mobility for workers, internally (within the same firms), and externally (towards other companies). In exchange for this loss of guarantees, the strategy

21. For the impact of ILO Conventions in national regulation *see* J. Lopez, 'Beyond the National Case: the Role of Transnational Labour Law in Shaping Domestic Regulations' (2007) 3 *Comparative Labour Law & Policy Journal*, 547-563.
22. 'Towards Common Principles of Flexicurity: More and Better Jobs through Flexibility and Security', European Commission, Jul. 2007.
23. This is clear for the European Commission. *See* the document 'Termination of Employment Relationships. Legal situation in the Member States of the European Union', 2006.

offers a promise of employability. Employability as the capacity of workers to shorten the transition periods between jobs is based on training: workers have to be trained in other skills to improve their capability to move in the labour market. What remains unclear are the responsibilities of firms in the field of training.

During the transition periods the Green Paper posits unemployment benefits, to be provided by the welfare systems of individual Member States' welfare systems, as the solution. Training and welfare state unemployment programmes are the basis of the security that the Green Paper offers as a recipe for the modernization of labour law. The Americanization of the EU in this regard is obvious.[24] Cooperation in the implementation of flexibility is required from the workers,[25] but there is no sight of collective rights in the Green Paper.

The idea of employability transfers the responsibility for transition periods to workers and welfare state systems. To implement flexibility, Member States have transformed national systems in other ways, but have not modified the unemployment institutions to respond to the new challenges that flexicurity implies for unemployment.[26] The new strategy offers workers no guarantee of training, which is supposed to be one of the basic elements of the new relationship between capital and worker.[27]

The European Trade Union Confederation (2007) has denounced the increase in precarious jobs (which create a more segmented labour market), social exclusion, and new barriers in terms of rights. In this scenario, the vulnerability of women is increasing.

2.3. Equality and Anti-Discrimination Policy for the Next Decades: New EU Regulations in Maternity and Parental Leave

The Commission has pointed out the increased difficulty that women are facing in reconciling their professional and private lives and the unequal division of domestic and family responsibilities. The rate of employment of women between the ages of 20 and 49 falls by fifteen points when they have a child, while that of men

24. 'More than two decades have passed since the modern layoff first appeared as a mass phenomenon in the American life. Until this happened, companies tried to avoid layoffs. There were a sign of corporate failure and a violation of acceptable business behavior', *see* L. Uchitelle, *The Disposable American. Layoffs and Their Consequences* (New York, Knopf, 2006). IX.
25. *See* in this sense H. Collins, 'Flexibility and Stability of Expectations in the Contract of Employment' (2006) 4 *Socio-Economic Review*, 139-153.
26. *See* Table 5.1, unemployment benefits systems: policy reforms over the 1994-2004, OCDE Economic Surveys, 2005.
27. In the United States, '[u]nder the new employment relationship, the problem is no longer employer breaches of implicit promises of job security , but rather employer breaches of other implicit promises such as training, skill development , networking opportunities', *see* K. Stone, 'Thinking and Doing – the Regulation of Worker's Capital in the United States' (2006) 4 *Socio-Economic Review*, 135.

increases by six points. Moreover, increasing demands for labour flexibility are having a disproportionately large impact on women.[28]

As mentioned already, the current strategy on family friendly policies in the EU is linked to the EES and the modernization of the welfare state systems. It is within this recognition of the need to increase the employment of women that the EU introduced the need to implement policies on the reconciliation of work and family life. In this sense, the EU regards the aging of the world population as one of the greatest challenges faced today by the welfare state, particularly with respect to its ability to ensure the future viability of pensions, The rights of women are understood as part of the economic and employment policy, an approach that further implies the submission of women's rights to market goals.

As noted above, Directives 92/85 and 96/34, have played a very important role in entitling women to rights and reconciling work responsibilities and family lives. But it is important to realize that, while these regulations were crucial in the 1990s they need to be updated to continue to be effective in reaching the goal of equality between women and men.

There is great variety in the models of social protection among EU Member States, not only with respect to the amount of social expenditure but also with regard to the proportion destined to families and children. The EU model fails to offer a supranational concept of family[29]and lacks a definition of dependency, leaving a puzzle of regulations in the Member States and an obstacle to implementing gender-mainstreaming policies.[30]

---

28. Report from the Commission to the Council, the European Parliament, the European Economic and Social Committee and the Committee of the Regions on Equality between Women and Men, COM (2007) 49 final.
29. The first complexity is that the notion of family, as the subject of rights, has multiple meanings at the Member State level. In some countries (fundamentally in Mediterranean Europe) a family is defined essentially as the married couple and their children, whereas in other countries it includes unmarried heterosexual couples or homosexual couples as well. Other countries focus their attention not on the concept of family but of household. It would be beneficial for EU legislation to include a definition of family as a subject with rights, more in agreement with new social realities (as a 'natural and fundamental unit of society' in the United Nations' definition). It would also be useful to clarify the objectives underpinning various measures such as maternity leave, parental leave and family care as well as the effects of these measures on equal treatment. *See* M.S. Aguirre and A. Wolfgram, 'United Nations Policy and the Family: Redefining the Ties That Bind: a Study of History, Forces and Trends', (2002) 16 BYUJ.
30. The attention to children has taken center stage in the design of measures that facilitate attending to their dependence situation through parental childcare allowances that some Member States (Austria, Finland, France, Germany, Luxembourg, and Sweden) pay to those parents who look after their children, whether full or part time. The beneficiary is, then, the person who looks after the child even if that person is not one of the parents. There are conditions to meet in order to qualify. They relate to the place of residence of the child, the level of income, and in some cases, the relationship to the social security system as well. Some countries pay special attention to situations where only one of the parents looks after the child, recognizing in these cases specific allowances (as in Denmark, France, Iceland, Liechtenstein, Sweden) or where the child is disabled (Austria, Denmark, France, Greece, Iceland, the Netherlands, Portugal, Spain), large families (Austria, France, Greece, Italy, Luxembourg, Spain), multiple births (Finland, France, Ireland, Luxembourg, Norway, Spain, Sweden),or low income families (France and

The EU legislation contains no definition of dependency. At the EU level there is an effort to attend to the situation of dependency that arises with the birth or adoption of a child but there is very little legislative attention focused on other situations of dependency such as those generated by age or illness. This absence leads us to characterize the EU legal policies on co-responsibility as deficient.[31]

The role of collective bargaining is very clear in the group of directives that treat conciliation between work and family life, such as Directive 96/34 on parental leave, which includes leave to attend to the care of family members. In this sense, it establishes that Member States and/or the social negotiating partners will adopt the measures necessary to authorize workers to be absent from work – in accordance with national legislation, collective bargaining agreements, or practice – in situations of urgent family matters in the case of sickness or accident. Member States and/or the social negotiating partners may further establish the conditions for access to this right.

Involving collective social actors in the achievement of equality is a positive thing but it is necessary to work not only through social dialogue but also with hard and binding EU and national regulations. It is crucial to understand the differing goals of maternity protection, parental leave and family friendly policies to succeed in the application of gender mainstreaming. For example, there are Member States where maternity protection is mixed with parental leave – if we look at the duration and the definition of the leave – but only the mother is recognized as the beneficiary (while allowing her to transfer the leave to the father for some weeks).

There is a vicious circle: women get lower pay and worse conditions because they look after their dependent relatives and are therefore more likely to be pressed to leave work. The freedom of Member States to determine whether the leave is to be remunerated has important consequences. Where the leave is unpaid, it is reasonable to assume that women, rather than men, will be using it to stay at home to look after the children, given the discrimination in pay and working conditions. Parental leave for men is particularly important as an instrument to avoid the separation of women from the labour market for long periods. Furthermore, the EU has to work harder to recognize the implications on equal treatment of situations that generate dependency among the elderly or the sick. Along these lines, it is necessary to reinforce policies of equal treatment and guarantees against discrimination for those who care for dependent people who are not children. In

---

Ireland). For the analysis of these policies *see* G. Esping-Andersen, 'A Child-Centred Social Investment Strategy' in G. Esping-Andersen, A. Hemerijck and J. Myles (eds), *Why We Need a New Welfare State* (Oxford, Oxford University Press, 2002), 26-68.

31. The Council of Europe in its Recommendation No. 98 of the Committee of Ministers to Member States, defines dependence as 'a state in which people find themselves when, for reasons linked to the lack or the loss of physical, psychic or intellectual autonomy, they have the need for significant assistance and/or help in order to carry out the common tasks of everyday life'. EU law contemplates only two concepts – namely maternity leave and parental leave – in contrast with a far wider scope in the legislation of Member States.

short, there is a need to offer protection against any mistreatment arising from the care of a dependent.[32]

EU laws pay less attention to the care of elderly or sick relatives than of children. In order to attain equal treatment of women and men in their professions and similar levels of labour participation it is important to focus more on situations of dependency among the elderly and the sick with a gender mainstreaming perspective. However, the literature emphasizes the importance of a more comprehensive analysis of the situation of elderly people.[33]

3. EQUALITY BY GENDER, AND COLLECTIVE RIGHTS AS SOLIDARITY: THE CHAPTER OF FUNDAMENTAL RIGHTS

The EU is worried about women, but women are also very concerned with the future of women's rights. The combination of decentralization of regulations and law courts and a flexible employment approach suggest many problems for an improvement of equality. The lack of EU regulations concerning a woman caregiver when she herself falls into a situation of dependency is very revealing.[34]

---

32. P.K. Runkles-Pearson, 'The Changing Relations of Family and the Workplace: Extending Antidiscrimination Laws To Parents and No Parents Alike' (2002) 77 *NYUL Review*, 833. J.C. Williams, 'Beyond The Maternal Wall: Relief For Family Caregivers Who Are Discriminated Against On The Job', 26 *Harvard Women's LJ*, 77.
33. J. Myles, 'A New Social Contract for the Elderly?' in G. Esping-Andersen, A. Hemerijck and J. Myles (eds), above n. 30, 130-173.
34. A helpful item to reflect on this point is Recommendation (91) 2 of the Committee of Ministers of European Council Member States with respect to Social Security for those workers without a professional status (people with family responsibilities at home and volunteers), which considers that protection for such people requires the introduction of specific rights to social security. This Recommendation takes as its point of departure the need to recogzise the carers' rights to social protection. The Recommendation establishes in the first place that all such people should be protected in case of sickness, maternity, injury, old age, and family needs. In contrast to EU social law, the Recommendation addresses the treatment of dependence in a global (that is to say comprehensive) way. It states that persons who interrupt or delay the start of their occupational activity for a given period to exercise family responsibilities in looking after children, or dependent disabled or old persons should be given credit for the period in question (in accordance with prescribed procedures) for the purpose of entitlement to invalidity and old age benefits. This approach is very important in designing co-responsibility policies. The Recommendation, also deals with part-time contracts from the standpoint of equal treatment. Thus, the Recommendation establishes that periods of part-time work should be considered as periods of full time work in order to fulfil the qualifying period required for entitlement to sickness/maternity, old age and invalidity benefits and family benefit when the part-time work is chosen to exercise family responsibilities. Moreover, the benefits should be brought up to the level that full time occupational activity would give them during the period in question. Equally, persons who do not engage in any occupational activity to devote themselves for a given period to family responsibilities, should be given credit for the period in question for the purpose of entitlement to benefits and the calculation of those benefits.

A window of opportunity in the troubling scenario that the EU faces in the evolution of equality and anti-discrimination is the Charter of Fundamental Rights,[35] which permits the emergence of crucial pieces in the construction of democratic societies.

The Charter in its Preamble proclaims that dignity, liberty, equality and solidarity are indivisible and universal values. The Charter also dedicates its entire Third Chapter to equality, prohibits discrimination by sex (Article 21), and recognizes that the principle of equality between men and women (Article 23) will be guaranteed in all arenas including employment, the workplace and remuneration for work. Alongside this, the chapter on solidarity offers guarantees for the family in the legal, economic, and social spheres and also maintains – in the interest of reconciling work and family life – that all people have the right to protection against any termination of employment due to maternity, as well as the right to paid maternity leave and to parental leave in the event of the birth or adoption of a child.

The Charter integrates collective rights. Equality and anti-discrimination, and the intersection with collective rights is crucial.[36]

In conclusion, the development of policies on equality and anti-discrimination at the EU level should not be conceived exclusively as a requirement of employment policies. The right to equal treatment between men and women forms part of the workers' rights recognized in the Charter of Fundamental Rights. Equality and anti-discrimination polices by gender have to be constructed in a multilevel scenario made up by international, EU and national regulations – law and collective bargaining[37] – with the participation of governments and social actors and with the complicity of the judiciary. This should be the framework for the OMC, as a combination of regulations and policies[38] and techniques[39] serving the final goal of fomenting equality and solidarity in order to achieve societies in which women become real actors that decide about their own lives.

---

35. *See* the important role that the Charter plays in S. Scarponi, 'Introduzione: La Crisi della Sovranita Nazionales e le Transformazioni del Diritto del Lavoro' in S. Scarponi (ed.), *Globalizzazione e Diritto del Lavoro. Il Ruolo degli Ordinamenti Sovranazionali* (Milano, Giuffrè Editore, 2001), 7.
36. 'Grassroots movements and civil society organisations have contested the traditional status of the state as the sole actor in the process of construction and enforcement of international human rights', *see* B. Santos Rodriguez-Garavito, *Law and Globalisation from below. Towards a Cosmopolitan Legality* (Cambridge, Cambridge University Press, 2005).
37. For the evolution of collective bargaining *see* S. Sciarra, 'L'Evoluzione della Contratazione Collectiva. Apunti per una Comparazione nei Paesi dell' Union Europea' (2006) 4 *Rivista Italiana di Diritto del Lavoro.*
38. K. Wise, 'Caring for Our Parents in an Aging World: Sharing Public and Private Responsibility for the Elderly', (2002) 5 *NYUJ Legis.&Pub.Pol'y*, 563; J.C. Williams , 'Beyond the Maternal Wall: Relief for Family Caregivers Who are Discriminated Against on the Job', 26 *Harvard Women's LJ*, 77.
39. S. Sciarra, *Modernization of Labour Law: A Current European Debate* (International Institute for Labour Studies, Geneva, 2007).

References

Ashiagbor, D., *The European Employment Strategy: Labour Market Regulation and New Governance* (Oxford, Oxford University Press, 2005).

Aguirre, M.S. and Wolfgram, A. 'United Nations Policy and the Family: Redefining the ties that Bind: a Study of History, Forces and Trends' (2002), 16 *BYUJ. Publ.*

Caporaso, J.A., *The European Union. Dilemmas of the Regional Integration* (Notre Dame, University of Notre Dame, 2000).

Caruso, B. and Barbera, M., 'In Search of a New Language: Italian Labour Law Scholarship in the Face of the European Integration' (2007) NYU School of Law, *the Jean Monnet Working Papers Series.*

Collins H., 'Flexibility and Stability of Expectations in the Contract of Employment' (2006) 4 *Socio-Economic Review.*

Fishman, R., 'Introduction' in R. Fishman and A. Messina (eds). *The Year of the Euro. The Cultural, Social and Political Import of Europe's Common Currency* (Notre Dame, University of Notre Dame Press, 2006).

Fredman, S., 'The Ideology of the New Labour Law' in C. Barnard, S. Deakin and Morris, G.S., (eds). *The future of Labour Law. Liber Amicorum* (Oxford and Portland Oregon, Hart Publishing, 2004).

Flakner, G., Treib, O., Hartlapp, M. and Leiber, S., *Complying with Europe. EU Harmonization and Soft Law in the Member States* (Cambridge, Cambridge University Press, 2005).

Esping-Andersen, G., 'A Child-Centred Social Investment Strategy' in Esping-Andersen, G., Hemerijck, A. and Myles, J. (eds). *Why We Need a New Welfare State* (Oxford, Oxford University Press, 2002).

Joerges, 'Introduction and Overview' in Joerges, C. and Petersmann, E.U. (eds). *Constitutionalism, Multilevel Trade, Governance and Social Regulation* (Oxford-Portland, Oregon, Hart Publishing, 2006).

Hirschl, R., *Towards Juristocracy: The Origins and Consequences of the New Constitutionalism* (Harvard, Harvard University Press, 2004).

Lopez, 'J., 'Beyond the National Case: the Role of Transnational Labour Law in Shaping Domestic Regulations' (2007) 3 *Comparative Labour Law & Policy Journal.*

Myles, J., (eds). *Why We Need a New Welfare State* (Oxford, Oxford University Press, 2002).

Ross, G. and Martin, A., 'European Social Democracy and Monetary Integration' in Fishman, R. and Messina, A., (eds). *The Year of the Euro. The Cultural, Social and Political Import of Europe's Common Currency* (Notre Dame, University of Notre Dame Press, 2006).

Runkles-Pearson, P.K., 'The Changing Relations of Family and the Workplace: Extending Antidiscrimination Laws To Parents and No Parents Alike' (2002) 77 *NYUL Review.*

Santos Rodriguez-Garavito, B., *Law and Globalisation From Below. Towards a Cosmopolitan Legality* (Cambridge, Cambridge University Press, 2005).

Sciarra, S., 'Integration Through Courts: Article 177 as a Pre-Federal Device' in S. Sciarra (ed). *Labour Law in the Courts: National Judges and the European Court of Justice* (Oxford-Portland, Oregon, Hart Publishing, 2001).

– 'L'Evoluzione della Contratazione Collectiva. Apunti per una Comparazione nei Paesi dell' Union Europea' (2006) 4 *Rivista Italiana di Diritto del Lavoro.*

– *Modernization of Labour Law: a current European debate* (International Institute for Labour Studies, Geneva, 2007).

Scarponi, S., 'Introduzione: La Crisi della Sovranita Nazionales e le Transformazioni del Diritto del Lavoro' in S Scarponi, *Globalizzazione e Diritto del Lavoro. Il Ruolo degli Ordinamenti Sovranazionali* (Milano, Giuffrè Editore, 2001).

Schmitter, P.C., *How to Democratize the European Union and Why Bother?* (Oxford, Rowman &Little field Publishers, 2000).

Stone, K. 'Thinking and Doing – the Regulation of Worker's Capital in the United States' (2006) 4 *Socio-Economic Review.*

Williams, J.C., 'Beyond the Maternal Wall: Relief for Family Caregivers Who Are Discriminated against on the Job', 26 *Harvard Women's LJ.*

Wise, K., 'Caring for Our Parents in an Aging World: Sharing Public and Private Responsibility for the Elderly' (2002) 5 *NYUJ Legis.&Pub.Pol'y.*

Part II

Multilevel Governance Experiences on Employment Policies in a Cross-National Perspective

Chapter 5

The Reform of the Labour Market and of the Social Benefits for Unemployment in Germany

Maximilian Fuchs

1. INTRODUCTION

After the turn of the century Germany has undertaken far-reaching reforms in an attempt to improve the functioning of the labour market. I shall outline these reforms against the background of the employment guidelines which form part of the integrated guidelines for growth and jobs.[1] Main emphasis will be placed on those acts and provisions whose specific aim is the integration of the unemployed or of those who are threatened by unemployment. In other words, I will give an outline of the system of employment services and the system of economic benefits for the unemployed. But a few words have to be said on the reform of the labour law since it, too, has an impact on the labour market.

Guideline no. 21 requires the adaptation of employment legislation in order to promote flexibility combined with employment security, reviewing where necessary the different contractual and working time arrangements. In this context, the reforms concerning what is normally called atypical work figure most

1. C. Barnard, *EC Employment Law*, 3rd edn (Oxford, Oxford University Press, 2006), 118 *et seq.*

Roger Blanpain, Juan Pablo Landa, Brian Langille (eds), *Employment Policies and Multilevel Governance*, pp. 125–145.

prominently in Germany.[2] Part time, fixed term and agency work were put on a new legal basis. In a nutshell, the Act on Part Time Work 2001 brought as its most important element a subjective right for full time workers to pass to part-time work. Every kind of discrimination of part-time workers is banned.[3] With regard to fixed term contracts the new Act provides for a wide range of possibilities to make use of this kind of employment.[4] The legislator has decided for a mix of admissibility rules: on the one side fixed term contracts are admissible only in view of objective reasons laid down in the Act; and on the other side for a period of up to two years fixed term contracts are possible without objective justification. New enterprises are privileged insofar as they can hire workers within a time span of four years after starting up without any need of justification. The most intriguing alterations of the existing law have taken place in the area of agency work (temporary work). Nearly all former restrictions to this kind of employment have been abolished. The equality principle was introduced saying that temporary workers must be treated in the same way as workers in the user firm. But there are exceptions to this rule and in practice it is not the equality rule itself, but the exceptions to it which characterize the agency work sector.[5]

With regard to working conditions the legislator decided for the incorporation of the principle of equality of treatment of temporary workers and comparable workers in the user undertaking. The equality of treatment principle is protected by the law at two levels. Firstly equality of treatment grants the temporary worker an individual right. He can demand from the temporary work agency to be put on the same footing as comparable workers of the user firm. Secondly, another area of protection of the principle of equal treatment is given by the fact that the law created a link between authorization of an agency and the respect of this principle. This works as follows: Authorization will be refused when the applicant does not produce evidence for securing the principle. Afterwards, authorization can be withdrawn when the temporary work agency actually hires out workers without observing the principle. There are two exceptions to the equality rule, and I shall concentrate on the second one.

The second exception leads us into the area of collective agreements. The proposal for a EU directive on temporary work gives derogatory power to parties to collective agreements as long as an adequate level of protection is provided for temporary workers (*see* Article 5(3)). When in 2003 the German parliament reshaped the Act on Agency Work, it relied on this approach to address the

2. *See National Reform Program Germany 2005-2008, Implementation and Progress Report 2006* (15/8/2006), 37-38.
3. *See* M. Fuchs, 'Germany: Part Time Work – a Bone of Contention' in S. Sciarra *et al* (eds), *Employment Policy and the Regulation of Part-Time Work in the European Union. A Comparative Analysis* (Cambridge, Cambridge University Press, 2004), 121.
4. M. Fuchs, 'Germany' in B. Caruso and S. Sciarra (eds), *Flexibility and Security in Temporary Work: A Comparative and European Debate*, WP C.S.D.L.E. 'Massimo D'Antona'. INT – 56/2007, 28, available at <http://www.lex.unict.it/eurolabor/ricerca/wp/int/caruso_sciarra_n56-2007int.pdf>.
5. C. Weinkopf, *The Role of Temporary Agency Work in the German Employment Model*, Paper presented to the 26th Conference of the International Working Party On Labour Market Segmentation (Berlin, 8-10 Sep. 2005), 18.

problems of creating a workable framework for the relationship between temporary work agency and the worker. As a consequence, the Act allows derogations from the equality principle through collective agreements. And where the employer (temporary work agency) is not bound by a collective agreement due to a lack of affiliation to an employers' association, the contents of a collective agreement may apply because its contents, following a widely held practice, are deemed to be incorporated in full or in part into the individual contract of employment. This is clear evidence that with regard to agency work preference is given to the flexibility requirement.[6]

With a view to employment services and unemployment benefits (UBs) it is necessary to single out some of the most important messages contained in the guidelines which try to offer Member States coherent strategies to achieve the objectives set to overcome labour market weaknesses. This will allow us to evaluate the German system and to show to what extent European guidelines made an inroad into national legislation.

The programme the European legislator had in mind when addressing the unemployment problem is outlined in the preamble to Guideline no. 19:

> Facilitating access to employment for job seekers, preventing unemployment and ensuring that those who become unemployed remain closely attached to the labour market and increase their employability are essential to increase participation and combat social exclusion. This requires breaking down barriers to the labour market by assisting with effective job searching, facilitating access to training and other active labour market measures and ensuring that work pays, as well as removing unemployment, poverty and inactivity traps. Special attention should be paid to promoting the inclusion of disadvantaged people, including low skilled workers in the labour market, including for the expansion of social services and the social economy, as well as the development of new sources of jobs in response to collective needs. Combating discrimination, promoting access to employment for disabled people and integrating immigrants and minorities are particularly essential.

When we look at the realization of this programme we come across a series of elements which are linked to the shape of employment services and UBs. To call the attention upon a few of them I should point to what is said under the heading of 'improved adaptability of workers and enterprises', namely the need and support for transitions in occupational status, including training, self-employment, business creation and geographic mobility as well as addressing the issue of undeclared work. In the section 'increase investments in human capital through better education and skills' we read:

> Knowledge-based and service based economies require different skills from traditional industries; skills which also constantly need updating in the face of

6. K. Vitols, 'Reforming the German Labour Market: the Case of Temporary Agency Work' (2004), 8 *Competition & Change*, 375.

technological change and innovation. Workers, if they are to remain and progress in work, need to accumulate and renew skills regularly. The productivity of enterprises is dependent on building and maintaining a work force that can adapt to change.

Among the manifold steps to be taken in order to carry out these objectives it seems to be very important what is laid down in Guideline no. 24 by underlining the easing and diversifying access for all to education, training and knowledge by means of working time organization, family support services, vocational guidance and, if appropriate, new forms of cost sharing. Against this background we should now understand and evaluate the German system of employment services and UBs.

2. PROMOTION OF EMPLOYMENT

Over the years Germany had developed an extensive system of measures to reintegrate the unemployed into the labour market.[7] Despite this a new qualitative strategy has asserted itself in the last ten years focussing on a policy of active labour market measures. To a certain extent it is comparable to the new policy of the United Kingdom that has been implemented under Blair's government, the so-called 'New Deal'. The motto of the new strategy in Germany is 'promote and push' (*Fordern und Fördern*), that is, while, on the one hand, the unemployed person shall receive extensive support in finding a new job, on the other great effort is demanded of him, which entails sanctions in the case of non performance. The third Book of the Social Code (SGB III) is the legal basis for the individual measures.

2.1. Placement Services

Originally the so-called Federal Employment Agency (FEA) had the monopoly in placing unemployed persons in jobs. In the wake of the European Court of Justice's decision in the case Höfner/Makrotron,[8] this monopoly was revoked as not being in line with EU competition law. This opened the way for placement services being carried out by private persons or agencies. All such bodies require is approval by the FEA, such approval depending on the reliability of the private employment agency.[9]

The FEA and its regional authorities require exact data concerning the situation on the labour market if they are to provide effective employment services.

7. K-P. Wagner, 'Arbeitsförderung' in B. von Maydell and F. Ruland (eds), *Sozialrechtshandbuch*, 3rd edn (Baden-Baden, Nomos, 2003), 1173 *et seq.*; W. Eicher, in W. Spellbrink and W. Eicher (eds), *Kasseler Handbuch des Arbeitsförderungsrechts* (München, C.H. Beck, 2003), 2-14.
8. Case C-41/90, Höfner/Macroton, (1991) ECR I-01979.
9. M. Fuchs 'Vor §§ 292-301' in Gagel (ed.), *Sozialgesetzbuch III – Arbeitsförderung* (München, C.H. Beck, 2007), 7; B. Stindt, *Private Arbeitsvermittlung – Effizienzsteigerung für den Arbeitsmarkt durch mehr Kooperation und Wettbewerb* (Baden-Baden, Nomos, 2005).

To this end and to be in a position to follow the developments on the labour market the FEA has set up its own research institute, The Institute for Labour Market and Employment Research. This furnishes the FEA with accurate data, which can be used both for placing unemployed persons in jobs as well as for forming the basis of specific promotional measures.

2.2. Services Provided for the Benefit of the Unemployed and the Employed by the Promotion of Employment

2.2.1. Support in the Form of Consultation and Placement

Unemployed persons or such employed persons who are in danger of losing their jobs are in need of manifold consultations as well as financial support in the course of job placement. For this reason the law provides financial support for the compilation and postal expenses of job application documents (application expenses up to a maximum of EUR 260 per annum). In addition, travelling expenses incurred in connection with job interviews are reimbursed.

In order to improve the chances of unemployed persons, or such employed persons who are in danger of losing their jobs, the law has provided for measures that include aptitude tests and training schemes. Aptitude tests are intended to ascertain the knowledge and skills, the capabilities and career potential of those concerned in order to determine the professional activity for which they are best suited. Training schemes include not only training in job applications and consultation concerning the possibilities of job seeking, but most especially the teaching of knowledge and skills that facilitate the chances of finding a job. These schemes usually last for a minimum of four and a maximum of eight weeks. Expenses incurred, such as course and examination fees, travelling expenses and even child-care expenses for the unemployed person of up to EUR 130 per child monthly are paid by the FEA. German law meets the requirements of Guideline no. 19 'which asks for active and preventive labour market measures including early identification of needs, job search assistance, guidance and training as part of personalized action plans'.

Guideline no. 21 puts emphasis on geographic mobility. German law makes a contribution to this requirement with the so-called mobility programme. Very often it is only possible for an unemployed person to find a job within a certain distance from his/her place of residence. The law has provided for the promotion of mobility in finding jobs further afield with a whole bundle of benefits such as aid for living expenses until the first payment is received, payment of travelling expenses for entrance to the job and daily commuting to and from the place of work. If the need for an additional separate household is established, then a separation allowance is granted. To promote a move of the person concerned and his/her family, there is a removal allowance.

A special kind of job placement is carried out by so-called Personal Service Agencies (PSA). This instrument of labour market integration is a product of the

Hartz reform.[10] The way it works is like this:[11] A private agency installs a personal service agency as prescribed by the law. This means it takes on unemployed persons registered with the FEA with the aim of placing them in private enterprises. It is in fact a kind of temporary work. In a contract concluded between the FEA and the private agency, the latter undertakes to hire out the employee in temporary employment and in times when this is not possible to give the employee advanced training to enhance his/her qualifications. The agency receives a performance related remuneration as follows: in the first three months a so-called flat basic rate of EUR 1100 is paid, this then decreases to 70% and to 50% from the seventh to the ninth month. 200% of the flat basic rate is paid if the unemployed person is contracted out to a user undertaking or other employer procured by the PSA within the first three months. This goes down to 150% for months four to six and down again to 100% after six months.

2.2.2. Promotion of Self-Employment

In addition to the improvement of employability, the four aims of the EU Guidelines for Growth and Jobs and Guideline no. 21 include encouraging adaptability in businesses and their employees, strengthening policies for equal opportunities and the development of entrepreneurship. The aim of the EU is a continuous increase in the number of self-employed entrepreneurs. For this reason any system of protection against the risk of unemployment must set its sights not only on the placing of employees in jobs, but also on the prospects offered by self-employment. The so-called business creation allowance[12] fulfils this function.[13] It serves to secure livelihood and social security during the time after setting up a business. The granting of this benefit requires the previous existence of a claim to financial benefits in accordance with SGB III up until the start of self-employment or that a work creation scheme had been carried out. A claim to UBs must have existed for at least ninety days before the start of self-employment. Moreover, the self-employed person must prove that he/she has the necessary knowledge and skills to carry out the self-employed activity. In addition, a competent body (e.g., Chamber of Commerce and Industry, Chamber of Trade or other trade related chambers) must assess the intended business start up and approve its feasibility. These measures assure the interests of the FEA. The intention is to prevent anyone

10. M. Knuth, *Implementing the New Basic Allowance for Job Seekers in Germany*, Discussion paper (17/18 Apr. 2007), 2, available at <http://pdf.mutual-learning-employment.net/pdf/DE%2007/discussionpaper_DE_07.pdf.>.
11. P. Hartz *et al, Moderne Dienstleistungen am Arbeitsmarkt*, Bericht der Kommission (2003), 29.
12. Concerning the business creation allowance in general: <www.arbeitsagentur.de/nn_26400/Navigation/zentral/Buerger/Hilfen/Existenzgruendung/Existenzgruendung-Nav.html>.
13. *Bericht 2005 der Bundesregierung zur Wirksamkeit moderner Dienstleistungen am Arbeitsmarkt*, BT-Drs. 16/505; *Die Wirksamkeit moderner Dienstleistungen am Arbeitsmarkt, Bericht 2006 des Bundesministeriums für Arbeit und Soziales zur Wirkung der Umsetzung der Vorschläge der Kommission Moderne Dienstleistungen am Arbeitsmarkt (ohne Grundsicherung für Arbeitsuchende)*, available at <www.bildungsverband-online.de/hartz-bericht-erlaeuterungen.pdf>.

from taking up a kind of formal self-employment that in fact has no prospect of economic success.

If all requirements are fulfilled the business creation allowance is paid in two steps. An allowance amounting to the last UB received plus EUR 300 a month as a contribution to social security for a period of nine months. EUR 300 a month as a contribution to social security can be granted for a further six months if an intensive business activity and full time occupation is proved.

2.2.3. Measures for the Promotion of Professional Qualification

Measures to promote professional qualification serve to a great extent the aim of the promotion of employment via active employment policies to prevent or even reduce unemployment. They facilitate enhanced professional mobility, make professional development easier and contribute to better adaptation to changing economic structures. The law distinguishes between occupational training and advanced occupational training in these programmes.[14] Occupational training concerns a first professional qualification. Occupational training is eligible for benefits if carried out by an institute recognized and approved by the Occupational Training Act. However, the benefits are only granted if the trainee lives away from his/her parents or a parent and if the training institute cannot be reached within reasonable time from the home of the parents or parent. The benefits include a financial contribution to the costs of upkeep as well as accommodation, travelling expenses and the training fees (course fees etc.). This programme is, however, income related. The income of the trainee, his/her spouse and his/her parents is taken into consideration in compliance with a rating scale that is exactly defined in the Act.

Advanced training is concerned with programmes that tie in with already existing professional knowledge, skills and capabilities. Pursuant to the legal wording, the promotional measures for advanced occupational training shall be granted if the advanced training is necessary for the professional integration of the applicant in the case of unemployment, to prevent an imminent job loss or where the lack of a professional qualification justifies the necessity of the advanced training. The same is true here for the state aided costs as is the case with occupational training. An additional payment of EUR 130 per month and child is granted for childcare.

The integrated guidelines continuously stress that employment services should pay particular attention to the inclusion of disadvantaged people. Where handicapped persons are concerned, the Act has a separate section providing extensive promotional possibilities for the integration of handicapped persons into the working world.[15] Another disadvantaged group that has problems with integration into the labour market are unemployed persons that have reached the

14. W. iewald in Spellbrink and W. Eicher (eds), *Kasseler Handbuch des Arbeitsförderungsrechts* (München, C.H. Beck, 2003), 106.
15. A. Bauer and J. Bungart, *et al.*, 'Berufliche Teilhabe für Menschen mit Behinderungen – ein Positionspapier' (2007), 58 *TuP*, 74.

age of 50.[16] Germany has introduced a whole series of provisions to improve the situation of this group. In so doing it has not always kept to the path that accords to European legislation, if one considers the Mangold case,[17] for example. There is one promotional instrument that is of interest in this connection. Unemployed persons over the age of 50 who are claiming UBs receive a monetary incentive if they take up new employment. This monetary benefit amounts to 50% of the difference between the net income earned before he/she became unemployed and the net income in the new job. The intention behind this regulation is to provide an incentive for the persons concerned to perhaps accept a lower paid position.

2.3. Employer Benefits

There is whole section given over to employer benefits in the SGB III. This is not, however, concerned with subsidies aimed at the economic safeguarding of the company. The focus here is rather more on the creation and safeguarding of jobs. The benefits are in fact subsidies towards labour costs. They are intended as an incentive for the employer to take on new employees in need of support and should help to minimize any risk that this might involve, or even supposedly involve, for the employer.

As a basic principle the Act dictates that in order to integrate employees that have difficulties of various kinds in being integrated into the labour market, employers taking on such persons shall receive a subsidy towards the wages if the difficulties derive from circumstances linked with the employee's own person.[18] For this reason the amount and the length of the benefit depends on the degree of the employee's reduced performance and the individual requirements necessary for integration. If these requirements are fulfilled, the employer is entitled to a so-called integration subsidy. The employee should receive a professional qualification as a result of on the job training. On principle the FEA will assume 50% of the wage eligible for allowance for a period of twelve months. In the case of the severely handicapped or other handicapped persons the benefit can even go up to 70% for a period of up to twenty-four months.

As already mentioned, the development of entrepreneurship is an important aim of European employment policy. The so-called employment subsidy for start up companies is of particular interest in this connection. Employers that have been self employed for not more than two years can receive a subsidy for a newly created job if this is offered as permanent employment to an unemployed person receiving benefits. This requires that the employee had been receiving unemployment or similar benefits for in total at least three months immediately before he/she is hired and that he/she cannot be integrated into the labour market, or not permanently so, without this benefit and that the employer has no more than five employees.

16. M. Kossens, 'Maßnahmen für ältere Arbeitnehmer' (2007), 62 *AuA*, 214.
17. Case C-144/04, Mangold, (2005) ECR 1-9981.
18. H.A. Köhler, 'Leistungen der Arbeitsförderung an Arbeitgeber' (2002), 40 *DStR*, 1533.

The employment subsidy can be paid for a maximum of two employees at the same time. The employment subsidy amounts to 50% of the wage eligible for allowance for a period of maximum twelve months.

Guideline no. 23 outlines that knowledge-based and service-based economies require different skills from traditional industries; skills, which also constantly need updating in the face of technological change and innovation. Workers, if they are to remain and progress in work, need to accumulate and renew skills regularly. The productivity of enterprises is dependent on building and maintaining a workforce that can adapt to change. Against this background the German law contains an interesting provision on promoting so called job rotation. Job rotation is understood as the release of one employee for reasons of advanced occupational training with the simultaneous employment of another employee to stand in for the time in question. The employer receives support in the form of a subsidy towards the wages of the newly hired stand in employee. The intention here is provide the chance of advanced occupational training by releasing employed persons for this purpose, while at the same time enhancing the chances of unemployed persons finding employment by providing them with a kind of probational employment in the form of temporary stand in jobs. In this case the employment subsidy is granted for the period of the stand in employment to the amount of at least 50% and maximum 100% of the wage involved. The period of the benefit for a stand in one and the same company must not exceed twelve months.

2.4. Promotion of Job Creation Programmes

This instrument for the promotion of employment is concerned with the creation of jobs on the so-called secondary labour market.[19] This term implies that, in addition to the general (primary) labour market, there are jobs whose performance is in the public interest but that cannot be fulfilled on a purely economic and commercial basis. This is what is referred to in Guideline no. 18 where we read that special attention should be paid to the expansion of social services and the social economy, as well as the development of new sources of jobs in response to collective needs. It is for this reason that requirements for benefits also follow along these lines of thought. The Act prescribes that the agencies involved in job creation measures for the employment of job seekers referred to them by the FEA shall receive subsidies, if the measures serve to reduce unemployment and allow unemployed persons the chance of employment, at least temporarily, in order to receive or renew employability and if the measures encompass additional jobs that are in the public interest and there is no potential threat to the economy as a result of the promotion, in particular if these measures are effected in times of high unemployment in the

19. Bieback in Gagel, *Sozialgesetzbuch III – Arbeitsförderung* (München, C.H. Beck, 2007), 40-41; M.Knapp, *Vom zweiten auf den ersten Arbeitsmarkt – Der Erfolg aktiver arbeitsmarktpolitischer Maßnahmen* (Wiesbaden, Dt. Universitätsverlag, 2005).

problem areas of the regional and occupational labour market sectors. Jobs are considered to be additional if they could not be performed, or not on this scale or only at a latter date, without this subsidy. Just a glance at these restrictive promotional requirements is enough to *see* that the lawmaker places great importance on the fact that the job creation programmes do not interfere with the primary labour market. A few practical examples shall serve to clarify the nature of such jobs. Environmental measures taken by a local authority, maintenance of a castle as an historical monument, the operation of an environmentally friendly telephone and the like were all approved as being in the public interest. The promotion takes the form of a flat rate subsidization of wage costs. The subsidy amounts to EUR 1300 for jobs that normally require a university or college qualification, EUR 1100 if a skilled trade qualification is required and EUR 900 otherwise.

2.5. Transfer Benefits

The European Commission has continuously referred to the necessity of restructuring processes within enterprises. Thereby it simultaneously stressed the need for due regard for the principles of employment security for the employee. Thus in Guideline no. 21 the Council calls for a better anticipation and positive management of change, including economic restructuring, so as to minimize their social costs and facilitate adaptation. In Germany, too, restructuring has been taking place in a great number of enterprises for many years; a trend that has had drastic consequences for the employees involved. The most recent significant, and here one is forced to say, scandal, was the closure of the mobile phone manufacturer BenQ that led to closure of the factory and resulted in 3000 job losses. For a long time now employment promotion legislation has been prepared for such situations.[20] In addition to the demands made under labour law in such circumstances, such as the involvement of works councils in setting up so-called redundancy programmes, employment promotion legislation wishes to make an accompanying contribution to the prevention of unemployment. The transfer benefits serve this purpose. The requirements and form that these benefits take are extremely complicated. At this place it is impossible to give a detailed account of the legal regulation here. It must suffice to say that in cases of major restructuring measures that would have led to employees losing their jobs, a so-called employment and qualification agency was often established to take on workers that were to be made redundant, a measure intended to prevent such a situation from arising. The role of such employment and qualification agencies is to find jobs for the employees in other companies, to contract them out or to advance their professional qualification. In times when a placement or contracting out is not possible, a so-called short time compensation provided for in the Act serves to secure the economic upkeep of

20. W. Spellbrink, 'Das Einstiegsgeld nach § 29 SGB II – oder von den Aporien moderner Gesetzgebung' (2005), 14 NZS 231 *et seq.*

the employee concerned. Additional financial support comes from the insolvency estate of the enterprise and from the European Social Fund.

3. ECONOMIC BENEFITS

3.1. UNEMPLOYMENT BENEFIT

Income support for the unemployed was traditionally provided for by two different schemes: UB as part of social insurance and unemployment assistance which is means-tested. Finally, for those unemployed who fell neither under the first nor the second type social assistance was awarded. The first type is the subject matter of this section. The second type will be treated next. Before outlining the UB scheme I should point out some features which characterize the present regulation and which give answers to the question of the extent to which our law on UB corresponds to what is expected by the Integrated Guidelines when it comes to shaping UB legislation in such a way as to meet employment objectives.[21] Obviously, in the first regard UB serves the interests of the insured persons. The benefit secures the livelihood of the applicant during the period of unemployment. In this regard, it does what a system of solidarity among the insured should bring about. But alongside the provisions, which reflect the solidarity in favour of the unemployed, we encounter provisions which put first the interests of the insurance carrier vis-à-vis the applicant in order to safeguard the sound functioning of the insurance operation. It is well known that for many years' systems of unemployment insurance have been criticized. Roughly speaking, critics argue that UB is a disincentive to work since it destroys or at least diminishes motivation to seek and find a new job. And this position has gained in importance in Germany. The debate was not restricted to academic circles. On the contrary, during the last decade the lawmaking bodies made it their philosophy.[22] As a consequence and, as we shall *see* later on, the favoured policy was to design restrictions intended to make the unemployed compete effectively for jobs, to make access to UB more difficult and to avoid payments at levels which mean that the unemployed may find discouraging to accept low paid jobs. In a nutshell, in the following study of the rules and principles governing UB we shall meet two strands of regulation: one which aims at safeguarding the economic maintenance of the recipient and another which tries to motivate people to go back to work thereby making a contribution to a sound economic basis of the insurance budget.

---

21. M. Knuth, *Implementing the New Basic Allowance for Job Seekers in Germany*, Discussion paper (17/18 Apr. 2007) 2, available at <http://pdf.mutual-learning-employment.net/pdf/DE%2007/discussionpaper_DE_07.pdf.>.
22. W. Spellbrink, 'Das Einstiegsgeld nach § 29 SGB II – oder von den Aporien moderner Gesetzgebung' (2005), 14 NZS 231 *et seq.*

3.1.1. Benefit Entitlement

In principle, there are three conditions for entitlement:[23]

(1) being unemployed;
(2) registering with the FEA; and
(3) completion of the qualifying period.

3.1.1.1. Unemployment

This consists of three elements:

(1) Lack of employment relation.
(2) Actively seeking work.
(3) Availability for work.

Pursuant to the wording of the SGB III the claimant has to use every possibility for getting a job. The Act provides for a (non-exhaustive) list of steps to be taken in the search for employment:

(a) follow a so-called integration agreement concluded with the FEA;
(b) use placement offers by the FEA and third parties;
(c) use the whole range of information sources offered by the FEA.

Availability for work is defined by law as the willingness to work at least fifteen hours a week. According to the legal wording, work means reasonable (*zumutbare*) work. What constitutes reasonable is set down in detail. The parameters to be taken into consideration are:

(i) work to be done must comply with statutory law, collective agreements, or health or safety regulations;
(ii) restrictions placed by the claimant on the rate of pay and the location of a job are allowed only within the following limits:
   - Work for which earnings are lower than 20% of his/her former income can be refused during the first three months of unemployment. In the following four months, the level is 30% and beginning with the seventh month of unemployment every job which is paid at least at the rate of the UB has to be accepted.
   - With regard to commuting times, what is expected from the recipient of UB is dependent on the relationship between daily working hours and commuting times: the recipient is not required to commute longer than two and an half hours upon a working time of more than six hours a day and two hours related to a workload of less than six hours per day. A duty to move outside of the geographical area for which commuting can be required arises in principle only after three months of

23. § 118 I SGB III.

unemployment, save unless it is clear from the beginning of the unemployment that there are no prospects of finding a job within this time frame.

3.1.1.2. Registering with the FEA

Registering is not only a mere formality. Through registration a narrow link is created between the FEA and the unemployed person which opens up a range of duties on the part of the unemployed person. For example, he or she has to make sure that he/she can be contacted quickly and easily, and any long absence from home has to be communicated to the FEA. In other words, the continuous presence of the unemployed is seen as a necessary prerequisite for missing no opportunity to act quickly on incoming job offers.

3.1.1.3. Completion of the Qualifying Period

Similarly to pensions, UB follows the insurance logic. As a consequence, it is necessary to comply with contribution conditions. The Act requires a twelve month insured employment relation within the two years preceding the occurrence of unemployment.

3.1.2. Period of Disqualification from Benefit

The contents of the current law show clear evidence of a tightening up of the entitlement conditions for UB. So far, we have spoken of rules which require discipline from the unemployed person after the granting of UB. But the duty to behave in a responsible way does not begin at this stage, it extends to periods before the occurrence of unemployment. Therefore claimants are disqualified from benefits in circumstances where they were responsible for the loss of their employment. This is a measure typical of insurance principles according to which an insured person must avoid behaviour which helps the risk insured to materialize. Otherwise, sanctions will follow to protect the interests of the insurance community.

As a rule the law states that the claimant is disentitled for a fixed period if he behaves in a manner contrary to the interests of the insurance (*sich versicherungswidrig verhält* is the legal wording) without good cause. The Act lists the grounds which constitute adverse behaviour exhaustively:

(1) voluntary termination of the employment relation;
(2) dismissal caused by misconduct;
(3) refusal to take reasonable work proposed by the FEA or to present himself/herself acceptably to an employer, provided that the claimant has been informed beforehand about the legal consequences of his/her behaviour;
(4) insufficient search for work;
(5) refusal to take part in training measures or the giving up such a measure.

The imposition of a disqualifying period is subject to the proviso that the claimant is not able to establish good cause (the burden of proof is on the claimant). The consistent case law of the Federal Social Court construes the term 'good cause' very narrowly. Its interpretation requires balancing the interests of the claimant against those of all other contributors to the insurance pool. In principle the reasons for the claimant's motives must be employment related and be of such a nature that they outweigh insurance necessities. In certain well-defined circumstances the courts have acknowledged overwhelming family interests as good cause.

The usual disqualifying period is twelve weeks. But there are exceptions to this rule. A relevant factor which may lead to the reduction of the full disqualifying period is, among others, the length of time the employment relation or the training measure was likely to have lasted. The reduction is graduated from twelve to six to a minimum of three weeks.

3.1.3. Amount and Duration of UB

UB is earnings related. Therefore, the first step in calculating the benefit is the assessment of the earnings. The daily gross earnings less income tax, social insurance contributions and the so-called solidarity contribution (in favour of the *Länder* of the former German Democratic Republic) are taken into consideration.

UB is a fixed percentage of the net earnings calculated in this way. The percentage is conditional upon the family situation of the claimant. The basic rate is 60%. It is 67% if he or she has a child who falls under the tax code.

The duration of payment of UB is dependent upon two factors:

(1) the length of the preceding employment relation;
(2) the age of the claimant.

Table 5.1 (which is taken from the Act) gives the duration of UBs (in months) as a result of both the duration of employment (in months) preceding unemployment and the minimum age (in years) of the unemployed:

Table 5.1. Duration of Unemployment Benefits

Employment (months)	*Minimum age (years)*	*Benefits (months)*
12	-	6
16	-	8
20	-	10
24	-	12
30	55	15
36	55	18
48	58	24

3.2. The Unification of Unemployment Assistance and Social Assistance for the Unemployed

As of 1 January 2005, the former separation of the benefit systems for unemployment assistance and social assistance for the unemployed was relinquished. There is now only one uniform basic protection for the unemployed, which is incorporated in the second Book of the Social Code (SGB II). This reform derives from proposals submitted by the Hartz Commission.[24] The numerous disadvantages of retaining two different schemes for the unemployed (outside of the insurance schemes) were emphasized in these proposals. Criticism was directed primarily against the additional expenses involved in this division and the resulting costs for the public authorities. Moreover, no sense could be seen in granting benefits based on different calculations and in differing amounts for one and the same need in the case of unemployment. Perhaps the most serious complaint was directed against the insufficient competence of local authorities when it came to integrating unemployed persons successfully into the labour market. The main argument here was that the local authorities usually restricted their focus to local labour markets or else they did not undertake any efforts to place people in jobs, or rather did not do so effectively. Instead, they concentrated on the payment of the financial benefits.

The lawmaker fell into line with the criticism submitted by the Hartz Commission. So it created a uniform basic security system for all those unemployed persons that had no right to UBs, that is, no insurance benefits. Whereby it placed competence for the provision of the benefits in the hands of the FEA, which upholds employment offices in the individual federal states (*Länder*) each one responsible for specific geographic areas. However, the reform did leave certain competences in the hands of the local institutions, competencies that are of considerable importance. I will come back to this in more detail later. When mapping out the benefits, the lawmaker was anxious to incorporate those elements from the existing separate systems that it regarded as the most advantageous for the successful integration of the unemployed into the labour market. To put it simply, it fell back on the previous law of social assistance with regard to the financial security of the unemployed and on the legal provisions of employment benefits and services for the unemployment insurance system in the case of integration into the labour market.

3.2.1. Benefits (Overview)

The new scheme provides for two types of benefits:[25]

(1) Employment services and measures (support for people in moving from receiving benefits to obtaining employment).
(2) Economic benefits (aimed at the maintenance of the applicant and his family).

24. P. Hartz *et al*, *Moderne Dienstleistungen am Arbeitsmarkt*, Bericht der Kommission (2003).
25. M. Fuchs and U. Preis, *Sozialversicherungsrecht*, (Köln, Dr. Otto Schmidt, 2005), 870.

3.2.2. Benefit Entitlement

The scheme encompasses people in the age bracket from 16-65 years of age. In order to be eligible for benefits they must be:

(1) capable of work;
(2) in need of help.

Capable of work is understood as anyone who is not by reason of disease or disablement prevented for a foreseeable time from performing any occupation for at least three hours per day on the usual terms of the general labour market. This legal definition is parallel to that under the Act on Pensions (which provides for invalidity allowances).

People in need of help are those who are not able to maintain themselves through the performance of reasonable work, or through their own personal income or capital; or cannot draw on other resources such as financial support from relatives or other social benefits.

3.2.3. Employment Services and Measures

The new Act sets as its main objective caring for jobseekers in a comprehensive way in order to bring them back into work. The first step in this direction is to entrust the unemployed person to a special case manager who is responsible for identifying the most appropriate strategy to be taken to find work and for ensuring adequate monitoring of the applicant's efforts. To this purpose a jobseeker's agreement has to be concluded between him/her and the FEA at the beginning of the search process, an agreement in which all the benefits awarded to the jobseeker are laid down on the one hand and all the steps to be taken in order to find work on the other. It is a fixed term agreement for a period of six months. On the basis of this agreement the jobseeker has the right or, as the case may be, the duty to make use of any kind of employment service offered by the case manager. The spectre of services may range from job offers to placements on a compulsory training scheme or employment programme. In other words jobseekers who fall under the SGB II scheme are placed on the same footing as the unemployed who draw on the UB (under the insurance scheme).

Beyond the use of these common services the SGB II expects stronger commitments from the jobseeker. The case manager may ask him to take specific activities which are not carried out by businesses, but which are in the general interest. They are often called EUR 1 or EUR 2 jobs because the jobseeker gets EUR 1 or EUR 2 per hour as a supplement to his/her economic benefit (for this *see* below). This small amount of money is not considered to be a consideration for the work performance, but as a modest compensation for additional costs incurred by the jobseeker in carrying out these activities. Here again we find clear references to the work to welfare strategy chosen by the Hartz Commission and in its wake by the lawmaking bodies. The logic behind it runs along the lines that the state has a duty to provide assistance to the unemployed through economic benefits and vocational training to facilitate a return to employment but, as a consequence, a recipient has a reciprocal duty to make the most of this assistance risking sanctions if he/she should refuse to do so.

To further stimulate the jobseeker to take employment, the Act grants – upon discretion of the FEA – a cash payment of approximately EUR 180 a month which can be awarded for up to twenty-four months (back to work bonus!).

Beside these traditional employment measures the Act includes benefits like:

(1) care for underage children or disabled persons;
(2) debt counselling;
(3) drug counselling;
(4) psychosocial care.

When I said above that the reform combined elements of the former separated schemes these three measures have their origin in the social assistance activities of local authorities. Since many unemployed persons face problems, which result from a high debt burden or drug addiction and which most frequently destroy that indispensable life basis necessary for taking up employment, help of this kind is badly needed to overcome difficulties. The same is true for child care (especially by single parents) or care for handicapped family members which may prevent persons from performing work.

3.2.4. Economic Benefits

The main cash payment is called unemployment benefit II (II expresses the difference to the unemployment benefit, so to say unemployment benefit I under the insurance scheme). UB II is composed of various elements:

(1) flat rate allowance: EUR 345;
(2) housing benefits (to cover the actual rent and the actual heating costs);
(3) contributions to the national health, care and pension schemes;
(4) specific supplements for specific needs (e.g., pregnancy, special food requirements, etc.).

From this list one can gather that the legislation secures elementary maintenance and provides for social security protection. Obviously the law supplements the aforementioned payments if the recipient lives with his family or other dependants (in a 'community of need' as the law puts it). The amount of payments for these other persons in need is dependent on their age.

3.2.5. Assessment of Income and Capital

The benefit entitlement laid down in the Act shows that economic benefits are means-tested. For lack of space, I cannot go into great detail of the provisions on the assessment of income and capital. It should be noted that these provisions were one of the reasons why the new Act was so heavily attacked, both during parliamentary discussion and after the Act was passed, mainly by trade unions, social rights groups and welfare organizations. Contrary to the former rules, the newly introduced scheme takes over the more rigid rules of social assistance. That means nearly every kind of income or capital is taken into consideration, disregard of financial assets is very restricted. This approach mirrors the general logic of the new scheme according to which incentives have to be created in order to bring people back into employment. A well known argument has it that too high jobseekers' allowances are disincentives to work. If benefits are too generous the unemployed prefer passive reception of money to remunerated jobs.

One important exception in which disregard of income takes place has to be underlined. As we have seen the fight against undeclared work is one of the elements which form part of the employment objectives formulated by the Integrated Guidelines. Among the manifold instruments to discourage undeclared work, one is to render it, at least partially, legal. The provision in the SGB II whereby a certain amount of income earned through dependent or self employed work is considered as legally irrelevant for the purposes of calculating the unemployment benefit II must be seen in this context. More precisely income from work up to EUR 100 is not taken into consideration, a further 20% of income exceeding EUR 100 but lower than EUR 800 is disregarded as well as a 10% portion of an income exceeding EUR 800 but lower than EUR 1100.

3.2.6. Sanctions

As a consequence of the work to welfare strategy or in its German version of the logic of *Fördern und Fordern* sanctions are the necessary corollary to the granting of benefits. The jobseeker receiving benefits under the SGB II scheme who is not ready to enter into a jobseeker's agreement, or does not abide by the duties set down in it, or refuses to take a job offered (including doing a EUR 1 job) is subject to reduction of benefits by 30%. Further violations lead to an additional reduction of 20%.

3.2.7. Competence for the Provision of Benefits

It has already been mentioned above that the law that came into force on 1 January 2005 had the intention of disposing of the hitherto different competencies for the provision of benefits to the unemployed (those not receiving unemployment benefit I) and creating one single competent body instead.[26] This competency was put into the hands of the FEA. It was, however, ruled that this general competency of the FEA was not in fact to be absolute.

What effect has the reform had? The SGB II is a federal law and thus regulates the requirements and contents of the benefits provided for the unemployed on a common national basis. By giving the basic competence to the FEA, the new law

26. T. Voelzke, 'Aktuelles aus dem Sozialrecht – Die Zusammenführung von Arbeitslosenhilfe und Sozialhilfe', *jurisPR-SozR* 2/2003 Anm. 4.

had intended to create an administrative body for the execution of the law that would be valid for the federation as a whole. Had the lawmaker implemented this principle consistently, it would have been forced to abolish the former activities and models for the qualification and placement of the unemployed into employment that had hitherto been installed and carried out by the local authorities (townships and counties). Indeed that was the original intention of the federal lawmaker. However, as the representation of the *Länder* (states) was required by both constitutional law and the *Bundesrat* (Federal Council) for the passing of the law, it was not possible to realize these plans. The *Länder* insisted on retaining substantial competence in this field.

What emerged was the following compromise. The FEA has a general competence. But competence is given to the local authorities for specific benefits: the care of underage children or disabled persons, debt and drug counselling, psychosocial care and the back to work bonus. Moreover, costs for rent and heating and specific supplements (e.g., pregnancy) are compensated on a local level.[27] Just looking at these benefits renders it immediately clear why they were placed under the competence of the local authorities. Not only tradition favoured this solution (as these fields had always been dealt with on a communal level), but also the many years of experience that had been gained here and where many successful models and projects had been created. It would probably have been impossible, or at least have taken a long time, for the FEA and its regional authorities to be in a position to deal with these tasks effectively. But most especially leaving these tasks in the hands of the previous competent bodies is in the interest of the persons concerned. Basically communal authorities inspire more trust in such delicate matters, they are less anonymous and easier to reach than the governmental administration of the FEA. The intention of the law with its regulation of competency was to realize the principle of what is designated as 'grassroots politics'. The consideration that the local bodies could judge most expediently the question as to which rented accommodation should be deemed adequate and which entailing costs could be assumed was decisive as far as the question of assuming the costs for rent and heating is concerned.

Apart from legally establishing partial division of competence, the law also aims at promoting cooperation between the FEA authorities and local bodies with a series of institutions and mechanisms. The most important institutions in this connection are so called partnerships. The law stipulates here as follows. For the purposes of a coordinated and effective performance of their tasks the FEA and the local authorities establish through special contracts partnerships within the job centres (job centres are specific units of the regional offices of the FEA whose task is to serve as a meeting point (*Anlaufstelle*) for anybody seeking a job or an apprenticeship). Once such a contract for establishing a partnership is established,

27. It should be noted that the Constitutional Court in 2007 declared this division of competence unconstitutional, because it violates the rules on the division of power between the federal state and the Länder, *see* decision of 20 Dec. 2007, 2 BvR 2433/04, NZS 2008, 198. As a consequence the legislature has to provide a new model until the end of 2010.

the responsibility for providing all benefits passes to this partnership. The idea behind creating such partnerships is clear. The intention is to bundle the expertise of the FEA and the partnerships with regard to the care and placement of the unemployed in order to facilitate a particularly effective and successful fulfilment of the tasks.

Attention should be given to one final point, the so-called Experimental Clause, which was incorporated into the new law. Divergent from the competence of the FEA, the Federal Ministry of Labour and Social Affairs can, within the scope of the experiment, transfer competences to the local authorities. In particular, the experiment is directed towards alternative models for the integration of job seekers in competition with the integration measures of the agencies of employment. This is most certainly an interesting experiment. FEA and local institutions shall compete in order to discern which works more successfully. For this reason the law obliges the ministry to simultaneously analyze the way in which the tasks are fulfilled by the approved local institutions as compared to the agencies of employment (so called effects analysis). In so doing the ministry has approved sixty-nine towns and counties in the whole of the federal territory for the fulfilment of this task. It is obliged to conduct the assessment of the experiences made on 31 December 2008 and to report upon them.

References

Barnard, C., *EC Employment Law*, 3rd edn (Oxford, Oxford University Press, 2006).

Bauer, A. and J. Bungart, *et al.* 'Berufliche Teilhabe für Menschen mit Behinderungen – ein Positionspapier' (2007), 58 *Theorie und Praxis der Sozialen Arbeit (TuP)*.

Bieback in Gagel, *Sozialgesetzbuch III – Arbeitsförderung* (München, C.H. Beck, 2007).

Eicher, W., in W. Spellbrink and W. Eicher (eds). *Kasseler Handbuch des Arbeitsförderungsrechts* (München, C.H. Beck, 2003).

Fuchs, M., 'Germany: Part-time Work – A Bone of Contention' in S. Sciarra *et al.* (eds). *Employment Policy and the Regulation of Part-Time Work in the European Union. A Comparative Analysis* (Cambridge, Cambridge University Press, 2004).

– 'Vor §§ 292-301' in Gagel, *Sozialgesetzbuch III – Arbeitsförderung* (München, C.H. Beck, 2007).

– 'Germany' in B. Caruso & S. Sciarra (eds). *Flexibility and Security in Temporary Work: A Comparative and European Debate*, WP C.S.D.L.E. 'Massimo D'Antona'. INT – 56/2007, 28, available at <http://www.lex.unict.it/eurolabor/ricerca/wp/int/caruso_sciarra_n56-2007int.pdf>.

Fuchs, M., and U. Preis, *Sozialversicherungsrecht* (Köln, Dr. Otto Schmidt, 2005).

Hartz, P., *et al*, *Moderne Dienstleistungen am Arbeitsmarkt*, Bericht der Kommission (2003).

Knapp, M., *Vom zweiten auf den ersten Arbeitsmarkt – Der Erfolg aktiver arbeitsmarktpolitischer Maßnahmen* (Wiesbaden, Dt. Universitätsverlag, 2005).

Knuth, M., *Implementing the new basic allowance for job seekers in Germany*, Discussion paper (17/18 Apr. 2007), available at <http://pdf.mutual-learning-employment.net/pdf/DE%2007/discussionpaper_DE_07.pdf>.

Köhler, H.A., 'Leistungen der Arbeitsförderung an Arbeitgeber' (2002) 40 *Deutsches Steuerrecht (DStR)*.

Kossens, M., 'Maßnahmen für ältere Arbeitnehmer' (2007) 62 *Arbeit und Arbeitsrecht (AuA)*.

W. iewald in Spellbrink & W. Eicher (eds). *Kasseler Handbuch des Arbeitsförderungsrechts* (München, C.H. Beck, 2003).

Spellbrink, W., 'Das Einstiegsgeld nach § 29 SGB II – oder von den Aporien moderner Gesetzgebung' (2005) 14 *Neue Zeitschrift für Sozialrecht* (NZS).

Stindt, B., *Private Arbeitsvermittlung – Effizienzsteigerung für den Arbeitsmarkt durch mehr Kooperation und Wettbewerb* (Baden-Baden, Nomos, 2005).

Vitols, K., 'Reforming the German Labour Market: the Case of Temporary Agency Work' (2004), 8 *Competition & Change*.

Voelzke, T., 'Aktuelles aus dem Sozialrecht – Die Zusammenführung von Arbeitslosenhilfe und Sozialhilfe', *jurisPR-SozR* 2/2003 Anm. 4.

Wagner, K-P., 'Arbeitsförderung' in B. von Maydell and F. Ruland (eds). *Sozialrechtshandbuch*, 3rd edn (Baden-Baden, Nomos, 2003).

Weinkopf, C., *The Role of Temporary Agency Work in the German Employment Model*, Paper presented to the 26th Conference of the International Working Party On Labour Market Segmentation (Berlin, 8-10 Sep., 2005).

Chapter 6

The Reform of the Public Employment Service in France: Modernization and New Governance Issues

Philippe Auvergnon & Philippe Martin

1. INTRODUCTION

The way the public employment service (PES) is organized in France is so complex and scattered that it seems to have no equivalent in Europe, as pointed out by the Marimbert Report.[1] Such a situation can be explained by both the social history and the cultural background of the institutions in charge of employment policies in France.

At this stage a brief description of the main institutions which are part of the French PES may be useful:

The state's services in charge of employment: the DGEFP (*Direction Générale de l'Emploi et de la Formation Professionnelle*) at national level. Placed under the authority of the Minister for Employment, it proposes guidelines for employment and the life long learning policies. The DGEFP is the administrative supervisor of the ANPE and AFPA. At regional and local level are the

1. J. Marimbert, *Le Rapprochement des Services de L'emploi: Rapport au Ministre des Affaires Sociales, du Travail et de la Solidarité*, Jan. 2004.

Roger Blanpain, Juan Pablo Landa, Brian Langille (eds), *Employment Policies and Multilevel Governance*, pp. 147–169.

DRTEFP and DDTEFP. Those are the 'external state's services' for employment and vocational training.[2]

The ANPE: the National Agency for Employment. This is a public institution whose main mission is job placement. The ANPE centralizes the vacancies and the job applications. It also produces statistics about the number of jobseekers. According to the legislation, the ANPE participates in the implementation of the employment policy which is defined by the public authorities. The local agencies are empowered to manage the jobseekers listing. They provide services of guidance in job seeking and of assistance for building occupational plans and help for the weakest jobseekers.

The UNEDIC: the national association for employment in trade and industry. Created in 1958, it is governed by a bipartite board composed by employers and by trade unions' representatives. At regional and local level, the ASSEDIC acts as an associated member of the UNEDIC. The UNEDIC manages the contributive unemployment benefits system created by the social partners through a national and intersectoral collective agreement approved by the Government. The ASSEDIC provides unemployment benefits; they also guide and help the unemployed to reintegrate the labour market. In the past, because of its autonomous nature, the UNEDIC was only 'associated' to the PES. It is now recognized as a main agent.

The AFPA: the Association for Adult Education. It is a private organization (association) created in 1949 and placed under the authority of the Ministry of Employment. The board of direction includes state/local authorities, employers and unions' representatives. The general mission of the AFPA is to provide vocational training programs for the adults. It specifically provides services of guidance, orientation, training, certification (qualifications and skills) and advice.

It could be said that, traditionally and culturally the French PES is:

(1) *Centralized.* As regards the public institutions – or the private ones placed under the authority of the Government, such as the AFPA – the role of the state remains prominent in France. The actions are framed, decided, mainly financed and controlled by the state. Employment policy is a national concern. Nevertheless, this does not exclude a local and 'territorial' approach of the

---

2. The DRTEFP acts under the authority of the '*Préfet de Région*'. Among various missions, it coordinates the regional PES, making sure that the programs for the reintegration of the long term unemployed and of young in difficulty are implemented, in collaboration with the ANPE, the AFPA, the DDTEFP and the social partners.

   The DDTEFP is usually known as the 'Labour Inspection'. It is also in charge of the implementation of some tools relating to employment policies. It acts in coordination with other members of the PES at local (departmental) level. The DDTEFP is empowered to control and to sanction the unemployed.

public action. The plans are governed at national level, but are generally coordinated at regional level. The 'regional PES' acts with the regional and local partners (public and private ones) which are put together by the '*Préfet de Région*' which is the state's representative at this level. As regards the organizations in charge of the unemployment benefit system, things are quite the same. The UNEDIC rules the whole system, and the territorial actions are mainly coordinated at regional level (regional organizations of the ASSEDIC).

(2) *Monopolistic*. The missions and objectives of the PES are basically conceived as missions of general interest which, in the French legal culture, excludes the possibility of acting in an open and competitive field. There is no business, no competition, and the institutions involved in the PES are not private companies. This can particularly be observed on the ground of the job placement which is the mission of the ANPE. The ANPE's activity has traditionally been monopolistic despite the fact that some organizations specially dedicated to job placement for some categories of jobseekers (executive, young people in difficulties, disabled, artists, sportsmen or women, . . .) have been in existence for years. However, the French system has had to adapt itself to EC laws which decree that job placement be no longer a monopolistic activity of the ANPE since 2005.

(3) *Scattered*. As shown by the presentation of the various institutions above, the missions and the functions of the PES are rather segmented: job placement; payment of the unemployment benefits; vocational training for the adults and the unemployed; implementation of the national employment policies, especially those aiming at reintegrating people in the labour market. In this pattern, the way the competences are legally fixed and determined is rather clear in some cases (the dichotomy between job placement and payment of the unemployment benefits and the respective competences of the ANPE and of the ASSEDIC). But in some cases, it is not that clear. For instance, the ANPE and the DDTEFP both have capacity to provide some measures in order to help some kinds of jobseekers (the weakest ones) to reintegrate the labour market.

This structural context has to be taken into account as the point is, by now, to know how the national PES can be modernized and reformed, in order to better fit the European targets and guidelines in the field of employment. This means that the PES must be more efficient as far as unemployment – and especially long-term unemployment – is concerned.

Within the European context, the French PES is actually faced with the trend towards decentralization and territorialization of the employment policies. One argument for this trend is that local public action is supposed to be more efficient, that it emphasizes the local responsibilities and helps to take into account the local particularities. Decentralization and territorialization of the employment policies is a big challenge because of the administrative structure and organization of the country,[3] but also because of the new levels for action and cooperation and the new areas for the implementation of some employment measures that appeared more recently, such as the '*bassins d'emploi*',[4] or the '*pays*'.[5] The French PES is also faced with a widespread tendency in Europe which consists of making the various players involved in the fight against unemployment share a unique or unified view about the employment policies. This requires a coherent relationship between the various measures and institutions dedicated to orientation (of the jobseekers), job placement, reintegration into the labour market, payment of unemployment benefits, and so on. It also requires an adequate coordination of those institutions with the systems providing social allowances as well as social and medical assistance. In a word, the point is to provide the PES with a new system of governance.

As it will be described below, the 'Cohesion Act' 2005, passed on 18 January 2005, deeply reforms the organization of the PES in France. This article first aims to display the various elements which previously intervened – both at national and at European level – and which certainly influenced the reconfiguration of the French PES. Then, it examines the new legal and institutional frame for the French PES as it aims at providing it with renovated governance. Finally, the typical challenges that are to be faced by the French system as regards the efficiency, in practice, of this new governance will be analyzed. Those are partnerships and decentralization issues.

2. THE SOURCES OF THE RECONFIGURATION OF THE FRENCH PES

The reform or the 'reconfiguration' of the French PES can be analyzed and explained taking into account two kinds of elements. Firstly, some initiatives to improve the collaboration between the different institutions have been put to the test over the past twenty years. As those initiatives were conceived 'from the inside' of the French administrative system, they can be called 'domestic' ones. Secondly, since the late 1990s some European influences have certainly played a part as the EU has promoted some dynamics of modernization of the PES in Europe.

3. There are 26 'Regions' (the main administrative division), 100 'Departments' and more than 36,000 municipalities.
4. A '*bassin d'emploi*' is geographic area in which the population usually finds jobs and the employers normally find the workforce they need for their undertakings. This concept was first used for statistics. However, the French regulation has created some new institutions at this level (*les comités de bassins d'emploi*) whose purpose is to build some kind of territorial social dialogue about employment.
5. The concept of '*pays*' (literally 'country') has been defined by the French legislation (1995). A '*pays*' is formed by several municipalities or by a group of municipalities. It constitutes a territory in which plans for development are elaborated. This area must be characterized by a geographic, economic, a cultural and a social cohesion.

2.1. Domestic Initiatives to Improve the Inter-institutional Collaboration

For years, the public authorities, the institutions but also the jobseekers had to deal with a PES which was not very well defined, legally speaking. A pattern was designed in 1984 by a simple *circulaire*[6] and some efforts were made to improve the inter-institutional collaboration, but they have been largely inefficient.

2.1.1. The Pattern Designed in 1984

Until then, the term 'public employment service' and the official list of the institutions which were members of the PES were defined by a *circulaire* of 7 March 1984 from the 'delegation for employment' of the Employment Ministry. According to this text, at national level, the PES was constituted by the DGEFP, the General direction of the ANPE and the General direction of the AFPA. At regional and local level, the PES was constituted by the 'external state services for employment and vocational training' and by the territorial directions of the ANPE and of the AFPA, under the authority of the state representatives (*préfets*). In this pattern, the UNEDIC and the ASSEDIC managed by the social partners were only associated members.

As it has already been noticed, in this pattern, the functions were very segmented: the external state's services were in charge of the implementation of the national employment policies and managed the main financial public aids for the integration into the labour market; the ANPE was in charge of the job placement; The UNEDIC and the ASSEDIC were in charge of the unemployment benefits; the AFPA was (and remains) the main instrument for providing qualifications and vocational training to the adults.

Moreover, the *circulaire* did not recognize the role of many national and local institutions or organizations which, actually, play an important part in the PES. For instance, some institutions dedicated to the reintegration of the disabled into the labour market,[7] or the *missions locales* (literally the 'local missions') initially created as a service aiming to take care of the young 'in difficulties' and whose missions evolved and now focus on integration and job placement for the young.[8]

6. A *circulaire* is an administrative document produced by an administrative head (Ministry services; General direction). It has no binding or legal effects for the population. It's an internal instrument that aims at easing the way the administration works.
7. Since 1975 the legislation has developed the role of special institutions which aim to help people with disabilities find a job and to remain on the labour market. These services are available free of charge.
8. The Local Missions: Associations that can be created by agreement between the State, local authorities, public institutions, no profit organisations, trade unions. They aim at social inclusion and occupational integration of young people (16-25 years old). In 2004, more than one million young people were received by the Local Missions and other similar institutions. Most of them (900,000) have had a personalized interview with an agent (adviser) during the year. 450,000 of the young people guided by the Local Missions found a job or entered a vocational training plan

The local bodies created by the *Departments* (local authorities) in 1988 which aim to reintegrate the people entitled to the RMI can also be mentioned.[9] Another point is that, since 1993, the *Regions* have been transferred the competences in the field of vocational training and therefore have become important players of the employment policies.[10] The municipalities are also supposed to play a part as they are now able to provide job placement actions under agreement with the state and the ANPE. The *circulaire* also failed to take into account the fact that the services of the Ministry of Employment and the ANPE have widely externalized to private bodies some of their services for jobseekers and for employers, such as advice, training, evaluation and guidance.

So the relationships between the various players, within the PES, were characterized by a kind of institutional rivalry. Plus, the French pattern for action on the labour market appeared as a real labyrinth for the jobseekers. In this context some instruments for a concerted and territorialized action were created.

2.1.2. The Instruments for a Concerted and Territorialized Action

The Government and the Parliament made many attempts during the 1990s to improve the collaboration between the various institutions and agents of the PES.

An inter-ministerial *circulaire*, in 1989, set up, in each *bassin d'emploi* (employment area), a new kind of agent: the coordinators for the employment and vocational training (*coordonnateurs emploi-formation*). Those agents are employed by the DDTEFP (the external state's services at departmental level) and their mission is to coordinate employment policy at a local level.

In the field of the policies for the integration of the young into the labour market, the Employment Act 1993 created a 'single office': the *espace jeune* ('the youth area'). But the collaboration between the partners (ANPE and Local missions) did not work very well.

In 1998, the task of registering the jobseekers was transferred from the ANPE to the ASSEDIC. This seemed more coherent as most of the jobseekers are supposed to be entitled to the unemployment benefit which is managed by the ASSEDIC. In fact, this led to 'statistical distortions' because the ASSEDIC do not have a total view of the reality of the unemployment.

(source: Dares, 'L'activité du réseau des missions locales et PAIO en 2003 et 2004: 45% des jeunes peu qualifiés accueillis dans l'année de leur sortie du système scolaire', doc. Mar. 2006 No. 12.3).

9. RMI: *revenu minimum d'insertion*, the minimum income. This is a social allowance granted to all people of up to 25 years old and whose income is under a threshold fixed by the law. People have to design a plan for their social or professional reintegration. Those plans are managed by local organisations and social workers acting under the authority of the *Conseils Généraux* (the local governments at *departmental* level). Since 2004, the *Conseils Généraux* are totally in charge of the RMI.
10. First, the *Regions* have been entitled to build the plans for the young people vocational training, which means they have to finance it. Since 2004, they also have to plan and to finance vocational training for adults.

In 1999, the ANPE and the AFPA were imposed by the Ministry of Employment to reach an agreement that aims at making both services more complementary.

However, the most relevant measure from the Government has been to impose a local coordination for the use of the financial aids provided by the state for the reintegration of the weakest into the labour market. This was made in 1998-1999, as the French Government was implementing the first National Plan for Employment, in application of the European Strategy for Employment. The principle consists of providing the external services with a global budget for the whole 'package' of financial aids; then, the local partners of the PES have to agree on a distribution for each 'employment area' (*bassin d'emploi*), based on a common diagnostic of the local needs. This global and territorial measure has strengthened the cooperation between the members of the PES.

The usual local partners

- The DDTEFP: Implementation of some integrating measures (for young people, disabled, long term unemployed, . . .); financial assistance for businesses dedicated to job integration; approval of local projects; control of the unemployed in coordination with the ANPE and the ASSEDIC.
- The ANPE (local agencies): Job placement. Since 2006, implementation of the 'PPAE'/Personalized plan for an access to the employment (for all kinds of unemployed people).
- The AFPA (local associations): Vocational training programs and actions.
- The ASSEDIC: Payment of unemployment benefits and, since 2001, various actions and aids for the reintegration of the insured unemployed, in cooperation with the ANPE and the AFPA.
- The municipalities: Able to provide job placement actions under agreement with the state and the ANPE.
- The Local Missions: Associations that can be created by agreement between the state, local authorities, public institutions, non-profit organizations, trade unions. They aim at social inclusion and occupational integration of the young people (16-25 years old). They act in cooperation with the ANPE for the implementation of the PPAE for the young.
- Local scheme for integration and employment: Associations that can be created by one or several local authorities. They act to help people with great difficulties towards achieving social and occupational integration (long term unemployed, unskilled young people, etc.). Help to define individual occupational plans. The Local scheme coordinates the various local players: Local Missions, Social Affairs, Municipalities, ANPE. They are involved in the partnership 'ANPE-*Alliance Villes Emploi*' in order to implement the PPAE for the people in difficulties.

Nevertheless, the local PES – at departmental level – remained rather inefficient: scarce reunions for the coordination; minor role for leading projects; no real integration of the AFPA (Association for the Adult Education) within the local PES. So it can be asserted that during the period 1984-2004, the PES was much more a concept for the Administration than a reality for the people, especially for the jobseekers.[11]

2.2. The Influence of the European Employment Strategy: Dynamics of Modernization of the PES in Europe

As mentioned above, things have changed more significantly since the European Union has given an impetus to the modernization of the PES, which includes the issue of the coordination of the various partners.

2.2.1. Some Guidelines for the Modernization of the PES in Europe

The modernization of the PES was not a specific objective of the first European guidelines for employment (1997). Nevertheless some of those guidelines directly concerned the institutions in charge of employment, vocational training and more specifically the institutions in charge of the reintegration of the unemployed into the labour market.

In the first guidelines, the relevant topics for the modernization of the PES were:

(1) Activation of unemployment benefits systems and of the vocational training and reintegration measures and policies.
(2) Partnerships and cooperation between the state or public institutions and the social partners at various levels in order to increase the employability of the jobseekers.

In 1998 (13 November), the European Commission approved a Communication which specially deals with the issue of the modernization of the PES in Europe: 'Modernizing Public Employment Services to Support the European Employment Strategy' (1998/641).

This Communication makes clear that the PESs have a major role to play in each Member State, in implementing the Employment Guidelines especially as regards the preventive strategy which consists of offering a new start to young people before six months of unemployment, and before twelve months for adults.

Thus the European framework stresses the need for more efficiency of the PES. Briefly speaking, modernizing the PES supposes that they will be able to coordinate the various services provided for jobseekers (and for employers) and to

11. Y. Rousseau, 'Du Monopole Public de Placement à un Nouveau Service Public de L'Emploi', (2005), 4 *Droit Social*, 456.

improve the quality of those services; it also supposes that partnerships with the other players on the labour market (especially the social partners) will be developed.

The Communication identifies some challenges for the adjustments of the PES. Some of them are particularly relevant as regards the French situation:

(1) Activating the unemployment benefits system implies that the relationships between this system and the job placement services are tightened. However, the Commission admits that managing unemployment benefits is not necessarily and totally compatible with the function and with the objectives of job placement.
(2) As a greater implication of the regional and local authorities is expected, the PES must be reorganized in order to become partners of the regional and local employment policies. Nevertheless, the Commission states that this 'regionalization' must be conciliated with the need for maintaining a unified national system (equal treatment, unified system of unemployment benefits).

With the Communication, the modernization of the PES has entered the European Employment Strategy. Since 2001, the European guidelines for employment invite the Member States to 'attend the progresses reached in the modernisation of the PES, to determine clear deadlines and to provide the staff with appropriate training'.

The EES was strengthened after the Barcelona Summit (15 and 16 March 2002). This led to the Council Decision of 22 July 2003 about the Guidelines for Members States' Employment Policies. Among the 'specific guidelines', remains the former objective of developing active policies for the unemployed, which implies 'modernising and strengthening the institutions of the labour market, especially employment services'. This idea is reiterated in the guidelines for employment 2005-2008 (guideline No. 20) approved by the Council Decision of 12 July 2005.

2.2.2. Coordination Processes through the PES European Network

As the European Commission had stated, in 1997, that it will support the cooperation between the PES in Europe, the national PES immediately expressed their will to build common approaches and views to face the new challenges.

On 16 November 1998, they adopted a 'Common statement of the Public Employment Services in Europe EU-EEA'.[12]

This document expresses a large consensus on the point that the missions of the PES must go much further than job placement. The PES must be able to foresee the needs for the local labour market. They must behave as 'service companies'

12. This statement was approved by the PES from nineteen countries.

acting in partnership with other protagonists in the labour market (social partners, educational and vocational training institutions, municipalities, institutions providing social benefits, private organizations).

The year 1997 also witnessed the creation a European network of PES heads (the general directors of the PES). This network has developed various actions such as:

(1) Comparing some practices about the use of new information and communication technologies, preventing long-term unemployment, the relationships between PES and private employment services, the PES action within a regional and local context and so on.
(2) Common mission statements about strategic and fundamental issues. One of them deals with the role of the PES in supporting the fight against long-term unemployment (22 June 2000).

Obviously, the European network of PES heads acts like a 'driving belt' of the main EU guidelines in both economic and social areas. From this point of view, the Mission Statement approved in Lahti (Finland) on 4 December 2006 by the network is very significant. The members of the network point out some problems and some challenges, so they define some objectives and strategies that are, in fact, totally convergent with the objectives of the EES and of the 'open method of coordination' about social inclusion.

The most interesting aspect of this coordinated reflexion and action through the European network of PES is the will to build a 'PES service model'. One of the key aspects of this model is the capability to act quickly on the basis of an early diagnostic of the situation of the individual towards employment: the so-called 'strong start' principle. This idea is expressed by the Mission Statement of Lahti;[13] it has been developed in a document called *Approaches of Public Employment Services (PES) to Long Term Unemployment. Draft report from seminar in Budapest 22-24 March 2006.*[14]

3. GOVERNANCE WITHIN THE NEW LEGAL AND INSTITUTIONAL FRAME FOR THE FRENCH PES

The 'Social Cohesion Act' 2005 has undeniably designed a new legal frame for the French PES. In this legal frame, the roles of each participant and the partnerships between them are identified; the legislation also deals with the issue of the local

13. Talking about the PES service model and the 'strong start principle', the document states that *an active work first approach should be adopted*, and that *activation measures, including guidance, should be linked to receipt of unemployment benefit to help with active job seeking*. The model should also be based on *multi-channel service delivery* and the use of *call centres* and internet self-services.
14. European Commission, Directorate General Employment, Social Affairs and Equal Opportunities, Unit EMPL.D.3 Employment Services, Mobility, Brussels, May 2006.

action of the PES and provides new instruments for a transversal approach to jobseekers' problems.

3.1. A Renovated Legal Frame for the Public Action

As usual in France, the main changes come from the legislation which means an act passed by the Parliament but prepared and proposed by the Government. However, as regards the reform of the PES, it has to be pointed out that a sort of a 'reallocation' of the traditional roles had been initiated by the social partners, through the renegotiation of the national agreement about the unemployment benefits regime.

3.1.1. The Missions of the Unemployment Benefits System as Redefined by the Social Partners: The Agreement of 2001

Since 1958, the function of the unemployment benefits system managed by the social partners has only been to compensate, to indemnify the workers who had lost their job. The agreements passed by the social partners were called 'agreements about the compensation in case of unemployment'. The theory of the social risks was applied and the regime worked just like a classical social insurance. However, the trade unions' and the employers' representatives who signed the agreement[15] of 1 January 2001 decided to fix a new objective to the regime: from now on, the regime aims both to help the unemployed to quickly find a new job and to provide them with compensation. Under the influence of the concept of *activation* (of the social security systems), the social partners have redefined the system. The reintegration of the unemployed becomes an objective in itself. In concrete terms, the UNEDIC and the ASSEDIC have set up various measures of guidance, advice, financial assistance, vocational training programs for the unemployed entitled to the regime. So it makes clear that the social partners have instituted themselves with missions of general interest that go further than the traditional mission which consists of paying unemployment benefits. They actually wish to play a part in the employment policies, as it is expressed in the preamble of the 2001 agreement: it deals with 'the necessity for reducing the level of the unemployment in France further than what is made possible by the current measures', and with 'the necessity to bring the demands and the supplies of employment closer together'. The social partners wanted 'new relationships for cooperation with the public authorities' to be established. In a way, the UNEDIC instituted itself as a main agent of the PES. As the 2001 agreement created a new tool, which is a kind of a jobseeker's agreement signed between the ASSEDIC and the jobseeker but which implies a

15. The agreement was signed in October 2000 by the MEDEF, the CGPME and the UPA which are the main employers' associations at national level and by the CFDT, the CFTC and the CFE-CGC which are three of the five main employees' trade unions. The CGT and FO didn't sign the agreement.

triangular relationship with the ANPE,[16] the UNEDIC and the ANPE, at national level, had to set an institutional agreement, in order to make the new system work in practice.[17] This was the beginning of a process continued and consolidated by the Social Cohesion Act 2005.

3.1.2. The 'Social Cohesion' Act 2005 and the Three Circles of the PES

Looking for a solution to the segmentation and the fragmentation of the PES, the lawmaker, in 2005, did not opt for the unification of the various institutions; it was decided to institutionalize the cooperation between them, especially between those in charge of the job placement and those in charge of the unemployment benefits regime.

Firstly, the law (new Article L. 311-1 of the Labour Code) defines the missions of the PES. Those are: job placement, compensation in case of unemployment, integration in the labour market, vocational training, help and guidance for the jobseekers. Then, the law shapes 'three circles' of the PES, according to the role of the various institutions and organizations which act, intervene or participate in the PES.

The 'first circle' is made of the institutions which really carry out the PES. These are the state's services in charge of employment, the ANPE and the AFPA. The law adds that the PES is also carried out by the organizations in charge of the unemployment benefits system. According to the law, this first circle has to be organized by a tripartite agreement between the state, the ANPE and the UNEDIC; the AFPA is included as it will have to sign the appendices of the agreement. The content of this agreement has been fixed by the law. The agreement will have to deal with: the territorialization of the employment policy; the methods of coordination between the state's services, the ANPE and the UNEDIC, which is a big issue pointed out by the Marimbert Report[18] and which poses the problem of the autonomy of both institution;[19] the creation of a new tool, the 'jobseeker single administrative file'; the implementation of 'measures for the activation of the passive expenditures from the unemployment benefits system'.[20]

---

16. Under the agreement 2001, the jobseeker first had to sign a document with the ASSEDIC called PARE, which is an individual plan to help the jobseeker to return to employment. Then, he had to sign another document called PAP (Project for a personalised action) with the ANPE. Having signed the PARE, the jobseeker and the ASSEDIC both committed themselves to carry out some actions framed by the ANPE. This system has been replaced in 2006 by a new tool called PPAE (*see* below n. 38).
17. A tripartite agreement was signed on the 13 Jun. 2001 by the State, the ANPE and the UNEDIC in order to implement the PARE.
18. Marimbert Report, *See* above n. 1.
19. Before the Act was passed, the Economic and Social Council had considered that it was fundamental to show respect for the freedom of choice of both institutions (Opinion of the CES, 6 Sep. 2004).
20. Article L. 354-1 du Code du travail.

The 'second circle' is constituted by the local authorities who are supposed to contribute to the PES, under the provisions of the Article L. 311-9 of the Labour Code. Some legal forms of this contribution previously existed:[21] the *Departments* are legally in charge of the social integration of the unemployed and the municipalities which can provide job placement services have already signed agreements with the state's services. However, the *Regions* will have to formalize their action and contribution to the PES.

In the 'third circle' are the public and the private organizations whose mission is to provide services of job placement, integration, vocational training, help and guidance, and which participate to the PES in this way. This includes the '*entreprises d'insertion par l'économique*' which are businesses aiming to reintegrate the long term unemployed in the labour market (they propose fixed term contracts of employment and provide services of guidance under an agreement with the state's services); also included in the third circle are the Temporary Work Agencies and the private agencies for job placement. So this area is now open and competitive, eventually.[22] This fits the European case law by the European Court of Justice (ECJ)[23] and also the provisions of the convention No. 181 of the ILO.[24] In a way, the law has just made official the role of many private and public organizations that already participated in the PES at local level. So this is a positive point, though the problems of coordination of those agents remain.[25] However, this poses a fundamental and theoretical problem in this country in which was born, a century ago, the 'theory of the public service', by Léon Duguit. Is this concept still valid, as regards the way the recent legislation describes the PES? For sure, the new concept of public service in France seems closer to the European concept of general interest services.

3.1.3. The Tripartite Agreement between the State, the ANPE and the UNEDIC of 2006

Under the Social Cohesion Act 2005, an agreement has to be set between the state, the ANPE and the UNEDIC. One object of this agreement is to fix 'the methods of the coordination for the actions of the services of the Employment Ministry, the ANPE and the organizations in charge of the unemployment benefits system respectively, and the way will be mutually communicated the information which

21. Since an Act passed in 1986 (*see* Art. L. 311-9 and Art. L. 311-10 of the Labour Code).
22. D. Soldini, 'Le service public de l'emploi et le droit de la concurrence' (2006), 6 *Droit Social*, 599. Let's notice that, at this time, few real private job placement agencies have appeared. Nevertheless and before the new regulation, one could consider that Temporary Work Agencies which are very developed in France have acted like private job placement agencies.
23. ECJ, C.-41/90, *Höfner*, 23 Apr. 1991.
24. The Convention No. 181 recognises *the part that can be played by private job placement agencies to help the labour market work correctly.*
25. M. Véricel, 'La Réorganisation du Service Public de L'Emploi' (2005), 8.9 *La Semaine Juridique*, I 1115.

are necessary to carry out theses actions. If such an agreement is not reached, those methods will be fixed by a public regulation'.[26]

The tripartite agreement was signed on 5 May 2006. In concrete terms, the main issue dealt with is the institution of a unified system to collect information about the jobseeker. The agreement states that the coordination of the information systems about the jobseekers requires the immediate implementation of a common access to a single administrative file that can be used by all the agents entitled to. The agents will have total or partial access to the data. So the 'DUDE' (*Dossier Unique du Demandeur D'Emploi*) was created – the jobseeker single administrative file – which contains the whole information collected by all the services and institutions that are members of the PES or which participate in it. This data file has to be updated in real time, which means every day for some kind of actions. The agreement also states that, 'on the operative ground, the services and the institutions which carry out the PES have at their disposal the technical means and the tools that facilitate permanent exchanges of information about the jobseeker single file'.[27]

3.2. Some New Instruments for a Transversal Approach to the Jobseekers' Problems

As it has been mentioned, the new legal frame not only establishes or institutionalizes the missions and the relationships within the PES; it also provides the agents with new instruments. Those instruments are supposed to achieve a transversal approach to the jobseekers' problems.

3.2.1. The 'Jobseeker Single Administrative File'

This new tool should improve the quality of the service for the jobseeker. The fact is that the situation has to be improved as regards the exchange of information about the jobseeker situation, between each institution in charge of the PES. For more than twenty years, the ANPE and the UNEDIC have experimented with some systems of common administration of the jobseeker file. First was implemented the 'GIDE system'.[28] But this system did not offer a total access to the data file, so the ANPE could not do its job properly. As a consequence, the ANPE decided, in 1996, to develop its own system for the management of the jobseekers listing; this system Gestion Opérationnelle des Demandeurs D'emploi (GEODE) had a common interface with the ASSEDIC one. However, this system never really worked. So it was urgent to build a real common and unified system.

26. Article L. 311-1 c) of the Labour Code.
27. Article 9 b) about the systems of information of the partners to the agreement between the State, the ANPE and the UNEDIC of the 5 May 2006 dealing with the coordination of the actions of the PES (*Liaisons Sociales*, 6 Jun. 2006, no. 8699, D4, 426).
28. GIDE: *Gestion Informatisée de la Demande D'Emploi*, computer-assisted management of the job seeking.

In 2006 was created the 'DUDE' . It is a single data file constituted by all the relevant information about the jobseeker, collected by all the institutions which are parts of the PES, updated daily. To be efficient, it requires the compatibility of each system of information – the ANPE one, the UNEDIC one and the one of the external state's services- so the agents of those three institutions can have a full access in real time to the whole data.[29]

In practice, it depends on the way the information is collected and recorded in the single data file. In 2007, some problems came from a certain lack of information from the ASSEDIC about the periods during which the jobseeker has been employed or unemployed, so the external state's services in charge of monitoring the jobseekers could not have a clear view of the situation. On the other hand, those services have had a correct access to the information coming from the ANPE about the content of the individual interviews between the agents and the jobseekers. But as both institutions have kept their own software, the agents confess that they still prefer using it,[30] so the situation is not really unified yet.

3.2.2. The 'Job Houses'

The Social Cohesion Act 2005, as regards the reconfiguration of the PES, deals with 'the role of the local authorities, of their groups and of the job houses'. According to the draft text which includes an explanation of the objectives of the law by the Government, the 'job houses' should be a new instrument for associating the local authorities (*Regions, Departments, municipalities, groups of municipalities*) to the action of the PES. So the 'job houses' are before all conceived as a tool for the so called multilevel governance of the PES. It cannot be excluded that the French Government was inspired by the 'job centres' which exist in other European countries (UK, Germany, Norway for instance), however, it's not that clear if the new legislation really wished to create a 'single employment office' for the jobseekers.

According to the Act 2005, the 'job houses' should fit the geographical area of the '*bassins d'emploi*' (local socio-economical area) and should not exceed the territory of a *Region*. The idea, which is clearly expressed by the 'Social Cohesion Plan',[31] is that the job houses should be useful to: inventory the human resources and to anticipate the local needs for employment (and for qualifications local vocational training programs so that can be planned); offer special services to the unemployed in difficulties previously oriented by the ANPE; regroup all the services and helps for the self-employment of jobseekers; federate all the partners

29. M. Véricel, *see* above n. 25, 1176.
30. This information was collected during an interview with an executive of the DDTEFP-Gironde on 29 May 2007.
31. In June 2004, the Minister for Employment presented a Social Cohesion Plan to the Government. So the action of the Government and the implementation of the Social Cohesion Act, especially on the financial ground, have been planned for five years.

of the employment policy in a single structure. Officially, under the terms of the Social Cohesion Act, the job houses:

> contribute to coordinate the actions of the public employment service and develop forecasting actions about the workforce needs and territory reconversion actions, especially in the case of industrial reorganizations. They also participate in the reception and in the orientation of the jobseekers, in the integration, the orientation for vocational training programs, guidance of the jobseekers and of the employees, in the help for setting up a business.[32]

Legally speaking, it has to be pointed out that founding job houses is not compulsory; creating a job house must be a voluntary decision from one or several local authorities. In fact, some kinds of job houses had already been instituted by some local authorities before. A regulation by the Ministry of Employment of 7 April 2005 states that, when a 'job house' is founded, the statutory members are: the local authorities who have initiated the project, the state representative, the ANPE and the ASSEDIC. The *Conseil régional* (local government at *regional* level), the *Conseil général* (local government at *departmental* level), the inter-municipalities and the municipalities can be constitutive members if they wish to. The local organizations which act in the field of the employment policies (the AFPA, the social partners, the Chambers of Commerce, the *local missions*, the *local scheme for integration and employment* and others) can be associated members. It is expressed by the regulation that some of those partners (the local missions, the local schemes for integration and employment) can evolve and transform themselves into 'job houses'. Some financial incentives from the state are provided.[33] The conditions to be entitled to the financial aid is, first, that the project of job house must be 'certified' and then, an agreement has to be signed with the state's services. In this case, the actions of the job house will be evaluated according to a legal process.

Formally, the new legal framework for the PES redesigns the relationships between the various 'players' in the field of employment policy and stresses the need for a territorial approach. From this point of view, multilevel governance seems to have entered the French system. However, this does not mean that those changes are really and immediately effective. Partnerships and decentralization remain real challenges for the French PES.

4. CHALLENGING PARTNERSHIPS AND DECENTRALIZATION IN THE FRENCH SYSTEM

The legislation institutionalizes partnerships between various institutions and organizations. Nevertheless, this frame is faced with the 'structural autonomy' of some

32. Article L. 311-10 of the Labour Code as modified by the Art. 1-5 of the Social Cohesion Act 2005.
33. Article L. 311-10 of the Labour Code and Regulation of the 22 Feb. 2005 (Official Journal, 24 Mar., 4929).

players, especially of the UNEDIC. Beyond the formal partnerships lies the reality: the part played by each 'partner' depends largely on its financial means and on the way it targets and spends those means. In this context, the UNEDIC seems to exert a certain but unofficial leadership.

Plus, the will and the trend to build local and territorial employment strategies pose the problem of decentralization in the field of the employment. In the French system, employment policy remains theoretically a national one. The recent legislation, however, makes things more complex and rather unclear. Do the 'job houses' solve this problem? In practice and at local level, things seem to be uncertain as regards the coordination of the PES. The role of the state is called into question.

4.1. Partnerships and Autonomy of the Various Players in the Field of the Employment Policies

The PES is supposed to work on partnerships between the main institutions. However, each of them has kept a 'functional' autonomy, since unemployment remains a non unified notion. There lies the problem. Nevertheless, the dynamics of activation of the social security systems leads to a more transversal approach and imposes a narrow connection between job placement actions and payment of unemployment benefits or social allowances. In this context, merging the ANPE and the UNEDIC could be a solution.

4.1.1. The Problem: A Segmented Approach to Unemployment

In spite of the coordination (tripartite agreement) and of the concept of new PES, the treatment of the unemployed population remains segmented. There are – legally speaking – several status for the unemployed, which means no real equal treatment towards the services that are supplied and no real continuity in their rights:

(1) The unemployed covered by the contributive system of unemployment benefits[34] are mainly in charge of the UNEDIC and the ASSEDIC. They represent 47, 5% of all unemployed people. The actions of the UNEDIC – paying benefits, financing vocational training and various measures of reintegration on the labour market, guiding people in cooperation with the ANPE – tend to be focused on its 'natural customers' (the unemployed entitled to social insurance), just because those actions are financed by the UNEDIC on the employees and employers' contributions.

(2) The other ones, those who are not entitled to the unemployment benefits regime have a right to non contributive social allowances which are

34. To be entitled to the unemployment regime, the jobseeker must have been employed – and must have paid contributions- for a certain period before he loses his job. He must have lost his job involuntarily, be able to work and be actively looking for a job.

financed by the state (ASS (*Allocation Spéciale de Solidarité*) for the unemployed who have run out their rights in the contributive system)[35] or by the local authorities – the *department* governed by the *Conseil Général* – now totally in charge of the RMI measure (minimum income linked to social inclusion measures and policies). The services that are offered to this group depend on their status. Generally speaking, the measures of reintegration in the labour market for the long term unemployed and the young are financed by the state and coordinated by its external services (DDTEFP) at local level; the training programs for the unemployed are financed by the regional authority; the measures of social integration linked to the RMI are assumed by the departmental authority.

So the point is 'who pays for whom and for which purpose?'

The purpose of the UNEDIC is to reach a quick reintegration of the unemployed into the labour market. So, even if the UNEDIC widely finances vocational training programs for the (entitled) unemployed, the objective is to make the workers' skills immediately fit the needs of the local labour market in a short-term economical perspective.[36]

For the ANPE, theoretically, the purpose is or should be to help people to find a convenient and quality job in order to reach a high and durable level of employment,[37] which implies long term strategies especially on the ground of vocational training. However, the ANPE only guides the unemployed but does not finance the measures.

The state's external services now focus on special groups and social categories: long term unemployed, young people, people with disabilities, and their action is both economical – the DDTEFP help and control the *entreprises d'insertion par l'économique* – and social. Nevertheless, there is a trend to limit some prerogatives of the DDTEFP, in the area of the employment policies, and to transfer those prerogatives to other players or institutions. For instance the DDTEFP were in charge of signing the special employment contracts linked to financial

35. ASS: *Allocation Spéciale de Solidarité* (literally special solidarity allowance). The non-contributive unemployment benefits assumed by the State (ASS, *Allocation d'Insertion* become ATA, *Allocation Equivalent Retraite*) are provided to 20% of the unemployed. The RMI covers the others.

36. Some empirical studies lead to the conclusion that the actions of the UNEDIC and ASSEDIC aiming to provide vocational training for the unemployed tend to 'format the jobseekers in direct relation with the very needs of the activity sectors in which the employment and wages conditions are more damaged'. *See* D. Gelot, C. Lévy and W. Pelletier, 'La nouvelle convention d'assurance-chômage: de la formation au formatage des demandeurs d'emploi' (2002), 6 *Droit Social*, 631.

37. Formally speaking, the Art. 136 of the European Community Treaty deals with – among other objectives – 'the development of human resources with a view to lasting high employment and the combat of exclusion'. The 'quality employment' issue began being developed with the Conference about the quality of employment launched by the Belgium Presidency in 2001; Ten criteria were established by the Laeken Council and the quality of employment has become one of the main objectives of the guidelines for employment 2003-2005 and for 2005-2008. One of those criteria is: skills, qualification, training and life long learning.

assistance and this prerogative has been transferred to the ANPE by the 'Social Cohesion Plan' 2005. At the same time, the financial means given to the DDTEFP for implementing some employment measures tend to be more and more limited.

Within the partnership between the state, the ANPE and the UNEDIC, it seems that the UNEDIC tends to assume a strong and rather central position. An explanation is the fact that the social partners, through the *agreement for indemnification and reintegration of the unemployed 2001*, have autonomously expressed their will to be an efficient player in the fight against unemployment in France. So in fact, the UNEDIC and the ASSEDIC tend to impose their own purposes on the other partners. Talking about guidance and actions of reintegration into the labour market, the ANPE plays its part. The new measure which appeared in 2006, the 'PPAE' ,[38] is opened to every unemployed person but is mainly financed by the UNEDIC. The result is a certain trend to put the ANPE agents under pressure for more control of the unemployed: those who miss a compulsory appointment with the agent are able to be excluded from the jobseekers' listing and of the guidance measures. Even the mission of controlling the unemployed – who are supposed to act positively to find a new job- and the power of imposing sanctions are now shared by the agents of the ASSEDIC and the local agents of the Ministry of Employment (DDTEFP). In fact, the state's external services are more and more likely to be activated by the ASSEDIC for controlling the unemployed. It is no longer a self action. According to some local agreements which implement the tripartite national agreement between the state, the ANPE and the UNEDIC, the DDTEFP commits itself to reach quantitative targets in terms of control.

4.1.2. A Solution: Merging the ANPE and the UNEDIC

Despite the partnerships between the main institutions of the PES, the administrative system remains too complex for jobseekers. Over the past few years, there have been many local arrangements between the ANPE and the ASSEDIC that aim to locate their offices in the same place in order to make it easier for the jobseekers. In 2007, those are 170 'single offices' which seem to work properly.[39] The Ministry of Employment has had planned to reach the number of 400 at the end of 2008.

Nevertheless, some think that the best solution for the jobseekers would be to merge both institutions. The problem was posed in January 2007 by Dominique de

38. The PPAE measure begins with a diagnostic of the individual case of the unemployed person: how far is he from the employment? So the unemployed are classified (three categories). Then, they have a right – and a duty – to attend monthly meetings for personal guidance, having spent three months unemployed. The agent can prescribe actions of vocational training, measures of integration through special contracts of employment.
39. In the 'classical' dual system, the average time spent between the moment of the registration (ASSEDIC) and the first interview with an agent of the ANPE was twenty-one days; with the single office, this time decreased to seven days (source: *Semaine sociale Lamy*, 2 Apr. 2007, no. 1301, 2).

Villepin, Prime Minister at the time.[40] The social partners reacted negatively to this idea and adopted a common statement.[41] They fear the UNEDIC would become a 'state body' and argue that the independence of their system is the best guarantee for a correct use of the employers and employees' contributions.

The step towards a unified system was announced during the campaign for the presidential elections in spring 2007. For the new President, Nicolas Sarkozy, it is absolutely necessary to build 'a universal and integrated public service for all jobseekers whether they are entitled to the unemployment benefits regime or not'. The idea of the President is also to make the system of control on the job-seekers more efficient so that they cannot easily refuse a job or a vocational training program.

In October 2007, a social dialogue was initiated on this topic by Christine Lagarde, Minister of the Economy, Finance and Employment. According to the Minister, the jobseekers should have access to a single office and to a unique agent in charge of the reception, the registration, the payment of unemployment benefits and guidance in order to find a new job. Each agent should be in charge of about thirty jobseekers.[42] In December 2007, a law proposal about the reform of the PES was presented in the Parliament by the Government and the bill was passed on 13 February 2008. Basically, the new structure will be governed by an Advisory Council composed of state's representatives (five persons), the social partners (five employers' and five employees' representatives), two 'qualified personalities' and one local authority representative.[43] This new institution unifies the former ANPE and ASSEDIC bodies and will be in charge of the registration, the guidance, the payment of the unemployment benefits, and the control of the job-seekers. So it means that the allowances will be paid by this new body, at local level. Nevertheless, the UNEDIC remains as a bipartite manager of the unemployment benefit regime. The unified structure is to be financed by both the state and the UNEDIC.

However, merging the ANPE and the UNEDIC and building a 'universal and integrated public' would suppose a fundamental reform of the whole system of unemployment benefits and social allowances. Shall France follow the German path? One of the 'Hartz reforms', in Germany, has consisted of reorganizing and rearticulating the contributive and the non contributive systems of benefits and

40. 'Villepin relance la fusion ANPE-UNEDIC' (2007) 11 *Liaisons sociales*, , actualité sociale 13/07.
41. Newspaper *Les Echos* 12-13 Jan. 2007.
42. Currently, the ANPE agents are in charge of 120 or 130 jobseekers, so there is a discussion about how it can be possible to reduce this number – for a more efficient service- without increasing significantly the number of agents. At the moment there are 30,000 ANPE agents. The new service would integrate the 14,000 agents of the UNEDIC, but it will not be enough to reach the objectives.
43. The new institution should effectively function on 1 Jan. 2009. The regulation for the application of the law was passed on 29 Sep. 2008 (*décret n 2008-1010 relatif à l'organisation du service public de l'emploi*).

allowances for the unemployed, in order to 'activate' both.[44] Such a reform has not yet been implemented in France.

4.2. The Decentralization Issue

A large process of administrative and political decentralization has been implemented in France since the early 1980s. As a result, on the ground of employment policies, three areas of competences are generally identified:

(1) The state rules and leads employment policy.
(2) The regional authorities (*Region/Conseil régional*) rule and lead vocational training policies and programs.
(3) The local authorities (*Département/Conseil Général*) are in charge of social inclusion (RMI measure).

However, some recent legislation tends to modify this situation or to make it more complex.

4.2.1. The 'RMI Decentralisation Act' (18 December 2003)[45]

As the goal of the new regulation is to put stress on the reintegration of 'excluded people' into the labour market (rather than on mere social inclusion for people entitled to the RMI), the Local Authorities naturally asked for partnerships, at local level, with the ANPE. In some cases, the local ANPE behaved as a partner, but the major trend is to behave as a provider for services, so the local authorities have to pay for the guidance and job placement actions by the ANPE. Within this process, the action of the ANPE is made more territorial or territorialized. The consequence of this is that the way the ANPE is financed could itself become more and more territorialized.

4.2.2. The 'Social Cohesion Act' 2005 and the Job Houses in Practice

One of the missions of the 'job houses', according to the new regulation, is to 'associate the local authorities, to federate the action of the public and the private partners and to root the public employment service in the territories'. It seems that the legislation wishes to establish a kind of a collegial coordination (state/ANPE/

---

44. *See* M. Veil, 'Les Lois Hartz, Plus Qu'Une Réforme du Marché du Travail?'(2005) 92 *Chronique internationale de l'IRES*, 5-19.
45. Before the 2003 Act, the RMI was co-managed by the State (in reality by the '*Préfet*' which represents the state at local level) and by the local authority (the *Conseil* Général). With the new legislation, the president of the local authority is now totally in charge of governing the social inclusion policy and the reintegration in the labour market programs for the persons entitled to the RMI.

ASSEDIC/local authority). The problem is that creating a job house is a voluntary and, often, a political action at local level. As it is voluntary, some territories may have a job house when other ones do not. So, one could say that the French state no longer has under control its own implication in the national territory under control. Another point is that those who initiate the plan (the local authorities) are rather free to determine the content of their own project. Some job houses are likely to be involved in some kind of 'social action' towards the unemployed. This happens when the job house has been created through a transformation of a former Local Scheme for integration and employment. Some job houses are more likely to develop economical actions and to provide services for the employers and the firms.[46]

The job houses also suffer from the ambiguity of the legal frame:[47] the legislation suggests that the job house could be a kind of a single office for the unemployed. In fact, it is not and in some cases, partners such as the ASSEDIC show themselves a bit reluctant to provide the job houses with supplementary material means and staff. The negative side is that the job houses tend to be seen as a supplementary or a redundant level for public action, though it is theoretically a complementary one.

Anyway, the experimentation of the job house should be stopped in the future. The Minister of Economy, Finance and Employment announced, on October 2007, that the real way to provide the jobseekers with a unified service is to merge the ANPE and the ASSEDIC. So the job houses which have already been created and 'certified' shall remain, but the government will not finance any new projects.

4.2.3. The Role of the State in Question

Finally, the decentralization poses the question of the role of the state through the action of the DDTEFP, as it is pointed out by some researchers: 'The move towards decentralisation which affects the policy of guidance for jobseekers, in the wide sense of the concept, leads to call into question the role of the state's external services'.[48]

Sometimes, in practice, the legitimacy of the DDTEFP which was – till then – in charge of animating and coordinating the local players tend to be contested by some local authorities. The problem is, in this move towards decentralization, that the state has only kept competences in the field of the employment policies in the narrow sense of the concept. The result is that the state's external services are confronted with players who act on grounds which are no longer a state's competence (vocational training, social inclusion) and this makes things confused. So,

46. For instance: the Bordeaux job house.
47. The law is not clear about whether the 'job houses' actually belong to the public employment service or if they are simply an expression of the PES (Y. Rousseau, *see* above n. 11, 462).
48. A. Exertier and A. Germain, 'La Coordination Locales des Acteurs de la Politique D'Accompagnement des Demandeurs D'Emploi. Contexte et Enjeux des Récentes Redéfinitions du Rôle de l'Etat'. Colloque 'Etat et Régulation Sociale', 11-13 Sep.. 2006, Matisse-Université Paris 1.

after the 'Social Cohesion Act' 2005, the governance of the local/regional PES really seems to be in question.

Those remarks lead to a brief conclusion. Modernization and new governance seem to have played a part as key concepts for the reform of the French PES as far as the relationships between the various partners are concerned. One should think that they can produce positive effects especially if a correct integration of job placement and unemployment benefits services is achieved. However, things remain problematic as regards the territorial dimension, as the local action of the state in the field of employment seems weakened by now. The reorganization of the Ministries after the presidential elections of the spring 2007 – employment is no longer under the authority of the Labour Ministry and has been transferred to the Economy – has brought some uncertainties about the coherence of external state services which now depend on two different Ministries. If it can be taken for granted that the labour affairs remain a national policy – ruled by a national regulation (the Labour Code) – should one consider that the employment policies could be transferred to the local authorities? It is not sure that such a solution improves social cohesion. Territorial action is one thing but decentralization is quite another.

References

Exertier A. and Germain, A., 'La Coordination Locales des Acteurs de la Politique D'Accompagnement des Demandeurs D'Emploi. Contexte et Enjeux des Récentes Redéfinitions du Rôle de l'Etat'. Colloque 'Etat et Régulation Sociale', 11-13 Sep. 2006, Matisse-Université Paris, 1.

Gelot, D., Lévy, C. and Pelletier, W., 'La nouvelle convention d'assurance-chômage: de la formation au formatage des demandeurs d'emploi' (2002) *Droit Social.*

Rousseau, Y., 'Du Monopole Public de Placement à un Nouveau Service Public de L'Emploi', (2005) *Droit Social.*

Soldini, D., 'Le service public de l'emploi et le droit de la concurrence' (2005) *Droit Social* 2006.

Veil, M., 'Les Lois Hartz, Plus Qu'Une Réforme du Marché du Travail?'(2005) 92 *Chronique internationale de l'IRES.*

Véricel, M., 'La Réorganisation du Service Public de L'Emploi' (2005) *La Semaine Juridique.*

Chapter 7

Vocational Education Policies in the Process of Multilevel Governance: A French Perspective

Thierry Berthet & Pierre Iriart

1. INTRODUCTION

Vocational training policies are clearly considered an aspect of national active labour market policies, yet they are subject to regional regulation. European education and employment strategies also have considerable influence over this national/regional framework of public action.

The aim of this chapter is to highlight the ways in which the subsidiarity principle contributes to defining a framework for these policies. Subsidiarity is more than a simple way of organizing the distribution of competences among different levels of political bodies within the Union. This multilevel governance tool has apparently made a significant contribution to the emergence of a normative, cognitive and instrumental framework for both national and local public policies. From that perspective, the hypothesis underlying our analysis in this chapter is that the European influence is both normative and related to changes in public action theory and policy instruments.

This chapter will start by examining the impact of European employment and education strategy on the French national government, presenting the normative frame supporting the European vocational training policy and stressing its influence on both the texts and goals of the country's labour legislation and

Roger Blanpain, Juan Pablo Landa, Brian Langille (eds), *Employment Policies and Multilevel Governance*, pp. 171–183.

vocational education system. The next section explores the ways in which the regional vocational training systems have been changed by implementing the subsidiarity concept. On the one hand, this influence will be described as promoting new principles for public action: territorialization, individualization and governance. On the other hand, we will consider the implications of a new financial tool promoted by the European Union (EU): the new public procurement contracts code (NCMP), governing the contracts for training procured by regional public authorities.

Conclusions will be drawn from this analysis, stressing how these changes contribute to the development of active labour market policies.

2. EUROPEAN INFLUENCE ON THE FRENCH NATIONAL VOCATIONAL TRAINING SYSTEM

2.1. The Normative Framework of European Intervention

Vocational training is a rather recent field of action for the EU. The European Social Fund (ESF) is as old as the Union itself, but plays a somewhat marginal role as an instrument for funding national targeted actions. In certain cases, it makes an appreciable contribution and its role has been clarified since its integration into Community policies on education and training.

European competence in the field of vocational training developed during the 1980s, initially via the case law of the Court of Justice of the European Communities (CJEC). In the Gravier case, the court ruled (point 23) that:

> Although educational organization and policy are not as such included in the spheres which the treaty has entrusted to the Community institutions, access to and participation in courses of instruction and apprenticeship, in particular vocational training, are not unconnected with Community law.[1]

Competence is thus affirmed, but limited to the implementation of the principle of free movement of labour. Within that context, this decision ensures that workers and students can actually be trained in any part of the Union. The Maastricht Treaty (MT) broadened this competence. Article 3 of the Treaty gives the Union the responsibility of 'a contribution to education and training of quality and to the flowering of the cultures of the Member States'. More concretely:

> The Community shall contribute to the development of quality education by encouraging cooperation between Member States and, if necessary, by supporting and supplementing their action, while fully respecting the responsibility of the Member States for the content of teaching and the organization of education systems and their cultural and linguistic diversity (Article 149 M.T.).

1. CJCE 13 Feb. 1985, *Gravier v. Ville de Liège*, case No. 293/83, Rec. p. 593, *D.* 1985, IR 299, obs. L. Cartrou.

The Member States are committed to: 'work towards developing a coordinated strategy for employment and particularly for promoting a skilled, trained and adaptable workforce and labour markets responsive to economic change' (Article 125 MT). However, these competences do not assume a major change in national policies. Community intervention is, in theory, strictly subject to subsidiarity: 'in doing so the competencies of the Member States shall be respected' (Article 127 MT) and 'those measures shall not include harmonisation of the laws and regulations of the Member States' (Article 129 MT). As regards vocational training: 'the Community shall implement a vocational training policy', but this policy 'shall support and supplement the action of the Member States, while fully respecting the responsibility of the Member States for the content and organization of vocational training' (Article 150 MT).

Nevertheless, the EU plays a rather important role in the field of vocational training, by bringing together education and training and considering them in the broader context of the European Employment Strategy.

In most of the Union's Member States, the distinction between education and training stems from a difference in policy and aims: training focuses on supporting the integration and transfer of workers, while education essentially targets the school population. Community case law tried to break down these barriers at quite an early stage, for example, by considering that university courses leading to the exercise of an occupation constituted vocational training.[2] This merging of education and training was supported by the promotion of the Life Long Learning (LLL) concept and the incentive to develop learning from 'pre-school age to that of post retirement, including the entire spectrum of formal, non-formal and informal learning'.[3] LLL is both an approach and a new design of teaching methods, covering all the competencies useful for working activity, whether they are acquired within a formal and traditional framework, through practical experience, by distance learning, or any other method.

Furthermore, vocational training and education are considered to be instruments of social and employment policies. The Amsterdam (1997) and Lisbon (2000) Treaties assigned the European Employment Strategy the objective of turning the EU into a knowledge based economy supporting sustainable economic growth, quantitative and qualitative improvement of employment, and greater social cohesion. The Education and Training 2010 process comes under this objective, calling for a review of the actions of public authorities in the Member States. The open method of coordination aims at bringing the stakeholders together and leading them to develop integrated actions.

The EU does not impose standards on the Member States, but rather builds common policies. The Community authorities propose implementation criteria while supporting exchanges among Member States to promote the emergence of good practices. This provides a framework for the states to implement their own changes.

2. CJCE, 21 Jun. 1988, *Brown v. Secretary of State of Scotland*, case No. 197/96, Rec. 1988 p. 3205.
3. Resolution dated 27 Jun. 2002 on lifelong learning, *JOCE* 9 Jul. 2002, C 163/1.

2.2. The Implementation of the European Strategy in the French National System: The French System Traditionally Separates Education and Training, in Terms of both Recipients and Policy Makers

Education deals with children and young people, who are, by definition, outside the labour market. Its universal nature gives legitimacy to the fact that education policies are defined by the national government, with the assistance of local authorities on certain aspects. The Education Department establishes the curriculum and operational policies, as well as managing and paying the teachers. Local authorities are involved in decisions to open and close primary and secondary schools. They are also responsible for maintaining the buildings and managing non-teaching personnel in schools.

Vocational training is aimed at working and unemployed people. Competence in matters concerning professional training is shared by firms, social partners and regional councils, with very little state intervention.

Although it was designated a national obligation by the 1971 Act, vocational training is not the sole responsibility of the state. The national authority remains responsible for defining standards, direct or joint financing of training programmes, and the activities of state owned agencies, such as the AFPA (adult professional training agency). However, in theory the state is only one of the stakeholders in the vocational training system, especially as two decades of decentralization have given regional authorities general competence for people under 25 and the unemployed. Firms have funded vocational education since 1925 and, particularly, since 1971.[4] Since 1992, firms have been obliged to take responsibility for adapting workers' competencies to their job, which is only a limited obligation of qualification.[5] The funds thus mobilized can be used directly by companies for competence management or used to pay for training freely chosen by employees (i.e., not directly related to their current occupation). The social partners are also actively involved in vocational training policies. They contribute to the design of corporate training strategies via branch agreements and also manage the organizations responsible for collecting the training taxes (Organismes Paritaires Collecteurs Agréés, OPCA). As managers of the UNEDIC (the agency which pays unemployment benefits), they are also involved in financing training for job seekers.

Community policies have resulted in a reorganization of the vocational training system and have also played a central role in redefining its goals.

4. The legal contribution represents 1.6% of the gross annual wage bill in companies with at least twenty employees, 1.05% for companies employing between ten and twenty people, and 0.55% for companies with less than ten employees (Arts L 951-1 and L 952-1 Labour Code).
5. Soc. 25 Feb. 1992, *Expovit*, *Bull.* V, 122, *D.* 1992, 390, note M. Defossez, *Dr. soc.* 1992, 379; A. Lyon-Caen, 'Le Droit et la Gestion des compétences (1992), *Dr. soc.*, 573; M. Del Sol, 'Le Droit des Salariés à une Formation Professionnelle Qualifiante: des Aspects Juridiques Classiques, des Interrogations Renouvelées' (1994) *Dr. soc.*, 412 et seq. The obligation of adaptation was instituted by the legislator in Arts L 932-2 and L 321-1 of the Labour Code.

2.3. Redefining the Goals of Vocational Training

The French vocational training system is based on two approaches: continuing education and workforce adaptation.

The first aspect originated with Condorcet,[6] who, in 1792, proposed to develop training and education for adults, especially those with low skills. This led to the creation of the National Academy of Arts and Crafts (CNAM) in 1794; the 'elimination of illiteracy' strategy launched by Guizot (1833) and Duruy (1865); and initiatives aimed at the emancipation of the working classes by training, education, and cultural development, based on either socialist (Proudhon) or Christian social (Sangnier) principles. Training to enable workers to adapt to the changing needs of the economy or to provide a skilled workforce for firms is hardly more recent, as demonstrated by the paternalistic activities of firms like Wendel or Schneider in the nineteenth century; the development of apprenticeship by the Astier Act in 1919; and the 1949 foundation of the National Inter Industry Association for the Training of the Workforce, which became, in 1966, the Association for Vocational Training for Adults (AFPA), in charge of 'organizing and providing vocational training for adults'.

The 1971 Act combined these two approaches by including continuous vocational training goals in labour law, in order to adapt the workforce to technical changes and working conditions, promote social advancement, and contribute to cultural, economic, and social development.

The contemporary changes in vocational training system goals are related to European policies. Article L 900-1 in the Labour Law Act of 4 May 2004 assigns the following objectives to vocational training:

(i) assist in the professional integration of workers and their continued employment;
(ii) support the development of their skills and qualifications;
(iii) contribute to their economic and cultural development as well as their social advancement;
(iv) facilitate the return to work of people who have left their jobs to take care of dependent children, parents or spouses.

The further education aspect is maintained and confirmed by Article L 900-2, which includes among the objectives of permanent vocational training: 'the means to access culture, maintain or enhance qualifications or cultural development, and prepare to take on greater responsibilities'. However, it should be pointed out that, in fact, Article L 900-2 lists eight classes of possible objectives, the others being more directly focused on work activity.[7] At least from a

6. *Rapport sur L'Organisation Générale de L'Instruction Publique* (1792). Condorcet: www.assemblee-nationale.fr/histoire/7ed.asp
7. Including, in particular (1) socialization and preparation for work life; (2) adaptation and development of professional competences; (3) promotion in employment; (4) adaptation to changes in the work world; understanding corporate operations and challenges; and (5) profit sharing

quantitative point of view, attention is now focused on employment and the work environment. The problematic issue here is the ability to implement the principle of lifelong learning, which does not seem to fit in with actions financed by firms.[8] Individual training leave (Congé Individuel de Formation: CIF), on the contrary, provides opportunities for further education, but only if the organizations managing the funding retain it among their priorities.[9] In practice, they give priority to training for those who have lost their jobs.

Continuing education is thus enshrined in law, but, as in the European texts, it has only residual importance. The vocational training system is now essentially viewed as a tool for economic development and employment policy.

3. EUROPEAN ACTION AND TERRITORIAL REGULATION OF VOCATIONAL TRAINING

The influence of the EU policies on the French system of vocational training thus places the normative framework and goals of these policies on a national level. In France, however, vocational training policies have been decentralized to the regional authorities, which have become the main stakeholders in these policies. This second section analyses the influence of the Union on two dimensions of regional vocational training policies: principles of public action and financial instruments.

3.1. Subsidiarity as Promoting New Principles of Public Action on a Regional Level

Subsidiarity means that political answers to social problems should be determined as close as possible to the beneficiaries. According to this principle, the implementation of public policies requires new principles of public action.

These principles extend beyond the sector based, centralized framework, characteristic of the modern French nation state, to propose new forms of legitimacy. The reorganization of public action into a territory-based mode of governance is indicative of the search for new types of legitimacy. Framed by new methods of public management; the territorialization of public policies legitimizes local government representatives and tools. The dynamics of proximity ensure that this legitimacy remains compatible with the unity and indivisibility of the Republic. In other words, the assumed efficiency of a proximity-based public action justifies the gradual development of a state-centred model defining the general

mechanisms, employee savings schemes and shareholding; and more specific, health related courses.

8. Concerning adaptation to the workstation, changes in jobs, maintaining employability, and developing skills (see Art. L 932-1 Labour Code).
9. Article L 931-1 of the Labour Code specifies that a CIF may be taken to achieve a higher qualification, change job or industry, and to facilitate access to culture, social life, and voluntary responsibilities in associations.

interest. Three principles of public action, articulated with the concept of subsidiarity, characterize the regulation of vocational training and support the reforms which affect it: territorialization, individualization and governance. It should be stressed that this reshaping of public action must be understood as taking into consideration the erosion of the central government's legitimacy to define the general interest.

3.1.1. Decentralization of Vocational Training Policies

The logic of subsidiarity implies reinforcing the political capacity of local political bodies, based, in France, on a decentralization process. Territorialization relies on institutional transfers from the central government to decentralized administrations (devolution) or local communities (decentralization). In the field of vocational training, territorialization took the form of decentralization to the regional authorities. The first act of decentralization of training policies took place in 1982, in the context of a more general process of redistribution of powers between central government and local communities. A general competence for vocational training was thus decentralized to the regional authorities to support their efforts in economic development and regional planning.

The Five Year Act on work, employment, and vocational training formed the second part of this decentralization process. This text, presented by Michel Giraud, Minister for Labour in the Balladur government, and adopted on 20 December 1993, broadened the general competence of the Regions. The principal change consisted of giving the regional authorities broader competence for continuous vocational training of young people under 26. The regional authorities also became responsible for coordinating training and guidance policies by building a regional action plan (PRDF).

The third and last act in the decentralization of vocational training was triggered by a series of legislative texts. The Social Modernization Act of 17 January 2002 set up coordination committees for employment and vocational training in each region. The Local Democracy Act of 27 February 2002 broadened the scope of the PRDF to include adults, as well as the AFPA's training activities. Lastly, the Local Freedoms and Responsibilities Act of 13 August 2004 extended the regional authorities' responsibility for vocational training to the entire population, arranging a gradual transfer over three years of the AFPA training courses and reinforcing their role in issues concerning apprenticeship.

3.1.2. Individualization as a Logical Outcome of the Principle of Subsidiarity

Subsidiarity can be interpreted in various ways. One currently prevalent interpretation is that it increases the individual's responsibility, either as a recipient or policy maker. If subsidiarity consists of transferring responsibilities to the lowest possible level, there is considerable risk that the individual will end up by being this 'lowest common denominator'. This supports the hypothesis that the development of subsidiarity promotes individualization, thus undermining the importance of public authorities.

The difficulty for policy makers and grassroots bureaucrats is, above all, to manage the cultural shift from agent of the state to stakeholder, that is, to accept a change in the order of legitimacy. The legitimacy acquired via a position in a political institution or government agency is replaced by the individual's capacity to be influential. This transformation is accentuated by the multiplication and broadening of local decision-making arenas. Institutional legitimacy, which used to be strong in a sector-based mode of government, is weakened in a context of territorial governance. Government agents are in competition with other types of legitimacy (elected, economic, associative, etc.), so they are obliged to become players and build their own leadership in the local decision making arenas.

Obviously, this change affects not only government agents, but also the recipients of public programmes. This highlights another semantic slip: 'recipients' become 'users', or even 'clients'. Users are supposed to contribute by their individual efforts to the success of the public programme. Users are also stakeholders, who tend to become coproducers, jointly responsible for their employability, who thus cooperate to ensure the success of the training policy. The latest training systems, based on active labour market policies, leave increasing room for individual initiative. For example, the DIF (*Droit Individuel à la Formation* – individual training rights) or VAE (*Validation des Acquis de l'Expérience* – validation of learning outcomes) rely mainly on individuals for their implementation. This raises the issue of the social consequences of the current trend. For example, is the increasing individualization of training and recruitment methods, focused mainly on individual qualities and competencies, not likely to lead to greater discrimination? In any case, competition among individuals in the labour market, not only on a local or national, but also an international level, seems to have become deeply entrenched.[10] However, the dynamics of this situation are relatively unfair: while unemployment risk management is clearly individualized, training is still largely shaped by the administrative, financial, and organizational requirements of both political and professional organizations. Regulatory and prescriptive procedures tend to be reinforced in the activation dynamics, particularly for the unemployed, leaving little room for choice by users/recipients of training and placement agencies. Adapting the length and content of training courses to the specific needs of individuals remains the exception.

3.1.3. Governance

Reorganizing public policies to comply with subsidiarity principles has given a central role to territorial partnerships. This has resulted in the emergence of new local political arenas, where public action and private interests are mixed. The dominant perceptions related to public action in the field of training and

10. R. Castel, *L'Insécurité Sociale, Qu'est-ce Qu'être Protégé ?* (Paris, Editions du Seuil, 'République des Idées', 2003).

employment have led to extensive partnerships with stakeholders from the corporate and political worlds, as well as the social economy. The development of these hybrid decision-making bodies is, once again, justified by the need to maximize efficiency in combating unemployment.

In terms of political decision making and defining territory-based strategic policies, this dynamic is embodied in the involvement of players from civil society in circles formerly reserved for government elites. While, on a national level, the social partnership is a formalized system for building political compromises in the field of vocational training; on a local level, the involvement of private players in public decision making processes increases with the territorial focus of public action. This raises the practical question of the weak territorial structure of the social partnership.

On the level of policy implementation, this hybridization takes a different form: outsourcing. Contracting training activities to private operators is certainly not new. The former state training administration and the regional authorities never implemented these policies directly. Both public (Greta, AFPA) and private training organizations have always relied on outside trainers. Current changes concern the conditions for organizing this subcontracting. Since 2001, these have been based on the new public procurement code, which has considerably affected the relations between regional authorities and training organizations by shifting from a subsidy approach to the purchase of services. This reflects the increasing hybridization of public and private spheres and highlights the interest of analyzing the public policy instruments. These tools, particularly the financial instruments, provide a good indication of the changes induced by the implementation of subsidiarity in regional policies.

3.2. Instruments for Public Action and the Political Capacity of the Regions: Role of the New Public Procurement Code

In any consideration of European financial instruments, attention is naturally drawn to the structural funds and, in particular, the European Social Fund (FSE).[11] This instrument has been abundantly studied in its role as key vector for EU influence. On the contrary, the implementation of new methods for organizing both national and local financing of vocational training policies is seldom discussed. The New Public Procurement Code (*Nouveau Code des Marches Publics*, NCMP), promoted by the European Commission as an instrument for supporting the free competition objective, constitutes a powerful tool for regulating regional vocational training policies.

Although only recently applied (September 2001) and still in a process of recurring adjustments, the decision to include the public procurement of training within the scope of the NCMP has led to considerable changes in the regulation of

11. T. Berthet, 'Le Financement des Politiques de Formation Professionnelle' *Annuaire des Collectivités Locales* (Paris, GRALE, 2005).

the vocational training market. The introduction of a dominant dynamics of purchase of services into a market previously managed via routine subsidies to training organizations is a powerful lever for change. The NCMP has affected relations among all those involved in the regional vocational training system.

For the local authorities, this institutional innovation has transformed their position and its requirements, with a shift from coordinating and defining general trends to the role of sleeping partner. This has had a number of implications. First, the authorities have had to develop a set of new skills. Preparing calls for tender, drafting schedules of conditions, selecting applicants and monitoring services requires know how that most local authorities did not possess. One key point here concerns the definition of the regional demand for vocational training. Whereas, until 2002, regional authorities simply formulated general policies for the regional training system, the introduction of the NCMP obliged them to precisely define their needs very early in the process. They must obtain or coordinate data on local labour markets, social demand from individuals, and existing vocational training resources. However, unlike government ministries, the regional authorities rarely have internal research departments capable of assessing supply and demand on a regional level. They have had to develop ad hoc partnerships or set up internal departments to obtain and analyze this data.

These changes have also affected the vocational training organizations. New skills were required to respond to the proliferation of calls for tender. The resulting financial instability for these organizations has obliged them to devote staff to monitoring calls for tender, preparing applications, and financial engineering. Teaching and guidance activities, which were always vital and have become even more important now, in view of the increasing requirement for recipient placement have had to be supplemented by the development of project engineering and management skills.

The changes in the regional training system induced by the implementation of the NCMP have also affected relations between the public authorities and vocational education providers, bringing about sweeping changes in the relative positions of the stakeholders and the policy making process. There has been a shift from a bottom-up to a top-down approach; from selecting projects submitted to the regional authority for funding to the normative evaluation of responses to the annual call for tender.

However, the new standards prohibit joint policy development. Evaluation of needs, project design, preparing the call for tender, selecting providers; all these elements are now the exclusive province of the public authorities. Under the subsidy regime, joint development happened all the time.[12]

Vocational training organizations bitterly regret their change in status from partner to service provider.

The changes introduced by market driven regulation of training policies have brought about a drastic transformation in the relatively unstable political and

---

12. B. Schneidermann, 'Le Code des Marchés Publics, Nouvel Outil de la Qualité de L'Offre de Formation Professionnelle?' (Septembre-Octobre, 2002), 180 *Actualité de la Formation Permanente*, 112-114.

technical relationship between the local public authorities and their providers. The technical side of this process is important and provides a good indication of the nature and intensity of the changes involved. For example; the implementation of the new financial rules imposed by the NCMP has resulted in a reduction in advance payments to the recipients, from a maximum of 60% of the costs to a threshold of 5%, which has had considerable impact on the survival of training organizations. The financial risks are now totally borne by very unequal organizations in terms of size and engineering. This transfer of the financial advance from the sleeping partners to the providers has weakened the latter considerably. As argued by a delegate from the leading training organization union: 'The sudden shutdown of the advance system, coupled with the slow development of training activities has had a considerable impact on organizations. Those which do not have enough working capital, which is likely to be the case of many associations, could be facing deadly financial difficulties.'[13]

In other words, many of them do not have the cash flow to survive pending the final payment of their services. On the one hand, this difficulty is exacerbated by a set of rigid management rules which, for example, regulate the final payment on the basis of a 90% occupancy rate in the training courses at a very low fixed hourly rate. On the other hand, the requirements in terms of six-month follow-up and placement of the recipients are increasingly demanding. Consequently, these organizations are drowning under the flood of unbearable constraints.

Regional vocational training markets generally consist of several organizations of different sizes, with variable levels of internal resources. Only the largest organizations, with well-equipped financial engineering departments, can handle these constraints. The smallest organizations; in particular those in the third sector; have the greatest problems.

The risk of atrophy in innovation as regards course engineering has frequently been raised. The previous, subsidy based system left room for a bottom-up approach, where vocational education organizations were able to obtain funding for innovative courses. Innovation has suffered a crushing blow, as these organizations can no longer propose new ideas but are simply required to implement prescribed programmes. The cost of disclosure necessitated by regional financial practices and the development of public management have the most impact on the weakest, but also, frequently, the most innovative organizations.

There is no advantage for local authorities in this atrophy of their vocational training market. Several regional authorities have experimented a softening of the NCMP rules, despite pressure from their own financial staff. One good example is the attempt at stabilizing the regional market by granting accreditation to local organizations, entitling them to respond to calls for tender over a period of several years.[14]

---

13. R. Bourglan, 'Fédération des UROF: des Exigences de Clarification' (Septembre-Octobre, 2002), 180 *Actualité de la Formation Permanente,* 111-112.
14. P. Lardeur, 'Conseil régional Nord-Pas-de-Calais : L'Analyse des Besoins, Une Combinatoire' (Septembre-Octobre, 2002), 180 *Actualité de la Formation Permanente,* 100-101.

At the same time as they are trying to preserve their local vocational training markets, the regional authorities have gained a decisive advantage in terms of regulating capacity. This point deserves particular emphasis. As previously observed,[15] policy instruments imply much more than choosing or implementing neutral technical devices. Policy instruments contribute to the normative and cognitive dimension in policy-making and also represent strategic resources for players in the competition for political leadership. These changes in the financial relationship between public sleeping partners and service providers have had positive effects for the political authorities, by regulating capacity on the regional training market. With the implementation of the NCMP, the regional public authorities are now able to define clear priorities they intend to implement by choosing the organizations and services to suit their strategic policies. In this sense, it could be hypothesized that this tool reinforces institutional decentralization by giving regional authorities decisive means of intervening in the vocational training market.

4. CONCLUSION

The aim of this chapter was to point out the ways in which the EU concept of subsidiarity influenced the French national vocational training system.

Analysis of the normative framework provided by the Union revealed that the European strategy on vocational training was clearly subject to the subsidiarity principle. Furthermore, examination of the implementation of the European vocational education strategy on national level highlighted the fact that the EU was particularly influential in changing the cognitive framework of these policies. The goals and objectives of the French vocational education system have been adapted to suit European activation and LLL policies.

However, the EU strategy seems to have greater impact on a sub-national level. The promotion of new public management principles has supported the development of multilevel governance in vocational training policies. The implementation of the subsidiarity principle has reinforced a decentralisation movement initiated in the early 1980s. In a sense, the EU subsidiarity strategy has given greater legitimacy and power to a decentralization process that was often seen as contradictory to the founding principles of the French political system. However, appropriate tools are required to implement a strategy efficiently. The example of the NCMP demonstrates how new management tools can dramatically strengthen the political power of regional authorities. Important changes are not necessarily the result of major decisions; but may be brought about by technical modifications in policy engineering. The general use of calls for tender to regulate the regional vocational training market is a good example of this effect.

---

15. C. Hood, *The Tools of Government* (London, Mc Millan, 1983); P. Lascoumes and P. Le Galès, *Gouverner par les instruments* (Paris, Presses de sciences po, 2004).

One question remains about the French case: why was it possible to implement such an innovative process in the vocational education system, while it would be difficult to impose on labour market policies and impossible to imagine in general education?

One answer is probably inherent in the symbolic importance of the educational system in France, as a founding element of the republic. Another factor is the importance of public sectors in the organization of the French governmental system. Government action is divided into separate sectors (education, transport, agriculture, etc.); each with its own administration, values, norms, interest groups, etc. Vocational training is not a separate sector, but rather involves both education and employment. As a result, it offers less resistance to institutional innovation. The major reforms instituted by the national multi industry agreement in September 2003 received very little political attention, in contrast with the major conflicts that follow any attempt to reform the French education system. This inter institutional position of the vocational training system is a potential factor for easier acceptance of cognitive, institutional, and instrumental changes. This is probably one of the reasons why the European strategy has had such considerable impact on the French vocational training system, especially on a regional level.

References

Berthet, T., 'Le Financement des Politiques de Formation Professionnelle' (2005) *Annuaire des Collectivités Locales.*

Bourglan, R., 'Fédération des UROF: des Exigences de Clarification' (2002) *Actualité de la Formation Permanente.*

Castel, R., *L'Insécurité Sociale, qu'est-ce qu'être Protégé?* (Paris, Editions du Seuil, 'République des Idées', 2003).

Del Sol, M., 'Le Droit des Salariés à une Formation Professionnelle Qualifiante: des Aspects Juridiques Classiques, des Interrogations Renouvelées' (1994) *Droit Social.*

Hood, C., *The Tools of Government* (London, Mc Millan, 1983).

Lardeur, P., 'Conseil régional Nord-Pas-de-Calais: L'Analyse des Besoins, une Combinatoire' (2002), *Actualité de la Formation Permanente.*

Lascoumes, P. and Le Galès, P. *Gouverner par les Instruments* (Paris, Presses de Sciences po, 2004).

Lyon-Caen, A., 'Le Droit et la Gestion des Compétences' (1992) *Droit Social.*

Schneidermann, B., 'Le Code des Marchés Publics, Nouvel outil de la Qualité de l'offre de Formation Professionnelle?' (2002) *Actualité de la Formation Permanente.*

Chapter 8

Features and Limits of the Regionalization of Social and Employment Policies in Italy

Giancarlo Ricci

1. THE ITALIAN MODEL OF MULTILEVEL GOVERNANCE: THE STATE-REGIONS DUALISM

The concept of multilevel governance – which refers to specific ways of exercising public powers, characterized by the simultaneous presence of a number of institutional forces cooperating in decision making processes and the implementation of public policies – is becoming of increasing significance for juridical analysis.[1]

This is due above all to the fact that the multilevel governance model is eminently suitable for the architecture of transnational legal systems: *in a vertical sense* it describes the relationships between supranational, state, and possibly sub state organizations; *in a horizontal sense* it follows the dynamics of relationships between the private sector (in particular those of a collective nature) and the public sector.

It is certainly not by chance that the multilevel governance scheme is often referred to in connection with what is, at least as far as we are concerned, the most important supranational political and juridical body – the European Union. The

1. P. Bilancia and E. De Marco, *La Tutela Multilivello dei Diritti* (Milano, Giuffrè, 2004).

Roger Blanpain, Juan Pablo Landa, Brian Langille (eds), *Employment Policies and Multilevel Governance*, pp. 185–203.

complex network of relationships between the supranational body and the Member States, along with the presence of a wide range of other parties playing various significant roles in the EU, has in fact been considered as a highly significant example of the dynamics of multilevel governance.[2]

In this respect, multilevel governance appears to be an appropriate methodological tool for the explanation of new forms of interaction between the legal decision makers operating at a supranational level. This is above all the case of the Open Method of Coordination (OMC), a flexible regulation technique of recent birth by which supranational forces succeed in influencing national policies without recourse to *hard* sources (that is, excessively invasive in the sense that they intervene directly to impose conformity on decentralized regulatory systems), but rather by means of forms of coordination based on *soft* sources and procedures, 'aiming to have a direct effect on the contents and the expected results of policies',[3] although under the strict control of EU institutions, whose task it is to initiate and then monitor the results of the ongoing procedure.[4]

Multilevel governance mechanisms also operate, however, at a national level, characterizing the institutional workings of a number of democracies.[5] From this point of view, multilevel governance allows us to draw a clear picture of the endogenous dynamics of institutional relationships between the state and its territorial articulations, with particular reference to the complex distribution of competencies (legislative and administrative) between the various law making

2. L. Hooghe and G. Marks, *Multi-Level Governance and European Integration* (Oxford, Rowman & Littlefield, 2001); N. Bernard, *Multilevel Governance in the European Union* (The Hague, Kluwer, 2002); M. Telò, 'Il Metodo Aperto di Coordinamento. Dal Consiglio Europeo di Lisbona al Testo Costituzionale' (2004) 4 *Quaderni di Rassegna Sindacale*, 77-78.
3. B. Caruso, 'Il Diritto del Lavoro nel Tempo della Sussidiarietà (Le Competenze Territoriali nella Governance Multilivello)' (2004) *Argomenti di Diritto del Lavoro*, 807.
4. M. Barbera, *Nuove Forme di Regolazione: il Metodo Aperto di Coordinamento delle Politiche Sociali* (Milano, Giuffrè, 2006); M. Barbera and B. Caruso 'In Search of a New Language: Italian Labour Law Scholarship in the Face of European Integration', (2007) Jean Monnet Working Paper no. 11, <www.JeanMonnetProgramme.org>, 22 *et seq.* It is almost superfluous to recall the significance of the OMC in social law. It is, in fact, on the basis of this method that Title V of the EC Treaty on employment policy was implemented: A. Andronico and A. Lo Faro, 'Defining Problems: The Open Method of Coordination, Fundamental Rights and the Theory of Governance', in O. De Schutter and S. Deakin (eds), *Social Rights and Market Forces: Is the Open Coordination of Employment and Social Policies the Future of Social Europe?* (Bruxelles, Bruylant, 2005); K. Armstrong and C. Kilpatrick, 'Law, Governance, or New Governance? The Changing of Open Method of Coordination', (2007) 13 *Columbia Journal of European Law*, 649 *et seq.*; A. Benz, 'Accountable Multilevel Governance by the Open Method of Coordination?'(2007) 13 *European Law Journal*, 505 *et seq.*; S. Sacchi, 'Governance e Coordinamento Aperto delle Politiche Sociali' in M. Ferrera and M. Giuliani (eds), *Governance e Politiche nell'Unione Europea* (Il Mulino, Bologna, 2008), 271 and, more recently, the tuning of similar strategies concerning 'social inclusion' in M. Ferrera and S. Sacchi, 'Il Metodo di Coordinamento Aperto e le Capacità Istituzionali Nazionali: L'Esperienza Italiana' (2005) *Giornale di Diritto del Lavoro e delle Relazioni Industriali*, 65 *et seq.*
5. L. Bobbio, 'Governance Multilivello e Democrazia' (2005) 2 *Rivista delle Politiche Sociali*, 54.

centres (state and sub state).[6] In Italy, the recent reform of Title V (Article 114 *et seq.*) of the Constitution – commonly known as the 'federalist' reform, but perhaps more appropriately definable as 'regionalist decentralization' – has decidedly helped to include the Italian legal system among those featuring multilevel governance.[7]

This chapter will briefly describe the Italian institutional model and then analyze the distribution of legislative competencies, with reference to the issues and institutions of social law *lato sensu* (individual employment relationships, the labour market, welfare), verifying their degree of decentralization and lastly attempting to assess the overall results of the process of regionalization of social law.

2. FROM CENTRALISM TO REGIONALISM: POTENTIAL AND LIMITS OF THE 2001 CONSTITUTIONAL REFORM

In the original text of the Italian Constitution, the allocation of powers was typically centralistic. Only regions with a special statute were endowed with a limited autonomous model, via the attribution of exclusive and/or concurrent legislative competencies in social matters. This was the case of the autonomous statute of the Sicilian region, which gave the Regional Parliament exclusive responsibility for the legal and economic status of regional employees, as well as concurrent responsibility in the field of social legislation (employment relationships, welfare) in compliance with the minimum standards laid down by state law.[8]

These competencies were, however, rarely used, not least because they were subject to interdiction by the Constitutional Court: sheltering behind the principle of uniformity within the state system, the Court imposed considerable restrictions

6. Though the expression of 'multilevel government' is quite diffusely utilized by some authors (*see* R. Bin, 'La Prassi della Cooperazione nel Sistema Italiano di *Multilevel Government*' (2007) *Le Istituzioni del Federalismo*, 689; F. Leotta, *La Competenza Legislativa nei Sistemi Autonomisti* (Milano, Giuffrè, 2007), 99, who make a further distinction between national multilevel *government* and EU multilevel *governing*), the notion of 'multilevel governance' seems better equipped to describe the peculiar kind of cooperation occurring between institutional players who are not necessarily identified with governmental actors. Just to give an Italian example, the *Conferenza Unificata Stato – Regioni*, which is often recognized by the Constitutional Court as a pivotal instrument for the functioning of the principle of 'fair collaboration' between the state and the regions (*see* Constitutional Court ruling no. 50 of 7 Mar. 2008).
7. F. Pizzetti, 'La Tutela dei Diritti nei Livelli Substatali' in P. Bilancia and E. De Marco (eds), *La Tutela Multilivello dei Diritti* (Milano, Giuffrè, 2004), 207.
8. M. Marinelli, 'Federalismo e Diritto del Lavoro: il Caso della Sicilia' (2004) *Lavoro delle Pubbliche Amministrazioni*, 393; G. D'Alessio, 'Pubblico Impiego' in G. Corso and V. Lopilato (eds), *Il Diritto Amministrativo dopo le Riforme Costituzionali. Vol II*, (Milano, Giuffrè, 2006), 409. Wide ranging competencies were also granted by the statutes of other regions such as Trentino Alto Adige: G. Loy, 'Le Competenze delle Regioni a Statuto Speciale in Materia di Lavoro alla Luce della Modifica del Titolo V della Costituzione' in A. Di Stasi (ed.), *Diritto del Lavoro e Federalismo* (Milano, Giuffrè, 2004), 24.

on the use of these exclusive and concurrent competencies.[9] Thus, following the above example, Sicily and Trentino Alto Adige did witness a certain flourishing of legislation regarding the labour market, but it had little effect on labour law in the strict sense.[10]

In Italian regions with an ordinary statute, on the other hand, the process of decentralization of regulatory powers is a much more recent phenomenon. The regional dimension was greatly strengthened following approval of Constitutional Law no. 3 of 18 October 2001, which modified Title V of the Italian Constitution.

In the ensuing framework, the key constitutional provision is Article 114(1) of the Constitution, which outlines a model of organization that is no longer top-down (that is, hinging on the dominant role of the state) but bottom-up: 'The Republic comprises municipalities, provinces, metropolitan cities, regions and the state.' It follows that the regions and the state are placed on the same plane, the former being defined as 'autonomous bodies with their own statutes, powers and functions, according to the principles established by the Constitution' (Article 114(2) of the Constitution).

In addition, both bodies (the state and the regions) are entrusted with equal legislative powers: the exercise of these powers, however, is to be 'in compliance with the Constitution, as well as constraints deriving from the EU legal system and international obligations' (Article 117(1) of the Constitution).

As regards the identification of legislative competencies, a new article included in the Constitution – Article 117 – indicates, as a corollary to a detailed statement of matters that are responsibility of the state (first block), those for which the regions are endowed with concurrent responsibility, limited by 'the fundamental principles reserved for state legislation' (second block), with the residual attribution of legislative powers to the regions in all matters not expressly reserved for the state (third block). The unitary nature of the system is ensured by Article 120 of the Constitution, which, in view of certain objectives such as 'the protection of basic levels of service concerning civil and social rights', gives the Government power to replace regional bodies and other local authorities, with respect of the principles of subsidiarity and loyal collaboration.

It is evident that the aim of the reform was to enact 'an overall upgrading of autonomy'[11] and that to this end it adopted a technique that greatly modified the previous situation: on the one hand, the bodies making up the Republic (the state and its territorial organizations) are given equal status; on the other, the method whereby legislative powers are attributed is inverted: alongside competencies which are exclusively of the state and those which are concurrently the responsibility of the state and the regions, we have the criterion of '*residuality*', which theoretically entrusts the regions with responsibility for legislating in areas which are not explicitly outside their sphere of competency.[12]

9. As regards the case of Sicily, *see* M. Marinelli, above n. 8, 395.
10. *See* G. Loy, above n. 8, 25.
11. A. Ruggeri, 'Leggi Statali e Leggi Regionali alla Ricerca di una Nuova Identità' (2007) *Quaderni Regionali*, 404.
12. L. Torchia, 'La Potestà Legislativa delle Regioni' (2002) *Le Regioni*, 352 *et seq.*; F. Leotta, above n. 6, 255.

In practical terms, this scheme, which formally overturns the previous centralistic system, has proved to be affected by severe limits. The combination of named and unnamed competencies, further complicated by the use of various techniques of internal and/or transversal limitation of decision making powers, has conferred on the scheme such a degree of 'opacity'[13] as to assign the Constitutional Court the decisive task of producing models of interpretation capable of ensuring that application of Title V will be in harmony with the fundamental principles of the Constitution.

The involvement of the Constitutional Court in the process of 're-reading' Title V of the Constitution is significant from a quantitative viewpoint: in the years since the reform there has been a consistent increase in the number of appeals concerning conflict of competencies, both by the regions (against state laws) and the Government (against regional laws alleged to be prejudicial to the criteria of allocation).[14] From qualitative viewpoint, analysis of the outcome of constitutional jurisprudence indicates a trend towards redimensioning decentralization: a widespread opinion is that constitutional case law has privileged a sort of continuation of the centralistic pre-reform model[15] and that this trend is not to be considered a transient but probably a 'regular' phenomenon.[16]

In the following pages we will give details of the main outcomes (and the underlying argumentations) of constitutional case law relating to application of Article 117 of the Constitution in the area of labour law, dwelling in particular on three areas: the labour market and employment policies; individual employment relationships; welfare.

3. THE (PARTIAL) DECENTRALIZATION ACHIEVED: THE LABOUR MARKET AND EMPLOYMENT POLICIES

The nucleus of a regional labour law system in Italy preceded the 2001 reform and concerned competencies in the field of recruitment and active labour policies, as a consequence of the shift in responsibility for vocational training which underwent administrative (and, by the principle of parallelism, also legislative) decentralization from the 1970s onwards.[17] It is worth mentioning Law no. 56 of 1987, which set up regional employment agencies in the wake of experience gained in regions

13. *See* A. Ruggeri, above n. 11, 405.
14. T. Groppi, 'Il Titolo V Cinque Anni Dopo, ovvero la Costituzione di Carta' (2007) *Le Regioni*, 423; R. Bin, 'I Criteri di Individuazione delle Materie' (2006) *Le Regioni*, 890; *contra* B. Caruso and A. Alaimo, 'Il Conflitto tra Stato e Regioni in tema di Lavoro e la Mediazione della Corte Costituzionale: La Recente Giurisprudenza tra Continuità e Innovazione' (2007) *Rivista Italiana di Diritto del Lavoro*, part II, 596-597.
15. *See* T. Groppi, above n. 14, 421.
16. *See* A. Ruggeri, above n. 11, 416.
17. R. Salomone, *Il Diritto del Lavoro nella Riforma Costituzionale* (Padova, CEDAM, 2005), 54.

with a special statute.[18] It was a promising regulatory experience which aimed to make various competencies in the area of active employment policies and vocational training converge on regional offices, but was in fact frustrated by the persistently centralistic connotation of the system, which hindered any real process of integration between coordination by the state and regulatory powers at a regional level.[19]

Of far greater significance was Legislative Decree no. 469 of 1997. It implemented Article 1 of Law no. 59 of 1997, and entrusted peripheral institutions with important functions in matters concerning the labour market. These ranged from transferring responsibility for employment agencies and active labour policies to the regions and local authorities to the opening up of 'employment services' to the private sector, thus eliminating the monopoly of the public sector.

The decentralization achieved by the 1997 reform aimed to give rise to a new framework, overcoming a centralism that was apparently egalitarian but in fact excessively bureaucratic and inefficient. Articles 1 and 2 of Legislative Decree no. 469 of 1997 thus entrusted the regions with functions and tasks concerning employment agencies and active labour policies. More specifically, the regions were given the task of legislating in these sectors and generally overseeing collaboration and cooperation between local authorities (provinces and municipalities).

From a chronological viewpoint it is important to point out that the process of institutional decentralization in responsibility for employment services took place in two stages.[20]

3.1. Under the Original Constitution

Decentralization of functions from the state to the regions and local authorities started within the previous constitutional framework. It was accompanied by a reinforcement of the competencies allocated to *employment centres*, which were no longer to deal merely with registering documents relating to the recruitment of employees, but were given responsibility for active labour policies aiming to promote vocational guidance and training for the unemployed. Besides Legislative Decree no. 469 of 1997, we should also mention the significant Legislative Decree no. 181 of 2000. These decrees brought about what was to be known as *administrative federalism.*

18. M. D'Antona, 'Possibili Agenzie per l'Impiego. Stato e Regioni nel Mercato del Lavoro' (1988) *Lavoro e Diritto*, 385 *et seq.*; M. D'Antona and G. D'Auria, 'L'Agenzia regionale per l'Impiego: Posizione Istituzionale e Profilo Normativo' (1990) *Rivista Italiana di Diritto del Lavoro*, part I, 127 *et seq.*
19. *See* R. Salomone, above n. 17, 60.
20. *See also* G. Ferraro, 'Nota Introduttiva' in G. Ferraro (ed.), *Sviluppo e Occupazione nell'Europa Federale. Itinerari Giuridici e Socioeconomici su Regioni e Autonomie Locali* (Milano, Giuffrè, 2003), 7; A. Alaimo, 'I Servizi all'Impiego e l'Art 4 Cost. Dopo le Recenti Riforme del Mercato del Lavoro' (2004) *Giornale di Diritto del Lavoro e delle Relazioni Industriali*, 271.

3.2. Under the Modified Constitution

The second part of the reform took place within the modified constitutional framework introduced by Constitutional Law no. 3 of 2001. It completed the process of decentralizing legislative and administrative powers regarding public employment services. It also delegated private concerns, duly authorized at a national or regional level, with the role of mediating between demand and supply in the labour market. Here the main reference is Legislative Decrees no. 297 of 2002 and no. 276 of 2003, which introduced what was known as *regulatory federalism.*

In a vertical sense, the process briefly outlined here is closely connected with the supranational level. The acceptance in Italy of efficiency-based models of management of the labour market (no longer tied to a state monopoly), alongside an increase in the proactive functions of public authorities pursuing decentralized *workfare* policies, not to mention the involvement of the private sector, was given a substantial boost by the well known *Job Centre II* case.[21] It was subsequently confirmed by the *Carra* judgment,[22] and was also decidedly influenced by the guidelines provided by the European Employment Strategy (EES). The latter, in fact, provided inspiration for the reform, at times dictating its contents verbatim, by establishing decentralized employment services as a requisite for the implementation of active employment policies. In this respect, 'the European Employment Strategy was intentionally, strategically and selectively used to justify the reforms, from both the functional and regulatory point of view'.[23]

On the domestic front, on the other hand, the progressive reform of employment agencies and services – especially when consolidated by means of the 2002 and 2003 decrees – has its roots in the new text of Article 117(3) of the Constitution. It entrusts the regions with concurrent responsibility for 'protection and security in employment'. Despite the rather 'cryptic' nature of the definition,[24] which 'seems to emerge from a void, with no history behind it',[25] the expression is generally taken to include the labour market, giving the regions the possibility to regulate it, with particular reference to the structure and functions of employment services.[26] The Constitutional Court, in its ruling no. 50 issued on 28 January (undoubtedly the most important judgment so far concerning the division of responsibilities regarding the labour market between the state and the regions), explicitly confirmed that the wording 'protection and security in

---

21. *Job Centre coop. Arl.*, Case no. 55/96 [1997] ECR I-7119.
22. *Criminal Proceedings against Giovanni Carra and Others*, Case no. 258/98 [2000] ECR I-4217.
23. *See* M. Ferrera and S. Sacchi, above n. 4, 63.
24. *See* R. Salomone. above n. 17, 81.
25. F. Carinci, 'Riforma Costituzionale e Diritto del Lavoro' (2003) *Argomenti di Diritto del Lavoro*, 52.
26. *See* M. Pallini, 'Sub Art 117 della Costituzione' in G. Amoroso, V. Di Cerbo and A. Maresca (eds), *Il Diritto del lavoro. Vol I Costituzione, Codice Civile e Leggi speciali* (Milano, Giuffrè, 2007), 444.

employment' referred to 'employment services and especially employment agencies'.[27]

The point is to establish with a reasonable degree of certainty the extent to which regions have concurrent responsibility in the matter. The minimalist hypothesis is that regional legislative powers operate within the traditional bounds of the 'fundamental principles' laid down by state legislation: in other words, state law provides a general framework within which more specific regional legislation can be implemented. However, from a reading of constitutional case law there emerge unmistakeable signs that regional legislative power is subject to limitations that go beyond such 'fundamental principles'. Constitutional Court ruling no. 50 of 2005, in fact, states that regional responsibility for employment services may in reality interfere in various circumstances with the 'exclusive' competencies of the state, listed, as mentioned previously, in Article 117(2) of the Constitution. The most significant interference may regard 'satisfaction of the social right to employment' (in this case it is the state which establishes 'basic levels of service concerning social rights' that have to be met throughout the state territory), or 'application of the system of civil and penal sanctions' connected with violations of the regulations governing private mediation, which may have further implications for the 'protection of competition'.[28]

From an analysis of the regional legislation approved to date in the area of employment services, there emerges a 'virtuous' relationship between state and regional sources. Specific regional legislation would appear to have achieved a balanced integration of national 'framework' provisions.[29]

Despite this, however, there have been cases in which regional legislation has overstepped the established limits and has been submitted for evaluation by the Constitutional Court. Although the resulting judgments do not necessarily appear to indicate a 'recentralization' of competencies, they do show the Constitutional Court's wish to safeguard respect of the 'fundamental principles' laid down by the state.

A significant area of contention involving legislation regarding employment services has been the conditions governing maintenance of the unemployed status required for application of active employment policy provisions (especially the

27. A. Trojsi, 'La Potestà Regionale in Materia di Lavoro' (2007) *Rivista Giuridica del Lavoro*, part I, 653.
28. *Ibid.*, 658.
29. *See* A. Alaimo, above n. 20, 267; D. Garofalo, 'Lo Status di Disoccupazione tra Legislazione Statale e Provvedimenti Regionali' (2006) *Diritto delle Relazioni Industriali*, 637 *et seq.* The Constitutional Court defused a possible cause of conflict regarding the division of responsibilities in the authorization of private mediation in the labour market. In a double ruling, the Court identified the correct relationship between competencies: state law is to regulate the details of the system of authorization holding at a national level (Constitutional Court ruling no. 50 of 28 Jan. 2005), whereas the regions are not prevented from drawing up regional registers of authorized subjects, or from regulating the system itself as long as they do so in respect of the fundamental principles established by state legislation (Constitutional Court ruling no. 406 of 7 Dec. 2006). For a theoretical discussion, *see* B. Caruso and A. Alaimo, above n. 14, 585 *et seq.*

'support services' offered by employment centres). In its ruling no. 268 of 13 July 2007, the Constitutional Court declared constitutionally illegitimate a regional law that had introduced a system more favourable to workers: it allowed an unemployed person to retain unemployed status in the event of his/her accepting an offer of fixed term employment or temporary employment lasting up to twelve months, irrespective of the income involved. In contrast, the corresponding national provision (Article 4 of Legislative Decree no. 181 of 2000, as amended by Article 5 of Legislative Decree no. 297 of 2002) established that the condition for maintenance of the unemployed status was a certain earnings threshold (Article 4(1)(a)) and that the unemployed status was 'suspended' (but not lost) in all cases of fixed term or temporary employment lasting less than eight months (Article 4(1)(d)). The regional legislation had thus safeguarded workers with fixed term contracts of up to a year from the disadvantages deriving from loss of the unemployed status (i) by excluding the income threshold; and (ii) by extending the suspension period for the whole duration of the contract.

In its ruling, the Constitutional Court limited the sphere of regional legislation, equating the criteria for ascertainment of the unemployed status, as established by state legislation, with fundamental principles with which regional legislators could not but comply,[30] without allowing any regional adjustment aiming to introduce more favourable conditions for workers.

This excessive rigidity shown by the constitutional judges leads the observer to refer to partial decentralization of legislative functions regarding the labour market, not to mention certain 'centralistic' trends supported, as has been seen, by Constitutional Court case law. This topic is resumed in the concluding section below.

4. UNSUCCESSFUL DECENTRALIZATION: INDIVIDUAL EMPLOYMENT RELATIONSHIPS

The decentralization of legislative powers acquires even more complex implications when the regulation of individual employment relationships is considered.

As mentioned previously, before the constitutional reform of 2001, only regions with a special statute had power to legislate on matters of 'social legislation', and therefore those regarding employment relationships. The shift of competencies towards the regions following the reform immediately raised doubts as to the possibility of a territorial differentiation between the 'juridical statutes' of subordinate employment.[31]

30. In ruling no. 268 of 2007, the Constitutional Court stated that 'in the case being examined, the definition of the unemployed status, with the establishment of circumstances leading to its loss, is of a polyvalent nature and constitutes the premise for an undefined and virtually indefinable number of rules pertaining to the various hypotheses and modalities of regulation of the demand and supply of labour'.
31. L. Mariucci, 'Federalismi e Diritto del Lavoro' (2001) *Lavoro e Diritto*, 415.

The starting point is once again the new version of Article 117 of the Constitution, where regions are allocated concurrent responsibility for 'protection and security in employment'. Does this provision mean that regions may also legislate upon matters concerning individual employment relationships as long as they observe the fundamental principles laid down by the state? And what is the role played in this framework by Article 117(2) of the Constitution, which recognizes the state as having exclusive responsibility for the 'civil system', in addition to 'establishing basic levels of service concerning the civil and social rights that are to be guaranteed throughout the national territory'?

The issue is of paramount importance for the overall framework of the labour law system, not least because, unlike what happens in employment services, there is no tradition in Italy of institutional decentralization in the field of individual employment relationships.

It would be inappropriate to dwell on all the different academic opinions. According to most,[32] however, exclusive state responsibility for the civil system would appear to exclude any possibility of regional intervention regarding work relationships. This reflects a sort of *idem sentire* about the necessity of 'preserving the most significant and sensitive issues of the matter within the sphere of state legislation'.[33]

In the light of this opinion, shared responsibility for 'protection and security in employment' would appear to boil down to the previously described possibility of regulating the labour market with state laws while still allocating specific matters (for example, vocational training) to the residual exclusive competency of the regions.[34]

Although reassuring,[35] this prevailing opinion does not solve an institutional problem of far greater complexity. The problem of the interweaving of state and regional competencies as regards individual employment relationships involves a number of cases in which national or regional legislation has regulated issues that are difficult to frame clearly within the division of powers outlined by Article 117 of the Constitution:

(a) In at least one case, state legislators explicitly excluded the possibility of the regions legislating upon a certain issue as it came under state responsibility. This was the case of the working hours regulations.[36] Legislative

32. For a summary *see* M. Pallini, above n. 26, 429.
33. M. Cinelli, 'Sussidiarietà e Modello di Sicurezza Sociale' (2004) *Rivista di Diritto della Sicurezza Sociale*, 452-453.
34. In this sense, the constitutional notion of 'protection and security in employment' refers to the definition of 'security' established in Europe in the context of the debate on *flexicurity*, rather than coinciding with the classical meaning of 'job security'. Active employment policies, in fact, are one of the four basic components of *flexicurity*, more specifically identified as 'security in transition' from one job to another (T. Wilthagen, F. Tros and H. van Lieshout, 'Towards Flexicurity? Balancing Flexibility and Security in EU Member States' (2004) 6 *European Journal of Social Security*, 113-136).
35. For a critical approach, however, *see* B. Caruso, above n. 3, 840.
36. G. Ricci, *Tempi di lavoro e tempi sociali. Profili di regolazione giuridica nel diritto interno e dell'UE* (Milano, Giuffrè, 2005), 268.

Decree no. 66 of 2003, implementing an EU directive, expressly stated that the provisions of the decree 'are aimed at regulating in a uniform manner throughout the national territory' the issue of working hours. Implicit confirmation of the radical exclusion of regional responsibility is given by the exclusion of the education sector from the scope of application of the law. As stated by a Ministry circular implementing the decree (Circular no. 8 of 2005), this is accounted for by the fact that the regions share responsibility for matters pertaining to education, from which it would appear that the regions are allowed to legislate on working hours in the schools sector, albeit within the framework of the fundamental principles established by the state.

(b) Regional legislators also intervened to regulate a recently emerging phenomenon: *mobbing*. For a better understanding of this, it should be said that in Italy mobbing (seen as the employer's abuse of power and harassment of employees) is a concept defined by case law, not regulated by statute. Some Italian regions have therefore introduced specific regulations, to provide for administrative measures to protect the workers involved (the setting up of advice bureaux, anti-mobbing initiatives, etc.). These regulations were brought before the Constitutional Court for violation of Article 117 of the Constitution. The Constitutional Court adopted a rigid, restrictive interpretative approach. It first confirmed the constitutional illegitimacy of a regional law (more specifically, a law introduced by the region of Lazio) which supplied a definition of mobbing.[37] It subsequently made an exception for other regional regulations which only disciplined aspects of a procedural nature without any attempt to interfere in the juridical definition of the case in point (laws passed by the Abruzzo, Umbria and Friuli Venezia Giulia regions):[38]

---

37. More specifically, Art. 2 of the Lazio regional law defines mobbing as follows: 'for the purposes of this law, *mobbing* refers to protracted discriminatory or harassing acts and behaviour towards employees, public or private, by an employer, by any other party in a position of superiority, or by other colleagues, which constitute a regular form of psychological persecution or moral violence'; the definition was followed by examples of employer behaviour that could be defined as mobbing.
38. *See* respectively Constitutional Court rulings no. 22 of 27 Jan. 2006; no. 238 of 22 Jun. 2006; no. 239 of 22 Jun. 2006. For a theoretical discussion, M. Belletti, 'I Criteri Seguiti dalla Consulta nella Definizione delle Competenze di Stato e Regioni e il Superamento del Riparto per Materie', (2006) *Le Regioni*, 905 *et seq.*; G. Ciocca, *Devoluzione e Diritto del Lavoro* (Milano, Giuffrè, 2008), 110 *et seq.*

    The regions are attributed a modest role by a more recent law – no. 123 of 3 Aug. 2007 – on the reorganization of regulations concerning health and safety in the workplace. Article 1(1), in fact, establishes that government power to adopt legislative decrees is to guarantee 'uniform protection of workers throughout the national territory through the respect of basic levels of service concerning social and civil rights', but 'in compliance with Article 117 of the Constitution and the statutes of regions with a special statute'. Considering the various constraints affecting regional competency, it seems evident that it is limited to promotion, support and supervision rather than direct regulation (G. Natullo, 'La Disciplina della Sicurezza sui Luoghi di Lavoro nel Labirinto delle Competenze Legislative di Stato e Regioni' in P Pascucci (ed.),

The orientation against regulatory decentralization, with reference to issues affecting individual work relationships, was confirmed by the Constitutional Court when dealing with the regulation of apprenticeship contracts. The detailed regulations drawn up by national legislation concerning this type of contract (the contents of which refer essentially to training) were considered to be constitutionally in compliance with Article 117 of the Constitution, as its object was traineeship 'in' companies, of an obligatory nature given the type of contract, and thus to be regulated by the state (Constitutional Court ruling no. 50 of 2005).[39] A regional law can legitimately regulate aspects regarding training 'outside' companies (Constitutional Court rulings no. 406 of 7 December 2006; no. 425 of 19 December 2006; no. 21 of 2 February 2007).[40] This is a typical case in which the Constitutional Court, in the presence of a concurrence of competencies,[41] applied the so-called principle of prevalence in its decision.[42]

The analysis carried out so far highlights a tendency – in the first case of a legislative nature, in the other two the interpretative orientation of the Constitutional Court – towards centralizing legislative powers concerning individual employment relationships.[43] The latter can be regulated at a regional level only with difficulty, on the basis of claims regarding territorial differentiation and principles of the Constitution such as equality, territorial uniformity of the discipline, etc.[44]

It would not, however, be fair to say that the Constitutional Court does not take into any account the regulatory space left to decentralized authorities. There have been situations in which the court has evaluated *subordinate* as opposed to *prevailing* interests, imposing an 'obligation to coordinate initiatives by the holders of various interests through practices of loyal collaboration',[45] variously interpreted as limitations of state powers (Constitutional Court ruling no. 219 of 8 June 2005, regarding community service jobs; no. 50 of 7 March 2008, concerning national

---

Il Testo Unico sulla Sicurezza del Lavoro (Roma, Ministero della Salute e Ispesl, 2007), 36 *et seq.*; V. Speziale, 'La Nuova Legge sulla Sicurezza del Lavoro' (2007) CSDLE 'Massimo D'Antona' Working Paper no. 60, 6 *et seq.*, <www.lex.unict.it/eurolabor/ricerca/wp/default.htm>; M. Lai, 'Sicurezza del Lavoro e Riforma del Titolo V della Costituzione' in A. Di Stasi (ed.), *Diritto del Lavoro e Federalismo*, (Milano, Giuffrè, 2004), 311 *et seq.*

39. Moreover, the Constitutional Court sanctioned the constitutional legitimacy of the regulation of the national system of civil servants and public managers' training, thus excluding the regional training facilities, which are still entrusted to the legislative competence of Regions (*see* Constitutional Court ruling no. 75 of 28 Mar. 2008).
40. A regional law is unconstitutional when it regulates aspects directly affecting the contents of an employment contract (e.g., establishing minimum working hours in the initial period of training: Constitutional Court ruling no. 24 of 6 Feb. 2007).
41. *See* F. Carinci, above n. 25, 79 in which he speaks of 'shared' competencies.
42. *See* R. Bin, above n. 14, 896; G. Ciocca, above n. 38, 165 *et seq.*
43. For example, F. Carinci, 'Il principio di Sussidiarietà Verticale nel Sistema delle Fonti' (2006) *Argomenti di Diritto del Lavoro*, 1518-1519.
44. *See* B. Caruso and A. Alaimo, above n. 14, 597-598.
45. *See* R. Bin, above n. 14, 897.

financing of funds for social policies, education and family) and regional powers (Constitutional Court ruling no. 24 of 6 February 2007).

5. IMPROBABLE DECENTRALIZATION: THE SOCIAL SECURITY SYSTEM

The welfare system in Italy is guaranteed by the Constitution. Article 38(2) does not make explicit mention of social security but entrusts 'bodies or authorities appointed or integrated by the state' with the task of meeting workers' needs in all cases of industrial accidents, sickness, invalidity, old age and involuntary unemployment.[46] This provision reflects the intention to give social security the status of a social right of citizens, in an egalitarian dimension, with respect to which the responsibility of the state is of primary importance.[47]

It thus seems consistent that the revised Article 117(2)(o) of the Constitution should have entrusted the state with exclusive responsibility for social security. It ensures basic guarantees of social security and insurance, contrasting the risks connected with employment or financial insecurity upon retirement.

The situation becomes more complicated, however, when Article 117(3) of the Constitution gives the regions shared responsibility for 'supplementary social security' but at the same time makes no provisions regarding 'social services', so that they are to be considered as the exclusive responsibility of the regions (Article 117(4) of the Constitution).

This division of responsibilities leads to a number of practical problems.

Firstly, the Italian welfare system includes not only various forms of pensions paid by social security authorities but also income support measures for the unemployed, as they concern the consequences of unemployment and thus do not involve ascertainment of actual poverty or need. It follows that the responsibility for regulating situations of fundamental significance for 'social protection', for example unemployment benefits, should be exclusively the preserve of state legislation.[48] In the same way, the state has powers to regulate the allocation of

46. G. Ciocca, 'Il Sistema Previdenziale ed il Federalismo' (2003) *Argomenti di Diritto del Lavoro*, 741.
47. A. Poggi, 'La Previdenza Complementare e Integrativa del Nuovo Titolo V della Costituzione tra Politiche Locali e Cittadinanza Sociale' (2002) *Rivista di Diritto della Sicurezza Sociale*, 329; E. Ales, 'Diritti di Cittadinanza Sociale e Livello Essenziale di Prestazione nel Nuovo Disegno Costituzionale: Brevi Considerazioni sull'Uguaglianza Solidale' (2002) *Rivista di Diritto della Sicurezza Sociale*, 349-361.
48. *See* Ciocca, above n. 46, 755; also M. Persiani, 'Devolution e Diritto del Lavoro' (2003) *Argomenti di Diritto del Lavoro*, 36; *contra* Carinci, above n. 25, 80. It being understood that many of the competencies *ex* Art. 117, although variously divided between the state and the regions, make up, as G.G. Balandi puts it, an 'integrated system of support in the labour market' including vocational training (exclusively the responsibility of the regions), active measures governing the labour market (shared responsibility) and transfers of income (basically the exclusive responsibility of the state, with the exception of welfare measures): *see* G.G. Balandi,

training and income support funds, as these also, according to the Constitutional Court, come under the general welfare system.[49]

The re-expansion of regional responsibility for 'supplementary social security', for which it has concurrent competency, does not seem to go beyond a theoretical level. The only state law regarding supplementary social security, following the constitutional reform, which formally granted the regions power to set up 'forms of supplementary pensions in compliance with the relative national laws' (Article 3(1)(d), Legislative Decree no. 252 of 5 December 2005), appears to be so analytical and detailed as to make different forms of regulation at a regional level highly improbable.[50] This would seem to be in line with the need to supplement basic pensions in an era of crisis involving the state welfare system: on the principle of equality, it justifies the prevalence of state intervention which, despite Article 117 of the Constitution, leaves minimal space for regional legislation.

Whereas welfare is for the time being the general responsibility of the state, the same does not apply to social services, which are not mentioned by the Constitution and for which the regions are to be considered exclusively responsible.[51] The regions can therefore not only legislate on social services but also regulate specific forms of financial support for persons and families at risk of social exclusion, as in the case of basic income.[52]

This does not, however, preclude the responsibility of the state, in the presence of certain conditions, for establishing 'basic levels of service' concerning the right to welfare services.[53] However, this concept does not include the financing, by state law, of funds for social policies, family and education, since these measures do not identify any basic level of services, constituting on the contrary mere financing of expenditure in regional matters (assistance and social services), in breach of the constitutional limits on legislation and financial autonomy of the regions (Constitutional Court ruling no. 50 of 7 March 2008).

'La Tutela Sociale nel Mercato' in M.V. Ballestrero (ed.), *La Stabilità Come Valore e Come Problema*, (Torino, Giappichelli, 2007), 192 *et seq.*

49. *See* Constitutional Court ruling no. 50 of 2003, § 12; *see also* R. Salomone, above n. 17, 199.
50. P. Passalacqua, 'La Previdenza Complementare nel Prisma della Sussidiarietà tra Disegno Costituzionale e Legislazione Ordinaria' (2007) *Rivista di Diritto della Sicurezza Sociale*, 77 *et seq.*
51. This is on the basis of the *dichotomy* which separates social security and welfare (*see* M. Cinelli, above n. 33, 464). As regards the 'protection of health', on the other hand, the state and the regions have concurrent competencies (*see* G. Ciocca, above n. 46, 757).
52. *See* M. Pallini, above n. 26, 447; A. Durante, 'Il Reddito di Cittadinanza: Verso un Nuovo Modello di Protezione Sociale?' (2006) *Rivista Giuridica del Lavoro*, 417 *et seq.* Confirming this, the Constitutional Court ruling no. 423 of 29 Dec. 2004, which judged constitutionally illegitimate the establishment by national legislators of conditions for access to a particular form of 'basic income' (the so-called 'Reddito di ultima istanza').
53. C. Lagala, 'Le Regioni e il Sistema di Sicurezza Sociale dopo la Legge Costituzionale n. 3 del 2001' (2002) *Rivista di Diritto della Sicurezza Sociale*, 374-375.

6. CONCLUSION

From a comparative analysis it emerges that even national systems of a 'federalist' institutional nature (Germany, Belgium, Spain) provide for mechanisms, based on institutional weights and counterweights, so as to avoid a lack of balance in favour of decentralized authorities, with a consequent marginalization of the state in decision-making processes.[54] Clauses such as those concerning national interest, uniformity of the legal and territorial system, and principles of equality are too cogent (and equally essential for the inherent structure of European constitutional systems) for them not to curb centralistic trends even in federally based systems.

In such a situation, it comes as no surprise that in the Italian system, currently structured on a semi regional basis, the drive towards decentralization should be relatively limited in scope. It has mainly taken root in sectors which were involved in the transfer of functions from the state to the regions before the 2001 reform (recruitment and employment services, labour market regulations), while individual employment relationships and welfare remain firmly in the hands of the state.

It is not, however, necessarily true that this model – which formally aspires towards a high degree of legislative uniformity, capable of avoiding the risk of fragmented protection and the ensuing effect of social *dumping* at a territorial level – is one which will provide greater guarantees for employees. Some examples will better clarify this statements:

(a) First of all, let us refer once again to Constitutional Court ruling no. 268 of 2007 concerning the unemployed status. In this case, although the Court's reference to fundamental principles with regard to the criteria for defining the unemployed status formally complies with the Constitution, it hinders the introduction of regulations that are more favourable for workers at a regional level, and indeed leads to a downgrading of levels of protection in the labour market. The Court might perhaps have considered national laws regarding the unemployed status as a 'basic level of service', defining a legal standard that could be improved on by regional legislators.[55]

(b) Or again, let us reflect briefly on the ruling in which the Constitutional Court declared the Lazio Region law concerning mobbing to be illegitimate. The ruling not only appears to be exorbitant, given the moderate scope of the law.[56] It also fails to appreciate that the region filled in a serious gap in the legal system in a sector (the protection of health and

54. *See* Pallini, above n. 26, 435.

55. F Liso, 'Il Collocamento Ordinario da Funzione Pubblica a Servizio. Appunti' in *Rappresentanza, Rappresentatività, Sindacato in Azienda ed Altri Studi. Studi in Onore di Mario Grandi*, ed. CEDAM (Padova, CEDAM, 2003), 425-426; *also* M. Cinelli, 'Sussidiarietà e Modello di Sicurezza Sociale' (2004) *Rivista di Diritto della Sicurezza Sociale*, 456; A. Poggi, above n. 47, 348.

56. *See* B. Caruso, above n. 3, 858 *et seq.*; V. Roppo, 'Diritto dei Contratti, Ordinamento Civile, Competenza Legislativa delle Regioni. Un Lavoro Complicato per la Corte Costituzionale' (2005) *Corriere Giuridico*, 1306.

safety) for which the regions have concurrent responsibility, which is not regulated by state laws despite is practical significance, and which relies in short on the creative logic of case law.[57] Nor was it possible to claim a lack of 'fundamental principles' established by the state (the 'framework law'), as these are widely 'to be found in the legal system, albeit not organised and arranged in a single place but existing in a fluid state'.[58]

This means simply that there is no assuredly good 'centralism' countered by an assuredly bad (regionalist or federalist) 'decentralization' or vice versa. In socially and institutionally complex systems (and in an era of multilevel governance), it is difficult for centripetal trends, or centrifugal trends within the system itself, to be governed on the basis of a 'systemic' rule. It is, on the contrary, necessary to adjust regulatory tools, techniques and modalities to the aims to be pursued, on the basis of dynamic evaluations that take into account the relationship of instrumentality between the 'best place' for the rule (and the procedure) to be allocated and the 'highest degree of satisfaction' of the (socially significant) interest pursued. Such prognostic judgments, albeit in an institutional context featuring rules of coordination, are not easy to formulate and may seriously jeopardize the 'certainty of law'. But at the same time they appear necessary to reduce the risk that the methods used to attribute practical competencies will prove to be mere operations of institutional engineering, incapable of increasing the chances of a better functioning system in terms of social justice, efficient services and the guarantee of fair competition.

References

Alaimo A., 'I Servizi all' Impiego e l'Art 4 Cost. dopo le Recenti Riforme del Mercato del Lavoro' (2004) *Giornale di Diritto del Lavoro e delle Relazioni Industriali*, 249-284.

Ales E., 'Diritti di Cittadinanza Sociale e Livello Essenziale di Prestazione nel Nuovo Disegno Costituzionale: Brevi Considerazioni sull'Uguaglianza Solidale' (2002) *Rivista di Diritto della Sicurezza Sociale*, 349-361.

Andronico A. and Lo Faro A., 'Defining Problems: The Open Method of Coordination, Fundamental Rights and the Theory of Governance', in O. De Schutter and S. Deakin (eds), *Social Rights and Market Forces: Is the Open Coordination of Employment and Social Policies the Future of Social Europe?* (Bruxelles, Bruylant, 2005).

Armstrong K. and Kilpatrick C., 'Law, Governance or New Governance? The Changing of Open Method of Coordination' (2007) 13 *Columbia Journal of European Law*, 649-678.

57. A. Leone D'Agata, 'Federalismo e Diritto del Lavoro' (2004) *Rivista Critica di Diritto del Lavoro*, 499.
58. *See* B. Caruso, above n. 3, 863.

Balandi G.G., 'La Tutela Sociale nel Mercato' in M.V. Ballestrero (ed.), *La Stabilità Come Valore e Come Problema* (Torino, Giappichelli, 2007).

Barbera M., *Nuove Forme di Regolazione: il Metodo Aperto di Coordinamento delle Politiche Sociali* (Milano, Giuffrè, 2006).

Barbera M. and Caruso B., 'In Search of a New Language: Italian Labour Law Scholarship in the Face of European Integration' (2007) Jean Monnet Working Paper no. 11, <www.JeanMonnetProgramme.org>.

Belletti M., 'I Criteri Seguiti dalla Consulta nella Definizione delle Competenze di Stato e Regioni e il Superamento del Riparto per Materie' (2006) *Le Regioni*, 903-931.

Benz A., 'Accountable Multilevel Governance by the Open Method of Coordination?' (2007) 13 *European Law Journal*, 505-522.

Bernard N., *Multilevel Governance in the European Union* (The Hague, Kluwer, 2002).

Bilancia P. and De Marco E., *La Tutela Multilivello dei Diritti* (Milano, Giuffrè, 2004).

Bin R., 'I Criteri di Individuazione delle Materie' (2006) *Le Regioni*, 889-901.

Bin R., 'La Prassi della Cooperazione nel Sistema Italiano di *Multilevel Government*' (2007) *Le Istituzioni del Federalismo*, 689-706.

Bobbio L., 'Governance Multilivello e Democrazia' (2005) 2 *Rivista delle Politiche Sociali*, 51-62.

Carinci F., 'Riforma Costituzionale e Diritto del Lavoro' (2003) *Argomenti di Diritto del Lavoro*, 17-84.

Carinci F., 'Il principio di Sussidiarietà Verticale nel Sistema delle Fonti' (2006) *Argomenti di Diritto del Lavoro*, 1496-1541.

Caruso B., 'Il Diritto del Lavoro nel Tempo della Sussidiarietà (Le Competenze Territoriali nella *Governance* Multilivello)' (2004) *Argomenti di Diritto del Lavoro*, 801-865.

Caruso B. and Alaimo A., 'Il Conflitto tra Stato e Regioni in Tema di Lavoro e la Mediazione della Corte Costituzionale: La Recente Giurisprudenza tra Continuità e Innovazione' (2007) *Rivista Italiana di Diritto del Lavoro*, part II, 569-598.

Cinelli M., 'Sussidiarietà e Modello di Sicurezza Sociale' (2004) *Rivista di Diritto della Sicurezza Sociale*, 447-476.

Ciocca G., 'Il Sistema Previdenziale ed il Federalismo' (2003) *Argomenti di Diritto del Lavoro*, 739-768.

Ciocca G., *Devoluzione e Diritto del Lavoro* (Milano, Giuffrè, 2008).

D'Alessio G., 'Pubblico Impiego' in G. Corso and V. Lopilato (eds), *Il Diritto Amministrativo Dopo le Riforme Costituzionali. Vol. II* (Milano, Giuffrè, 2006).

D'Antona M., 'Possibili Agenzie per l'Impiego. Stato e Regioni nel Mercato del Lavoro' (1988) *Lavoro e Diritto*, 385-392.

D'Antona M. and D'Auria G., 'L'Agenzia Regionale per l'Impiego: Posizione Istituzionale e Profilo Normativo' (1990) *Rivista Italiana di Diritto del Lavoro*, part I, 127-156.

Durante A., 'Il Reddito di Cittadinanza: Verso un Nuovo Modello di Protezione Sociale?' (2006) *Rivista Giuridica del Lavoro*, 403-431.

Ferraro G., 'Nota Introduttiva', in G. Ferraro (ed.), *Sviluppo e Occupazione nell'Europa Federale. Itinerari Giuridici e Socioeconomici su Regioni e Autonomie Locali* (Milano, Giuffrè, 2003).

Ferrera M. and Sacchi M., 'Il Metodo di Coordinamento Aperto e le Capacità Istituzionali Nazionali: l'Esperienza Italiana' (2005) *Giornale di Diritto del Lavoro e delle Relazioni Industriali*, 51-83.

Garofalo D., 'Lo *Status* di Disoccupazione tra Legislazione Statale e Provvedimenti Regionali' (2006) *Diritto delle Relazioni Industriali*, 637-653.

Groppi T., 'Il Titolo V Cinque Anni Dopo, Ovvero la Costituzione di Carta' (2007) *Le Regioni*, 421-431.

Hooghe L. and Marks G., *Multi-level Governance and European Integration* (Oxford, Rowman & Littlefield, 2001).

Lagala C., 'Le Regioni e il Sistema di Sicurezza Sociale dopo la Legge Costituzionale n. 3 del 2001' (2002) *Rivista di Diritto della Sicurezza Sociale*, 363-381.

Lai M., 'Sicurezza del Lavoro e Riforma del Titolo V della Costituzione', in A Di Stasi (ed.), *Diritto del Lavoro e Federalismo* (Milano, Giuffrè, 2004).

Leone D'Agata A., 'Federalismo e Diritto del Lavoro' (2004) *Rivista Critica di Diritto del Lavoro*, 479-502.

Leotta F., *La Competenza Legislativa nei Sistemi Autonomisti* (Milano, Giuffrè, 2007).

Liso F., 'Il Collocamento Ordinario da Funzione Pubblica a Servizio. Appunti' in *Rappresentanza, Rappresentatività, Sindacato in Azienda ed Altri Studi. Studi in Onore di Mario Grandi* (Padova, CEDAM, 2003).

Loy G., 'Le Competenze delle Regioni a Statuto Speciale in Materia di Lavoro alla Luce della Modifica del Titolo V della Costituzione Italiana', in A Di Stasi (ed.), *Diritto del Lavoro e Federalismo* (Milano, Giuffrè, 2004).

Marinelli M., 'Federalismo e Diritto del Lavoro: Il Caso della Sicilia' (2004) *Lavoro nelle Pubbliche Amministrazioni*, 391-414.

Mariucci L., 'Federalismi e Diritto del Lavoro' (2001) *Lavoro e Diritto*, 403-417.

Natullo G., 'La Disciplina della Sicurezza sui Luoghi di Lavoro nel Labirinto delle Competenze Legislative di Stato e Regioni' in P. Pascucci (ed.), *Il Testo Unico sulla Sicurezza del Lavoro* (Roma, Ministero della Salute e Ispesl, 2007), 35-41.

Pallini M., 'Sub Art. 117 della Costituzione', in G. Amoroso, V. Di Cerbo and A. Maresca. (eds), *Il Diritto del Lavoro. Vol. I. Costituzione, Codice Civile e Leggi Speciali* (Milano, Giuffrè, 2007), 418-453.

Passalacqua P., 'La Previdenza Complementare nel Prisma della Sussidiarietà tra Disegno Costituzionale e Legislazione Ordinaria' (2007) *Rivista di Diritto della Sicurezza Sociale*, 47-91.

Persiani M., '*Devolution* e Diritto del Lavoro' (2003) *Argomenti di Diritto del Lavoro*, 19-40.

Pizzetti F., 'La Tutela dei Diritti nei Livelli Substatali', in P. Bilancia and E. De Marco (eds), *La Tutela Multilivello dei Diritti* (Milano, Giuffrè, 2004).

Poggi A., 'La Previdenza Complementare e Integrativa del Nuovo Titolo V della Costituzione tra Politiche Locali Cittadinanza Sociale' (2002) *Rivista di Diritto della Sicurezza Sociale*, 309-348.

Ricci G., *Tempi di Lavoro e Tempi Sociali. Profili di Regolazione Giuridica nel Diritto Interno e dell'UE* (Milano, Giuffrè, 2005).

Roppo V., 'Diritto dei Contratti, Ordinamento Civile, Competenza Legislativa delle Regioni. Un Lavoro Complicato per la Corte Costituzionale' (2005) *Corriere Giuridico*, 1301-1316.

Ruggeri A., 'Leggi Statali e Leggi Regionali alla Ricerca di una Nuova Identità' (2007) *Quaderni Regionali*, 401-449.

Sacchi S., 'Governance e Coordinamento Aperto delle Politiche Sociali', in M. Ferrera and M. Giuliani (eds.), *Governance e Politiche nell'Unione Europea* (Bologna, Il Mulino, 2008).

Salomone R., *Il Diritto del Lavoro nella Riforma Costituzionale* (Padova, CEDAM, 2005).

Speziale V., 'La Nuova Legge sulla Sicurezza del Lavoro' (2007) CSDLE 'Massimo D'Antona' Working Paper no. 60, < www.lex.unict.it/eurolabor/ricerca/wp/default.htm>.

Telò, 'Il Metodo Aperto di Coordinamento. Dal Consiglio Europeo di Lisbona al Testo Costituzionale' (2004), 4 Quaderni di Rassegna Sindacale, 71-96.

Torchia L., 'La Potestà Legislativa delle Regioni' (2002) *Le Regioni*, 343-363.

Trojsi A., 'La Potestà Regionale in Materia di Lavoro' (2007) *Rivista Giuridica del Lavoro*, part I, 651-671.

Wilthagen T., Tros F., and van Lieshout H., 'Towards Flexicurity? Balancing Flexibility and Security in EU Member States' (2004) 6 *European Journal of Social Security*, 113-136.

Chapter 9

Centralization and Decentralization within the Spanish Model of Social Federalism: The Examples of Social Assistance and Employment Policies

Antonio Baylos, Jaime Cabeza & Maria Jose Romero

1. THE SPANISH MODEL OF SOCIAL FEDERALISM AS AN OPEN PROJECT

It is widely agreed that the political model for the structure of the Spanish state based on the 1978 Constitution is a federal model. There is an extensive doctrinal debate as to what may be regarded as federalism. From an examination of political systems it may be deduced that a federal system is one where, 'as opposed to centralized systems where there is a sole central authority, there are two (or more) levels of government, so that elements of shared government are combined with common institutions and regional self government within the constituent units'.[1] Amongst the wide range of non unitary political forms, the so called Spanish 'state of Autonomous Regions' is a notable example of asymmetric decentralization, a 'federation in all but name', with seventeen Autonomous

1. For all, R.L. Watts, *Sistemas Federales Comparados* (Marcial Pons, Madrid, 2006), 105.

Roger Blanpain, Juan Pablo Landa, Brian Langille (eds), *Employment Policies and Multilevel Governance*, pp. 205–221.

Regions authorized by the Constitution to exercise an extensive level of self government.[2]

Said asymmetry is not only evident in the way that different areas of government are attributed to the Autonomous Regions, with the resulting strain when it comes to maintaining the cultural identity of those regions defined as 'nationalities' – a variety of the 'stateless nations'.[3] The power of self-government is also asymmetric with regard to content. In social protection matters, that is, protective public action through the Social Security system and the collection of welfare activities for social inclusion, the Spanish model maintains a strong centralizing component.[4] The framework for the distribution of powers between the central government and the regional self-government is based on (i) separating the legislative and executive levels, which entails a boost for centralization at the legislative level; and (ii) the acknowledgement of a decentralized area at the execution and administration level of the social protection system.

The reason behind the centralizing principle in matters of social protection lies in the concept of the welfare state and in the principles of equality and solidarity that make it up. The potentially decentralized structure of social protection may come into conflict with said principles of equality and solidarity. There will be unequal situations from the very moment that it is possible to establish different models of social protection, either from a territorial perspective, or from a material perspective. In contrast, a more unitary concept of the state ensures that all citizens are able to enjoy the guaranty of public protection against situations of need, irrespective of the territory where they reside. This is the justification of social protection as a 'state function', which imposes homogeneous content on all territories that make up the Spanish state.

This centralizing tension, encouraged by an important and influential doctrinal sector,[5] has been endorsed to a great extent by the Spanish Constitutional Court in a series of decisions through the 1980s and 1990s. This case law interprets the attribution of competences according to sections 148 and 149 of the Spanish Constitution by confirming the national scope of social protection policies and the confinement of the Autonomous Regions' powers to the management or execution of these policies. Equality and solidarity function as political principles that

2. *Ibid.*, 130-131.
3. On this subject, M. Guibernau, 'Naciones sin Estado: Escenarios Políticos Diversos', in M. Barañano (Dir.), *La Globalización Económica. Incidencia en las Relaciones Sociales y Económicas* (CGPJ, Madrid, 2002), 263 *et seq.*
4. Critically B. Suarez Corujo, *La Protección Social en el Estado de las Autonomías* (Iustel, Madrid, 2006), 28.
5. Fundamentally, L.E. de la Villa and A. Desdentado, 'Delimitación de Competencias Estado-Comunidades Autónomas en la Constitución de 1978 (Las Relaciones Laborales y la Seguridad Social)', in AA.VV *Derecho del Trabajo y de la Seguridad Social en la Constitución* (CEC, Madrid, 1980); A. Desdentado, 'El Régimen Económico de la Seguridad Social y las Autonomías' (1983) 38 *Revista Española de Derecho Administrativo*, whose line is continued in innumerable studies on Spanish pro labour policies which maintain this centralizing posture, even in contradiction with some decisions from the Constitutional Court relating to regional competence in matters of social protection that we look at later.

unify the scope of legal protection. At the same time, they form a part of the social protection system itself as basic principles of social security, an institutional safeguard provided for in the Constitution. Solidarity applies to the entire national community without discrimination.[6] Equality of rights and duties in matters concerning social security extends up to the territorial limit of the state. It makes uniformity of 'living conditions' compulsory beyond the territory of the different Autonomous Regions, that is, in the enjoyment of the social protection rights guaranteed in equal measure in the whole of the national territory.[7]

The drive for centralization on this basis has been reinforced, from an economic perspective, in accordance with the notion of the economic unity of the market. This subject is relevant for at least two reasons. Firstly because it is possible to observe a certain shift from the legitimization of a centralized model of social protection (based on the welfare state and its capacity to offer a standardized and uniform treatment of welfare services for all citizens), towards the economic matrix that directly relates market unity and social cohesion. The principles of 'unity of the national economic order' and of 'market unity' are fundamental to the territorial organization of the state and of the distribution of competences in economic matters. The statement of inter territorial solidarity as an articulating principle of the 'unity of the state and the Autonomous Regions' derives from them.[8] The framework for the distribution of powers and competences between the state and the Autonomous Regions must be interpreted on the basis of the unity of the economic and social order so that the 'unity' of the social security system be imposed. This notion implies uniform regulation throughout the national territory to ensure, above all, 'unity of treasury' and financial solidarity of the system, by way of attributing to the state the exclusive competence over the economic regime of the social security, without prejudice to complementary and subordinated powers of the Autonomous Regions.

The second significant element is that the shift towards market unity as a form of legitimization is fundamentally led by social intermediaries, that is, business associations and the most representative trade unions. The view of the business sector and of the national confederations of trade unions (CCOO and UGT) on this matter converges on the idea of a unitary vision of competences for social protection. Legitimization of the social security system, both at a legislative and at a governance level, ought to pertain to the state – without prejudice to the implementation of these rules by the Autonomous Regions. This sort of 'social Jacobinism' is very deeply entrenched in the thinking of trade unions, and has been echoed by Spanish business, historically pro state and hostile to nationalistic political thinking. The argument is doubly important for what it does not explicitly say.

6. J. Aparicio, *La Seguridad Social y la Protección de la Salud* (Civitas, Madrid, 1988), 105.
7. *Ibid.*, 139-140.
8. The most useful document in order to verify the economic ground for the unity of the market is contained in the Report drawn up by the Spanish Economic and Social Council on this subject, at CES, Unidad de Mercado y Cohesión Social, Informe 3/2000, Consejo Económico y Social, Madrid, 2000.

The fact is that by way of this pursuit of centralization of social protection, social intermediaries safeguard their position as direct interlocutors with the state in the reformulation of the social security model. Incidentally, this constitutes a characteristic of the Spanish model that was already present in 1990, when the historic negotiations for the creation of a second level of benefits took place, which gave rise to the Non Contributory Benefits Act.[9]

Whatever the underlying reason behind, this view, subject to social agreement with trade unions and business leaders, concentrates on the economic benefits supplied by the social security system. It cannot extend to those services which may be termed as social assistance. Neither to those economic benefits that guarantee a certain basic minimum to those who cannot access social security benefits, whether contributory or non-contributory. These areas may be regulated and managed by the regions, possibly because their raison d'être is not to be found in the notion of social citizenship qualified by work, but rather in the poverty and social exclusion as the 'frontier land' of the welfare state.

A new element is added to the definition of this model of social federalism biased towards centralizing positions in the determination of the content and scope of social protection. In the process of integration of states in the EU (with the surrender of sovereignty that this requires), social policy has been gradually integrated into a scheme of legislative harmonization by way of European regulations – normally directives – which impose a generalized result in all Member States. It therefore concentrates on the normative power of the state as a key element in order to achieve normative harmonization in the EU. As from the Treaty of Amsterdam, and fundamentally from the Lisbon Summit for the determination of the European Employment Strategy, there exists a regulatory technique known as the open method of coordination which, at least with regard to social regulation – but not in employment regulation as such – tends to polarize the sources of European law.[10] Convergence in the strategic objectives of the EU – in matters of employment, although subsequently this procedure has been extended to many other areas – reinforces the role of the Member States and their leading position in drawing up their internal policies.[11] The success of this regulatory procedure, and

9. The trend is more marked as from the start of the new century, and specifically as from the so called Agreement for the Improvement and Development of the Social Protection System of April 2001. *See* J. Aparicio, 'La Evolución Regresiva de la Seguridad Social en el Período 1996-2002: hacia el Seguro y el Asistencialismo' (2002) 19 *Revista de Derecho Social*, 22-23; J. Aparicio and J.L. Monereo, 'El Derecho a la Seguridad Social', in J.L. Monereo, C. Molina, Mª. N. Moreno (eds), *Comentario a la Constitución Socio-Económica de España* (Comares, Granada, 2002), 1507 *et seq.*
10. Out of so many reflections on the OMC, the essay by S. Sciarra, 'The Convergence of European Labour and Social Rights: Opening to the Open Method of Coordination' is always of interest, in G. A. Bermann and K. Pistor (eds), *Law and Governance in an Enlarged European Union, Columbia Law School* (New York, Hart Publ., Oxford and Portland, Oregon, 2004), 163 *et seq.* And this despite the relative 'decadence' of this method of European juridification since the Brussels Summit of 2005 and the Barroso Commission.
11. J. Cabeza, 'Estrategia Europea, 'Estado Autonómico y Política de Empleo' in Asociación Española de Derecho del Trabajo y de la Seguridad Social (AEDTSS) *XVIII Congreso Nacional de Derecho del Trabajo y de la Seguridad Social* (Laborum, Murcia, 2007), 22 *et seq.*

its application to matters as decisive as the whole issue of social cohesion, reinforces the position of the state as sovereign power with wide normative and regulatory capacity over the social protection system. The Report of the European Economic and Social Committee on the subject of 'Social Cohesion: Fleshing Out a European Social Model'[12] insists on this idea by linking the 'responsibility for promoting cohesion and social justice' to the states and their governments to the provision of 'systems of social protection that ensure adequate coverage or social protection against the main risks' at levels that allow 'the prevention of poverty and social exclusion'.

Nonetheless, this is not a closed model. Each of the factors mentioned also produce tendencies that pull in an opposite direction. At the political level, it is obvious that there has been a change in thrust with respect to the makeup of the spaces allocated for self-government with the renegotiation of the Statutes of Autonomy in some regions. The Statute of Autonomy of Catalonia became a highly symbolic case all through 2006 to the beginning of 2007, until its approval by referendum on 18 June 2006, replacing the statute in force since 1979. The new statute has been challenged before the Constitutional Court in an atmosphere of intense political bickering.[13] There are also the cases of the Statute of Autonomy of the Basque Country, also in 2006, the approval of the Statute of Autonomy of Andalusia in referendum in 2007, or proposals to reform the Statute of Galicia, among others. In all cases, the consolidation of more decentralized perspectives in the area of social policy is constant.

The unity of the market is quite possibly the principle that has suffered precisely the greatest erosion. This is because of the segmentation of the labour market and the consequences of the breakdown of basic withholding in social security systems, like the Spanish one. Inequalities are what generate precarious jobs in all their aspects, including in their psychological and cultural aspects,[14] but also in those areas related to training and worker qualifications, which are obstacles to opportunity and new needs for services that are a part and parcel of a postmodern and aged society.[15] This creates a crisis for withholding as a way that technically embodies the solidarity that is the expression of the social security system. What is more, this crisis of principles has caused the rigid separation of the sources of financing of the Spanish system. This, together with the taking on traits typical of insurance, has accentuated the assistance aspects of social security.[16] The other

12. Opinion of the European Economic and Social Committee on Social Cohesion, Fleshing out a European Social Model, *Official Journal of the European Union* C 309 of 16 Dec. 2006, 119-125.
13. Political disagreement on the self-disqualification of one of the judges who was to rule on the constitutionality of the Statute of Catalonia in the middle of a tremendous smear campaign against the judge, as it was considered a lynchpin in the far right's strategy to stop the policy plans of the Spanish government on this issue.
14. M. Bresson, *Sociologie de la Précarité* (Armand Colin, Paris, 2007).
15. A. Lettieri, 'Jonas o della crisi dei sistema pensionistici', in G. Giovannini (ed.), *Il Futuro delle Pensioni. Demografía, Sostenibilità, Ideología* (Hediese, Roma, 2002), 9 *et seq.*
16. J. Aparicio, above n. 9, 41-43.

side of this trend is the correlative strengthening of the private/collective dimension of the supplementary protection and the contracting out through private insurance contracts.[17] This contracting out is a distinctive characteristic of today's trends, strongly linked to the market perspective in so far as it deals with a process of approaching social protection as a business.[18] In this complex context notions of equality and solidarity, contemplated from the centralization or decentralization prism in a federal system, are empty ideas that lack real meaning. In a market that is fractured and dislocated in social categories and with such different levels of access to protection, the unity principle of organization of the social protection has lost any reference to a homogenous labour market. The foundation of the principles of equality and solidarity in the market may produce a result different from that expected. A market constructed around the borders of the nation state permits at its core very significant and unequal disparities of protection not only vertically but also horizontally, in some of its own territories.[19]

Lastly, the European construction of social cohesion and the employment policies also open a broad space for regional government action. This occurs not only because the open method of coordination can only be productive 'to the degree that it encourages participation in the decentralized territories'.[20] Regional government organs are also given 'growing competences in the design, development and application of employment policies' – a question that in addition converges with a certain 'territorialization' of the combined economic and employment policies.[21] On the subject of social cohesion, the axis of Community action and its own aims affects the regions that make up the different states of the EU as pointed out in Article 158 of the ECT when affirming that in order to strengthen economic and social cohesion it must 'reduce the differences between the levels of development of the different regions and the delay of regions or less favoured islands'. This is then set out in the regulation of the structural funds, aimed directly at the *infra* state institutions located at the regional level.

This role in relation to the EU is explicitly assumed by the different rules of the Spanish autonomous governments. All of them, but especially the rules resulting from the statutory reform of 2006-2007 mentioned above, establish that the autonomous region is not merely an entity of self-government that acts in the scope of the national community, but also a 'reference space' in the EU. This implies, on the

17. J.L. Monereo, *Público y Privado en el Sistema de Pensiones* (Tecnos, Madrid, 1996).
18. J. López Gandía, 'La Protección Social de los Funcionarios Públicos. Regulación Actual y Perspectivas ante los Sistemas Privados de Pensiones' (2004) 25 *Revista de Derecho Social*, 31 *et seq.*
19. As confirmed by the analysis of the differentials of unemployment and income in the different Spanish regions. Specifically, the turnout of the unemployed and temporary employees and the meeting point between these two categories is seen to be a characteristic of the Spanish labour market and is located especially in certain regions of Spain – like Andalusia and Extremadura.
20. J. Cabeza, above n. 11, 43.
21. *Ibid.*, 43.

other hand, the incorporation of values, principles and European rights in the sphere of the political decision of the region.[22]

The tension between unity and diversity is therefore a model in itself, still open under Spanish law, where those principles are frequently asymmetrical. An example that reveals very significantly the regulatory tensions found in the Spanish model is social assistance and its complementary division.

1.1. Social Assistance as an Example

Social assistance represents a technique of protection inherited from public charity and the battle against generic poverty, refined and improved as it has evolved.[23] Social assistance is clearly differentiated from social security, which protects the worker and is based on the notion of professions, even though in the future the system will revolve around the citizen, whom it will protect from certain situations of need. Social assistance, as part of the assistance of social security 'does not have as its object the fight against poverty, but rather against exclusion'. It seeks to ensure the individual 'a position of security and independence with respect to the negative market effects'.[24] The boundary between both concepts is not easy. This is principally due to social security getting some traits of social assistance, such as protection, that have a universal character. Initially, the benefits of social assistance[25] were of a discretional nature, while the social security benefits produced full individual rights for its beneficiaries.

The Spanish system of social assistance is based on two different subsystems. On the one hand, a subsystem is understood independently or outside the social security system, and entrusted to the self-government of the Autonomous Regions. This subsystem is a 'mechanism for groups of the population which [social security] does not cover and that operates by means of techniques different from those of the social security. At present (. . .) social assistance is characterised by its sustainability, apart from all contributory obligations or previous economic collaboration

22. Hence, the Statute of Andalusia (2007) establishes in Art. 1.4 that 'the European Union is the area of reference for the Autonomous Community, which accepts its values and oversees the compliance with its objectives and respect for the rights of European citizens'. The Statute of the Valencia Community (2006) says more of less the same, but spells out that the Valencia Community is a 'region of Europe'. Article 3.2 of the Statute of the Autonomy of Catalonia (2006) states that 'Catalonia has in the Spanish state and in the European Union its own political and geographic space of reference and incorporate the values, the principles and the obligations arising from the fact that it forms part of them'.
23. J. Vida Soria, 'Asistencia Social en el Sistema de la Seguridad Social Española' (1968) 21 *Revista de Trabajo*, 23 *et seq.*
24. A. Márquez, *Seguridad Social y Protección Social: Un Enfoque Conceptual* (Serv. Publicaciones Universidad de Málaga, Málaga, 2002), 177.
25. L.E. De La Villa and A. Desdentado, *La Reforma del Sistema Español de Seguridad Social*, 2nd edn (Fundación IESA, Madrid, 1985), 97 where *social assistance* is defined as 'a set of mechanism of protection, not based on withholding contributions, that covers all citizens in state of need and does not award demandable rights'.

from the recipients or beneficiaries'.[26] On this basis, it appears that there exists a well-defined scope, at least of what does *not* constitute part of this concept. The loopholes or deficiencies produced by the social security system constitute social assistance even if the absence of all contributory elements is its main characteristic, whilst its existence is, on the contrary, the characteristic element of social security.[27] Social services and non-contributory economic benefits for situations of poverty or lack of income are therefore the roots of this system. However, in parallel and in conformity with the maturity of social security systems, these also incorporate in their protective action measures of social assistance (and, since 1990, in a systematic manner), a network of non contributory benefits, especially in the area of disability and retirement. Naturally, these types of benefits are governed by the principles of unity and homogeneity, derived from the principles of equality and solidarity, centralized as state competence. The separation of these two spheres has been criticized by a significant part of the doctrine that departs from a unitary focus of social assistance that includes the autonomous social assistance in the social security system. This thesis, based on the recognition by numerous Autonomous Regions of the right to an insertion income or minimum salary to cover the basic cost of living[28] continues to have broad support. It defends the integration in the social security system of new situations of need such as dependency.[29] Article 41 of the Spanish Constitution infers the existence of a social assistance system *within* the social security system that follows the dynamic and expansive character of the latter. It goes beyond the contributory path and the ensuring of risks and is meant to defray situations of need not covered by a pension. This assistance 'outside' the system of social security contemplates benefits which are not set forth by the rules of the social security system and are within the exclusive competence of the Autonomous Regions.[30]

The case is that this separation operates in a dynamic manner, but the borders between the benefits of social security and those of social assistance have been blurred because of the universalization of social security, which has brought into its scope criteria that are more akin to social assistance. The recognition of actual rights to benefits and services in social assistance has also contributed to that.

---

26. Sixth ground of the STC 76/1986 of 9 Jun.
27. In 1990, non-taxable benefits were treated in this way: the legislator by virtue of Art. 41 of the Constitution guarantees assistance and benefits for all independently of the amount withheld from the individual. This introduced into the social security system a mixed model, by introducing the element of assistance, in L. Hurtado Gozález, 'Asistencia Social y Seguridad Social: Sus Fronteras Actuales' (1993) 25 *Actualidad Laboral*, 45; F. García-Nuñez Serrano 'Los Complementos Autonómicos: ¿Seguridad Social o Asistencia Social?' (2002), 34 *RMTAS*, 143.
28. J.L. Monereo and C. Molina, *El Derecho a la Renta de Inserción. Estudio de su Régimen Jurídico* (Comares, Granada, 1999), 191 *et seq.*
29. J. Cabeza, 'Cuestiones Sobre el Seguro de Dependencia' in AESS, *La Economía de la Seguridad Social. Sostenibilidad y Adaptabilidad del Sistema* (Laborum, Murcia, 2006), 40 *et seq.*; E. Rodríguez, 'El Contenido Constitucional de la Dependencia' (2006) 36 *Revista de Derecho Social*, 106 *et seq.*
30. *See* the fifth ground of the decision by the Constitutional Court STC 239/2002 of 11 Dec. 2002 (the STC decision).

For the Constitutional Court, social assistance is a 'group of actions and protective techniques that remain at the periphery of social security', but the measures of social assistance can have an effect on people who are already beneficiaries of social security benefits. This has in fact occurred in the case of the Autonomous Region of Andalusia which set up a major supplement for the non-contributory pension for retirement and disability of the social security system. Certain political sectors and social spokespersons criticized this payout and had the question brought before the Constitutional Court. Its decision 239/2002 of 11 December 2002 had various dissenting opinions, evidencing the sensitivity of this subject. The Constitutional Court's decision leans towards prudent decentralization. It was badly received by the conservative government of the Popular Party, which very improperly, in our opinion, decided to reform the social security law in a way contrary to the direction set forth by the Constitutional Court. The change of government in 2004 brought a new law reform, in alignment with the decisions on the constitutionality of the distribution of competences issued by the Constitutional Court.

The analysis performed by the Court's decision deserves a mention, due to its clarity of exposition. The court found that the Spanish system of social security is based, from the historical moment of the enactment of the Constitution, 'on a double pillar: the contributory principle and the coverage of risks that would have effectively been produced' as established in the General Social Security Act of 1974 (GSSA), whose Articles 15 and 20 regulated the obligatory nature of the contributions and the protective action of the system. However, in addition, the social security system relates to the 'situations or states of need' in the constitutional formula of Article 41. Hence, it is conceived as a function of the state in order to attend to situations of need that may escape the contributory coverage.[31] In the area of social assistance, this is included as a benefit supplementary to those foreseen by Articles 20.2, 36 and 37 of the GSSA. It had a residual characteristic and its recognition was discretional. In addition, it includes social assistance outside of social security, provided by the state, the province and the town halls, which is mentioned as a protective instrument in situations of need for the groups not covered by the social security.

The social security system may include in its scope not only the contributory benefits existing since 1978, but also a non-contributory protection, the only one which can guarantee assistance and social benefits for all citizens in situations of need. The Constitutional Court interprets the rule in a new way, upon widening the scope of social security. The Article 41 of the Spanish constitution establishes a 'system of social protection entrusted to public powers that is, although not solely, a fundamental axis of the social security system with an imperative characteristic, which coexists with other supplementary ones'. Moreover, it highlights:

> the neutrality of the legal provision from the perspective of the distribution of competences, since, if the social security system must take into account the

31. The dissenting opinion differs from this line of thought. Conde (the second judge) considers 'the taxation principle of the conceptual binomial principle and covering risks, as a synthesis of the structural elements characterising preconstitutional social security'.

> distribution of competences at its core, those that correspond respectively to the state and the Autonomous Communities in said area, the remaining segments of social protection that are not included in that system also lead to the distribution of competences that result from the measure of social protection involved in each case.[32]

Regarding social assistance from this second perspective, the Constitutional Court stated that the existence of assistance inside the social security system at the time of enacting the Spanish Constitution and its Article 41 (the guarantee of 'sufficient assistance and social benefits'), obligates the social security system to correct the mistake made by the legislator when using the term social assistance in a general manner, by understanding that the provision of Article 148(1)(20) of the Spanish Constitution referred, in principle, to social assistance outside social security.[33]

In short, there may be disturbances between social assistance and social security assistance as a result of the widening of their respective scopes. The universal nature of social security and the widening of its field of protection and assistance is produced by (i) the incorporation of non-contributory benefits to the social security system (Act 26/1990) that borrows essentially from assistance elements, subject to the computation of economic earnings and financed by taxes; but also (ii) by supplements to the pension of the surviving spouse that have assistance elements and are nurtured by fee contributions and earnings of social security.[34] Therefore, the inclusion of social assistance in the system of social security must be contemplated with caution. It is not decisive as regards the division of competences, or with respect to the division with 'insurers not included in social security' or with funds and pension plans, since it is possible to receive social security benefits and other supplementary ones from private insurers or from pension funds.[35]

Thus, 'nothing shall impede from the perspective of constitutional legitimacy' that the Autonomous Communities with competence in the subject of 'social assistance' provide assistance to groups of persons in situations of need – even though they may already be receiving assistance benefits from the social security system – as long this does not affect its economic regime.[36] Moreover, it is understood that it is a requisite of the social legal state that those who do not have their minimum needs covered by the non-contributory part of the social security system have access to other benefits and aid of a different nature, this assistance within the system coinciding with Article 148.1.20 of the Constitution.

Therefore, this 'union' cannot prevent the Autonomous Communities from acting in this 'common space', especially if it is considered that in 'certain economic situations, the scope of the social security protection, could involve

32. The citations belong to the sixth ground of the STC decision. In this respect, once again the dissenting opinion takes precedence, refuting the novel significance of Art. 41 of the Spanish Constitution.
33. *See* the seventh ground of the STC decision.
34. *See* the eighth ground of the STC decision.
35. *See* the sixth ground of the STC decision.
36. *See* the seventh ground of the STC decision.

assistance or benefit limitations that require supplementation with other sources in order to ensure the principle of sufficiency to which Article 41 refers.' The topic is important because by means of this constitutional interpretation, the application of a certain type of social federalism, more decentralized, to this new phase of social protection would imply 'to abandon old principles of control and centralised administrative hierarchy and depart from true frameworks of financial autonomy and management guided by the principles of coordination and faithful inter-administrative collaboration'.[37] At present, the legislative advances in this area are fruit of the permanent adaptation to new social circumstances. These changes must be considered as the result of the dynamism towards the achievement of (i) subjective universality of coverage;[38] and (ii) objective universality, understood as protection in face of situations of need. The conceptualization of these social risks constitutes, in our opinion, the centre of the debate, since there does not seem to be an end to their definition and scope, and that is linked to the true problem: to ensure the level of protection, needs must be covered by the social security system[39] and by social assistance.

1.2. Employment as an Example

Employment policies may be the clearest example of all the complexities intrinsic to a model such as the Spanish one. This is undoubtedly one of the areas where each territorial administration plays a more structuring role – or a destructuring one, depending on the point of view. In such an environment, as is the case of social work benefits, legislative competences may end up being concurrent.

The Autonomous Communities may have the power to foster the economic development of the region within the goals set by the national economic policy under paragraph 13 of Article 148.1. In turn, paragraph 17 of Article 149.1 recognizes the basic legislation and economic regime of the social security system as an exclusive competence of the state, without prejudice to the Autonomous Communities' power to execute the provision of the relevant services. Prior to that, paragraph 7 of the same Article recognizes the same exclusive competence of the state in matters of labour legislation, without prejudice to the executive competences of the Autonomous Communities.

On these grounds, it has always been difficult to distinguish the competences of the state from those of the Autonomous Communities in matters relating to employment. And even beyond the issue of competence, there is doubt as to whether the duality of presumably competent administrations may have affected

37. J.P. Landa Zapirain, 'La Organización de la Sanidad Pública ante la Jurisprudencia Constitucional: una Reflexión sobre este Modelo de Reparto Competencial entre el Estado y Comunidades Autónomas y sobre su Posible Extensión a otros Ámbitos de la Protección Social' (1999) 6 *Revista de Derecho Social*, 131-133.
38. All citizens and even residents in the state covered by the social security system.
39. J. Aparicio, 'Sobre la Suficiencia de las Prestaciones con Ocasión de las Recientes Reformas del Sistema de la Seguridad Social' (2002) 17 *Revista de Derecho Social*, 235 *et seq.*

the quality of public services. Although from another viewpoint, there seems to be a generalized acceptance that greater proximity of public services to citizens has improved the management of active employment policies.

In practice, the difference between the scope of competence of the state and of the Autonomous Communities has given rise to a situation in which the state is entitled to the regulation and management of the passive employment policies – that is to say, the provision of unemployment benefits – whereas the Autonomous Communities are entitled to the active employment policies. This needs explaining by a brief review of the legal background.

The first milestone after the Constitution of 1978 was Law 51/1980 of 8 October on employment. This statute brought together under the same legal framework all the regulations for employment and unemployment. It was passed right at the historic moment when the first generation of Statutes of Autonomy was being enacted. At that time the debate about the competence over employment and unemployment did not have much weight.

Four years later Law 31/1984 of 2 August was adopted, governing unemployment benefits. This statute dealt exclusively with the passive side of employment, that is, unemployment benefits. It was anchored on social security regulations, which in turn warranted, in principle, that the relevant legal competence correspond exclusively to the state. It was not until the consolidated drafting of the General Law of the Social Security by Royal Decree 1/1994 of 1 June that benefits in case of undesired lack of employment were covered by the basic provisions governing the social security system. There is no doubt, though, that the Law of 1984 caused the definitive separation between active and passive policies, since they have never been joined together in a legal text ever since. However, we need to qualify some aspects of this separation.

After the entering into force of the Amsterdam Treaty and the ensuing Luxembourg Summit the Commission, the Council and the Kingdom of Spain entered into a fruitful dialogue.[40] At the time, there was an economic cycle of great expansion that for once translated economic growth into employment growth. Nevertheless, perhaps it was no coincidence that as from 1997 the transfer of employment services to the Autonomous Communities had begun. The offices of the former National Employment Institute (INEM, its acronym in Spanish) started to depend little by little on the autonomous administrations. This transfer has now reached its conclusion, well in tune with the European policy of regional authorities getting involved in employment affairs. The INEM now has been divested of all power but for the management of unemployment benefits.

Ever since, the issue of competence has required a greater coordination between the state and the autonomous communities. Even the Constitutional Court has had to rule whether the competent authority to impose sanctions relating to administrative infringements by beneficiaries of unemployment benefits is the

40. On this subject, E. Terradillos Ormaechea, 'La Interacción entre Políticas Activas de Empleo y Políticas Económicas en la Unión Europea. El Juego del Método Abierto de Coordinación y sus Efectos sobre la Política de Empleo Española' (2005) 62 *RMTAS*, 59 *et seq.*

state or the Autonomous Community (STC 195/1996 of 28 November). Nevertheless, the outcome of this cleavage of active/passive policies may not be a negative thing, though the value judgment may have become blurred because of the significant decrease in unemployment rates experienced back then.

In the early 1990s there grew a closer connection between employment policies and social security benefits across Europe, more aimed at finding jobs and 'employability' for the subjects of such benefits. Parallel to other European laws, the Spanish social security legislation brings on board important nuances of employment in its regulations on unemployment benefits with the labour reform of 2002. Successively, the Royal Decree Law 5/2002 of 24 May, and the Law 45/2002 of 12 December bring forward instruments that are well known in Europe and in general at the International Labour Organization (ILO) and Organization for Economic Cooperation and Development (OECD): commitment to activity, suitable employment offers, active reintegration subsidies, capitalization programmes for taxable benefits, geographic mobility programmes or benefit/salary compatibility. These are tools regulated under the consolidated drafting of the General Law of the Social Security, though with an unmistakable flair of active policies – with the peculiarity that their management corresponds to the state and not to the Autonomous Communities.[41] And, by the way, the success of these intricate policies must be considered a limited one, not to say very disappointing, for two obvious reasons. Firstly, because when the Law 45/2002 came into force there was no real debate or sufficient reflection on the articulation of said measures and the general design of employability policies. And secondly, because the design of more or less appropriate measures was not accompanied by enough material and human resources to support reintegration programmes and individualized attention, which might have allowed for instruments such as the commitment to activity to become nothing but an increase of bureaucracy.

There is a programme that merits particular mention. Full unemployment benefit is paid out in one single instalment, something that has often changed in the last few years: either to foster individual business start-ups by unemployed persons, or to adapt it to other purposes, such as for migrants returning to their home countries. In any case, the dynamics of regulatory changes have had a lot to do with the relative success of such kind of measures.

In the meantime, and once the transfer of the management of active employment policies to the Autonomous Communities was completed, the problem of adapting employment legislation – the outdated Law 51/1980 – to the constitutional design began. This situation was not accompanied by enough reflection either. It ended up with a new law which was technically correct but did not meet the great challenges brought about by employment issues. This is the Law 56/2003 of 16 December.[42]

---

41. A general reflection of the intentions in F. Valdés Dal-Ré, *Las Tendencias de Contractualización en el Sistema Español de Protección Social* (2002) 20 *Revista de Derecho Social*, 13 *et seq.*
42. *See* F. Cavas Martínez, 'El Entramado Institucional del Empleo en las Vertientes Pública y Privada', in AA.VV *Estrategia Europea, Estado Autonómico y Política de Empleo* (MTIN, Madrid, 2008), 183 *et seq.*

It is fair to acknowledge the important contribution of this statute to the standardization of many an aspect which had hitherto been dubious. *Inter alia*, the setting up of an institutional fabric, the National Employment System, provided with bodies that involve the autonomous authorities as well as the social partners, in particular, the Sectoral Conference on Labour Affairs and the General Council of the National Employment System. More specifically, the former is in charge of drafting the National Action Plans for Employment. We also have to highlight the explicit recognition of the local dimension of employment policies. In sum, certain guidelines that tie in perfectly with the Community dimension, issues of good governance and the involvement of regional authorities, social partners and civil society.

On the other hand, the Law 56/2003 defines and recognizes the remit of the employment services to the Autonomous Communities. In addition, it makes reference to the three basic instruments of employment policy: labour mediation, active employment policies and the coordination between active policies and protection through unemployment benefits.

We ought to make reference to the shades of grey found in this statute. Management of passive employment policies is entrusted to the state employment service, an autonomous body that takes over the duties of the defunct INEM. The active policies 'attached' to the passive ones brought forward by the reform of 2002 depend on it. So a social security benefit, such as the unemployment benefit, is managed by a state body different from the regional organizations that manage the remainder of benefits. This despite the fact that in the early 1990s some budget laws had programmed the disparition of the INEM as the body in charge of managing unemployment benefits.

With regards to labour mediation, the statute entrusts this to the public employment services of the Autonomous Communities or to the relevant cooperating bodies and duly authorized employment agencies. As a consequence, managing employment opportunities corresponds to the Autonomous Communities, with the peculiarity that the regulations providing for the non-profit nature of said employment agencies remain in force – Article 16 of the *Estatuto de los Trabajadores* and the RD 735/1995, of 5 May.[43] This non-profit nature was not revisited when the Kingdom of Spain ratified ILO Convention No. 181 on private employment agencies. In general terms, the issue is in much need of regulatory updating in Spain. Temporary job agencies are theoretically excluded, despite the fresh winds that blow across Europe, perhaps intensified by the new Directive 2008/104 of 19 November. The management of the institutions of the Autonomous Communities may in all likelihood be burdened by legislation that could be qualified as obsolete. In practice, the contribution of private employment agencies has been

---

43. Relevant to these regulations, R. Escudero Rodríguez and J.R. Mercader Uguina, 'Las Agencias de colocación y los servicios integrados para el empleo. La aplicación de Nuevos Medios Técnicos a la gestión de la Seguridad Social. La selección de personal laboral en las Administraciones Públicas' (1995) 2 *Relaciones Laborales*, 1199 *et seq.*

and continues to be incidental, in contrast to the efforts carried out to improve the quality of public services, whatever existing deficiencies there may be.

Among the active employment policies, training for employment enjoys special relevance, particularly the traditionally known as occupational and ongoing training – now for the unemployed and for people with jobs. A core issue in the European Strategy's approach to employment, training has been one of the most disputed battlegrounds between the state and the Autonomous Communities, particularly with regard to the management of vocational training. On this matter, the Constitutional Court has issued several decisions, particularly decision 95/2002 of 25 April and decision 190/2002 of 17 October. Despite the fact that both recognize that the regulatory competence lies with the state (for it is a genuine labour matter), the Court considered that to exclude the Autonomous Communities from the management of ongoing training was not in line with the constitutional system of competence-sharing. This in turn caused somewhat of a regulatory stir, which has now concluded with the enactment of the Royal Decree 395/2007 of 23 March, generating a new set of measures,[44] but where further friction between both territorial bodies will most likely happen again. In the meantime, this subsystem is to be funded essentially from the vocational training fees collected by the General Treasury of the Social Security, despite the fact that they are not considered as social security dues. It is precisely such a difference in nature that has given rise to claims that the management thereof should be transferred to the Autonomous Communities, especially in the Basque Country.

However, conflicts over competence in matters of training for employment are not actually excessive. This situation of relative calm springs from the particular contribution of the social partners at the state level, as the system meets most of their expectations. It is only in such areas where trade unions' and employers' organizations at the regional level prevail – once again the Basque Country stands out – that there is an open confrontation to the established model, to the extent that alternative pillars have been instituted under the auspices of the Basque government itself.

The final reflection is that there probably is a certain deficit in terms of the overall regulation on employment in the Autonomous Communities. The impression is that the fear to impinge on state competences has placated initiatives in this matter, to the point that the Autonomous Communities have forfeited their entitlement to competences to this respect. The outcome has been, more often than not, that measures adopted by these territorial administrations have been excessively contingent, anchored only on programmes from concrete political impulses and not on regulation with a greater vocation of permanence.

44. On this issue, F. Camas Roda, *La Formación Profesional en los Ámbitos Educativo y Laboral* (Aranzadi, Pamplona, 2007).

References

Aparicio, J., *La Seguridad Social y la Protección de la Salud* (Civitas, Madrid, 1988).

– 'La Evolución Regresiva de la Seguridad Social en el Período 1996-2002: Hacia el Seguro y el Asistencialismo', (2002) 19 *Revista de Derecho Social.*

– 'Sobre la Suficiencia de las Prestaciones con Ocasión de las Recientes Reformas del Sistema de la Seguridad Social' (2002) 17 *Revista de Derecho Social.*

Aparicio J. and J.L. Monereo, 'El Derecho a la Seguridad Social', in J.L. Monereo, Molina, C. and M[a]. N. Moreno (eds), *Comentario a la Constitución Socio-Económica de España* (Comares, Granada, 2002).

Bresson, M., *Sociologie de la Précarité* (Armand Colin, Paris, 2007).

Cabeza, J., 'Cuestiones Sobre el Seguro de Dependencia' in AESS, *La Economía de la Seguridad Social. Sostenibilidad y Adaptabilidad del Sistema* (Laborum, Murcia, 2006).

– 'Estrategia Europea, 'Estado Autonómico y Política de Empleo' in *XVIII Congreso Nacional de Derecho del Trabajo y de la Seguridad Social,* (Laborum, Murcia, 2007).

Camas Roda, F., *La Formación Profesional en los Ámbitos Educativo y Laboral,* (Aranzadi, Pamplona, 2007).

Cavas Martínez, F., 'El Entramado Institucional del Empleo en las Vertientes Pública y Privada', in *Estrategia Europea, Estado Autonómico y Política de Empleo* (MTIN, Madrid, 2008).

CES, *Unidad de Mercado y Cohesión Social, Informe 3/2000* (Consejo Económico y Social, Madrid, 2000).

Desdentado, A., 'El régimen económico de la Seguridad Social y las Autonomías' (1983) 38 *Revista Española de Derecho Administrativo.*

de la Villa L.E., and A. Desdentado, 'Delimitación de Competencias Estado-Comunidades Autónomas en la Constitución de 1978 (Las Relaciones Laborales y la Seguridad Social)' Centro de Estudios Constitucionales, *Derecho del Trabajo y de la Seguridad Social en la Constitución* (CEC, Madrid, 1980).

– *La Reforma del Sistema Español de Seguridad Social,* 2nd edn (Fundación IESA, Madrid, 1985).

Escudero Rodríguez R. and J.R. Mercader Uguina, 'Las Agencias de colocación y los servicios integrados para el empleo. La aplicación de Nuevos Medios Técnicos a la gestión de la Seguridad Social. La selección de personal laboral en las Administraciones Públicas' (1995) 2 *Relaciones Laborales.*

García-Nuñez Serrano F., 'Los Complementos Autonómicos: ¿Seguridad Social o Asistencia Social?' (2002), 34 *RMTAS.*

Guibernau, M., 'Naciones sin Estado: Escenarios Políticos Diversos', in M. Barañano (Dir.), *La Globalización Económica. Incidencia en las Relaciones Sociales y Económicas* (CGPJ, Madrid, 2002).

Hurtado Gozález, L., 'Asistencia Social y Seguridad Social: Sus Fronteras Actuales' (1993) 25 *Actualidad Laboral.*

Landa Zapirain, J.P., 'La Organización de la Sanidad Pública ante la Jurisprudencia Constitucional: una Reflexión Sobre este Modelo de Reparto Competencial entre el Estado y Comunidades Autónomas y Sobre su Posible Extensión a otros Ámbitos de la Protección Social' (1999) 6 *Revista de Derecho Social.*

Lettieri, A., 'Jonas o della crisi dei sistema pensionistici' in G. Giovannini (ed.), *Il Futuro delle Pensioni. Demografía, Sostenibilità, Ideología* (Hediese, Roma, 2002).

López Gandía, J., 'La Protección Social de los Funcionarios Públicos. Regulación Actual y Perspectivas ante los Sistemas Privados de Pensiones' (2004) 25 *Revista de Derecho Social.*

Márquez, A., *Seguridad Social y Protección Social: Un Enfoque* Conceptual (Serv. Publicaciones Universidad de Málaga, Málaga, 2002).

Monereo, J.L., *Público y Privado en el Sistema de Pensiones* (Tecnos, Madrid, 1996).

Monereo J.L., and C. Molina, *El Derecho a la Renta de Inserción. Estudio de su Régimen Jurídico* (Comares, Granada, 1999).

Rodríguez, E., 'El Contenido Constitucional de la Dependencia' (2006) 36 *Revista de Derecho Social.*

Sciarra, S., 'The Convergence of European Labour and Social Rights: Opening to the Open Method of Coordination' in G.A. Bermann and K. Pistor (eds), *Law and Governance in an Enlarged European Union* (Columbia Law School, New York, Hart Publ., Oxford and Portland, Oregon, 2004).

Suárez Corujo, B., *La Protección Social en el Estado de las* Autonomías (Iustel, Madrid, 2006).

Terradillos Ormaechea, E., 'La Interacción entre Políticas Activas de Empleo y Políticas Económicas en la Unión Europea, El Juego del Método Abierto de Coordinación y sus Efectos sobre la Política de Empleo Española' (2005) 62 *Revista del Ministerio de Trabajo y de Asuntos Sociales.*

Vida Soria, J., 'Asistencia Social en el Sistema de la Seguridad Social Española' (1968) 21 *Revista de Trabajo.*

Watts, R.L., Sistemas Federales Comparados (Marcial Pons, Madrid, 2006).

Chapter 10

The Jobseeker's Allowance: A British Perspective on Job Activation

Jo Carby-Hall

1. INTRODUCTION

1.1. Methodology

The Jobseeker's Allowance (JSA) Act of 1995 (with the Regulations of 1996, enacted under it) provides for a unified law on the topic and replaces the previous unemployment benefit, and to a certain extent, income support which has been relegated to being a 'fall back' benefit for jobseekers who are, or remain, unemployed.

One of the aims of this legislation was at the time, and still is, to encourage the unemployed back to work, but it is suggested that the main aim was, and is, to place robust financial restrictions on this social security benefit by tightening up the conditions of entitlement. Means testing is another feature introduced (in the case of the income-based allowance limb of the benefit) to save money to the detriment of those diligent persons who have worked and saved!

With regard to disqualifications for entitlement to JSA, something will be said briefly on the resulting appeals system, using cases decided under the old unemployment benefit law. Since much of the old law on the subject has been inserted into the 1995 legislation, those cases decided under the old laws are still valid.

Roger Blanpain, Juan Pablo Landa, Brian Langille (eds), *Employment Policies and Multilevel Governance*, pp. 223–244.

It will be noticed that the JSA rules are specific, practical and technical in nature; they therefore encourage a descriptive approach and thus do not allow for scholarly analysis and theoretical discussion.

Taking into account these 'limitations' it is proposed to treat briefly the historical milestones followed by an explanation and description of two relevant matters which will be discussed in this chapter, namely the New Deal schemes and the Jobcentre Plus notions.

There will then follow a discussion on the JSA concept on the claimant's eligibility to receive this benefit, special provisions for young persons of 16 and 17 years of age and joint claims. The rates of JSA, additional benefits and back pay will be discussed, followed by sanctions and disqualifications. Some concluding thoughts will round off the discussion.

1.2. Historical Milestones

In their book entitled 'Law and Society in England, 1750-1950'[1] the learned authors, Cornish and Clark point out[2] that the National Insurance Act 1911 provided for compulsory insurance against unemployment and ill health. Such compulsory insurance was initially limited to certain specified industries. In the course of time, additional industries were included followed by a consolidation of the legislation.

The 1911 legislation was overtaken by events. As a result of the reforms proposed by the Beveridge Commission culminating in the 1946 legislation which created the 'Welfare State' and which became operative as from 1948, unemployment benefit became one of the main benefits of the welfare state. That benefit was a contributory benefit paid on a flat rate during the first year of unemployment. Were the unemployed claimant's needs to be greater than the benefit received, for example because of dependants, unemployment benefit could be increased by income support. This latter benefit was of course, means tested.

During the time of the Thatcher government there was a thorough review of the welfare state system which was costly on the government coffers. Thus, unemployment benefit and benefits provided to those who were sick over a long period of time and therefore incapacitated, came under the scrutiny of the then government. The Social Security (Incapacity for Work) Act 1994 treated incapacity, whereas the Jobseeker's Act passed a year later, in 1995, provided for an allowance for jobseekers subject to certain legal conditions being met.[3]

The Social Security (Incapacity for Work) Act 1994 had the effect of restricting sickness benefits by removing a significant number of persons off these benefits. Where those persons had been removed from the incapacity benefits lists they

1. W.R. Cornish and G. de N. Clark, *Law and Society in England, 1750-1950* (London, Sweet & Maxwell, 1989).
2. *Ibid.*, 447-472.
3. *See* the government White Paper entitled 'Jobseeker's Allowance' Cmnd. 2687 (1994).

would have been deemed capable of work. If however they were not able to find employment, then they would have been entitled to claim unemployment benefit and in appropriate instances, income support. This resulted in further financial strains being placed on those latter benefits. It therefore became necessary to 'tighten the screw' once more to alleviate such financial strains occurring.

The Jobseeker's Act of 1995 was an attempt[4] by the government to alleviate these financial strains by creating a unified JSA to replace both unemployment benefit and income support. The aim was obviously a cost-cutting measure by the government in that it restricted social security benefits. Other aims were, firstly, to encourage people to actively seek employment; secondly, to make it harder for the unemployed to obtain benefits through the tightening of entitlement conditions; thirdly, by the creation of a variety of 'New Deal' programmes applicable to a variety of age/status groups who are unemployed; in the fourth instance, to discourage the culture of persons claiming and relying on social security benefits; and finally to discourage social benefits fraud which has made headlines on several occasions.

1.3. New Deal Schemes

Something needs to be said of the New Deal schemes mentioned above since these programmes are tied up, and have important links, with the measures under the Jobseeker's legislation that an unemployed person needs to take to find employment.

The New Deal has celebrated its tenth anniversary in 2008 and according to the government, since 1998, when the first New Deal scheme came about, more than 1.8 million persons have been helped into jobs as a result. Furthermore, 300,000 lone parents have gone back to work which has helped lift 600,000 children out of poverty. The numbers claiming incapacity benefit decreased and long-term unemployment for young persons has been virtually eliminated.[5]

The New Deal launched in January 1998 was the first of twelve pilot schemes of a modern approach to welfare.

During the 1980s and 1990s the United Kingdom experienced mass unemployment.[6] Changes and new approaches were required on the labour market. At the heart of these were the various New Deal schemes.

4. *See* the discussion by A Bryson in 'Jobseeker's Allowance: Help or Hindrance to the Unemployed?' (1995) 24 ILJ, 204.
5. Source: Gordon Brown in the Foreword of 'Transforming Britain's labour market. Ten years of the New Deal' (2008) at <www.dwp.gov.uk/welfarereform/docs/PMNewDeal2-01-08.pdf>.
6. During those years unemployment exceeded three milion persons on two occasions. As for inacapacity benefit, between 1979 and 1997 the number of persons claiming incapacity benefit (and invalidity benefit which proceeded incapacity benefits) doubled with the number of lone parents on income support rising by some 700,000. By 1997 unemployment and inactive persons on social security benefits rose to some 5.5 million. More than a million persons were on

1.3.1. New Deal for Young People

The first New Deal introduced in January 1998 was targeted at long-term youth unemployment, these being persons of between 18 and 24 who had been claiming JSA (or National Insurance credits) for more than six months. Since then, no longer has there been the option of remaining indefinitely on unemployment benefits. The New Deal for Young People Pathfinders (NDYP) ensured for the first time that every youth claiming JSA over a period had to participate compulsorily in 'meaningful activity designed to improve their chances of getting a job'.[7]

1.3.2. New Deal 25 plus (ND 25+)

Building on the New Deal for Young People, there was introduced in July 1998, New Deal 25 plus, targeted at persons claiming JSA for two years or more. In April 2001, the scheme was enhanced by providing assistance to persons aged over 25, who have been unemployed for eighteen out of the last twenty-one months. Since June 2007, anyone aged 25 to 59 claiming JSA (or national insurance credits) for eighteen out of the past twenty-one months has been mandated to all aspects of New Deal 25 plus.

1.3.3. New Deal for Lone Parents (NDLP)

Since October, 1998 there was the introduction of NDLP which provides support[8] for lone parents who wish to return to work. This new deal is thus voluntary.

1.3.4. New Deal for Partners

From April, 1999, New Deal for Partners was introduced to give assistance to partners claiming benefits. Such assistance may include the tackling of barriers to work.

1.3.5. New Deal 50 plus

New Deal 50 plus was introduced in April, 2000 and is designed to help the long-term unemployed and economically inactive persons who are over 50 and who have been claiming specified benefits for six months or more. This scheme aims at getting the over 50s back to work.

Jobseeker's Allowance for more than one year, which included 85,000 young persons 'languishing on benefit…, with no job and no future in prospect.' In 'Transforming Britain's labour market' (2008) at p. 3 (DWP).

7. In April 1998, there was created too the New Deal for Young People National Rollout.
8. 'Support includes assistance ranging from informal support and advice to financal and practical assistance with training for a job as well as childcare.

1.3.6. New Deal for Disabled People (NDDP)

The NDDP was introduced in July 2001. Provided mainly by the private and voluntary sector, NDDP gives access to job broking advice and support to Incapacity Benefit claimants and disabled persons seeking to re enter the labour market. In October 2003 the Pathways to Work programme was introduced in pilot areas for new incapacity benefit claimants. This programme is focused on what claimants can do, not what they cannot. This scheme gives access to training, condition management, a return to work credit and personal adviser support.

As briefly examined above, it is obvious that there are numerous types of New Deals covering a variety of age and status groups. A key feature of the New Deal is to help customers obtain the job they want and at the same time to help employers to get the workers/skills they need. Although different, they all share some common features. One of these is that every New Deal participant has a personal adviser.[9] Another is the emphasis on the needs of the individual who is out of work.[10] Yet another is the partnership between the public, private and voluntary sectors.[11] Rights and responsibilities[12] are other common features of the New Deal system. Jobcentre Plus integrates benefits and employment services ensuring that their customers receive their rights and meet their responsibilities. Jobcentre plus takes overall ownership of the individual's experience of the welfare-to-work system and the New Deals, helping customers to navigate the system.[13]

1.4. Jobcentre Plus

The reader will find in the pages which follow numerous references to an organization called Jobcentre Plus. Something needs to be said of its background functions and aims.

9. Whose job is to assist the claimant to seek a job or overcome personal barriers to obtain a job.
10. For example, to take a new look at his/her personal situation; to take the skills and experience already acquired and build on those so as to have better opportunities for work.
11. All New Deals are delivered in close partnership with the private and voluntary sectors. Those latter provide most of the support available through the New Deal for Disabled People as well as the other New Deals. The Department of Work and Pensions and Jobcentre Plus work with some 600 providers with contracts worth some GBP 1 billion a year, in 'Transforming Britain's labour market' (2008) at p. 5.
12. Personal advisers assist in motivating, encouraging and buliding up the expectations of the individual. In return for the help provided through the New Deal system and the financial support provided through the social security system, society expects participants to do their utmost to obtain and keep a job. The rights and responsibilities attached to different benefits and different New Deals vary. Whereas the NDYP and ND25 + are mandatory, the other New Deals are voluntary. The basic philosophy however remains the same, namely to get and/or encourage persons back to work.
13. In 'Transforming Britain's labour market' (2008) at p. 5.

Jobcentre Plus is the hub around which the whole of JSA revolves. This body, local branches of which will be found throughout the United Kingdom, controls every aspect of JSA.

Jobcentre Plus which is part of the Department of Work and Pensions (DWP) is a government agency whose function is to assist persons of working age who are unemployed, to return to work; this being part of the government's welfare to work policy. This organization also assists employers to fill vacancies in their establishments. The government's policy is 'to promote opportunity and independence for all through modern, customer-focused services'. Jobcentres are situated in England, Scotland and Wales. The Northern Ireland JSA is claimed at the Social Security Agency.

The key objectives of Jobcentre Plus are various; one of the most important being the giving of assistance to the unemployed and to those who are economically inactive to return into employment. In other words, this organization attempts to increase the supply of labour by encouraging persons to work, this being the best form of welfare.

Another objective is to calculate the correct JSA benefits using some of the complicated formulae to be discussed briefly below. At the same time, Jobcentre Plus attempts to protect the JSA system from fraud and exploitation by its customers.

A third objective is to fulfil employers' needs by filling job vacancies promptly and efficiently by a well trained, well prepared and motivated workforce.

Another objective is to assist its customers facing barriers to employment, such as the handicapped or socially disadvantaged, to compete effectively in the labour market by training, advising and encouraging them and by boosting generally their morale. In such a manner they are assisted to both return to, and remain in, employment.

A fifth aim is to ensure that those receiving benefits fulfil their responsibilities and respect the duties required of them. At the same time Jobcentre Plus aims at providing support and giving assistance to those who are out of work.

Other objectives relate to the inside workings of Jobcentre Plus to make it a more effective, efficient and productive organization, such as to improve on a continual basis 'quality, accessibility, and delivery of services' to its customers.

Yet a further objective is to assist, without discrimination, its ethnic minorities and economic migrants, of which there are many, particularly from the Accession 8 countries which joined the EU on 1 May 2004 and Bulgarian and Romanian economic migrants since 1 January 2007.

2. JOBSEEKER'S ALLOWANCE

2.1. Some Preliminary Notions

The main benefit for persons who are unemployed is the JSA. The JSA can provide financial assistance to a claimant who is unemployed and looking for work.

JSA is of two types. The non means tested-contribution based JSA is the first type. It consists of a personal allowance based on the national insurance contributions a claimant has paid over two tax years.[14] This JSA is paid for up to 182 days only. The second type is the income-based JSA which is means tested. Whether or not a claimant receives it depends on his/her income as well as savings. Furthermore, if there are other members in the claimant's household, their income and savings are taken into account. This type of JSA, means tested as it is, discourages work and savings, both with regard to the claimant and his/her household. Thus the conscientious claimant is encouraged not to save or work! The benefit is thus designed for the claimant and his/her household to receive the minimum level of income which the government sets.

2.2. Eligibility

The conditions for JSA are applicable to all persons who claim this benefit. They are also applicable to a partner if a joint claim is made. Entitlement to JSA is governed by the Jobseekers Act 1995 provisions and the Regulations.[15]

To obtain JSA the claimant must normally be capable of, and available[16] for work. The norm is that the claimant should normally be immediately available to work for a minimum of 40 hours a week.[17] A JSA claimant is enabled to refuse unacceptable work, but only in circumstances where he/she has a reasonable chance of obtaining alternative employment. Such 'unacceptability' would normally refer to his/her normal or previous employment terms and conditions and can only last for a maximum of thirteen weeks. With regard to wages, after six months' unemployment, restrictions as to the claimant's acceptable level of wages are not allowed.[18]

---

14. The benefit year starts on the first Sunday in January and concludes the following January on the Saturday immediately before the first Sunday of January. Contribution-based JSA is not affected by any savings but earnings from part time jobs or an occupational or personl pension may affect the amount of JSA the claimant receives. If the claimant's earnings are high he/she will not be able to obtain a contribution-based JSA. Furthermore, any contribution-based JSA the claimant receives will be for that individual. A partner of the claimant will receive nothing if the claimant is claiming as a member of a couple. The claimant may, however, obtain income-based JSA on top of his/her contribution-based JSA if the claimant has a partner or due to personal circumstances, as for example, if the claimant is caring for a disabled person or is disabled himself/herself. To be noted is that where a claimant applies for JSA, the Jobcentre Plus Office will work out which of the two types of JSA will be paid. Thus contribution-based JSA may be paid on its own, and income-based JSA may be paid on its own. There can however be a mixture of both types of JSA.
15. Jobseeker's Allowance Regulations (1996) SI 1996/207.
16. Jobseeker's Act 1995, s1.
17. Jobseeker's Allowance Regulations (1996) SI 1996/207, Regulation 6. The claimant need not start work 'immediately' if he/she is a carer or performing voluntary work, but he/she must be available for work with a week's notice and available for a job interview within 48 hours' notice.
18. *See* the consolidated Regulations, 7 to 9 and 16.

Should a claimant have a medical condition, a restriction to a particular type of job or to working during specified hours is allowable. Medical evidence has to be produced, however. If the claimant's medical condition or disability is such that it would be difficult to find suitable employment, JSA may not be applicable and other benefits would need to be claimed.

A second condition for eligibility is that the claimant must be actively seeking work.[19] This means that he/she must take steps each week to find employment and/or improve the chances of obtaining work. Thus while the claimant is receiving the JSA he/she is expected to draw up a curriculum vitae giving details of any work experience, qualifications, special skills, activities, interests, etc. More active steps need to be taken by the claimant such as contacting prospective employers and keeping records of what the claimant is doing to seek employment as for example, reading advertisements for vacancies and registering with employment agencies.

The claimant would normally have to visit the local Jobcentre Plus office at least fortnightly. During that visit the claimant would be required to sign a declaration to the effect that he/she is seeking employment, is available for work, and that there have not been any changes of circumstances which would affect JSA entitlement. The declaration is an important part of the administrative procedure as to whether or not JSA would be granted.

Furthermore, during that visit discussions will take place (a) as to whether or not the conditions for JSA are still being met and what the claimant must do to continue receiving that benefit; (b) on how the claimant is progressing with the actions enumerated in the Jobseeker's Agreement (*see* below) and whether that agreement needs to be updated; (c) on whether suitable vacancies exist for the claimant; (d) on the availability of training courses, job search programmes or other services which would prove useful to obtain employment; and (e) any other opportunities and benefits which may be available. The Jobcentre Plus may telephone the claimant should opportunities for jobs, training, etc. present themselves. There could well be a link up in these circumstances with regard to claimants who are subject to the New Deal schemes[20] especially if the claimant has been unemployed for a number of months.

A third condition is that the JSA claimant has paid enough National Insurance contributions in the case of contribution-based JSA.[21] Alternatively, that the claimant has income or savings below a certain level of income-based JSA.[22] To receive-income based JSA the claimant must be a UK Channel Islands, Isle of Man or the Republic of Ireland resident. An overseas citizen or a recent arrival into the UK may find it difficult to claim JSA.

---

19. Jobseekers Act,1995, s. 8. There was a robust tightening up of this provision in 1989. *See* too Regulations above n. 15, 18 to 22.
20. For a brief discussion on the New Deal programmes *see* above. New Deal programmes can include work experience and/or training.
21. *See* above for a brief discussion. Before the claimant is entitled to contribution-based JSA he/she must have paid contributions over the last two complete years before the benefit year in which a claim is made.
22. *See* above for an explanation.

A fourth condition is that the claimant should usually be 18 years old and under pensionable age.[23] A claimant aged 16 or 17 years will not normally be able to receive benefits as an unemployed person. There is however certain circumstances where a person falling into that age group may be entitled to JSA so long as certain conditions are met. Some of these conditions are that the claimant is part of a couple with responsibility for a child or if he/she would be experiencing serious hardship if JSA were to be refused.

The fifth condition is that the claimant will have to enter into a jobseeker's agreement with the local Jobcentre Plus office. A jobseeker's agreement is a document which states that the claimant has agreed a *modus operandi* to find employment. The claimant must sign on at the Jobcentre Plus office at least every fortnight so that the office can check whether the claimant meets the conditions in the agreement and examine whether the claimant needs further assistance to find work. If the Jobcentre Plus office believes that the claimant is not respecting the agreement terms, benefits may be either cut or stopped altogether.

The sixth condition is that the claimant must not be engaged in remunerative work. Under the JSA legal provisions, this means that the claimant must work for less than 16 hours a week.[24] The claimant must therefore either not work at all or work for less than 16 hours a week.

The Regulations[25] provide for special rules as to whether or not a claimant is deemed to be in remunerative work.

In the seventh instance, a claimant cannot claim JSA if he/she is in full-time education at school or in higher education. A part time student may[26] be eligible in certain circumstances.

3. SPECIAL RULES FOR THE UNEMPLOYED 16 AND 17 YEAR OLDS

Unemployed 16 and 17 year olds are not entitled generally to income-based JSA. 'Generally' is used judiciously for in certain circumstances this group may be able to claim income-based JSA, but only over a short period of time.

The circumstances in which that group may be eligible are threefold. First, if the 16/17 year olds are living away from their parents because they are forced to do

23. Pensionable age means 60 for a woman and 65 for a man.
24. Or in the case of the claimant's partner twenty four hours a week. *See* Regulations above 15, regulation 51. Thus the partner must either not work at all or work less than 24 hours a week. If the claimant is working less than 16 hours a week and the partner less than 24 hours a week the amount of JSA received will depend upon the total earnings. If the claimant earns too much, the claimant would not be able to receive contribution-based JSA. This corroborates what has been said earlier regarding means testing and its discouragement to work/save. The claimant and the partner may have to seek a full-time job as part of the conditions of qualifying for JSA.
25. Regulations 52 and 53.
26. A part time student wishing to claim JSA would be advised to consult a Jobcentre Plus or a Citizen's Advice Bureau, because the rules are complicated and depend upon the circumstances of the claimant him/herself.

so and are leaving local authority provided accommodation; second, if they form part of a couple and have a child; thirdly, if by not being able to obtain JSA, severe hardship would ensue.

Nevertheless, in these three circumstances certain conditions need to be met. These include, the 16 and 17 year old being actively looking for work or training; agreeing to and signing a Jobseeker's Agreement; not having income and/or savings above the legally prescribed level; being able to work normally for 40 hours a week; being capable of work; being out of work, or working under 16 hours a week; and be a resident of the United Kingdom. The 16/17 year old must also not be in full-time education, for example, in school or at college,[27] and not receiving income support.[28]

To qualify for JSA the 16/17 year old must also be registered with the Connections Service or Careers Service for employment and training.[29] Young persons of 16/17 years have the same obligations as others seeking JSAs, namely regular visits to the Jobcentre Plus; entering and signing a Jobseeker's Agreement; attending interviews, etc.

Like in the case of adults seeking a JSA, young persons have the obligation to report to the Jobcentre Plus any material change of circumstances, as for example, carrying on voluntary work; obtaining a job; going on holiday; caring duties; change of address, telephone number, etc.

Where the young person is in the breach of the income-based JSA conditions, for example, by not being available for work, refusing to agree to and sign a Jobseeker's Agreement; is not actively looking for work and/or training; etc. he/she will be denied JSA.

---

27. Termed as 'relevant education'.
28. Briefly, 'income support' is an income related benefit which provides financial help for persons between the ages of 16 to 60 who work less than 16 hours a week; are not in full-time education (but there are some exceptions); do not receive JSA; reside in the UK; are not under immigration control; have income and/or saving below the statutory minimum; and in addition meet a variety of conditions.

    The conditions are numerous and consist of, *inter alia*, being a single parent; expecting a baby due in 11 weeks or less or experiencing pregnancy related illness; having had a baby in the previous 15 weeks; caring for someone who cannot look after him/herself; being a registered blind person; appealing against a decision relating to capability for work; being ill or disabled resulting in inability to work; having an obligation to go to court as a witness, or someone otherwise involved in the court proceedings or as a member of a jury; being a deaf or disabled student; and being a refugee living in the UK for less than one year and who is in the process of learning English. Pupils of 16 and 17 who are still at school cannot generally qualify for income support, but there are some exceptions. These include single parents; persons in physical and/or moral danger; persons subject to a serious risk to physical and mental health; 16/17 year olds who do not have a living parent or guardian or live away from parents or guardians because there is no contact with them; or because of disability. Income support is normally payable on its own, but is sometimes paid to supplement earnings from part time employment or incapacity benefit.
29. In these circumstances, the 16/17 year old may qualify for a Young Person's Bridging Allowance. This allowance will be considered prior to consideration for eligibility to a JSA.

There could be a reduction of 40% for two weeks[30] in the amount of JSA received by the 16/17 year old where opportunities for work and/or training are unreasonably refused; where training or a training place is given up; where training is lost because of misconduct; or where there is a failure to attend or to apply for training or work.

Where a young person is benefiting from JSA due to severe hardship[31] that allowance may be stopped if the conditions on training opportunities and offers of employment are rejected without reasonable cause. Income-based JSA will also cease. Were the young person to claim again successfully an income-based JSA due to severe hardship, the allowance will be reduced during the two first weeks by way of penalty.

A young person who leaves voluntarily a job without good cause or is dismissed on grounds of misconduct, will lose JSA for a period of from one to twenty-six weeks, depending on the circumstances. Such a person who has had the allowance reduced or stopped will not be allowed to look for training or work, with training as an alternative to work or restrict his/her availability for work involving jobs which offer suitable training.

There are special rules for new job seekers.[32] Any previous occurrences regarding their training/work practices will be ignored for purposes of JSA benefits but if they turn down or leave training without just cause thereafter their benefits will be reduced.

4. JOINT CLAIMS AND JOBSEEEKER'S ALLOWANCE

A joint claim applies where the jobseeker has a partner. In the case of a joint claim for income-based JSA both persons of certain couples need to claim JSA together and each one of them normally has to seek employment and meet all the necessary conditions for obtaining JSA. Furthermore, the job seeker and/or the partner has to be 18 years old or over and born after 28th October 1957, and neither must have responsibility for a child. To claim exemption to JSA requirements an application form (JSA6) will need to be completed.

The philosophy behind this scheme is that both members of a couple are receiving advice and assistance on seeking work and/or training, etc from Jobcentre Plus and both are taking part in the necessary arrangements.

Exceptions to this philosophy are possible however in certain instances, where both persons in the couple are unable to observe all JSA requirements. Under these circumstances, one of the members of the couple may be exempted from observing

30. In some instances the reduction will be 20%.
31. This kind of benefit is awarded where the income-based JSA has been stopped.
32. These are defined as 16/17 year olds who having left full-time education, have not been employed or have not been self employed, for more than 16 hours a week; completed a training course, or left a training course for no good reason, or given up or lost a training place without a valid reason, or because of misconduct.

some of the requirements for a certain period of time. It should be noticed however that both members of the couple cannot be exempted at the same time.

During the time when a joint claim is in operation one member of the couple may apply to the Jobcentre Plus adviser to be exempted from observing certain JSA provisions, or to adapt the job or the working hours to fit in with a person's particular situation.

Such a situation could arise where one member of the couple is ill or suffers from a medical condition which prevents him/her from carrying normal work.[33] Another situation could be attendance in court as a member of jury, a Justice of the Peace, a witness or a person involved in judicial proceedings, as for example an expert witness.[34] A person who is over 60 years old or is below pensionable age and does not wish to work may be exempted from some JSA requirements.[35] A registered blind person can be exempted from some of the JSA requirements.[36] An exemption from some JSA regulations may be made to a carer. Complicated rules exist in this case[37] and proof[38] of being a carer will need to be produced.

Allied to the carer's exemption is also an exemption from some of the JSA requirements in circumstances where the person in a joint claim for JSA is working and living in a residential care home, nursing home or other residential care accommodation. In these circumstances the Jobcentre Plus does not consider the person to be working![39]

---

33. Of course a medical certificate from the hospital or general practitioner stating that the person is unable to work will need to be produced and forms Med 10 or Med 3 recpectively will need to be produced. Alternatively a self-certification form will need to be filled in. In these circumstances the person may be entitled to make an Incapacity Benefit claim, but if he/she does not wish to do so, but only wishes to claim exemption from meeting JSA requirements by reason of illness, then a medical practitioner's letter or medical certificate will need to be produced.
34. It should be noted that this does not apply in cases when one of the partners is a defendant in legal proceedings, as for example, being charged with a criminal offence. Proof of a summons with date(s) and any other documentation will need to be produced.
35. *See* below for further information.
36. A blind registration card will need to be produced as evidence. Where blindness is a temporary phenomenon and registration ends, the person will normally be exempted from JSA requirements for a further 28 weeks.
37. Some of these rules include that one of the persons in the couple is receiving carer's allowance or regularly cares for another person in one of the following situations, namely (a) the person who is being cared for is receiving attendance allowance; or (b) the care component of disability living allowance at the middle or highest rate; or (c) the person who is being cared for has claimed attendance allowance or disability living allowance within the past 26 weeks and no decision had yet been made. Were a negative decision to be made, the partner in the couple claiming joint JSA, will need to revert to observing the JSA requirements. In all the above cases, should the condition cease, the person claiming joint JSA will need to observe the JSA requirements after eight weeks.
38. Proof (a) from the person being cared for that he/she is obtaining attendance allowance or disability living allowance or has made an application to receive these allowances; (b) by means of the production of a carer's allowance order book or notice of award; (c) through a certificate stating that the carer's allowance, or attendance allowance, or disability living allowance ceased to be paid.
39. Proof is required in support of an application. It may consist of a letter from the care home, etc. stating that the person is employed by the home, the production of salary slips or other relevant

Where a trade dispute exists there is an exemption from some of the JSA requirements if one of the partners is either involved in; or is affected by it.[40]

A refugee who is on a course to improve his/her English is exempt from some JSA requirements. This exemption is limited to a maximum of nine months. There is a requirement that the Home Office confirms the refugee status; that the refugee is on a minimum 15 hour per week course to improve his/her English and thus make him employable; and that the refugee started the course within twelve months of entering the United Kingdom.[41]

Persons who are between 18 and 24 years of age and who are on a work based training young people programme are exempt from some of the JSA requirements.[42]

It should be noted that the exemptions to the JSA requirements in the above situations and any other relevant situations which may arise are only applicable to certain JSA requirements and that only one person in the joint claim may be exempted at a time.

Exemptions to the JSA rules lie in the following fields, namely (a) actively looking for work; (b) being capable of work; (c) entering into a jobseeker's agreement; (d) not being in full-time education; (e) being available to work at least 40 hours a week;[43] (f) being a resident in the United Kingdom.

As for the duration of the exemption this will depend entirely on individual circumstances. The Jobcentre Plus will use its discretion and advise the joint claimant accordingly.

5. RATES OF JSA

Having examined briefly the necessary conditions in order to qualify for JSA, and bearing these in mind, it is purposed to look at the rates payable to claimants.

Under the contribution-based JSA, it will be recalled that the unemployed claimant who has paid enough national insurance contributions and is available

---

evidence. A proof of address is also necessary. Statistics show that more than one million people care for more than one person; 1.25 million people provide more than fifty hours of care a week; 6 million persons (one in eight adults) are carers in the United Kingdom; there are over three million carers in the workforce; 58% of carers are women and 42% are men. (Source: Carers UK). *See also Financial Times*, 1 Feb. 2008 at p. 5.

40. Proof of the trade dispute need not be produced as the Jobcentre Plus will know of it through the media.
41. The above does not apply if the refugee has been granted exceptional leave to enter or stay in the United Kingdom. Proof of refugee status from the Home Office will need to be produced; as will confirmation of the date of arrival in the United Kingdom and confirmation that the refugee is on an English course with details as to duration and the number of weekly hours on the course.
42. Proof by way of placement papers or a letter from the organization which provides the training or the Careers Service or Connexions, will need to be produced to the Jobcentre Plus.
43. The requirement sometimes enjoys exceptions by reason of flexibility.

for and actively seeking work is entitled to this allowance for a maximum of 182 days irrespective of any capital the claimant or his/her partner has. If he/she has dependants, these latter are not entitled to any payment. Although the JSA allowances vary periodically,[44] at the time of writing a person under the age of 18 receives GBP 35.65 a week, whereas an 18 to 24 year old's entitlement is GBP 46.85. The over 25 claimant will receive GBP 59.15 a week.

The income-based JSA, unlike the contributions based JSA, is means tested and the rates payable therefore depend on the financial and personal circumstances of the claimant. The rates of income-based JSA are identical to those of the contribution-based JSA. Being means tested, and therefore depending on the circumstances of the claimant, this latter will receive from nothing to an amount up to the *maxima*.

The joint claims for JSA have been set up[45] to reduce the number of households in which partners are unemployed or working short hours. By setting up this scheme partners are encouraged to seek work and/or training in the case of the unemployed, and increase working hours and improve employment prospects, if in part time work. It will be recalled that both partners need to observe the conditions for receipt of JSA which, it is stressed, is income-based. Income-based JSA is payable for as along as the claimant's income is less than the *minimum minimorum* allowed by the government and all conditions for receipt are met.

In the case of joint JSA claims, if both partners are under 18 years of age they receive GBP 35.65. If they are both under 18 years old, but one of them is disabled, they receive GBP 46.86. Where they are both under 18, but have a child, they receive GBP 70.70. If one of the partners is under 18 and the other between 18 to 24 years of age, they receive GBP 46.85. Should one of the partners be under 18, but the other over 25 years of age, they receive GBP 59.15. Where both are over 18 years old then they receive GBP 92.80 per week.

Additional allowances are available for dependant children[46] and for other matters,[47] all of which are means tested.

Those with savings of GBP 16,000 or over will normally not qualify for income-based JSA. Those with savings of over GBP 6,000 (up to GBP 16,000) will receive lesser payments from the income-based JSA. In the case of joint claims, if a partner works over 24 hours a week on average, the claimant will most probably not get income-based JSA.[48] If the partner works less than 24 hours a week, the payment of the claimant may be diminished.

44. The latest rates being those effective as from 9 Apr. 2007.
45. The Welfare to Work programme introduced the joint claims concept in October 2002.
46. Where GBP 47.75 is payable from birth until the day before the child's nineteenth birthday subject to the means test.
47. For example housing costs, additional premium payments for claimants with dependants and special needs.
48. This is of course not applicable to the contribution-based JSA.

5.1. Additional Benefits

In addition to JSA payments, assistance may be available in respect of the costs involved while looking for, and/or entering into, employment. Thus where a JSA claimant is invited for an interview his/her travel costs may be defrayed under the scheme. Similarly if selected for a job, the JSA claimant may be entitled to a subsidy to enable him/her to purchase appropriate clothing for that job. An advance may also be available to help the jobseeker during the first month of employment and before he/she receives a first salary. This could include costs for accommodation such as rents and victualing.

These additional payments are discretionary and depend on a variety of criteria such as the length of unemployment, diligence of the JSA claimant, attendance, etc. Persons on New Deal schemes and on certain government training schemes may have such additional payment built into the respective scheme.

Depending upon whether or not the job seeker qualifies under the means testing concept, the income-based JSA claimant may be entitled to receive housing benefit which would help with the rent and Council Tax benefit which would reduce the amount of council tax payments. Free school meals for the JSA claimant's children, free medical prescriptions and benefits to pay for newborn babies are also available.

5.2. Backdating of JSA

It may also be possible to have the JSA backdated in specific circumstances. These specific circumstances are that the JSA claimant would have been entitled to claim JSA earlier, but did not do so because he/she has a good reason for this. Such reasons are provided for under the regulations and include wrong advice given as to whether or not the candidate is entitled to JSA. With the number of economic migrants entering the United Kingdom, the language barrier could be a valid reason for backdating JSA. The candidate would have to prove that during the time of backdating he/she would have met all the conditions necessary for qualifying for that benefit. It should be noted that JSA backdating can only take place for a maximum period of one to three months. This period is discretionary and will depend on the reason(s) given as to why backdating is sought.

6. SANCTIONS AND DISQUALIFICATIONS FROM JSA

The JSA is subject to both sanctions and disqualifications. Parameters of space do not allow for a full discussion of either sanctions or disqualifications. These two topics will thus be treated briefly.

With regard to sanctions, if the JSA claimant does not take up opportunities of employment offered or does not follow up a chance to acquire work or does not observe the conditions of a jobseeker's direction, or again, fails to apply for a job which has been pointed out by the Jobcentre Plus,[49] he/she may be sanctioned,[50] Depending on the severity of the claimant's act, the JSA may be either reduced from between one to twenty six weeks or stopped altogether. Sanctions exit in circumstances where the JSA claimant leaves his/her last job voluntarily without just cause[51] or where the claimant is dismissed because of misconduct.[52]

Sanctions are also applicable to training schemes and to employment programmes in cases where the claimant is subject to a New Deal[53] scheme and he/she does not take up the options offered under that scheme.

In the case of joint claims for JSA both claimants need to visit the Jobcentre Plus[54] to sign a declaration. If either claimants do not keep the appointment the sanction is that JSA payment could well be delayed or otherwise affected.

Similarly, with the failure to report to the Jobcentre Plus pertinent changes of circumstances[55] which would affect the joint claimants' allowance. Thus where

49. Jobseeker's Act 1995 s. 20 (3) and Jobseeker's Allowance Regulations 1996, Regulation 74.
50. Jobseeker's Act 1995, s. 19 (5).
51. Jobseeker's Act 1995, s. 19(6) (b) and see too Jobseeker's Allowance Regulations 1996, Regulations 72 and 73, for factors to be taken into account in a defence. Were the causes to be just that would amount to constructive dismissal which would justify leaving the employment voluntarily and therefore not being sanctioned under the JSA conditions. What amounts to leaving 'voluntarily' without 'just cause' was put admirably by Commissioner Munroe in case R (U) 4/87. He said '[a]n examination of the decisions on the topic leads me to think that in general it is only where circumstances are such that a person has virtually no alternative but to leave voluntarily that he will be found to have had just cause for doing so, rather as a person who throws his baggage overboard to make room in the lifeboat can claim on his luggage insurance' (para. 9). Cf. *Crewe v. Social Security Commissioner* [1982] 2 All ER 745. *See* too Jobseeker's Allowance Regulations 1996. Regulation 71, where the employer and employee agree to the severance of the contract of employment on a mutual basis, including dismissal by reason of redundancy. *See* case R (U) 3/91. A JSA claimant who has taken up 'on trial' employment after being unemployed for more than thirteen weeks may leave that employment from between the fifth week of that employment and the twelfth week. Under these circumstances, he/she will not be disqualified for JSA purposes for leaving his employment voluntarily. Jobseeker's Act 1995, s. 20 (3) and Jobseeker's Allowance Regulations, Regulation 74.
52. Therefore it is not unfair dismissal because the employer had good cause for dismissal. Jobseeker's Act 1995, s. 19 (6) (a). *See* too R (U) 2/77 and R (U) 2/74 and R(U) 4/78.
53. *See* above for an explanation of the various New Deal schemes.
54. Unless one or both claimants are exempted or are on a training course.
55. Pertinent changes of circumstances with regard to either or both of the claimants and which would affect JSA payment include the claiming of the socuial security benefits: the receipt of pensions, the receipt of a legacy, for example, a property, or an increase or decrease of savings; the amount of savings; or illness of either or both claimants and consuequent inability to take a job; the entering into paid, voluntery or unpaid work or entering into full or part time education or going on a training programme. Changes of address; going abroad to look for work; short or long absences; hospitalization, care or nursing home; change of status, for example break up of civil partnership, separation and divorce; living with another party or a party leaves or starts living in the claimant's home are all material changes which may affect JSA payments. A further change is where a claimant gets married or has a civil partnership. This latter expression means an arrangement which is formalized and gives partners of the same sex the legal status of a married couple. Finally, the fact that any children of the claimants have left school needs to be reported to the Jobcentre Plus as this would affect JSA payments.

either of the partners do not disclose a material change, the Jobcentre Plus will recover from either of the claimants any JSA which has been overpaid.

A change of circumstances does not necessarily mean that JSA payments would cease. In fact payments could be increased! If such changes are not reported however a claimant could well lose JSA benefits.

A deliberate and intentional non disclosure of a change of circumstances could amount to benefit (or tax credit) fraud and/or the giving of incorrect or misleading information could also amount to benefit fraud (or tax credit fraud). Benefit fraud is a criminal offence which could lead to prosecution or to financial penalties. Where a JSA claimant is being investigated for benefit fraud, JSA payments will be suspended. If convicted of benefit fraud on more than one occasion, the JSA benefits could be reduced or stopped altogether in the future.

A claimant of JSA who is ill should inform the Jobcentre Plus office a soon as possible. If the claimant is ill for up to two weeks his/her JSA benefit will not be affected. Nor will JSA payments be affected if a claimant is ill up to two times within any period of six months. Where the claimant is ill for over two weeks or for more than twice in any six months, he/she will no longer be entitled to JSA,[56] but after the illness is cured the candidate who meets all the JSA conditions can make a new claim for JSA.

Where a job seeker's direction[57] is given to a JSA claimant and he/she fails to follow it without good cause, JSA will be stopped for two weeks. Should the jobseeker's direction not be followed for a second time without just cause,[58] JSA will not be granted for a further four weeks.[59]

There is a right of appeal in disqualification cases and where the tribunal considers that the length of disqualifications is excessive, it may shorten the period. It appears that the failure for the tribunal to consider the length of disqualification is considered to be an error of law[60] which would give rise to further appeal to the Commissioner.

Finally, there is an important disqualification with regard to 'trade disputes' which needs to be treated. Were a strike is, or other forms of industrial action

56. Sickness or disability benefits may be claimed in these circumstances.
57. A jobseeker's direction is a formal instruction to the claimant to take specific action(s) to obtain a job. A jobseeker's direction will follow a failure by the JSA claimant to take the advice/ suggestions previously made by the Jobcentre Plus office to increase the claimant's chances to obtain work.
58. Regulation 72 (6) of the Jobseeker's Allowance Regulations 1996 makes it clear that 'just cause' could not be that the jobseeker's allowance would be higher than the salary that the claimant would receive had he been employed. Religious or conscientious belief could be a just cause for refusal to work as would physical danger/harm to health or mental stress; long travelling times (over one hour); high expenses for taking employment; etc. The time scale permitted for looking for a job of similar status is 13 weeks. Regulation 16 and 72 (5).
59. A hardship allowance may be claimed which yields a lesser sum than that of the JSA. Hardship allowances may be claimed in other circumstances where JSA is refused, for example, if there are uncertainties about availability for work, or actively seeking a job.
60. Regulation (I) 4/87. Furthermore, failure by the tribunal to give reasons for its decision also constitutes an error of law which would give rise to an appeal to the Commissioner.

are,[61] in progress JSA will not be paid to the jobseeker.[62] It should be noted that the disqualification only applies where the loss of employment arises out of a trade dispute[63] at the place of work of the claimant, such disqualification lasting during the whole time the dispute exists.

The claimant may however be able to claim JSA in circumstances where he/she is reemployed by another employer but loses his job in that new employment. It appears that the fact that the trade dispute with the first employer is still ongoing when the claimant loses his new employment, would not disqualify him/her from claiming JSA. The new employment need not be permanent, it could even be of a temporary nature.[64] Where the employee continues to be employed by the employer after the termination of the trade dispute, but loses that employment for reasons which are not connected with that trade dispute, he/she would not be disqualified from claiming JSA. The same would apply in circumstances where the employee is dismissed because of redundancy.[65] Similarly, if it can be shown that the employee was not interested in a direct manner, in the trade dispute.

Thus although the disqualification of entitlement to JSA lasts during the whole period of the trade dispute there are circumstances where a successful claim may be made even when the dispute is ongoing![66]

7. CONCLUDING THOUGHTS

7.1. The United Kingdom Needs a Future Vision!

In a Foreword, the Prime Minister said:[67]

> [n]ow as we look ahead, we need a reformed New Deal to help us face the challenges of the next decades. In the old days the problem may have been unemployment, but in the next decades it will be employability. If in the old days lack of jobs demanded priority action, in the new world it is lack of skills . . . In future the best welfare will no longer be the benefits you have today, but the skills you gain for tomorrow'.

61. For a fuller discussion on strikes and other forms of industrial action *see* J. Carby-Hall, 'Grève et Action Collective en Grande Bretagne' (2003), 3 *Revue Internationale de Droit Comparé*, 575-612.
62. Jobseeker's Act 1995, s. 14. This was also the case under the 'old' unemployment benefit laws.
63. *See* the definition in the Trade Union and Labour Relations (Consolidation) Act 1992, 237 and 238.
64. *See* case R (U) 6/74.
65. Under the provisions of the Employment Rights Act 1996 s. 139.
66. For further reading on the background of jobseeker's allowance, *see* White Paper entitled 'Jobseeker's Allowance' above n 3. For the general policy relating to JSA, *see* A. Bryson, above n. 4.
67. In 'Transforming Britain's Labour Market – Ten years of the New Deal' 2007 at p. 2.

He goes on to say '[w]e will combine tough sanctions for those who refuse to work or train with better and more targeted support for those most in need to give them the skills and advice they need to get back onto the jobs ladder, . . . for those on incapacity benefits, we will focus on capability and what people can do, not on disability and what they cannot do'.

The message is clear. A new approach is required for the future. That approach should focus on skills, in particular in areas where there are shortages. The move is from benefits into work and then into training and career enhancement.

According to the government, this strategy for progression includes five principles.[68] First, a stronger New Deal framework to move benefit claimants from being passive recipients to being active jobseekers. Second, Jobcentre Plus advisers will tailor employment and skills to meet the needs of employers and individuals. Third, local strategic partnerships consisting of public, private and third sectors working together to get the most disadvantaged into work.[69] In the fourth instance, employment will be at the heart of local regeneration programmes with the government providing GBP 1.5 billion to the most deprived areas. Finally, the setting up of a new adult advancement and careers service and the carrying out of early screening to identify and address benefit claimants' skills needs. There will be job focused training courses for those claimants who are long-term on JSA.

All the proposed measures mentioned above are commendable! There is little doubt that the JSA and New Deals need to move forward, particularly in training tailored to meet skill shortages which would result, hopefully, in fuller employment, in moving from a passive to an active welfare state where persons are able to find, and stay in, work.

The challenges are enormous[70] and can only be achieved if there is the necessary will, not only on the part of the government but also on that of employers who would need, it is submitted, more financial incentives to be proactive in helping achieve those goals;[71] of trade unions and of Jobcentre Plus offices which will need more government finance to meet effectively those future challenges, particularly since there are 4.5 million persons of working age on the

68. *Ibid.*, 9-10.

69. Local Employment Partnerships are an innovative way for Jobcentre Plus to work with employers to get their most disadvantaged clients into work. There are some 600,000 job vacancies in the United Kingdom. These could be filled in with employers agreeing to employ those disadvantaged persons in return for the Jobcentre Plus pledge that it will do more to ensure that their clients receive both the preparation and training necessary to meet employers' needs. There will also be some employers' in-house training.

70. *See* 'Ready to Work, Skilled for Work: Unlocking Britain's Talents' (Cmnd. 7316) Jan. 2008 which sets out these challenges which include employer-led reform and renewal; demand-led recruitment and skills and working with employers in the local communities, <www.official-documents.gov.uk/document/cm73/7316/7316.pdf>.

71. Namely employers working with the government to build up a new skills partnership for the future; the employer-led shaping of recruitment and skills services; demand-led recruitment and training of the workforce; and investment by employers in employees to open up job opportunities to a wider range of potential recruits.

United Kingdom with no qualifications, 5.2 million who are illiterate and 6.8 million who are unable to understand simple graphical and numerical information.

There is also the problem of the need for tougher measures to be used by employers to monitor sickness claims and force disabled persons to improve their employability.

The government's aim is to reduce by one million the claimants of incapacity benefits. Their reduction is to take place by 2010. Currently, there are 2.64 million receiving incapacity benefits.[72] The Organization for Economic Cooperation and Development (OECD) questioned why so many people in the United Kingdom moved out of unemployment benefit and into incapacity benefit. The answer could be that incapacity benefit is an easy option taken to reduce the unemployment figures! The OECD considered that employers should monitor long-term sickness absences and report these to the Jobcentre Plus and that 'the unemployed who are sick should go through a mandatory capacity assessment'. Disability benefit recipients who lose their entitlement but do not get jobs, should be followed up systematically and offered the support needed to return to employment.

Thus the government envisages a tough welfare-to-work policy whereby the long-term unemployed would be compelled to take permanent, rather than temporary, employment or work-related activity of some kind in return for the benefits they receive. Employers in the private and voluntary sectors would play a more significant role in the welfare-to-work programme with Jobcentre Plus playing an active part in this respect.[73] Contracts with private and voluntary sector employers will be of a longer duration.[74] Benefits received by claimants will be focused more heavily on job outcomes by not only getting the unemployed into work but also by keeping them in employment.[75]

Personalized support for the long-term unemployed will feature as a matter of course; thus any personal barriers faced by the claimant would be tackled by the Jobcentre Plus personnel. As the Pension's Secretary put it, 'if you can work you should work and that would be a condition of getting benefits'.[76]

Tougher sanctions than at present are proposed for those who refuse to either take a job or take the opportunities available for employment. Cuts in benefits have been suggested or the possibility of an option of permanent work for benefits.

These policies appear robust and objective but will they work? Hitherto, the government has struggled to keep the unemployed off benefits and in work! Jobcentre Plus offices have spent large sums of money in getting the unemployed into

---

72. According to the OECD this is three times the number claiming unemployment benefit! (Source: *Financial Times*, 19 Dec. 2007).
73. In accordance with the Freud report which talks of welfare-to-work market for private and voluntary providers of 'multi-billion' pounds. *See Financial Times*, 28 Feb. 2008 at p. 2.
74. The proposal is that initially the employment contract will be for a minimum duration of four weeks' full employment; the time factor will increase in the future.
75. It is thought that 'some 80% of the contract's payment will be dependent on actually getting people into work and keeping them there.' *See Financial Times*, 28 Feb. 2008 at p. 2.
76. Source: *Financial Times*, 20 Feb. 2008 at p. 2.

work but have been unable to keep them in work on a permanent basis[77] because of lack of skills.

There has been a vague suggestion by the government that an 'advancement agency' be set up by 2011 with the aim of helping low paid unskilled workers obtain better jobs. The aim is to boost the proportion of adults with 'Level Two' qualifications by 20 per cent by 2020 'to redress the UK's productivity gap with . . . rivals'.[78]

The hopes of successfully achieving the aims of these policies are questionable. The National Audit Office states that the proportion of people moving repeatedly between work and benefits has hardly changed since the 1980s! Although the New Deal schemes have had the effect of reducing JSA and other claimants, they 'do not stay in work once they have found it'. More than a quarter of benefit claimants who successfully find work return to JSA within thirteen weeks and 40% are back on benefits within six months.[79]

The National Audit Office report finds that 'it is shattering to realize that the percentage of people looking for jobs who made repeat claims for benefits has remained unchanged since the early 1980s'.[80]

The Deputy Director General of the Confederation of British Industries (CBI) suggested that the government had to show 'political leadership and drive through plans to use the private and voluntary sectors in welfare-to-work initiatives'.

'Political leadership' is what is required. Since the Labour government came into power in 1997 the number of claimants claiming incapacity benefit has risen to 2.8 million. More than half a million of these are under 35 years of age. This means that there are more persons claiming incapacity benefit than unemployment benefit. There appears to be a flaw in the benefits system in that those on incapacity benefit do not have to attend at a Jobcentre Plus. All they need to do is to obtain a medical certificate. Such a system encourages laziness, invites abuse and acts as a disincentive to work.[81]

It is pleasing to note that the government has introduced in October 2008 revamped tests relating to incapacity and new employment and support allowances. Thus a claimant's capabilities for work will be assessed in a more rigorous

77. The reason why the unemployed are unable to stay in permanent employment is that they lack the necessary skills which in turn denies them promotion and consequently an increase in their salaries.
78. Source: *Financial Times*, 20 Nov. 2007 at p. 4.
79. This has been confirmed by the report of the parliamentary public accounts committee. The chairman of the committee said '[f]ar too many people bounce back and forth between short-term employment and being on benefits'.
80. According to the NAO some two thirds of the 2.4 million new JSA claims each year are from repeat claimants. *See* too *Financial Times*, 14 Nov. 2007 at p. 2.
81. *See Financial Times*, 2 Jan. 2008 at 3, the article by David Turner entitled 'The intractables: ill, jobless and young' which gives a good account of the culture of not working on the part of young persons. He says 'There are families that have never worked, and where there is a culture of not working. That has a significant impact on young people.' *See also* the OECD findings on the international dimension of the problem of rising disability rates, in the *Financial Times*, 14 Jun. 2006 at p. 5.

manner and more support will be provided to those returning to work. It will be interesting to see whether this bolder approach to welfare reform will work.[82]

The government has a difficult job ahead. It will need to put enormous efforts, firstly to help the millions of persons who are currently on incapacity benefits back into work, and secondly, to tackle the skills gap for the unemployed.

It will be interesting to see if all those theoretical initiatives will come about and more importantly, succeed in practice! Did not the Secretary of State for Work and Pensions show his determination on the welfare-to-work policy when he said of the private/voluntary sector involvement 'here to stay and set to grow'?[83]

Acknowledgement

I am most grateful to Miss Jana Derska for word processing this chapter to a high degree of accuracy. Her efforts are much appreciated. Diane Ryland needs to be warmly thanked for the support she has given me in preparing these materials. Her proof reading talents are second to none. My thanks also go to a variety of Job-centre Plus offices and their staff who enlightened me on a variety of procedures and other practical matters relating to their daily work schedule. Without their assistance it would not have been possible to complete this work. The advice given to me by my social security colleagues on the legislation currently in force is received gratefully. For all errors, omissions and uncertainties which remain, I take full responsibility.

References

Brown, G., 'Transforming Britain's Labour Market. Ten Years of the New Deal' (2008) <http://www.dwp.gov.uk/welfarereform/docs/PMNewDeal2-01-08.pdf>.

Bryson, A., 'Jobseekers' Allowance: Help or Hindrance to the Unemployed?' (1995) 24 *Industrial Law Journal.*

Carby-Hall, J., 'Grève et Action Collective en Grande Bretagne' (2003) *Revue Internationale de Droit Comparé.*

Cornish, W.R. and de N Clark, G., *Law and Society in England, 1750-1950* (London, Sweet & Maxwell, 1989).

82. To be noted is the Conservative Opposition proposal of '[t]hree strikes and you're out rule for claimants on benefits who refuse a job offer.' The proposal is such that a benefits claimant would lose one month's benefits if he/she unreasonably turns down a job offer. Where he/she turns down such an offer for a second time three months' benefits would be lost. Should there be a third refusal the claimant will be refused all out-of-work benefits for a period of up to three years.

83. Source: *Financial Times*, 28 Feb. 2008 at 2. The welfare-to-work problem is not solely a British problem; it also has a global dimension. *See* the very interesting analysis on this aspect by Nicholas Timmins entitled 'The jobless multinationals' in the *Financial Times*, 28 Feb. 2008 at p. 11.

Chapter 11

Who Governs Labour Market Policy in Canada?*

Brian Langille

1. INTRODUCTION

This is a paper in two parts. Part One introduces readers to the Canadian constitutional law regarding the distribution, between the federal and the provincial/territorial governments,[1] of legislative and administrative powers over labour market policy. These rules of Canadian constitutional law are now fairly stable but their wisdom has always been, and is still, much contested. Part Two describes the resulting political reality regarding federal/provincial 'cooperation' in the management of these issues. Again, there is much contestation concerning the usefulness of current Canadian efforts in this critical area of the Canadian, or any modern Organization for Economic Cooperation and Development (OECD), economy. These two controversies, one about constitutional law and the other about the political negotiations which that law engenders and structures, are obviously and intimately related. The interesting question is whether rational readers, seeking more than yet

* Prepared for the Conference on 'The Implementation of Community Employment and Social Inclusion Policies in the Model of Social Federalism' June 21 and 22 Jun. 2007 at Oñati, Spain. I wish to thank Gail Elman for her excellent research assistance.

1. In what follows I refer, for reasons of simplicity and clarity, only to Federal and Provincial jurisdictions omitting references to the territories.

Roger Blanpain, Juan Pablo Landa, Brian Langille (eds), *Employment Policies and Multilevel Governance*, pp. 245–265.

another illustration of some of the controversies to which federal constitutional structures are prone, will find Canada's answers to both questions helpful as a positive example or merely as examples of approaches to be avoided. That turns out to be a somewhat more complex question than appears at first glance.

One result is, however, certain: one can obtain from reflection upon this particular aspect of our current Canadian circumstances some insight into the general reality of Canadian federalism and indeed Canada itself. This is precisely because so much of Canadian politics is expressed not in terms of 'what should be done' but 'which level of government (federal or provincial) should do it?' Perhaps only those of us brought up in federations have lost the ability to be surprised by the ease with which important issues of substance can be transmogrified into a question of political process. But, and this is at least potentially the positive side of the matter, to also see the importance of that shift of question. Living in a federation is both a blessing and a curse. It is a blessing because it is obvious that one of the central legal and political questions of our time is 'who governs?' Politics or the market? If politics, state based or not? Government or governance? If government, at which level of government – local, regional, national, international, or supranational? In answering these questions federations have a special claim to relevant experience as the question of the level of governance is ever present. A well-developed theory for rational allocation of powers within a federation should be of more general use in confronting the question 'who governs?'. Moreover, the question 'who governs' has particular salience in connection with labour market policy. International economic integration along with revolutions in production techniques, the organization of firms, and in communications technology – in a word, 'globalization' – has put enormous pressure on existing labour market policies and indeed the whole idea of state based government in the teeth of the new economic dispensation. The idea of international labour law has witnessed a remarkable revival. So to have non-state-based initiatives in the form of consumer driven monitoring systems, corporate social responsibility initiatives, international trade union solidarity, and so on. But living in a federation is also a curse because the ever present possibility of the shift from substance (what is to be done?) to one of process (who is to do it?) is exploitable for other than sound and rational policy reasons.

It is in this light that an examination of the relationship between the rules of Canada's constitution, on the one hand, and Canadian labour market policy, on the other, is undertaken.

2. PART ONE: THE CONSTITUTIONAL RULES OF THE GAME

An analysis of the legal framework for determining which level of government has the power to regulate labour market policy in Canada begins with the an examination of the distribution of legislative powers, as listed in sections 91 and 92 of the

Constitution Act, 1867.[2] The general rule in Canada is that labour relations falls within provincial jurisdiction under section 92(13) of the Act – because it is considered a matter of 'Property and Civil Rights in the Province'. However, there are a number of ways in which the federal government has gained jurisdiction over labour relations, and thus, is able to establish labour market policy. First, section 91 of the *Constitution Act* explicitly establishes federal jurisdiction over certain undertakings, such as the postal service (section 91(50)), the military (section 91(7)), federal civil servants (section 91(8)), navigation and shipping (section 91(10)), fisheries (section 91(12)), and banking (section 91(15)).[3] Additionally, sections 91(29) and 92(10) constitutionally grant the Parliament of Canada power over undertakings involving inter-provincial and international transportation, as well as, works declared to be for the general advantage of Canada. Second, the *Constitution Act* has been amended twice to increase the scope of federal authority over labour market policy. Third, the preamble to section 91, allows Parliament to make laws for the peace, order, and good government of Canada.[4] Finally, the 'federal spending power' allows the federal government to directly affect provincial labour markets and labour market policy through federal government spending of federal funds.

2.1. The Division of Powers

In 1925, in the *Snider* decision[5] labour relations were held to be a matter of 'property and civil rights in the province' – section 92(13) of the *Constitution Act*, 1867.[6] The *Snider* decision dealt specifically with legislation concerning industrial disputes. Following *Snider*, many subsequent decisions extended the application of provincial jurisdiction beyond industrial disputes legislation[7] to, for example, labour standards legislation[8] and the allocation of mandatory union funds.[9] In the same year that the *Snider* decision was delivered, the Supreme Court of Canada, confirmed that the government of Canada had authority over the regulation of the hours of employment for federal government employees.[10] The Supreme Court would go on to specify that the provincial legislature could not

2. The Constitution Act, 1867 (U.K.), 30 & 31 Vict., c. 3 [Constitution].
3. *Ibid.*
4. Hereinafter referred to as the POGG power.
5. *Toronto Electric Commission v. Snider*, [1925] 1925 A.C. 396 [*Snider*].
6. *Constitution*, above n. 2.
7. P. Hogg, *Constitutional Law of Canada*, 4 th edn, looseleaf (Scarborough, ON, Carswell, 1997-2006) [Hogg].
8. *Reference re: Weekly Rest in Industrial Undertakings Act*, [1937] A.C. 326 [*Labour Conventions*].
9. *Oil, Chemical and Atomic Workers International Union, Local 16-601 v. Imperial Oil Ltd.* [1963] S.C.R. 584 [*Oil, Chemical Workers*].
10. *Reference re: Legislative Jurisdiction over Hours of Labour* [1925] S.C.R. 505 [*Hours of Labour*].

legislate a federal employee's hours of work or wages.[11] Additionally, Parliament could regulate labour relations in all those industries which were within the federal legislative competence,[12] including the federal private sector, and it was not a necessity that employment be exclusively in connection with a federal work.[13]

It is important to recognize that neither, the Parliament of Canada or a Provincial Legislature, is capable of delegating to the other explicitly,[14] or receiving from the other by acquiescence,[15] the powers vest in the *Constitution Act*. Further, the courts have continually asserted that there is inter-jurisdictional immunity,[16] whereby employees and employers in one jurisdiction are immune from legislation of the other jurisdiction.[17] The leading decision on inter-jurisdictional immunity is *Bell Telephone*,[18] in which, the Supreme Court held that Quebec's legislation could not apply to employer-employee relationships coming within a class of subjects under federal jurisdiction. The *Bell Telephone* case supplies the test for determining whether there is inter-jurisdictional immunity to a specific piece of legislation – the vital part test. The vital part test examines whether the law 'affects a vital part of the management and operation of the undertaking to which it relates'.[19] The Court notes that legislation respecting the employment contract, such as rates of pay or hours of work, will always be considered a vital part. The *Bell Telephone* decision was reaffirmed in a 1988 trilogy of cases dealing with occupational health and safety legislation,[20] in these cases the Court held that the vital part test did not require that the provincial statute impair of paralyze the federal undertaking.[21] The concept of inter-jurisdictional immunity does not apply to Worker's Compensation. Prior to *Snider*, in *Canadian Pacific Railway*,[22] the Privy Council held that Workmen's Compensation, although under provincial jurisdiction, applied to employees who were otherwise under federal jurisdiction with respect to all other aspects of employment regulation.

---

11. *Reference re: Minimum Wage Act (Saskatchewan)* [1948] S.C.R. 248.
12. *Re Industrial Relations and Disputes Investigation Act (Canada)* [1955] S.C.R. 529 [*Stevedores Reference*].
13. *Letter Carriers' Union of Canada v. Canadian Union of Postal Workers* [1975] 1 S.C.R. 178 [*Letter Carriers*].
14. *Nova Scotia (Attorney General) v. Canada (Attorney General)* [1951] S.C.R. 31 [*Nova Scotia Inter-delegation*].
15. *Snider*, above n. 5.
16. *See* generally: N. Finklestein, *Laskin's Canadian Constitutional Law 5 th Edition* (Toronto, The Carswell Company Limited, 1986).
17. Hogg, above n. 7.
18. *Quebec (Commission du Salarie Minimum) v. Bell Telephone Co. of Canada* [1966] S.C.R. 767 [*Bell Telephone*].
19. *Ibid.*, at para. 19.
20. *Bell Canada v. Quebec (Commission de la sante de la securite du travail)* 51 D.L.R. (4th) 161 [*Bell Canada*]; *Alltrans Express Ltd. v. British Columbia (Workers'/Workmen's Compensation Board)* [1988] 1 S.C.R. 897 [*Alltrans*]; *Canadian National Railway Co. v. Courtois* [1988] 1 S.C.R. 868 [*Courtois*].
21. *Bell Canada*, above n. 20, at para. 316.
22. *British Columbia (Workmen's Compensation Board) v. Canadian Pacific Railway Co.* [1920] A.C. 184 [*Canadian Pacific Railway*].

2.2. The Constitutional Amendments

There have been two amendments to the *Constitution Act*, which drastically affected the regulation of labour market policy.[23] In 1940, section 91(2A) – unemployment insurance – was added to the powers of Parliament and, in 1951, there was the addition of section 94A, which gave Parliament the power to 'make laws in relation to old age pensions and supplementary benefits, including survivors' and disability benefits.'[24] Both of these amendments followed Privy Council[25] and Supreme Court decisions[26] on the matters. Unemployment insurance represents a case where federal power has been detached from more general provincial power through constitutional amendment.[27] Section 94A presents one of the few, if not only, areas of labour market policy where there is concurrency between the two jurisdictions. Section 94A allows Parliament to enact legislation related to old age pension, but states that 'no such law shall affect the operation of any law present or future of a provincial legislature'.[28] In fact, in the province of Quebec, the Quebec Pension Plan is operative. The rest of the provinces have chosen not to set up pension plans; instead, the Canada Pension Plan covers workers.

The Supreme Court has recently revisited the unemployment insurance power.[29] The Quebec government challenged the constitutional validity of sections of the *Employment Insurance Act* allowing a woman who is not working because she is pregnant, and a person absent from work to care for a newborn or an adopted child, to receive employment insurance (EI) benefits. The question before the Court was whether the power to provide maternity benefits was within section 91(2A). The Court held that the sections of the *Act* are constitutional and are part of the jurisdiction assigned by section 91(2A). The Court said that the benefits were the replacement of employment income of insured individuals whose income is reduced because of pregnancy or the birth or arrival of a child.[30] The decision indicates that the scope of a power can be increased where it is deemed 'the natural evolution of that power' and required to adapt to the new realities of the workplace.[31]

---

23. It is important to note that neither of these areas could fall under the federal spending power, because they require the contribution of employees and employers and as such, are not simply the governmental spending of money.
24. *Constitution*, above n. 2.
25. *Reference re: Employment and Social Insurance Act (Can.)* [1937] A.C. 355 [*Unemployment Insurance*].
26. *Nova Scotia Inter-delegation*, above n. 14.
27. *Reference re Employment Insurance Act (Can.), ss. 22 and 23* [2005] 2 S.C.R. 669 [*Employment Insurance*].
28. *Constitution*, above n. 2.
29. *Employment Insurance*, above n. 27.
30. *Ibid.* And *see now CSN v. AG Canada* (SCC, unreported, 12 Dec. 2008) confirming this point and upholding 'active' measures for the unemployed.
31. Hogg, above n. 7, 15-50.

2.3. The POGG Power

The federal government can potentially gain legislative authority over the labour market policy through the Peace, Order and Good Government (POGG) power. The POGG power has two branches: the emergency branch and the national concern branch. In two cases the POGG power has been affirmed with respect to labour regulations. Under the emergency branch temporary legislation regulating wages was upheld[32] and under the national concern branch atomic energy was held to be a matter of national concern and labour relations significantly connected.[33] Whether the federal government will be able to enact permanent labour market policy, because what the policy addresses is, itself, a matter of national concern, is unknown. In a number of cases already discussed the courts denied the federal government jurisdiction under the POGG power.[34] However, there is indication that there may be grounds for finding certain policy a matter of national concern where the matter has singleness, distinctiveness and indivisibility.[35]

2.4. The Federal Spending Power

There is one other, and as we shall see, rather large, caveat to the rule of inter-jurisdictional immunity, which is the federal spending power. The federal 'spending power' is not explicitly listed in the *Constitution Act*, but is inferred from 'the powers to levy taxes (section 91(3)), to legislate in relation to public property and public debt (section 91(1A)), and to appropriate federal funds (section 106)'.[36] The federal spending power enables federal Parliament to spend money in areas that are under provincial jurisdiction. This spending is not in violation of the distributions powers because it is open to both levels of government and does not involve compulsion.[37] However, the federal government can have significant influence. Hogg explains:

> When the federal government contributes to a shared-cost programme which lies within the legislative authority of the provinces, the same is true: federal funds are applied to provincial objects. If, in addition, those federal funds are granted on condition that the programme accord with federal stipulations, then those stipulations will effectively regulate the programme even though it lies outside federal legislative authority.[38]

32. *Reference re Anti-Inflation Act* [1976] 2 S.C.R. 373.
33. *Ontario Hydro v. Ontario (Labour Relations Board)*, [1993] 3 SCR 327. Note: The decision was also made on the grounds of s. 92(10)(c).
34. For example *Snider*, above n. 5, and *Labour Conventions*, above n. 8.
35. *See R. v. Crown Zellerbach* [1988] 1 S.C.R. 401. [Crown Zellerbach].
36. Hogg, above n. 7, 6-17.
37. *Ibid.*
38. *Ibid.*, 6-16.

There has been some serious discussion on the limits of the spending power.[39] However, Professor Hogg, widely regarded as Canada's preeminent Constitutional academic, notes that in *Re Canada Assistance Plan*[40] there:

> is a rather clear affirmation both of Parliament's authorize grants to provinces for use in fields of provincial jurisdiction and the power to impose conditions on recipient provinces. Provided the Parliament's intervention does not go beyond the granting or withholding of money, there is no unconstitutional trespass on provincial jurisdiction.[41]

The Supreme Court has explicitly stated on two occasions that the federal spending power does not bring employees into the federal jurisdiction, and thus, the federal government cannot determine their conditions of employment as part of a spending scheme. In the *Brown* case[42] the issue was whether a federally funded job creation program could infringe on provincial jurisdiction over labour relations. A Community Centre participated in a federal job creation program, which provided wage subsidies for the employment of persons receiving benefits under the *Unemployment Insurance Act*, 1971. The program involved an agreement between the Community Centre and the federal government whereby the Centre would be designated as the employer and the government would continue to pay the unemployment insurance benefits, which the Centre would top up according to a wage schedule in the agreement. The wage rates were in line with provincial minimum wages, however, the dispute arose because a number of workers felt they were wrongly classified into a lower wage bracket. When the case reached the Supreme Court, the Court held the employees to be under provincial jurisdiction. Specifically, the Supreme Court reasoned that:

> [T]he federal head of power regarding unemployment insurance cannot be said to be the source of the power to establish federal job creation programs, nor can it be the source of constitutional authority to override provincial competence in the area of wage and labour relations.[43]

The Court held that the power to establish a job creation scheme is derived from the federal spending power. However, the Court noted that although the federal government can spend money in order to create jobs, such grants could not be construed as an intention to remove provincial labour law jurisdiction over the project. Justice L'Heureux-Dube wrote, 'I find it difficult to believe that simply by providing federal money to promote employment in a region or sector the federal government can obtain jurisdiction over the workers employed by virtue of the

---

39. M. Jackman, 'The Constitutional Basis for Federal Regulation of Health' (1996) 5 *Health Law Review*, 3-10. *See also* A. Petter, 'Federalism and the Myth of the Federal Spending Power' (1989) *Canadian Bar Review*, 68.
40. *Re: Canada Assistance Plan* [1991] 2 S.C.R. 525.
41. Hogg, above n. 7, 6-19.
42. *YMHA Jewish Community Centre of Winnipeg Inc. v. Brown* [1989] 1 S.C.R. 1532 [*Brown*].
43. *Ibid.*, at para. 44.

grant.'[44] Thus, provincial labour laws were held to apply to the project. Further, the court refused to categorize the job creation program as a federal undertaking.

The same reasoning with respect to federal spending was applied in an earlier decision, *Four B Manufacturing*.[45] In this case the issue was what jurisdiction applies to employees of a corporation carrying on business on an Indian Reserve. The corporation was a federally subsidized corporation, owned by Aboriginal shareholders, and employing a majority of Aboriginal employees. The majority of the Supreme Court held that provincial laws applied as there was nothing about the business that would allow the operational nature of the business to be characterized as federal.[46] The Court noted that there is no substance to the argument that a federal subsidy could bring the company within federal jurisdiction.[47]

3. PART TWO: THE REALITY OF CANADIAN FEDERALISM AND CANADIAN LABOUR MARKET POLICY

Canada has thus ended up with a constitutional 'default rule',[48] as North American lawyers like to say, of exclusive provincial jurisdiction over labour market issues, a rule to which there are few exceptions. The Federal government has no general constitutional jurisdiction and its main point of entry to labour market policy is via its 'spending power'. What are we to make of this quite extraordinary set of judicially created rules?

First, it obviously was not supposed to turn out this way. The founders of Canada had a completely different vision of the distribution of powers. In a speech in 1865 Sir John A. MacDonald, Canada's first Prime Minister, made this very clear, stating:

> Ever since the union was formed the difficulty of what is called 'State Rights' has existed, and this had much to do in bringing on the present unhappy war in the United States. They commenced, in fact, at the wrong end. They declared by their constitution that each state was a sovereignty in itself, and that all the powers incident to a sovereignty belonged to each state, except those powers which, by the constitution, were conferred upon the general government and Congress. Here we have adopted a different system. We have strengthened the general government. We have given the general legislature all the great subjects of legislation. We have conferred on them, not only specifically and in detail, all the powers which are incident to sovereignty, but we have expressly

44. *Ibid.*, at para. 51.
45. *Four B Manufacturing Ltd. v. United Garment Workers of America*, [1980] 1 S.C.R. 1031 [*Four B Manufacturing*].
46. *Ibid.*
47. *Ibid.*
48. R. Howse, 'The Effect of Jurisdictional Issues on the Application and Administration of Part III' 2. Prepared for the Federal Labour Standards Review 2006. Unpublished. [Howse].

> declared that all subjects of general interest not distinctly and exclusively conferred upon the local governments and local legislatures shall be conferred upon the general government and legislature . . . We thereby strengthen the central parliament and make the Confederation one people and one government, instead of five peoples and five governments, with merely a point of authority connecting us to a limited and insufficient extent . . . There are numerous subjects which belong, of right, both to the local and the general parliaments. In all these cases it is provided, in order to prevent a conflict of authority, that where there is concurrent jurisdiction in the general and local parliaments . . . and that when the legislation of the one is averse to or contradictory of the legislation of the other, in all such cases the action of the general parliament must overrule, ex necessitate, the action of the local legislature.[49]

A reading of the constitutional text makes it clear that this was the constitutional result obtained. As for the interpretation of that text by the Privy Council in the *Snider* case, in which this vision of a string central government was turned on its head, F.R. Scott, one of Canada's most distinguished constitutional scholars, put it this way almost fifty years ago:

> Perhaps the simplest way of commenting upon this extraordinary judicial performance is to say that it was wrong. . . . With that wrong we are still wrestling[50]

Although one might debate the wisdom of MacDonald's vision, and the constitutional text that embodied it, not many lawyers would dispute Scott's point about the perversity of the interpretation in *Snider*.

Second, the real life impact or result of this set of rules is that the federal government's jurisdiction in labour matters, outside of the specific constitutional amendments mentioned above, most critically that regarding unemployment insurance, is limited to its own employees and employees in a very limited set of specific industries which the constitution itself allocates to the federal sphere – banking, telecommunications, transborder shipping and aeronautics, and a few others. Our most recent estimate of the net real world result of this state of legal affairs is that 1.132 million workers, or 8.4% of the Canadian workforce, are in the federal sphere, the rest in provincial jurisdiction.[51] Thus provincial jurisdiction includes Canada's resource, manufacturing, technology, biomedical, services outside of banking, and most other major sectors of the economy.

Third, the constitutional rules create a system of parallel laws. In the federal sector and each province there are human rights codes, minimum standards laws,

49. In J. Ajzenstat, *et al.* (eds), *Canada's Founding Debates* (Toronto, Stoddart Publishing Co. Ltd., 1999), 282-283.
50. F.R. Scott, 'Federal Jurisdiction Over Labour Relations – A New Look' (1960) 6 *McGill Law Review*, 153. [Scott].
51. H. Arthurs, *Fairness at Work* (Report of the Federal Labour Standards Review, 2006), 8.

health and safety regimes, collective bargaining legislation, and so on.[52] There is a great deal of commonality in all of these laws – although also a great deal of detailed difference. The common features greatly outweigh the differences. This is also true across all of the provincial jurisdictions and the federal sphere. At the level of basic structure of rights, entitlements, and processes to realize them there is still an identifiable core of Canadian labour policy – is spite of the constitutional division of labour just described.

Fourth, there is a well-established set of critiques of this constitutional reality. Some of the major lines of criticism can be briefly outlined as follows:

(1) The Conceptualization Critique
Many commentators have voiced the view that the central problem with the *Snider* and the other early decisions granting of exclusive jurisdiction over labour market regulation to the provinces as matters of 'property and civil rights', is that it conceives of the labour relationship as a matter of private contracting and not as a matter of public economic policy. As Scott put it, the author of the *Snider* decision 'kept his mind on the private law aspects of the matter being dealt with and did not see the larger realities. . . .'[53] This critique may seem abstract, but it is in my view at the core of many of our current problems of how best to conceptualize labour law and policy, and thus a rational approach to the question of 'who governs?' the field.

(2) The Decentralizing Critique
This critique has a number of dimensions. First, labour relations in Canada is remarkably decentralized and it is argued that the constitutional rules 'help reinforce the strong atomistic tendencies of North American industrial systems, which generally favour plant-level rather than enterprise or sectoral level bargaining'.[54] Second, it is argued that this decentralization of collective bargaining ' . . . has militated against the participation of labour in central decision-making about labour policy.'[55] Arthurs claims that our rules 'diminish the authority and perhaps the influence of the Canadian Labour Congress and has inhibited the creation of a national labour-based political alignment.'[56] Third, there is the yet

52. With the exception of Workers Compensation – where there is no parallel federal scheme (although it has the constitutional competence to establish such a system) and federal workers are by federal law, and provincial agreement, covered by provincial law. This is for reasons of economies of scale, given the small federal workforce in any province. *See* R. Haddow and T. Klassen, *Partisanship, Globalization, and Canadian Labour Market Policy: Four Provinces in Comparative Perspective* (Toronto, University of Toronto Press, 2006), 69 [Haddow and Klassen].
53. Scott, above n. 50, 160.
54. H. Arthurs, 'Labour and the Real Constitution' (2007) 48 *Les Cahiers des Droit*, 2. [Arthurs].
55. C.Tuohy, *Policy and Politics in Canada: Institutionalized Ambivalence* (Philadelphia, Temple University Press, 1992), 166.
56. Arthurs, above n. 54, 11.

larger claim that the constitutional rules explain why in comparative studies Canada ranks 'near the bottom in terms of corporatist development.'[57]

(3) The 'Big Issue/Small Jurisdiction' Critique
Which – the constitution notwithstanding – sometimes occur on a nationwide basis.'[58] This was a point FR Scott made in his original critique regarding a national strike in the packing industry in 1947 where the collective labour laws of eight provinces regulated the single strike.[59] (The relevance of this critique was brought home once again in 2007 when a national strike in the movie making industry across Canada created an exact modern parallel in which the legality of the strike, and government responsibility for mediating a resolution, remained completely obscure.) As Scott put it 'This strike gave a revealing example of the anarchy that results from big issues being left to small jurisdictions.'[60]

(4) The Disempowering of Labour/Race to the Bottom Critique
The claim here is that Canada's constitution forces labour (and others such as environmental groups) to spread their resources, for lobbying and so on, 'thinly, thereby reducing their capacity to influence policy' while the 'power of business interests seems to be reinforced by the same structures.'[61] This latter point often reinforced by a reference to the collective action problems faced by individual provincial jurisdictions as they compete to attract or retain capital investment. It is a common argument that the resulting incentive to downward regulatory competition empowers capital vis-à-vis labour.[62]

(5) The Unfairness Critique
Others see a simpler line of critique, one that avoids game theoretic or other procedural complications engendered, and focuses directly on the question 'Why should a man or a woman in Canada have to settle for inferior labour standards simply because he or she lives and works in the "wrong" part of the country?'[63]

(6) The International Labour Law Critique
Canada's constitutional law creates a unique predicament at the international level – for example in relationship to the ratification of ILO (International Labour Organization) conventions. This is for the following reasons. We know that labour law is a matter of provincial

57. G. DiGiacomo, 'Federalism and Labor Policy in Canada' (2001) Queens University Working Paper at 13 and works cited there [DiGiacomo].
58. Arthurs, above n. 54 at 11.
59. Scott, above n. 50, at 161.
60. *Ibid.*, at 162.
61. DiGiacomo, above n. 57, at 12.
62. *See*, e.g., J. Fudge, 'Labour Law's Little Sister: The Employment Standards Act and the Feminization of Labour'(1991, Canadian Center for Policy Alternatives); S.Choudhry, 'Recasting Social Canada: A Reconsideration of Federal Jurisdiction Over Social Policy' (2002) 52 *University of Toronto Law Journal*, 163 [Choudhry].
63. DiGiacomo, above n. 57, 12.

jurisdiction. But treaty making is a federal executive power. The third complicating rule is that treaties have no direct application – they must be implemented through domestic legislation. Thus even though the federal government can ratify ILO Conventions it cannot bring Canadian law into compliance with them without not only the agreement of all of the provinces, but actual legislation in all provinces.[64] Many believe that this explains Canada's poor ratification record.

This brief outline of some of the Canadian debates about some of the controversies driven by our set of constitutional rules is meant simply to provide some of the context of our current reality. There is not space here to review the merits of these controversies. It should be noted however that many of the critiques can easily be contested. For example, the idea that provincial jurisdiction over labour market issues in Canada causes or explains our model of decentralized collective bargaining begs the obvious question – why is the same decentralization evident in the US, where the opposite rule of federal jurisdiction over labour issues is in place? The argument about the race to the bottom is an extremely familiar one to students of federal regimes whether in relation to corporate, environmental, labour, or other issues. It is interesting to note however that some time ago one of Canada's most distinguished labour and constitutional lawyers, Paul Weiler, famously took the positive view of provincial competition, agreeing with Louis Brandeis that the provinces should be seen as 'laboratories for legal experimentation' in industrial relations.[65] In 2004 Eric Tucker concluded that Weiler's optimism has turned out to be well placed concluding that '. . . there has been no race to the bottom' in Canadian labour law while the situation in the United States, with a central federal jurisdiction, looks much closer to the bottom. Tucker concludes that the 'simple lesson to be learned is that a regime that creates the structural conditions for regulatory competition may still have strong labour laws, while a more centralized one may not.'[66]

There have been serious academic engagements with these critiques and responses on the part of Canadian lawyers, political theorists, and others. These debates continue and some academics have made heroic efforts to impose theoretical reason upon our legal reality.[67] And as we have seen, from time to time the Supreme Court of Canada has tempted us with hints of a renewed federal power particularly under the 'peace order and good government' heading in cases such as *Crown Zellerbach*.[68] But as Robert Howse has recently written the promise these

64. *See*, e.g.,: J. Eayrs, 'Canadian Federalism and the United Nations' (1950) 16 *Canadian Journal of Economics and Political Science*, 172.
65. P. Weiler, *Reconcilable Differences: New Directions in Canadian Labour Law* (Toronto, Carswell, 1980), 11.
66. E. Tucker, 'Great Expectations Defeated: The Trajectory of Collective Bargaining Regimes in Canada and the United States Post NAFTA' (2004) 26 *Comparative Labor Law and Policy Journal*, 97, 107 [Tucker].
67. *See*, e.g.,: Choudhry, above n. 62.
68. *See Crown Zellerbach*, above n. 35.

cases once held out seems to have diminished subsequently.[69] The rules of the game are now widely seen to be stable if hotly debated. It is within this framework of constitutional norms that Canada's current efforts at labour market regulation take place. This is our world.

3.1. Some Basic Truths and Reminders

We should, before examining the current efforts at what Canadians often refer to as 'cooperative federalism' regarding labour market issues, recall the following basic truths. First, the constitution could always be amended to secure a larger federal role. Second, there are obvious ways that the provinces can achieve uniform legislation.[70] But these require political agreement and will to do so. It is probably fair to non-Canadian readers to simply assert at this point that for some time there has not been, at the present there is not, and for the foreseeable future there will not be such a political agreement in Canada. Far from it although Canada is a highly decentralized federation our current political reality appears to be one of a drift to further decentralization. Scott, in what has become a famous passage in Canadian politics and law, made this point nicely in 1960. Describing the failure of the multiple provincial jurisdictions involved in the national packers strike in 1947 to agree upon a common response to he wrote:

> Nothing came of the meeting except a good lesson in federalism; even the appointment of a common conciliator could not be agreed upon. The delegates went sorrowfully home, nursing their provincial autonomies.[71]

It would be an easy argument to make that all of the provinces have been nursing it very carefully in recent years. Again, for non-Canadian readers, it is probably fair to note simply that the one political reality which hovers over and dominates all Canadian thinking and discussion of division of powers, constitutional amendment, and national identity, is, in a word, Quebec. The struggle of nationalists and federalists in Quebec and elsewhere has constituted the central political drama of modern Canada. The question of whether Quebec can maintain its linguistic, social and political identity within Canada – and the efforts of both sides to secure their desired outcome – cast a long shadow over the strategy of all provinces and the federal government. As we shall see, it had, in the mid 1990s, when a sovereignist government in Quebec lost a referendum by a the narrowest of margins, a profound impact over the issue of labour market and employment policy in

69. Howse, above n. 46, 10.
70. For a clear example *see* Scott, above n. 50, who describes how shortly after the *Snider* decision the federal government rewrote the impugned legislation so that it applied only to the federal sphere, but also to 'any dispute which is within the exclusive jurisdiction of any province and which by the legislation of the province is made subject to the provisions of this Act' – as Scott put it 'The provinces were invited to legislate *Snider* away'. And they did – a situation which lasted until the end of World War II.
71. Scott, above n. 50, 162.

Canada – an impact which dominates our current federal labour market policy reality.

But it is also the case that one cannot understand the substance of Canadian political debates without seeing that in spite of the legal reality of 'exclusive provincial jurisdiction' over labour and social policy in general (including medical care, education, and so on) the federal role has been, as Sujit Choudhry rightly observes, 'all the more remarkable'[72] precisely because of these constitutional limitations upon its jurisdiction. The federal 'spending power' has proved to be an astounding constitutional development. It has allowed the federal government to either, depending on one's view, 'provide leadership' to, or 'unilaterally intrude' upon core areas of provincial jurisdiction including education, medical care, labour market and employment policy. The reality of Canadian constitutional law has been that it has allowed a legal distinction to flourish. This is the distinction between financing social policies on the one hand, and control of their design and delivery on the other. As Choudhry nicely puts it, the current assumptions:

> hold that the Constitution draws a sharp distinction between jurisdiction over the financing of contributory social insurance and social services, and jurisdiction over their design and delivery. Short of explicit constitutional amendment (as occurred in the case of unemployment insurance and pensions), federal jurisdiction is thought to be confined to the former realm, largely exercised through the use of the so called federal spending power, whereas provincial jurisdiction encompasses both the former and the latter areas.[73]

In a very real sense it is the argument made available by this set of constitutional rules – to the effect that when the federal government utilizing its spending power makes conditional grants to provinces or direct grants to individuals or institutions (such as universities) and thus goes 'over the heads of the provincial governments'[74] in areas of provincial jurisdiction, it is circumventing the constitution – which has, perhaps unsurprisingly, or perhaps not, gained political currency and come to dominate our 'normal' constitutional discourse. This is partly the explanation of, and explained by, the rise of more regional parties in the Federal Parliament whose platforms are often overtly based on avoiding federal interference in local affairs, the negotiation in 1999 of the Social Union Framework Agreement in which the federal government and nine provinces agreed to some limits on the Federal Government spending power, the creation by the Provinces of a new political and extra-constitutional body they have named 'the Council of the Federation' to coordinate their efforts to 'take an increasingly hard line towards Ottawa's unilateral actions,'[75] and of a much heightened rhetoric about what is

72. Choudhry, above n. 62, 164.
73. *Ibid.*
74. T., MacIntosh, 'Intergovernmental Relations, Social Policy, and Federal Transfers after Romanow' (2004) 47 *Canadian Public Administration*, 27 and 41 [MacIntosh].
75. *Ibid.*, 27.

known in Canada as the 'fiscal imbalance' (between Ottawa and the provinces – vertical imbalance – and between the provinces – horizontal imbalance).[76]

Of course it is important to note that the spending power cannot cure all ills. For example Canada still has, in spite of years of contrary policy analysis, no national securities commission. This is not an issue which can be remedied through conditional or direct grants. But in many policy areas concerning employment and social inclusion – that is, regarding Canada's social union – it has had a profound impact. Medicare – our public (national) health care system rests on the foundation of the spending power as medical care is a provincial jurisdiction. So too in post secondary education, an explicitly provincial area of competence, the federal government has had a profound impact on research funding, funding for hiring of faculty, and loans to students. The federal government make two sorts of transfers to the provinces – 'equalization payments' which are transfers, based on complicated formulae, from the richer provinces to the poorer provinces – and 'equal per capita transfers'of which there are now two, the Canadian Health Transfer (for healthcare) and the Canadian Social Transfer (for social programs and education).[77] What makes this possible is that Ottawa 'draws away more taxes from Canadians than it spends on programs that fall under its jurisdiction.'[78] MacIntosh notes that in the 2003 Federal Budget, in addition to the Canada Social Transfer, 2.5 times the amount of that Transfer was spent *directly* (i.e., not through the province) by the Federal government on education and other social programs.

3.2. What Has All of This Meant For Employment Policies?[79]

Writing in the 1980s several of Canada's most distinguished public policy analysts drew attention to the fact that Canada's labour market policy was perversely weighed in favour of passive policies aimed at compensating those out of work, largely through the federal Unemployment Insurance Act (as it was then called), as opposed to active labour market policies (ALMPs) aimed facilitating a return to the

76. *See* T. Courchene, 'Vertical and Horizontal Imbalances: An Ontario Perspective' Presentation to the Standing Committee on Finance, House of Commons, 4 May 2005 [Courchene].
77. *See* J. Milway, 'Fixing Fiscal Federalism to Improve Canada's Productivity Performance' (Fall, 2005) 11 *Productivity Monitor*, 14 and 16-17.
78. Courchene, above n. 76, 2.
79. For those interested in much more detail, *see* the following: A. Noël (ed.), *Federalism and Labour Market Policy: Comparing Different Governance and Employment Strategies* (Montreal, McGill-Queen's University Press, 2004); T.A. MacIntosh, *Federalism, Democracy and Labour Market Policy in Canada* (Montreal, McGill-Queen's University Press, 2000); A.Sharpe and R. Haddow, *Social Partnerships for Training: Canada's Experiment with Labour Force Development Boards* (Centre for the Study of Living Standards, Caledon Institute of Social Policy, School of Policy Studies, Queen's University, 1997); T. Klassen, *Precarious Values: Organizations, Politics and Labour Market Policy in Ontario* (Montreal, McGill-Queen's University Press, 2000); A. Johnson, *Continuities and Discontinuities: The Political Economy of Social Welfare and Labour Market Policy in Canada* (Toronto, University of Toronto Press, 1994).

workforce.[80] A number of studies also pointed to the growth in unemployment and especially of the long term unemployed.[81] On the policy front the logic of a shift to ALMP was clear and largely accepted, especially in light of 'the growing acceptance that Canada's future economic success will be increasingly bound up in the human capital.'[82] But on the federalism front the ALMP issue was caught up in the same web of legal and political realities described above. The federal government claimed a role and was prepared to use its spending power. The result was a familiar one 'namely that over much of this period [the 1980s and much of the 1990s] the federal and provincial governments bickered with one another regarding which order of government should design and deliver active policies.'[83] Key to this dispute was Quebec which strongly maintained that this was a provincial issue of education and social policy.

In the 1990s several developments altered this reality and resulted in a new federal/provincial arrangement – essentially an offer of complete devolution to the provinces of design and delivery of ALMPs, but with federal funding remaining intact. One key event was the reduction of federal government spending on social programs in the 1990s – including the transfers to the provinces and directly on Unemployment Insurance – as a part of then Finance Minister Martin's efforts (successful in the end) to balance the federal budget during that period. (These reductions in transfers are also part of the explanation for increased federal/provincial discord noted above). It was not until 2001 that the cash value of the Social and Health Transfers returned to 1995 levels.[84] Another key event was, as noted above, the Quebec referendum of 1995 in which the Parti Quebecois government in Quebec lost a (qualified) referendum on separation by the slimmest of margins. The federal liberal government of Jean Chretien quickly agreed to take the ALMP irritant off the table and to 'take no new initiatives in this field without provincial consent.'[85]

The net result of these political turns was a major set of reforms to the Federal Unemployment Insurance Act in 1996. First, it was symbolically renamed – becoming the Employment Insurance Act. And Part II of the EI Act 'overhauled the job creation and training measures funded from the EI budget'.[86] But the more significant event was the federal government's offer to the provinces to devolve the jurisdiction over ALMPs to the provinces – including design as well as implementation if desired – with the federal government generally vacating the field, except

80. *See* M. Trebilcock, M. Chandler and R. Howse, *Trade and Transitions: a Comparative Analysis of Adjustment Policies* (New York, Routledge, 1990).
81. H. Lazar, *Shifting Roles: Active Labour Market Policy in Canada Under The Labour Market Development Agreements* (Canadian Policy Research Network, 2002) at 4 [Lazar].
82. *Ibid.*, at 5.
83. *Ibid.*
84. *See* MacIntosh, above n. 74, at 31.
85. *See* R. Haddow, 'Canadian Federalism and Active Labour Market Policy' in F. Rocher and M. Smith (eds), *New Trends in Canadian Federalism*, 2nd edn(Ontario, Broadview Press, 2003), 243 at 252 [Haddow].
86. *Ibid.*

for the transfer of funds, all under what became called a Labour Market Development Agreement (LMDA), to be negotiated between the federal and each provincial government. Some governments – Quebec and now (from 1 January 2007) Ontario among them – have opted for the complete devolution model. Others have opted for a 'co-managed model'. There is not space here to describe the obvious complexities of all of these arrangements.[87] Two points of more general interest can be noted. First, the Federal Government has retained a role in ALMP by continuing to fund, what are, at least sometimes, 'corporatist' Sector Councils aimed at planning human resource strategies. Quebec maintains its own unrelated set of committees. Second, the federal government has at least the potential to monitor, through reporting requirements, and thus learn and promote best practices under the various LMDAs. From a European perspective these two data points may seem interesting but the consensus is that any such efforts are for many reasons, some of which have been canvassed here, are a very pale imitation indeed of 'the open method of coordination'[88] or corporatism.[89]

There are other aspects of the Canadian federal scene which further add to its complexity in relation to labour market issues. The weak legal state of Canada's federal government has general implications for both the social and economic union. While there is very real and difficult to absorb (at both ends) mobility of labour (currently from the east coast to the Alberta oil fields) internal barriers such as provincial control of access to certain forms of employment – the legal profession is a prime example of provincial protectionism constructing significant barriers to inter-provincial mobility of labour – are significant. So too are local residency period requirements for certain benefits. The Social Union Framework agreement pledged to address this issue of internal mobility and it is reported that some success has been made in relation to the latter. Meanwhile several provinces have acted 'regionally' negotiating what look remarkably like internal 'free trade agreements' addressing issues of trade, investment and labour mobility. The most recent and controversial of these is the Trade, Investment and Labour Mobility Agreement (TILMA) negotiated between Alberta and British Columbia, Canada's two most westerly provinces and scheduled to come into effect this year.[90] The agreement is seen by its critics as a kind of 'internal NAFTA (North American Free Trade Agreement)' and they allege that it advances a neoconservative agenda which favours investors, is damaging to local regulatory autonomy, and is undemocratic.[91] Its promoters see it as a second best solution to the failure of national

87. Haddow, above n. 85, provides a very detailed account – up to 2002. *See also* Lazar above n. 81.
88. *See* T. Hanniman, 'Human Capital Formation, Policy Formation and Canadian Federalism: Possible Lessons from the European Union and the Open Method of Coordination' (University of Wisconsin, Dept of Political Science, unpublished) [Hanniman].
89. A. Schneider and R. Klassen, 'Decentralization and the Status Quo in Ontario and Bavaria: Variations in Active Labour Market Policy Reform in Sub National Jurisdictions of Canada and Germany' (2004) Canadian Centre for German and European Studies, York Univ. Working Paper 9. *See also* Schneider in Haddow and Klassen, above n. 52.
90. *See* 'Barrier Busting'. *The Economist*, 10 Mar. 2007 at p.35.
91. 'Asking for Trouble' *Canadian Centre for Policy Alternatives* (Ottawa) Feb. 2007.

efforts to attack the same barriers, including labour mobility barriers based on non recognition of credentials. It remains to be seen whether TILMA is the beginning of a larger patch work of regional arrangements across the country, or something truly national.[92]

4. CONCLUSION

Canada's constitutional law and its constitutional practices are complex. There is no question that in the areas of job creation and ALMP we have, for reasons just described, come to a very complex, and from the perspective of comparative federalism, a very decentralized, result. As we have seen the legal reasons that have brought us to our current reality are suspect and the motivations for action within that legal framework political, in the most robust sense of that term. But the question which remains is whether this is a useful reality. This of course depends upon the answers to some obvious questions. There are, of course, the overt political calculations. Quebec is still part of Canada and it seems it will be for the foreseeable future. Some will take the view that they are willing to pay a price for this result. But the question remains whether a price is being paid. Developments in regulatory theory,[93] and Canadian labour law history,[94] suggest that the current dispensation will at least have the advantage of local experimentation, and thus also the possibility of continuous learning and improvement.[95] Canada is a big, complex, multicultural, and relatively successful society in which such a result is to be welcomed. If labour market and human capital policy are central to economic progress then there is a case for an open method of experimentation if not coordination. The interesting question is how much room the federal government has to monitor local experiments and advance learning and best practices in light thereof. There is some reason for hope here as this was precisely the path that our national health system followed – a local experiment expanded by the spending power. On the other hand, there are real internal provincial barriers to Canada's claim to being an open and mobile society, certainly for some and in geographic terms. These will

92. At the very moment of finalizing this manuscript an important development seems to have occurred. Press reports in Canada indicate that on 5 Dec. 2008 agreement had been reached in Ottawa on a national labour mobility agreement. The essence of the agreement appears to be the removal of barriers to movement between provinces presented by certain local professional qualification requirements. (The list of professions to be covered is not yet known.) The idea is that, for example, a doctor qualified to practice in Ontario can now move to practice in another province without any need for further qualification – in effect a mutual recognition system rather than a single national standard. This is viewed, politically, as a victory for the original authors of the TILMA agreement, i.e. the provinces of British Columbia and Alberta, at least on the labour if not the investment side. (*see* 'Provincial labour barriers to fall' The Globe and Mail, 6 Dec. 2008, A-4.).
93. *See* Hanniman, above n. 88.
94. *See* Tucker, above n. 66.
95. Sable, 'Rolling Standards' in G. Politakis (ed.), *Protecting Labour Rights as Humans Rights: Present and Future of International Supervision* (ILO, 2007).

not be resolved except through inter-provincial agreement. Again the positive take would be that the TILMA may be replicable.[96]

Our well established constitutional rules are, as we have noted, deeply suspect. But the legal reality they have constructed much less obviously so. The surprising availability of both central, and to some extent conditional (even if, in some cases, simply in the selection of policy areas to be explored) funding, and local control and implementation is at the very least capable of rational defence. The conceptual (seeing the problem as one of private contracting and thus a matter or 'property and civil rights' within provincial jurisdiction) and legal (an overt misinterpretation of the constitutional text) errors of *Snider* and the other early cases with which we have lived for so long, may have been overtaken by other developments in legal, especially modern regulatory, theory which have cast doubt both on the existence of some of problems to be solved (races to the bottom in regulation) and the solution to it (central and uniform regulatory control). The general lessons may simply be: first, to affirm that, as it has been famously said, predictions are always difficult, especially about the future; and second, that legal errors, even large constitutional ones, can have unintended consequences.

References

Ajzenstat, J., *et al. Canada's Founding Debates* (Toronto, Stoddart Publishing Co. Ltd., 1999).

Arthurs, H., 'Labour and the Real Constitution' (2007) 48 *Les Cahiers des Droit.*

Choudhry, S., 'Recasting Social Canada: A Reconsideration of Federal Jurisdiction Over Social Policy' (2002) 52 *University of Toronto Law Journal.*

Canadian Centre for Policy Alternatives, 'Asking for Trouble' (Ottawa) Feb. 2007.

Courchene, T., 'Vertical and Horizontal Imbalances: An Ontario Perspective' Presentation to the Standing Committee on Finance, House of Commons, 4 May 2005.

DiGiacomo, G., 'Federalism and Labor Policy in Canada' (2001) Queens University Working Paper.

Eayrs, J. 'Canadian Federalism and the United Nations' (1950) 16 *Canadian Journal of Economics and Political Science.*

Economist 'Barrier Busting', 10 Mar. 2007.

Arthurs. H, *Fairness at Work* (2006) Report of the Federal Labour Standards Review.

Finklestein, N., *Laskin's Canadian Constitutional Law*, 5th edn (Toronto, The Carswell Company Limited, 1986).

Fudge, J., 'Labour Law's Little Sister: The Employment Standards Act and the Feminization of Labour' (Canadian Centre for Policy Alternatives, 1991).

Haddow, R. 'Canadian Federalism and Active Labour Market Policy' in Rocher F. and Smith M. (eds), *New Trends in Canadian Federalism* 2nd edn (Ontario, Broadview Press, 2003).

96. As it now seems to have been – *see* above n. 92.

Haddow, R. and Klassen, T. *Partisanship, Globalization, and Canadian Labour Market Policy: Four Provinces in Comparative Perspective* (Toronto, University of Toronto Press, 2006).

Hanniman, 'Human Capital Formation, Policy Formation and Canadian Federalism: Possible Lessons from the European Union and the Open Method of Coordination' (University of Wisconsin, Department of Political Science, unpublished).

Hogg, P., *Constitutional Law of Canada*, 4th edn, looseleaf (Scarborough, ON, Carswell, 1997-2006).

Howse, 'The Effect of Jurisdictional Issues on the Application and Administration of Part III' p. 2 Prepared for the Federal Labour Standards Review 2006, unpublished.

Jackman, M., 'The Constitutional Basis for Federal Regulation of Health' 5 (1996) 2 *Health Law Review.*

Johnson, A.F. *Continuities and Discontinuities: The Political Economy of Social Welfare and Labour Market Policy in Canada* (Toronto, University of Toronto Press, 1994).

Klassen, T.R., *Precarious Values: Organizations, Politics and Labour Market Policy in Ontario* (Montreal, McGill-Queen's University Press, 2000).

Lazar, H., *Shifting Roles: Active Labour Market Policy in Canada under the Labour Market Development Agreements* (Canadian Policy Research Network, 2002).

MacIntosh, T., 'Intergovernmental Relations, Social Policy, and Federal Transfers After Romanow' (2004) 47 *Canadian Public Administration.*

MacIntosh, T.A., *Federalism, Democracy and Labour Market Policy in Canada* (Montreal, McGill-Queen's University Press, 2000).

Milway, J., 'Fixing Fiscal Federalism to Improve Canada's Productivity Performance' (Fall, 2005) 11 *Productivity Monitor.*

Noël, A. (ed.), *Federalism and Labour Market Policy: Comparing Different Governance and Employment Strategies* (Montreal, McGill-Queen's University Press, 2004).

Petter 'Federalism and The Myth of the Federal Spending Power' (1989) *Canadian Bar Review* 68.

Sable, 'Rolling Standards' in G. Politakis (ed.), *Protecting Labour Rights as Humans Rights: Present and Future of International Supervision* (Geneva, ILO, 2007).

Schneider and Klassen (2004) 'Decentralization and the status quo in Ontario and Bavaria: Variations in active labour market policy reform in sub national jurisdictions of Canada and Germany' Canadian Centre for German and European Studies, York Univ. Working Paper 9.

Scott, F.R. 'Federal Jurisdiction Over Labour Relations – A New Look' (1960) 6 *McGill Law Review.*

Sharpe, A. and Haddow, R. (1997) *Social Partnerships for Training: Canada's Experiment with Labour Force Development Boards* Centre for the Study of

Living Standards, Caledon Institute of Social Policy, School of Policy Studies, Queen's University.

Trebilcock, M., Chandler M., and Howse R., Trade and Transitions: A Comparative Analysis of Adjustment Policies (New York, Routledge, 1990).

Tucker, E., 'Great Expectations Defeated: The Trajectory of Collective Bargaining Regimes in Canada and the United States Post NAFTA' (2004) 26 *Comparative Labor Law and Policy Journal.*

Tuohy, C., *Policy and Politics in Canada: Institutionalized Ambivalence* (Philadelphia, Temple University Press, 1992).

Weiler, P. *Reconcilable Differences* (Toronto, Carswell, 1980).

BCLR – BULLETIN OF COMPARATIVE LABOUR RELATIONS

Vol. Title/Author/Year/ISBN

1. Roger Blanpain, *Individual Employment Contracts: Collective Agreements*, 1970.
2. Roger Blanpain, *Social Planning*, 1971 (ISBN 90-312-0018-2).
3. Roger Blanpain, *Guaranteed Income Funds*, 1972 (ISBN 90-312-0019-0).
4. Roger Blanpain, *Employee Participation at the Level of the Enterprise*, 1973 (ISBN 90-312-0020-4).
5. Roger Blanpain, *Vastheid van Betrekking: Staking en Bezetting*, 1974.
6. Roger Blanpain, *Labour Law and Industrial Relations (International Bibliography)*, 1975 (ISBN 90-312-0023-9).
7. Roger Blanpain, *Multinational Enterprises*, 1976 (ISBN 90-312-0024-7).
8. Roger Blanpain, *Worker's Participation in the European Company*, 1977 (ISBN 90-312-0044-1).
9. Roger Blanpain, *Women and Labour*, 1978 (ISBN 90-312-0077-8).
10. Roger Blanpain, *European Conference on Labour Law and Industrial Relations: Multinational Enterprises*, 1979 (ISBN 90-312-0091-3).
11. Roger Blanpain, *Job Security and Industrial Relations*, 1980 (ISBN 90-312-0147-2).
12. Roger Blanpain, Greg Bamber & Russell Lansbury, *Technological Change and Industrial Relations: An International Symposium*, 1983 (ISBN 90-312-0205-3).
13. Roger Blanpain, James Janssen van Raay & A. Moulty, *Worker's Participation in the European Community: The Fifth Directive*, 1984 (ISBN 90-654-4187-5).
14. Roger Blanpain, *Equality and Prohibition of Discrimination in Employment*, 1985 (ISBN 90-654-4215-4).
15. Roger Blanpain, *Restructuring Labour in the Enterprise: Law and Practice in France, F.R. of Germany, Italy, Sweden and the United Kingdom*, 1986 (ISBN 90-654-4283-9).
16. Roger Blanpain & E. Kassalow, *Unions and Industrial Relations: Recent Trends and Prospect: A Comparative Treatment*, 1987 (ISBN 90-654-4294-4).
17. Roger Blanpain & Marco Biagi, *Trade Union Democracy and Industrial Relations*, 1988 (ISBN 90-654-4394-0).
18. Roger Blanpain & Jelle Visser, *In Search of Inclusive Unionism*, 1990 (ISBN 90-654-4439-4).
19. Roger Blanpain, *Flexibility and Wages: A Comparative Treatment*, 1990 (ISBN 90-654-4461-0).

20. Roger Blanpain, Stephen Frenkel & Oliver Clarke, *Economic Restructuring and Industrial Relations in Industrialised Countries*, 1990 (ISBN 90-654-4488-2).
21. Roger Blanpain & Friedrich Fürstenberg, *Structure and Strategy in Industrial Relations,* 1991 (ISBN 90-654-4559-5).
22. Roger Blanpain, Amira Galin & Ozer Carmi, *Flexible Work Patterns and Their Impact on Industrial Relations*, 1991 (ISBN 90-654-4572-2).
23. Roger Blanpain, *Workers' Participation: Influence on Management Decision-Making by Labour in the Private Sector*, 1992 (ISBN 90-654-4600-1).
24. Roger Blanpain, Brian Brooks & Chris Engels, *Employed or Self-Employed*, 1992, (ISBN 90-654-4613-3).
25. Roger Blanpain Tiziano Treu, *Industrial Relations Developments in the Telecommunications Industry*, 1993 (ISBN 90-654-4642-7).
26. Roger Blanpain & Marco Biagi, *Industrial Relations in Small and Medium Sized Enterprises*, 1993 (ISBN 90-654-4696-6).
27. Roger Blanpain & Marco Biagi, *Participative Management and Industrial Relations in a Worldwide Perspective*, (ISBN 90-654-4769-5).
28. Roger Blanpain, Jacques Rojot & Hoyt N. Wheeler, *Employee Rights and Industrial Justice*, 1994 (ISBN 90-654-4804-7).
29. Roger Blanpain & Ruth Ben-Israel, *Strikes and Lock-Outs in Industrialized Market Economies*, 1994 (ISBN 90-654-4841-1).
30. Roger Blanpain, Kazuo Sugeno & Yasuo Suwa, *The Harmonization of Working Life and Family Life*, 1995 (ISBN 90-411-0064-4).
31. Roger Blanpain & Laszio Nagy, *Labour Law and Industrial Relations in Central and Eastern Europe*, 1996 (ISBN 90-411-0298-1).
32. Roger Blanpain, *Labour Law and Industrial Relations in the European Union*, 1997 (ISBN 90-411-0527-1).
33. Taco Van Peijpe, *Employment Protection under Strain*, 1998 (ISBN 90-411-0528-8).
34. Roger Blanpain, Takashi Araki & Ryuichi Yamakawa, *The Process of Industrialization and the Role of Labour Law in Asia*, 1999 (ISBN 9-041-1104-7-X).
35. Roger Blanpain & Marco Biagi, *Non-standard Work and Industrial Relations*, 1999 (ISBN 90-411-1117-4).
36. Roger Blanpain, *Private Employment Agencies: The Impact of ILO Convention 181 (1997) and the Judgment of the European Court of Justice of 11 December 1997*, 1999 (ISBN 90-411-1118-2).
37. Roger Blanpain, *Multinational Enterprises and the Social Challenges of the XXIst Century: The ILO Declaration on Fundamental* Principles *at Work, Public and Private Corporate Codes of Conduct*, 2000 (ISBN 90-411-1280-4).
38. Roger Blanpain, Ryuichi Yamakawa & Takashi Araki, *Deregulation and Labour Law: In Search of a Labour Concept for the 21st Century*, 2000 (ISBN 90-411-1370-3).
39. Roger Blanpain, *The Council of Europe and the Social Challenges of the XXIst Century*, 2001 (ISBN 90-411-1543-9).

40. Roger Blanpain, *On-Line Rights for Employees in the Information Society, Use & Monitoring of E-Mail & Internet at Work*, 2002 (ISBN 90-411-1626-5).
41. Roger Blanpain, *The Evolving Employment Relationship and the New Economy: The Role of Labour Law & Industrial Relations*, 2001 (ISBN 90-411-1691-5).
42. Roger Blanpain, *Involvement of Employees in the European Union, Works Councils, Company Statute, Information and Consultation Rights*, 2002 (ISBN 90-411-1760-1).
43. Michele Colucci, *The Impact of the Internet and New Technologies on the Workplace: A Legal Analysis from a Comparative Point of View*, 2002 (ISBN 90-411-1824-1).
44. Roger Blanpain, *White Paper on the Labour Market in Italy: The Quality of European Industrial Relations and Changing Industrial Relations*, 2002 (ISBN 90-411-1841-1).
45. Roger Blanpain, Russell D. Lansbury & Young-Bum Park, *Impact of Globalisation on Employment Relations: A Comparison of the Automobile and Banking Industries in Australia and Korea*, 2002 (ISBN 90-411-1850-0).
46. Roger Blanpain & Antoine Jacobs, *Employee Rights in Bankruptcy: A Comparative-Law Assessment*, 2002 (ISBN 90-411-1942-6).
47. Roger Blanpain, Takashi Araki & Shinya Ouchi, *Corporate Restructuring and the Role of Labour Law*, 2003 (ISBN 90-411-1949-3).
48. Roger Blanpain, *Collective Bargaining, Discrimination, Social Security and European Integration*, 2003 (ISBN 90-411-2010-6).
49. Roger Blanpain & Luis Aparicio-Valdez, *Labour Relations in the Asia-Pacific Countries*, 2004 (ISBN 90-411-2239-7).
50. Roger Blanpain & Ronnie Graham, *Temporary Agency Work and the Information Society*, 2004 (ISBN 90-411-2252-4).
51. Roger Blanpain, *The Actors of Collective Bargaining: A World Report*, 2004 (ISBN 90-411-2253-2).
52. Roger Blanpain & Michele Colucci, *The Globalisation of Labour Standards: The Soft Law Track*, 2004 (ISBN 90-411-2303-2).
53. Roger Blanpain, Takashi Araki & Shinya Ouchi, *Labour Law in Motion: Diversification of the Labour Force & Terms and Conditions of Employment*, 2005 (ISBN 90-411-2315-6).
54. Roger Blanpain, *Smoking and the Workplace*, 2005 (ISBN 90-411-2325-3).
55. Roger Blanpain, *Confronting Globalization: The Quest for a Social Agenda*, 2005 (ISBN 90-411-2381-4).
56. Roger Blanpain, Thomas Blanke & Edgar Rose, *Collective Bargaining Wages in Comparative Perspective: Germany, France, the Netherlands, Sweden and the United Kingdom*, 2005 (ISBN 90-411-2388-1).
57. Roger Blanpain & Anne Numhauser-Henning, *Women in Academia & Equality Law: Aiming High – Falling Short?*, 2006 (ISBN 978-90-411-2427-6).

58. Roger Blanpain, *Freedom of Services in the European Union: Labour and Social Security Law: The Bolkestein Initiative*, 2006 (ISBN 978-90-411-2453-5).
59. Roger Blanpain, Frans Pennings & Nurhan Sural, *Flexibilisation and Modernisation of the Turkish Labour Market*, 2006 (ISBN 978-90-411-2490-X).
60. Roger Blanpain & Boel Flodgren, *Corporate and Employment Perspectives in a Global Business Environment* 2006 (ISBN 978-90-411-2537-X).
61. Roger Blanpain, Shinya Ouchi & Takashi Araki, *Decentralizing Industrial Relations and The Role of Labor Unions and Employee Representatives*, 2007 (ISBN 978-90-411-2583-3).
62. Roger Blanpain, *European Framework Agreements and Telework: Law and Practice: A European and Comparative Study*, 2007 (ISBN 978-90-411-2560-4).
63. Roger Blanpain, Jim Kitay, Leanne Cutcher & Nick Wailes, *Globalization and Employment Relations in Retail Banking*, 2007 (ISBN 978-90-411-2620-1).
64. Roger Blanpain, Russell Lansbury, Jim Kitay, Nick Wailes & Anja Kirsch, *Globalization and Employment Relations in the Auto Assembly Industry: A Study of Seven Countries*, 2008 (ISBN 978-90-411-2698-6).
65. Roger Blanpain & Michele Tiraboschi, *The Global Labour Market: From Globalization to Flexicurity*, 2008 (ISBN 978-90-411-2722-8).
66. Roger Blanpain, Michele Colucci & Frank Hendrickx, *The Future of Sport in the European Union: Beyond the EU Reform Treaty and the White Paper*, 2008 (ISBN 978-90-411-2761-7).
67. Roger Blanpain, Linda Dickens, *Challenges in European Employment Relations: Employment Regulation, Trade Union Organization, Equality, Flexicurity, Training and New Approaches to Pay*, 2008 (ISBN 978-90-411-2771-6).
68. Roger Blanpain, Hiroya Nakakubo & Takashi Araki, *New Developments in Employment Discrimination Law*, 2008 (ISBN 978-90-411-2782-2).
69. Roger Blanpain, Andrzej Marian Świątkowski, *The Laval and Viking Cases: Freedom of Services and Establishment v. Industrial Conflict in the European Economic Area and Russia*, 2009 (ISBN 978-90-411-2850-8).
70. Roger Blanpain, William Bromwich, Olga Rymkevich, Silvia Spattini, *The Modernization of Labour Law and Industrial Relations in a Comparative Perspective*, 2009 (ISBN 978-90-411-2865-2).
71. Roger Blanpain, Juan Pablo Landa & Brian Langille, *Employment Policies and Multilevel Governance*, 2009 (ISBN 978-90-411-2866-9).

www.ingramcontent.com/pod-product-compliance
Lightning Source LLC
LaVergne TN
LVHW011117300926
849160LV00008B/416
9789041128669